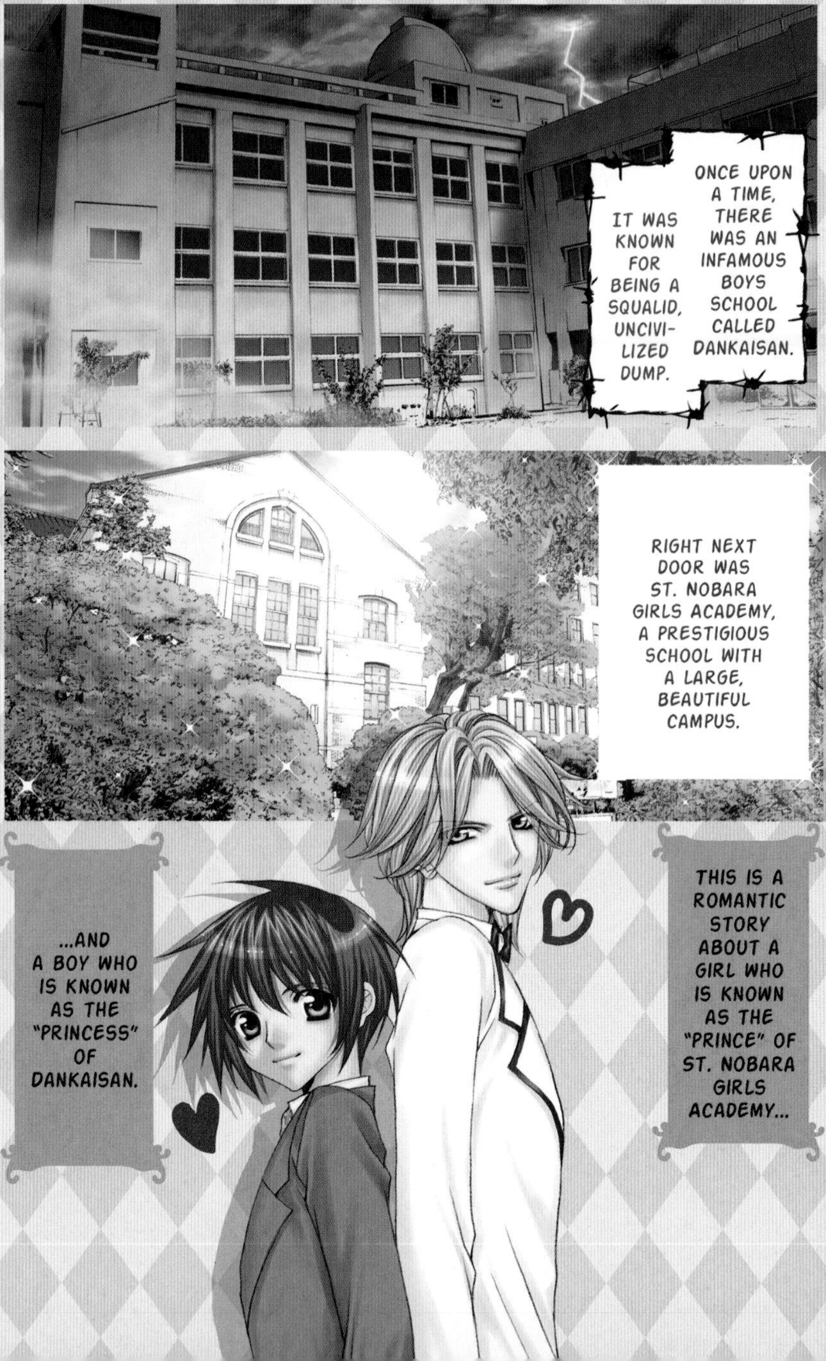
ONCE UPON A TIME, THERE WAS AN INFAMOUS BOYS SCHOOL CALLED DANKAISAN.
IT WAS KNOWN FOR BEING A SQUALID, UNCIVI-LIZED DUMP.
RIGHT NEXT DOOR WAS ST. NOBARA GIRLS ACADEMY, A PRESTIGIOUS SCHOOL WITH A LARGE, BEAUTIFUL CAMPUS.
THIS IS A ROMANTIC STORY ABOUT A GIRL WHO IS KNOWN AS THE "PRINCE" OF ST. NOBARA GIRLS ACADEMY...
...AND A BOY WHO IS KNOWN AS THE "PRINCESS" OF DANKAISAN.

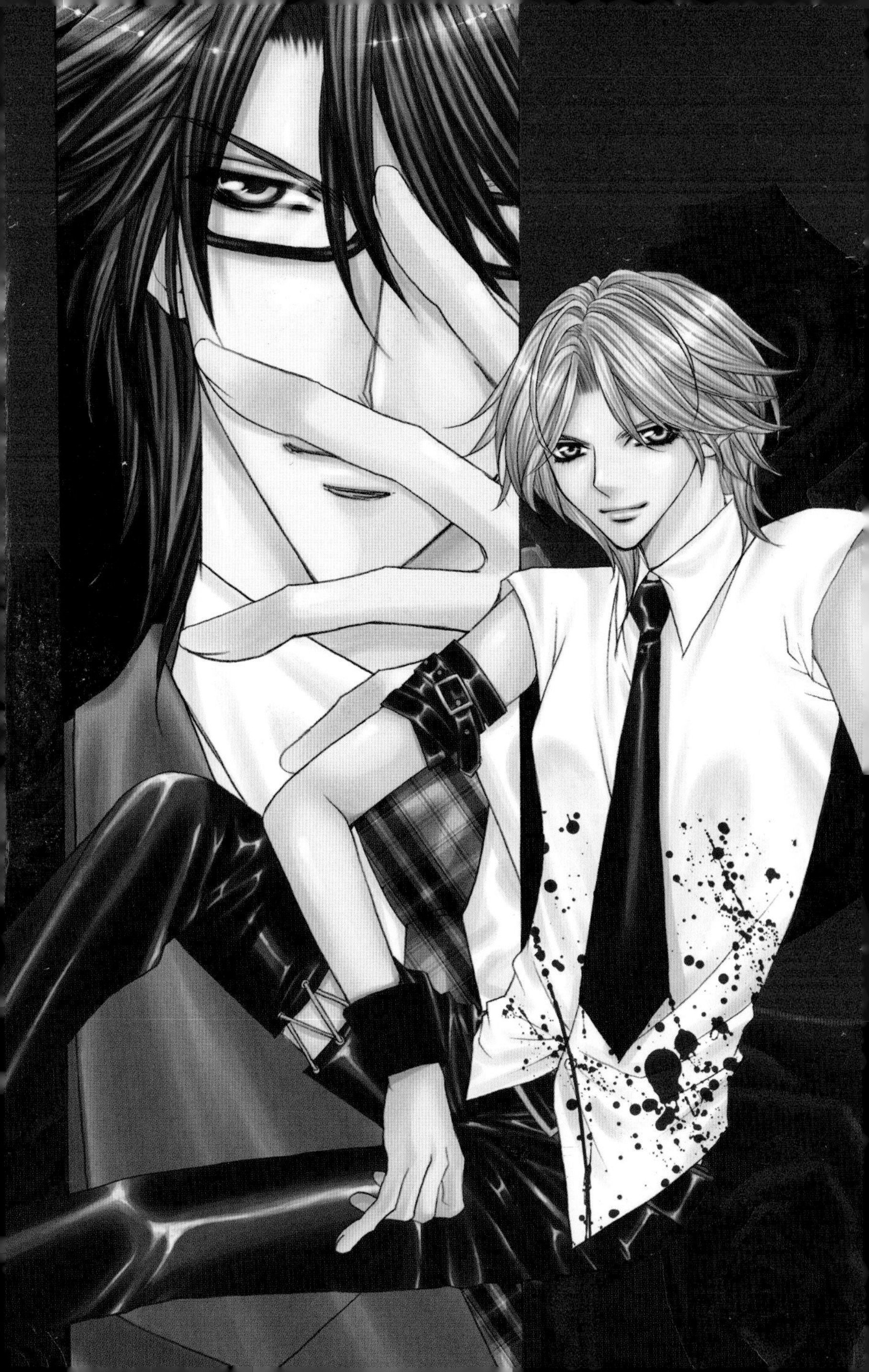

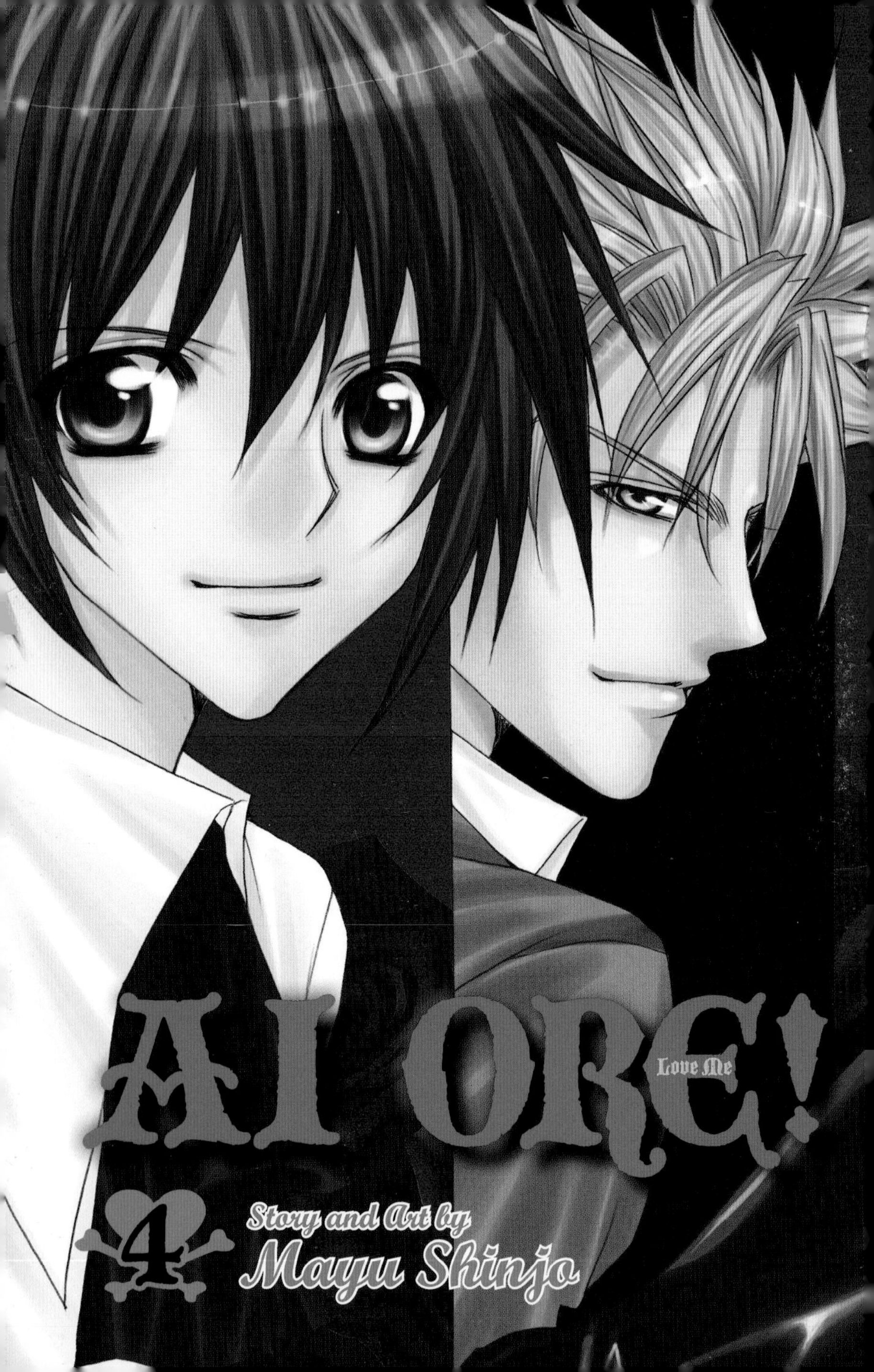
AI ORE!
Love Me
4
Story and Art by
Mayu Shinjo

AI ORE!
Love Me

4

Story Thus Far

❀ Mizuki Sakurazaka, the lead guitarist of indie girl band Blaue Rosen, is an extremely handsome girl. She is treated like a "prince" at St. Nobara Girls Academy. Her boyfriend, Akira Shiraishi, is an extremely cute boy who is considered to be the "princess" of his all-boys school, Dankaisan High. Akira joins Blaue Rosen as its lead singer but hides the fact he is a boy from the girls at Mizuki's school.

❀ Mizuki and Akira start dating, and although they've grown closer, Mizuki still hasn't told Akira how she feels about him. When she attends an arranged marriage meeting with Ran as a favor to her father, Akira believes he hasn't been manly enough for Mizuki and decides to stop dressing as a girl. Then, at a live gig, he announces to the audience that he's a boy and quits the band. Akira dresses as a cat boy to beg forgiveness from Mizuki, and she finally admits she loves him. Blaue Rosen is back together, but what will happen now that everyone knows Akira is a guy?!

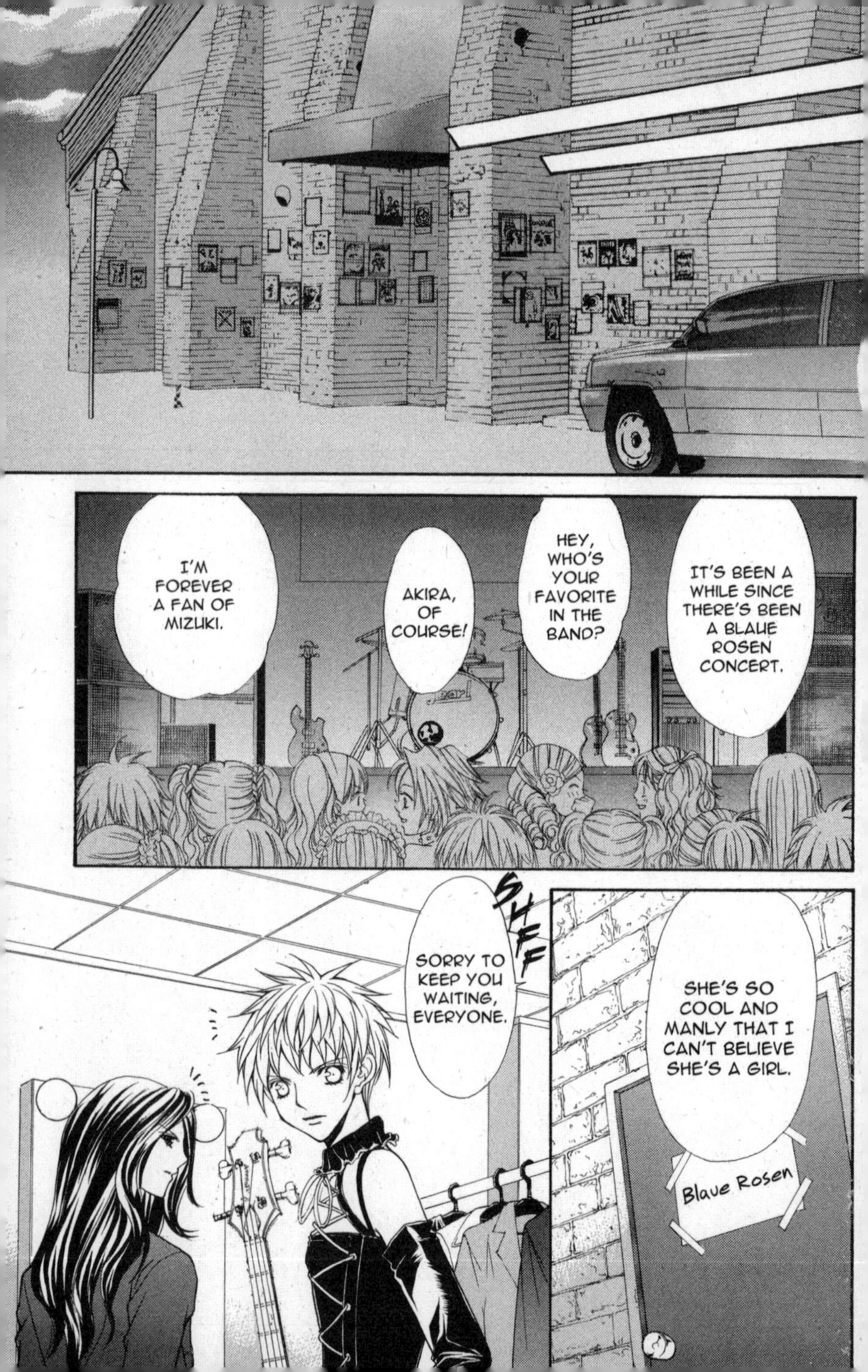
IT'S BEEN A WHILE SINCE THERE'S BEEN A BLAUE ROSEN CONCERT.
HEY, WHO'S YOUR FAVORITE IN THE BAND?
AKIRA, OF COURSE!
I'M FOREVER A FAN OF MIZUKI.
SHE'S SO COOL AND MANLY THAT I CAN'T BELIEVE SHE'S A GIRL.
Blaue Rosen
SHFF
SORRY TO KEEP YOU WAITING, EVERYONE.

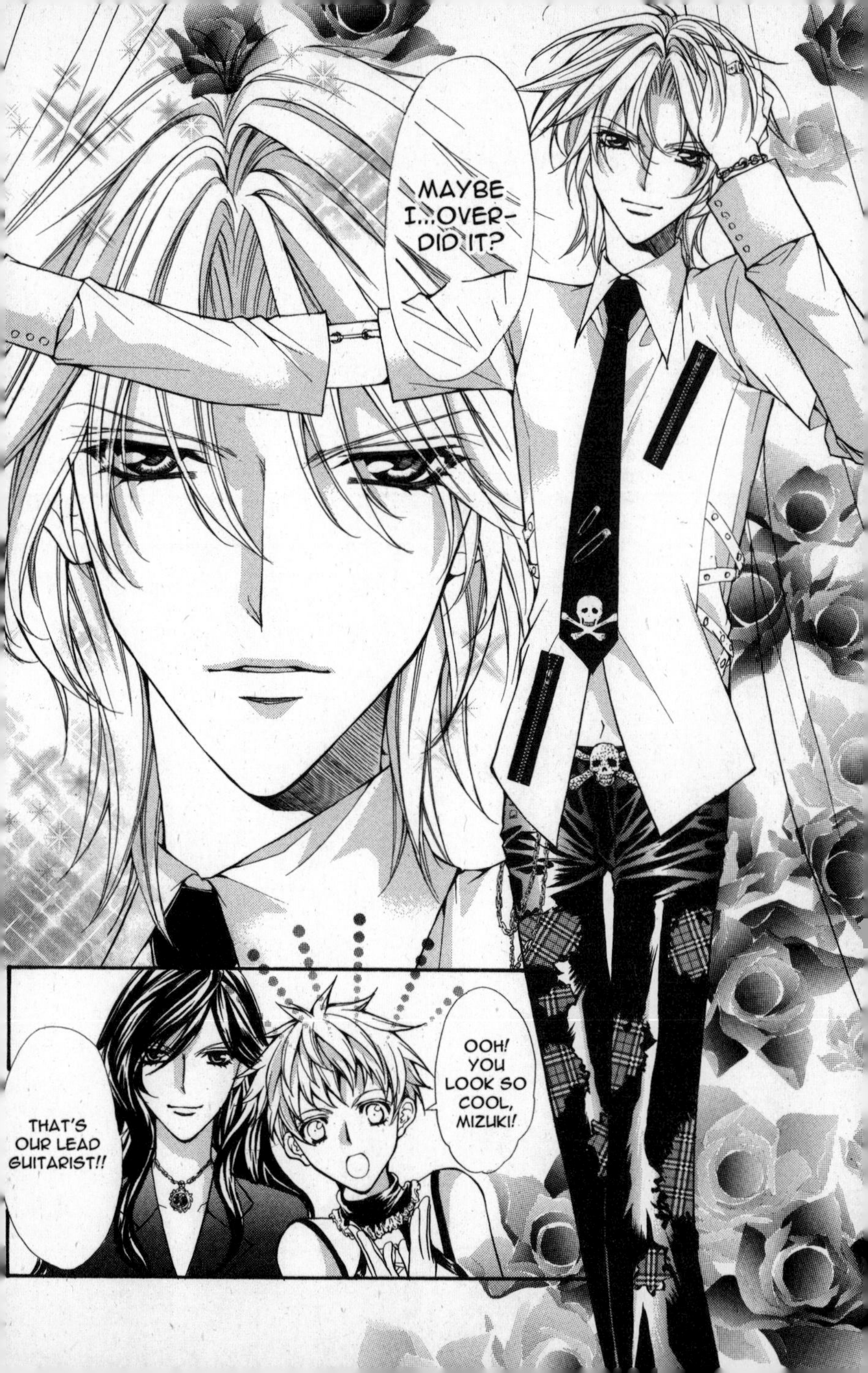
MAYBE I...OVER-DID IT?
OOH! YOU LOOK SO COOL, MIZUKI!
THAT'S OUR LEAD GUITARIST!!

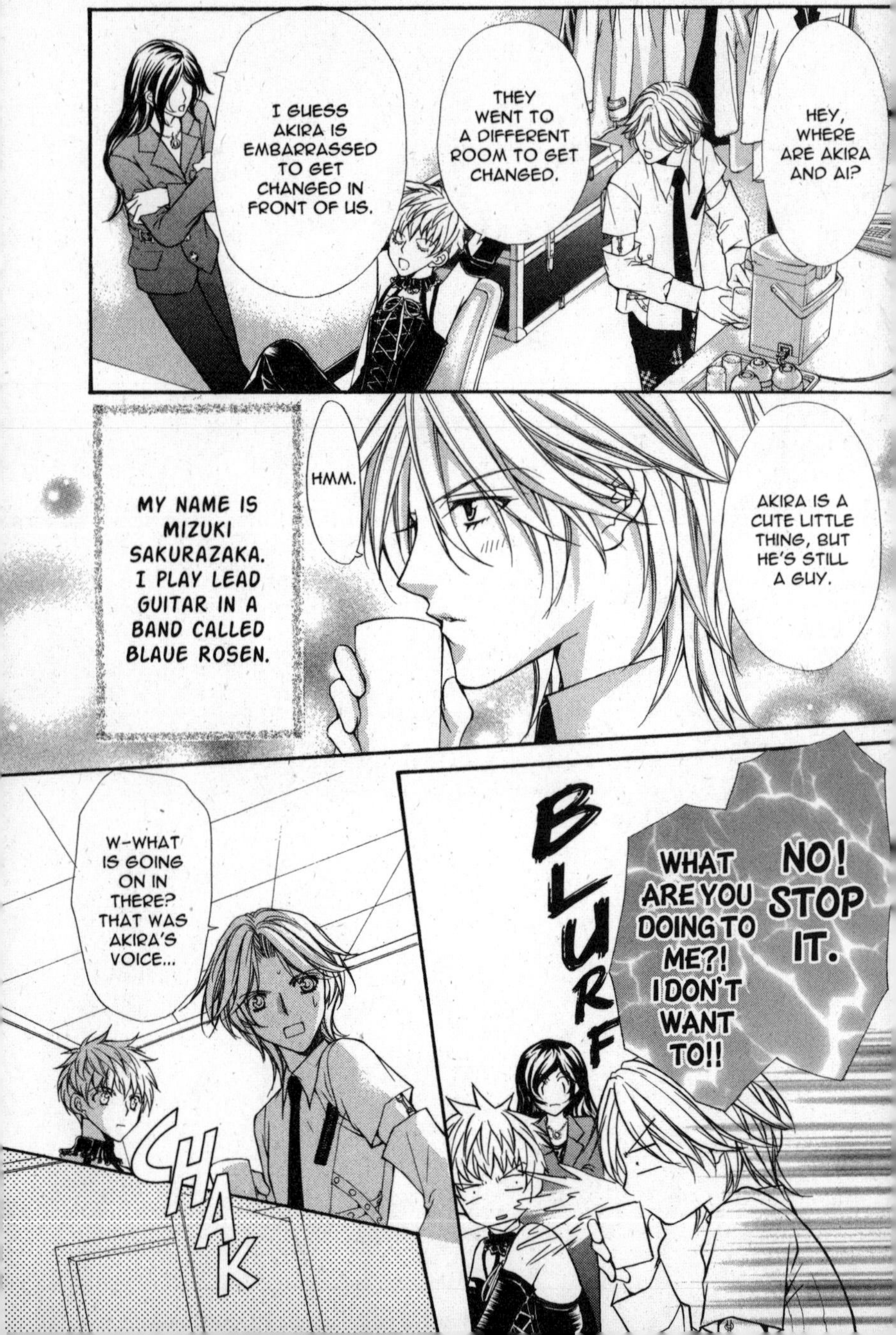
HEY, WHERE ARE AKIRA AND AI?
THEY WENT TO A DIFFERENT ROOM TO GET CHANGED.
I GUESS AKIRA IS EMBARRASSED TO GET CHANGED IN FRONT OF US.
AKIRA IS A CUTE LITTLE THING, BUT HE'S STILL A GUY.
HMM.
MY NAME IS MIZUKI SAKURAZAKA. I PLAY LEAD GUITAR IN A BAND CALLED BLAUE ROSEN.
NO! STOP IT.
WHAT ARE YOU DOING TO ME?! I DON'T WANT TO!!
BLURF
W-WHAT IS GOING ON IN THERE? THAT WAS AKIRA'S VOICE...
CHAK

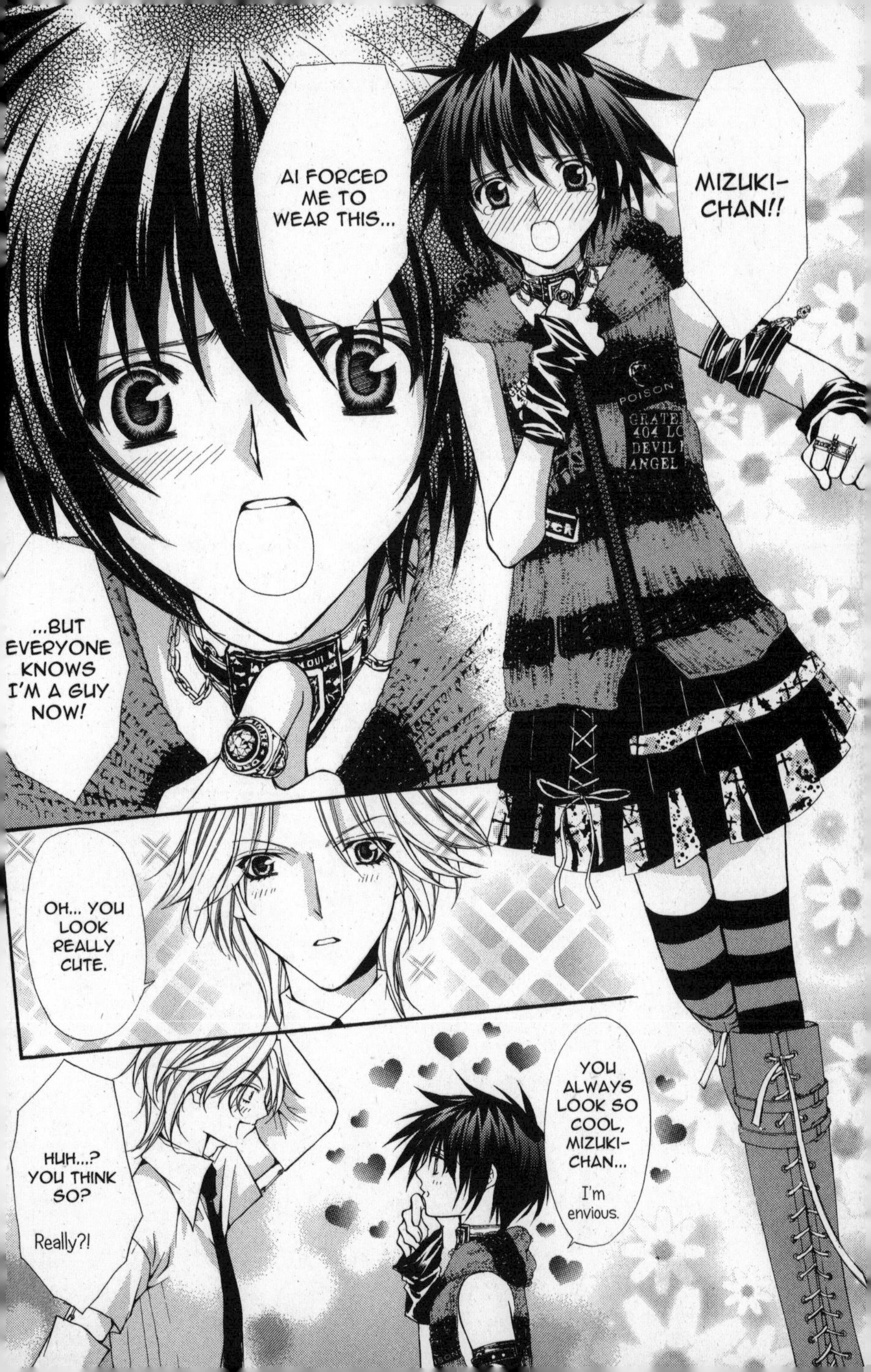
MIZUKI-CHAN!!
AI FORCED ME TO WEAR THIS...
...BUT EVERYONE KNOWS I'M A GUY NOW!
OH... YOU LOOK REALLY CUTE.
YOU ALWAYS LOOK SO COOL, MIZUKI-CHAN...
I'm envious.
HUH...? YOU THINK SO?
Really?!

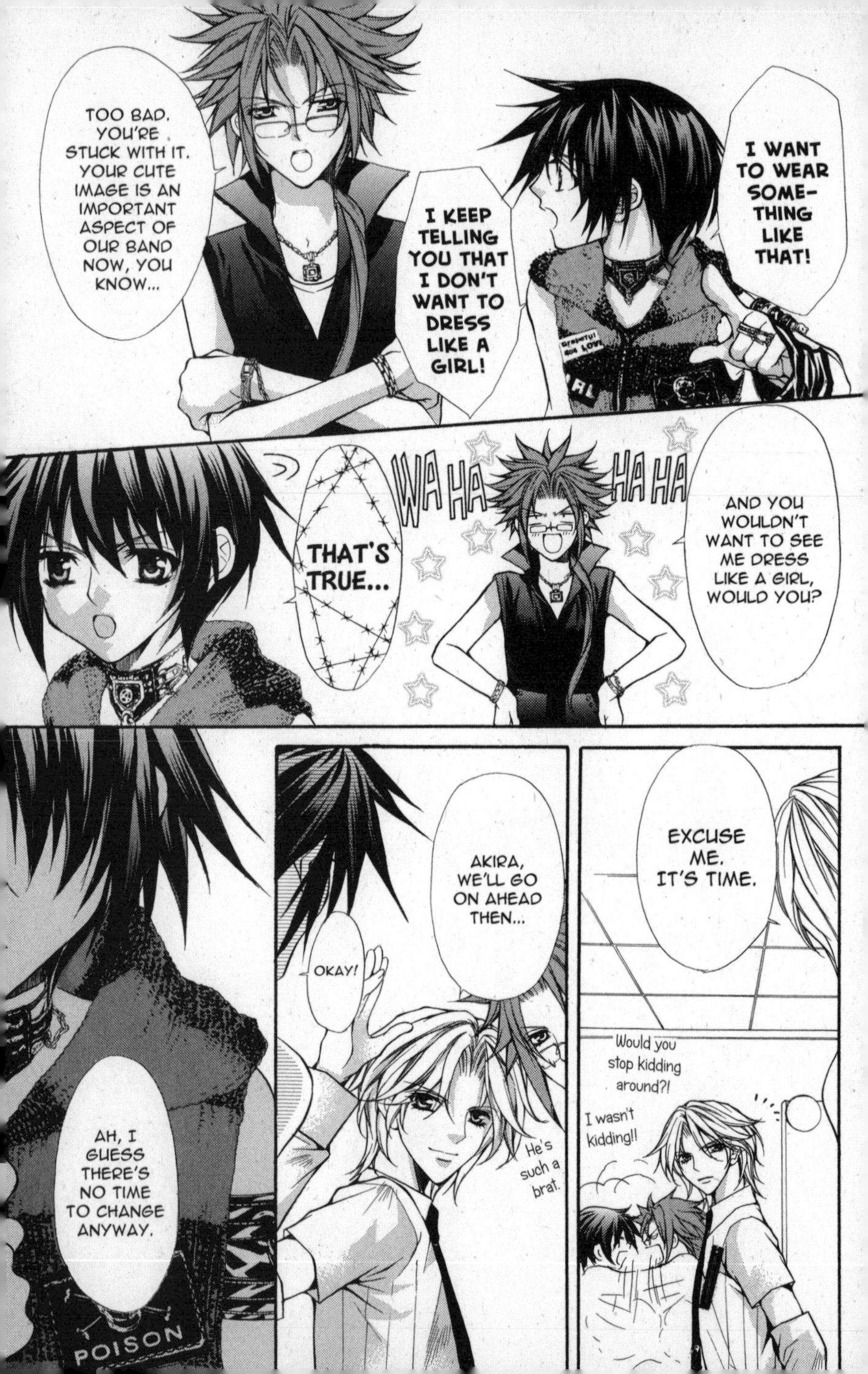
I WANT TO WEAR SOMETHING LIKE THAT!
I KEEP TELLING YOU THAT I DON'T WANT TO DRESS LIKE A GIRL!
TOO BAD. YOU'RE STUCK WITH IT. YOUR CUTE IMAGE IS AN IMPORTANT ASPECT OF OUR BAND NOW, YOU KNOW...
AND YOU WOULDN'T WANT TO SEE ME DRESS LIKE A GIRL, WOULD YOU?
WA HA HA HA
THAT'S TRUE...
EXCUSE ME. IT'S TIME.
Would you stop kidding around?!
I wasn't kidding!!
AKIRA, WE'LL GO ON AHEAD THEN...
OKAY!
He's such a brat.
AH, I GUESS THERE'S NO TIME TO CHANGE ANYWAY.
POISON

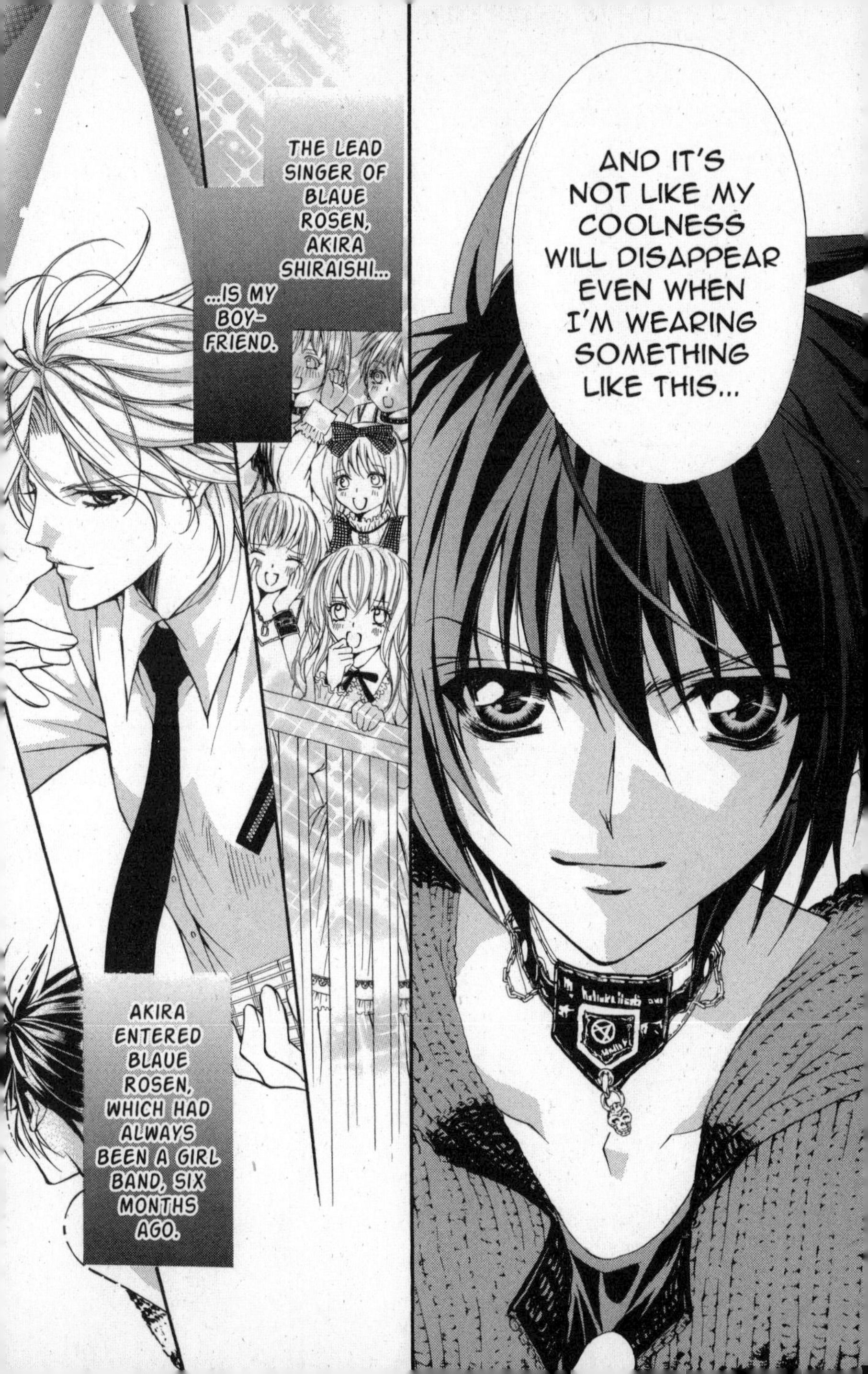
AND IT'S NOT LIKE MY COOLNESS WILL DISAPPEAR EVEN WHEN I'M WEARING SOMETHING LIKE THIS...
THE LEAD SINGER OF BLAUE ROSEN, AKIRA SHIRAISHI...
...IS MY BOY-FRIEND.
AKIRA ENTERED BLAUE ROSEN, WHICH HAD ALWAYS BEEN A GIRL BAND, SIX MONTHS AGO.

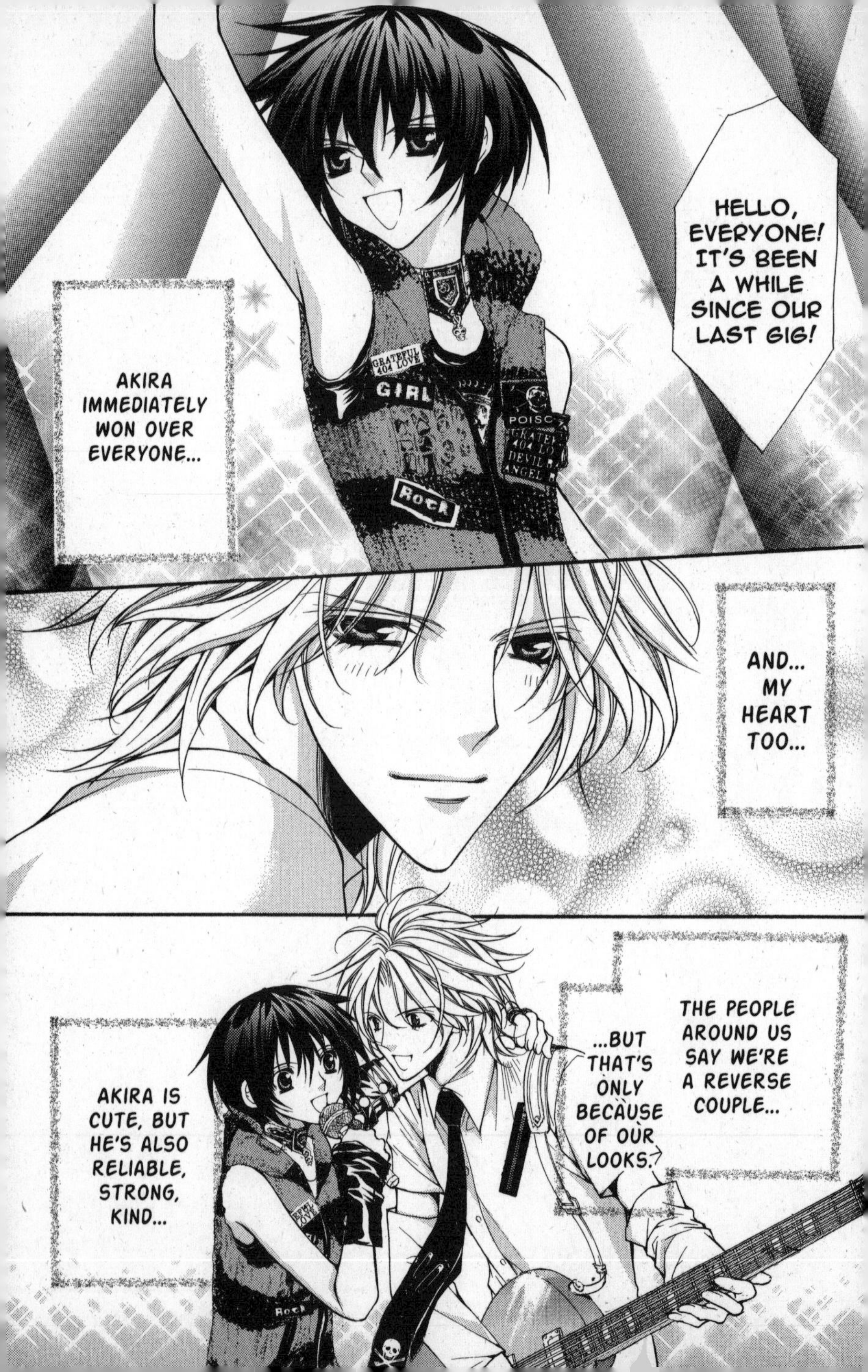
HELLO, EVERYONE! IT'S BEEN A WHILE SINCE OUR LAST GIG!
AKIRA IMMEDIATELY WON OVER EVERYONE...
AND... MY HEART TOO...
THE PEOPLE AROUND US SAY WE'RE A REVERSE COUPLE...
...BUT THAT'S ONLY BECAUSE OF OUR LOOKS.
AKIRA IS CUTE, BUT HE'S ALSO RELIABLE, STRONG, KIND...

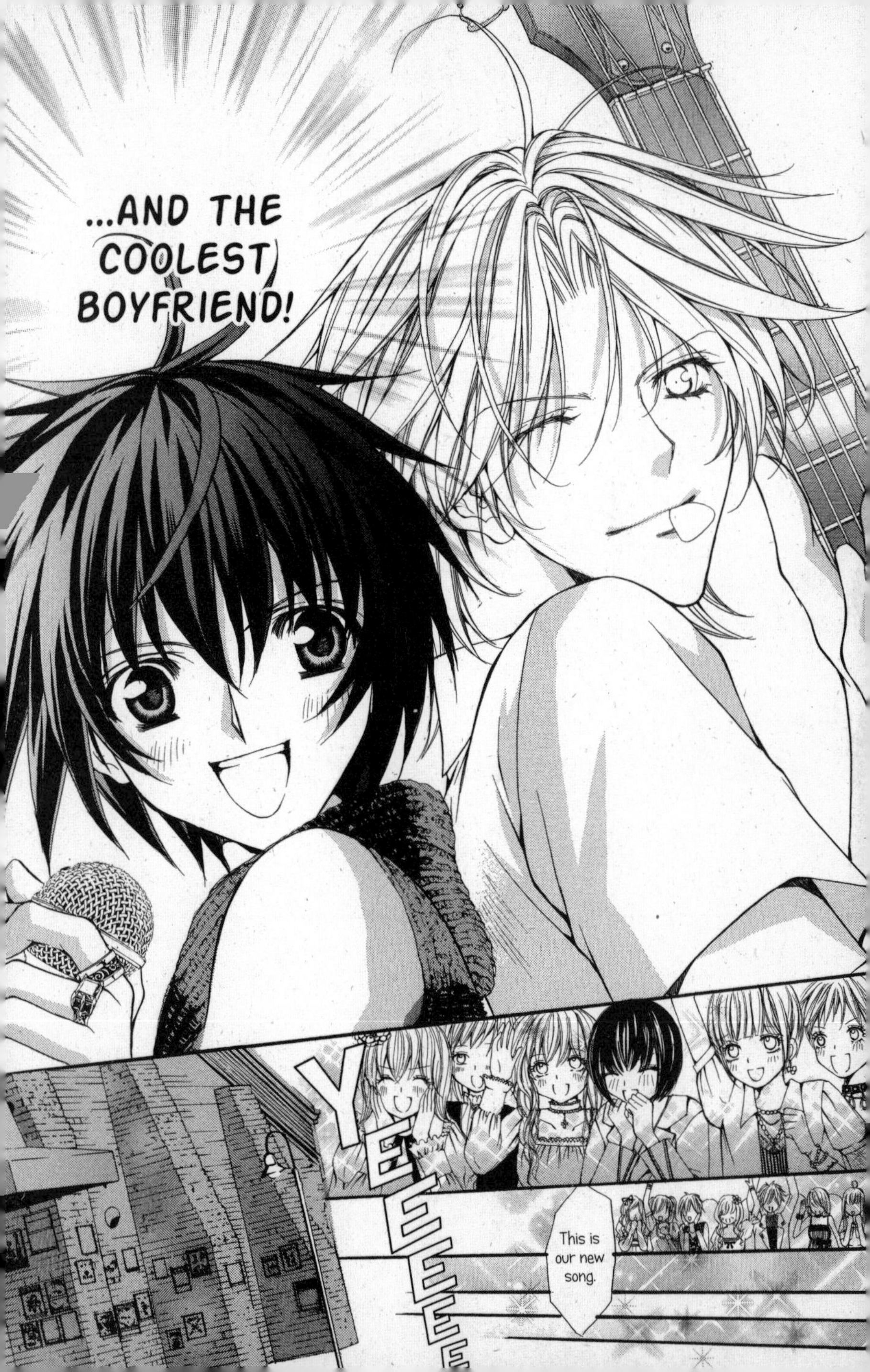
...AND THE COOLEST BOYFRIEND!
YEEEEEE
This is our new song.

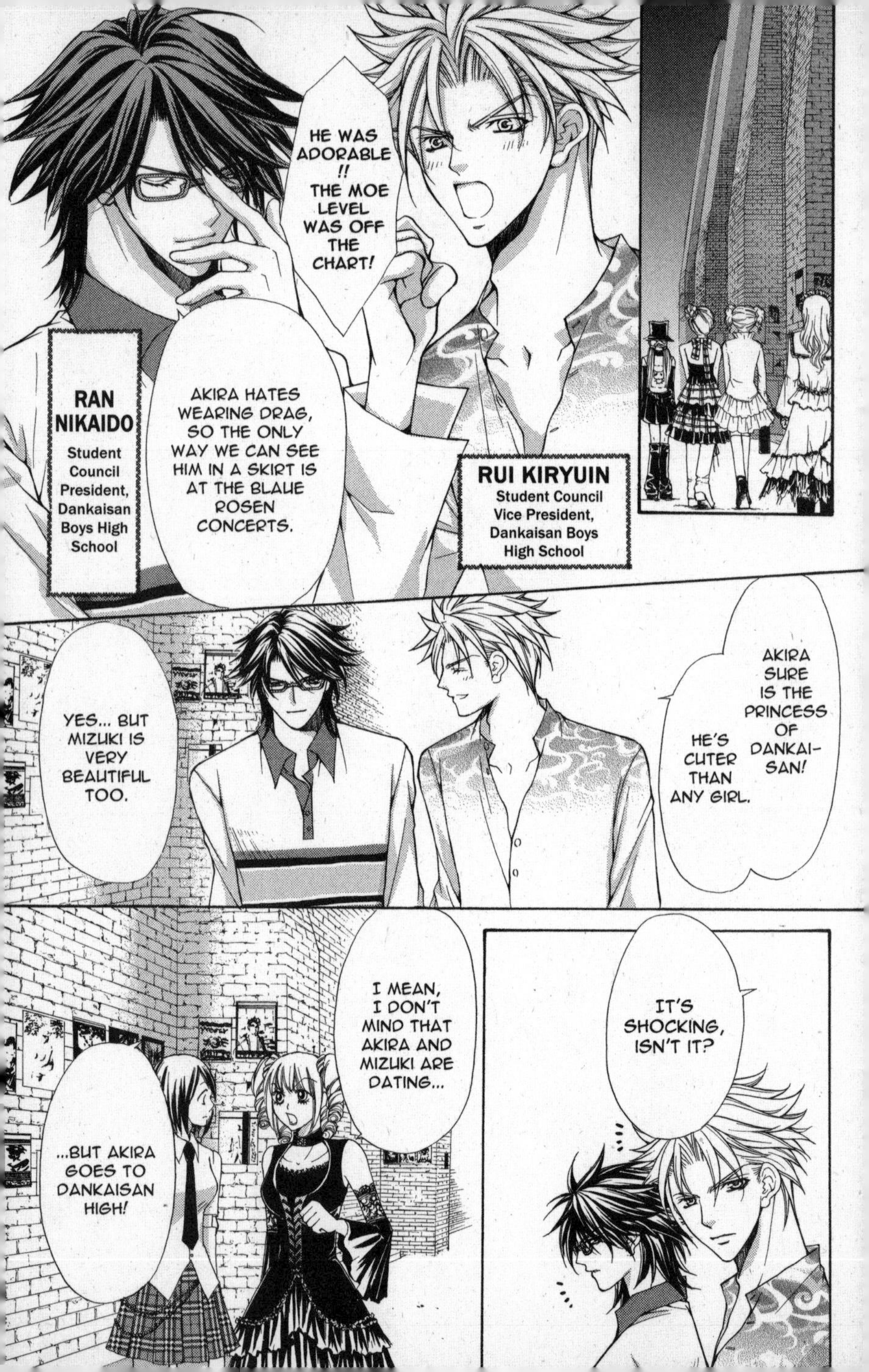
HE WAS ADORABLE!! THE MOE LEVEL WAS OFF THE CHART!
RUI KIRYUIN
Student Council Vice President, Dankaisan Boys High School
AKIRA HATES WEARING DRAG, SO THE ONLY WAY WE CAN SEE HIM IN A SKIRT IS AT THE BLAUE ROSEN CONCERTS.
RAN NIKAIDO
Student Council President, Dankaisan Boys High School
AKIRA SURE IS THE PRINCESS OF DANKAI-SAN!
HE'S CUTER THAN ANY GIRL.
YES... BUT MIZUKI IS VERY BEAUTIFUL TOO.
IT'S SHOCKING, ISN'T IT?
I MEAN, I DON'T MIND THAT AKIRA AND MIZUKI ARE DATING...
...BUT AKIRA GOES TO DANKAISAN HIGH!

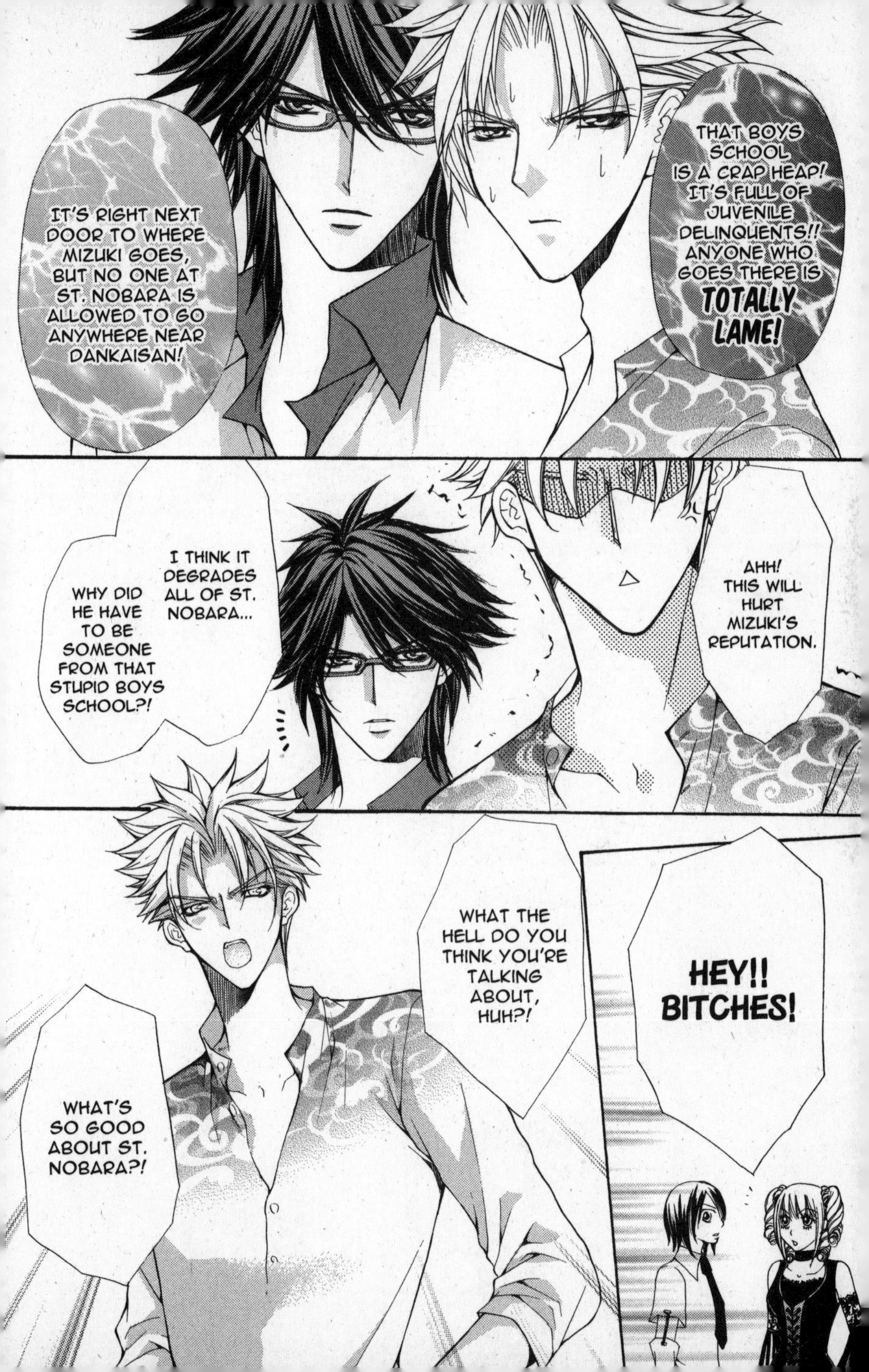
THAT BOYS SCHOOL IS A CRAP HEAP! IT'S FULL OF JUVENILE DELINQUENTS!! ANYONE WHO GOES THERE IS **TOTALLY LAME!**
IT'S RIGHT NEXT DOOR TO WHERE MIZUKI GOES, BUT NO ONE AT ST. NOBARA IS ALLOWED TO GO ANYWHERE NEAR DANKAISAN!
AHH! THIS WILL HURT MIZUKI'S REPUTATION.
I THINK IT DEGRADES ALL OF ST. NOBARA...
WHY DID HE HAVE TO BE SOMEONE FROM THAT STUPID BOYS SCHOOL?!
HEY!! BITCHES!
WHAT THE HELL DO YOU THINK YOU'RE TALKING ABOUT, HUH?!
WHAT'S SO GOOD ABOUT ST. NOBARA?!

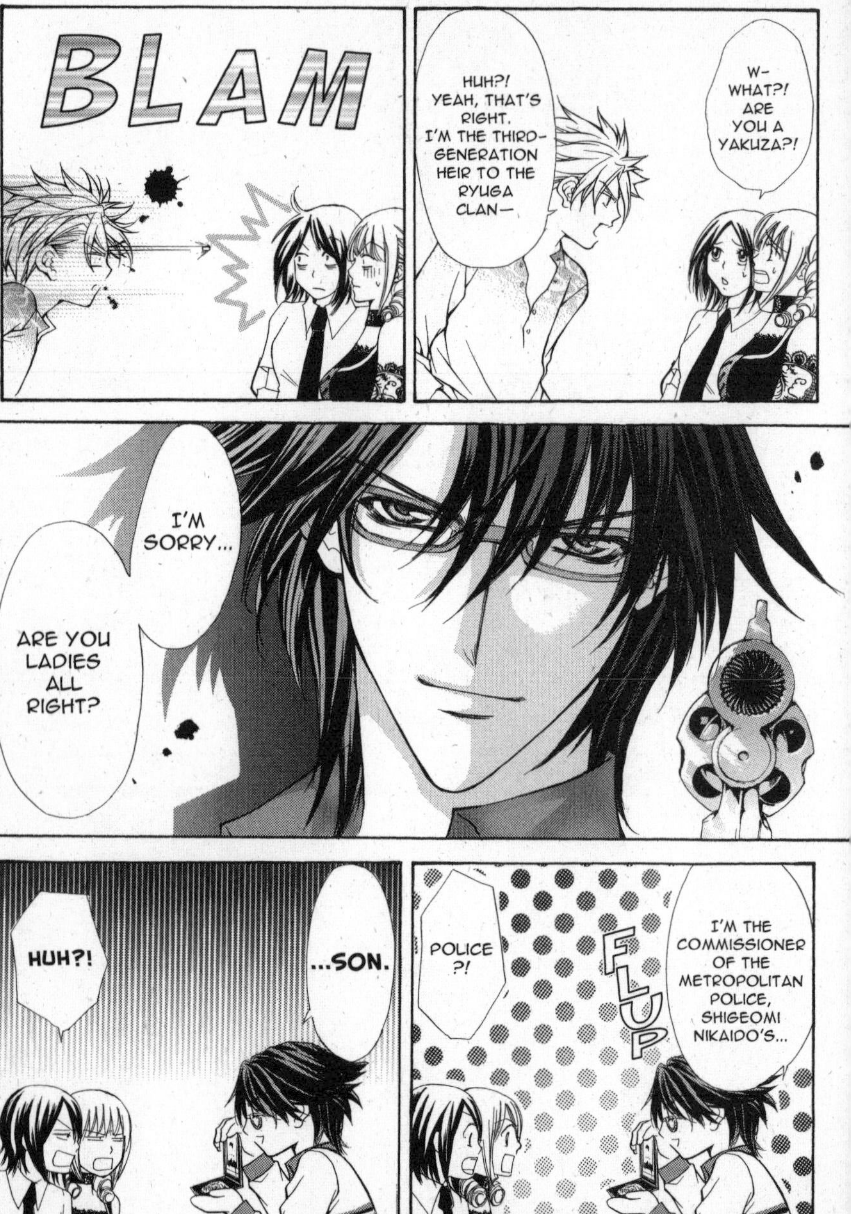
W- WHAT?! ARE YOU A YAKUZA?!
HUH?! YEAH, THAT'S RIGHT. I'M THE THIRD-GENERATION HEIR TO THE RYUGA CLAN—
BLAM
I'M SORRY...
ARE YOU LADIES ALL RIGHT?
I'M THE COMMISSIONER OF THE METROPOLITAN POLICE, SHIGEOMI NIKAIDO'S...
FLUP
POLICE ?!
...SON.
HUH?!

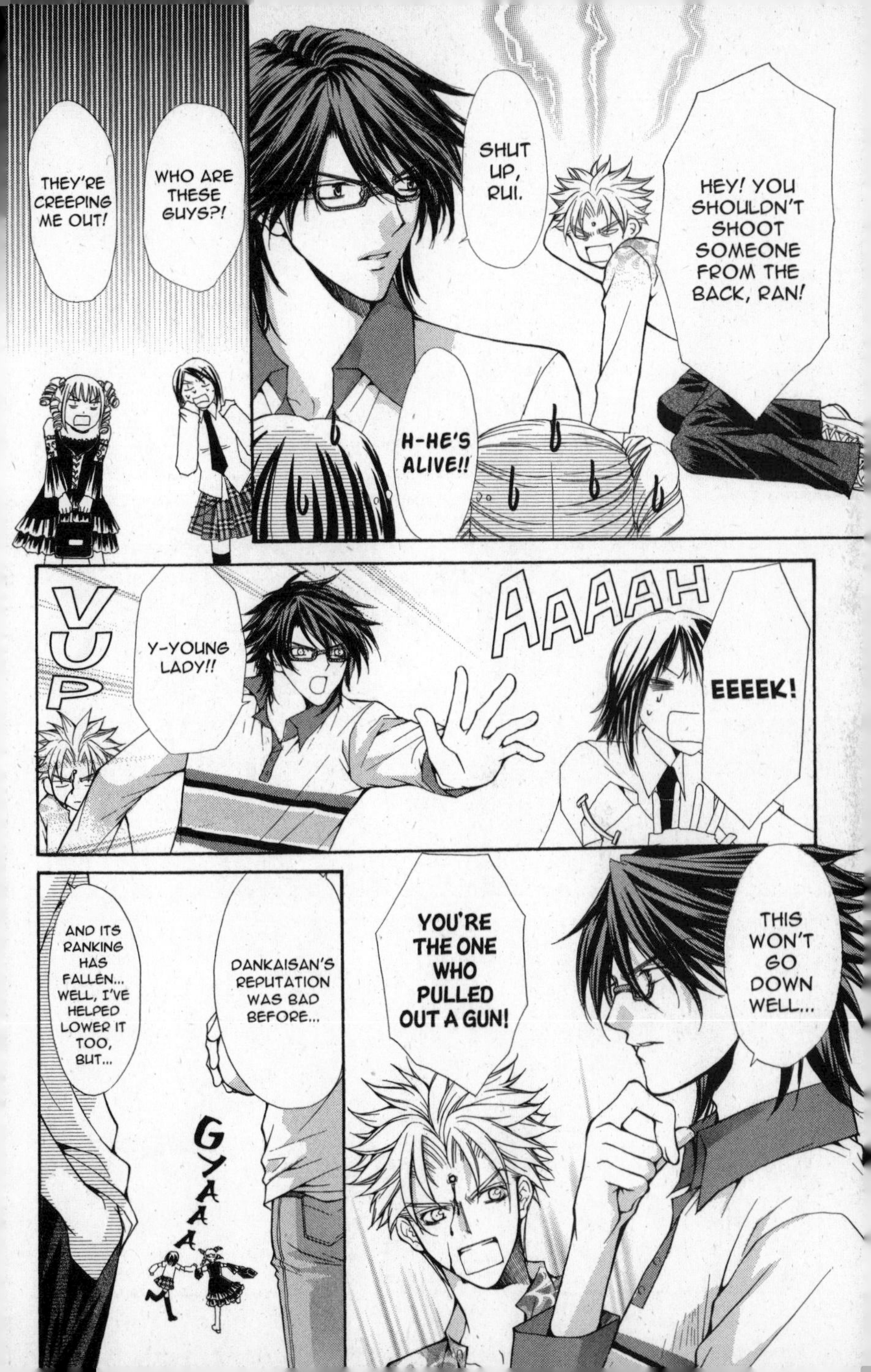
HEY! YOU SHOULDN'T SHOOT SOMEONE FROM THE BACK, RAN!
SHUT UP, RUI.
H-HE'S ALIVE!!
WHO ARE THESE GUYS?!
THEY'RE CREEPING ME OUT!
EEEEK!
AAAAH
Y-YOUNG LADY!!
VUP
THIS WON'T GO DOWN WELL...
YOU'RE THE ONE WHO PULLED OUT A GUN!
DANKAISAN'S REPUTATION WAS BAD BEFORE...
AND ITS RANKING HAS FALLEN... WELL, I'VE HELPED LOWER IT TOO, BUT...
GYAAAA

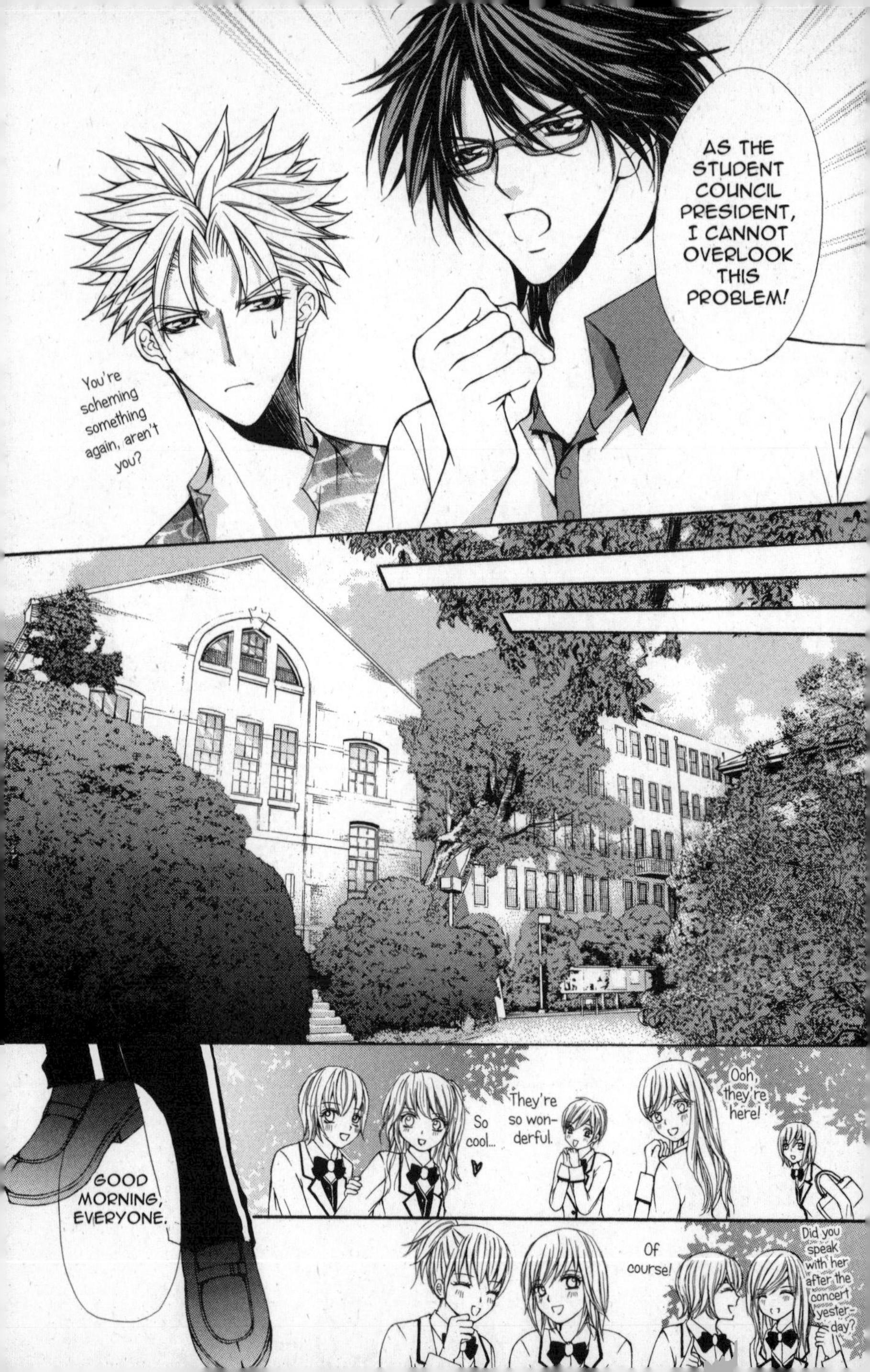
AS THE STUDENT COUNCIL PRESIDENT, I CANNOT OVERLOOK THIS PROBLEM!
You're scheming something again, aren't you?
Ooh, they're here!
They're so wonderful.
So cool...
Did you speak with her after the concert yesterday?
Of course!
GOOD MORNING, EVERYONE.

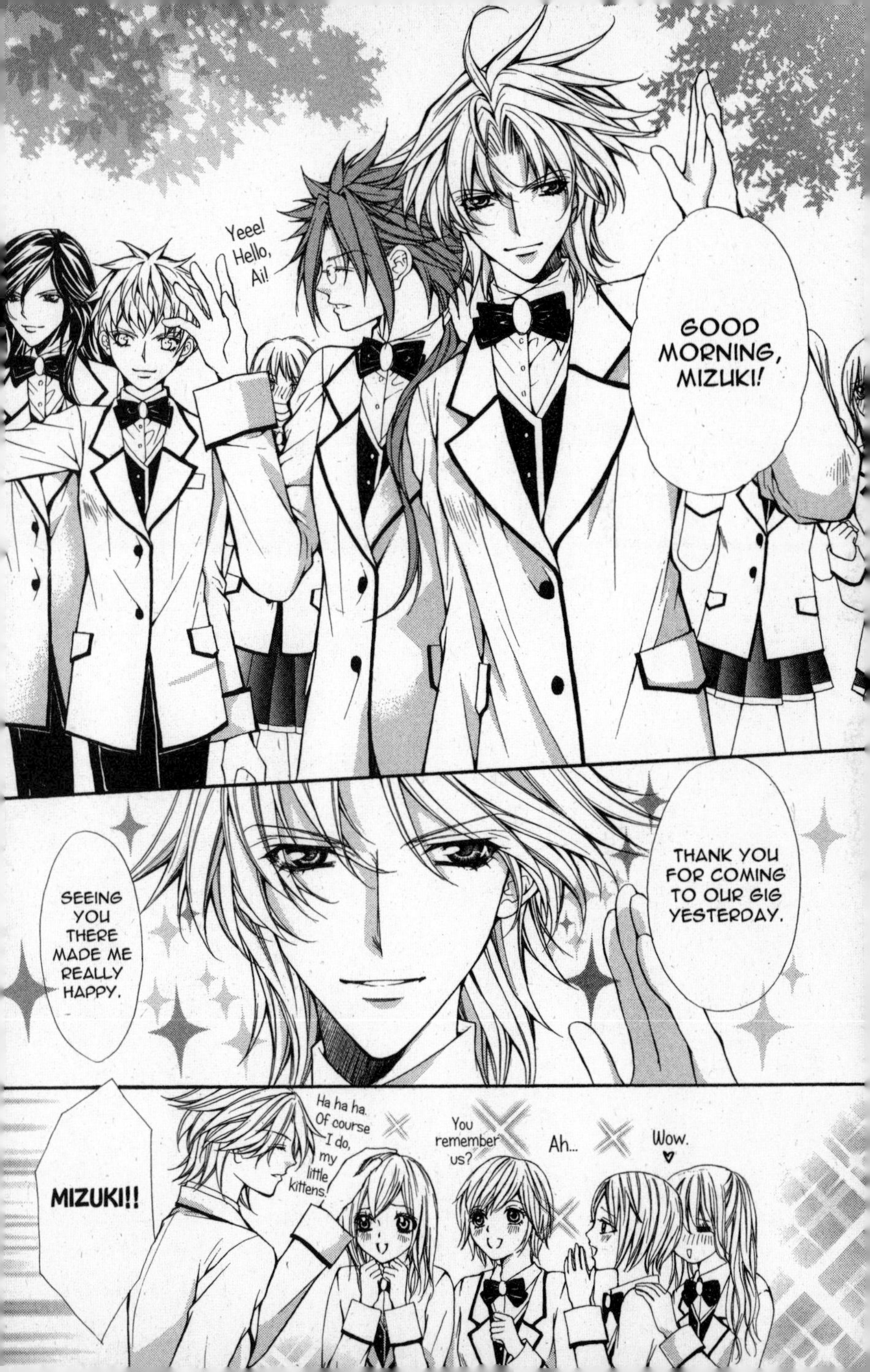
GOOD MORNING, MIZUKI!
Yeee! Hello, Ai!
THANK YOU FOR COMING TO OUR GIG YESTERDAY.
SEEING YOU THERE MADE ME REALLY HAPPY.
Wow. ♥
Ah...
You remember us?
Ha ha ha. Of course I do, my little kittens.
MIZUKI!!

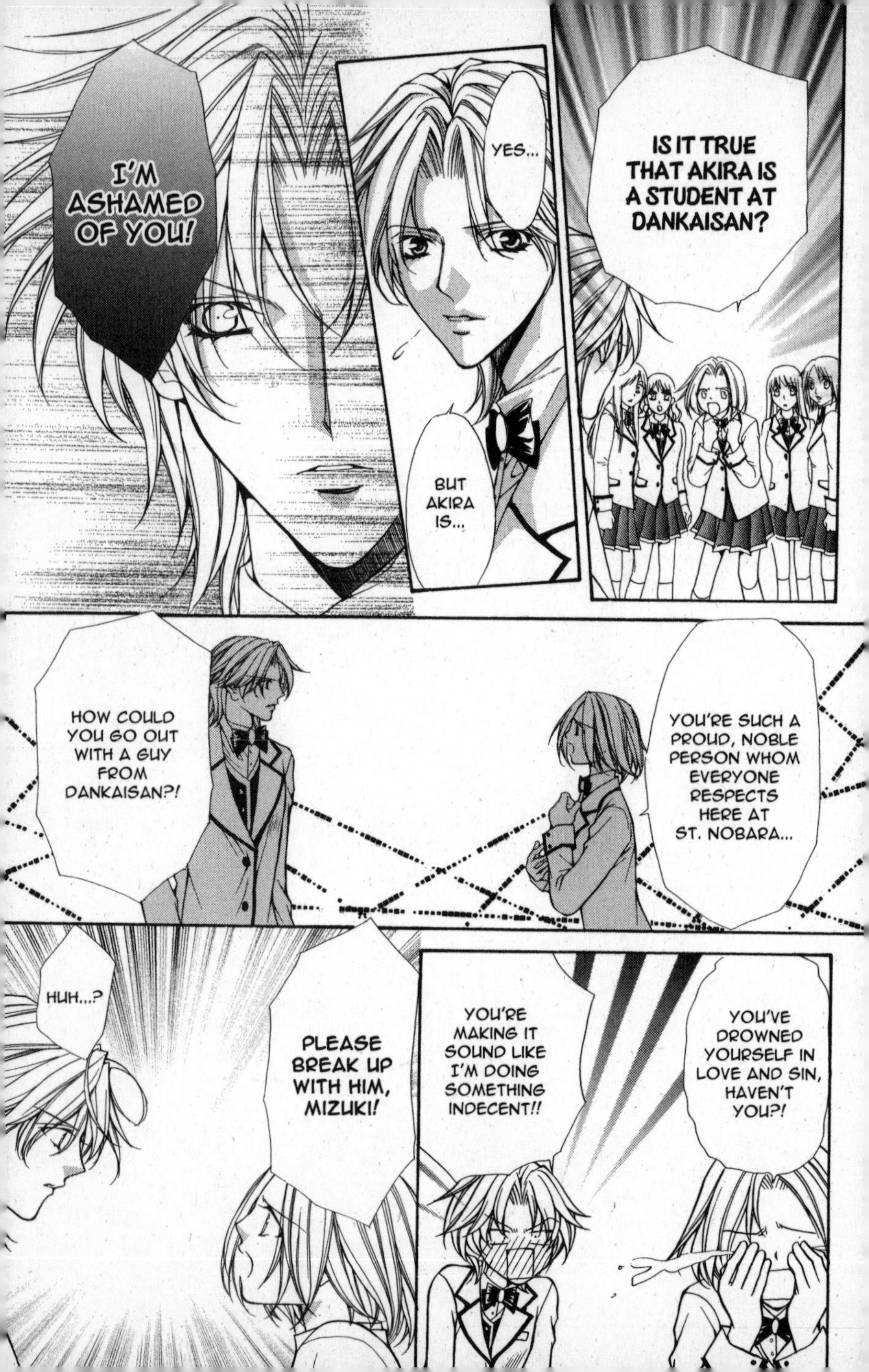
IS IT TRUE THAT AKIRA IS A STUDENT AT DANKAISAN?
YES...
BUT AKIRA IS...
I'M ASHAMED OF YOU!
YOU'RE SUCH A PROUD, NOBLE PERSON WHOM EVERYONE RESPECTS HERE AT ST. NOBARA...
HOW COULD YOU GO OUT WITH A GUY FROM DANKAISAN?!
YOU'VE DROWNED YOURSELF IN LOVE AND SIN, HAVEN'T YOU?!
YOU'RE MAKING IT SOUND LIKE I'M DOING SOMETHING INDECENT!!
PLEASE BREAK UP WITH HIM, MIZUKI!
HUH...?

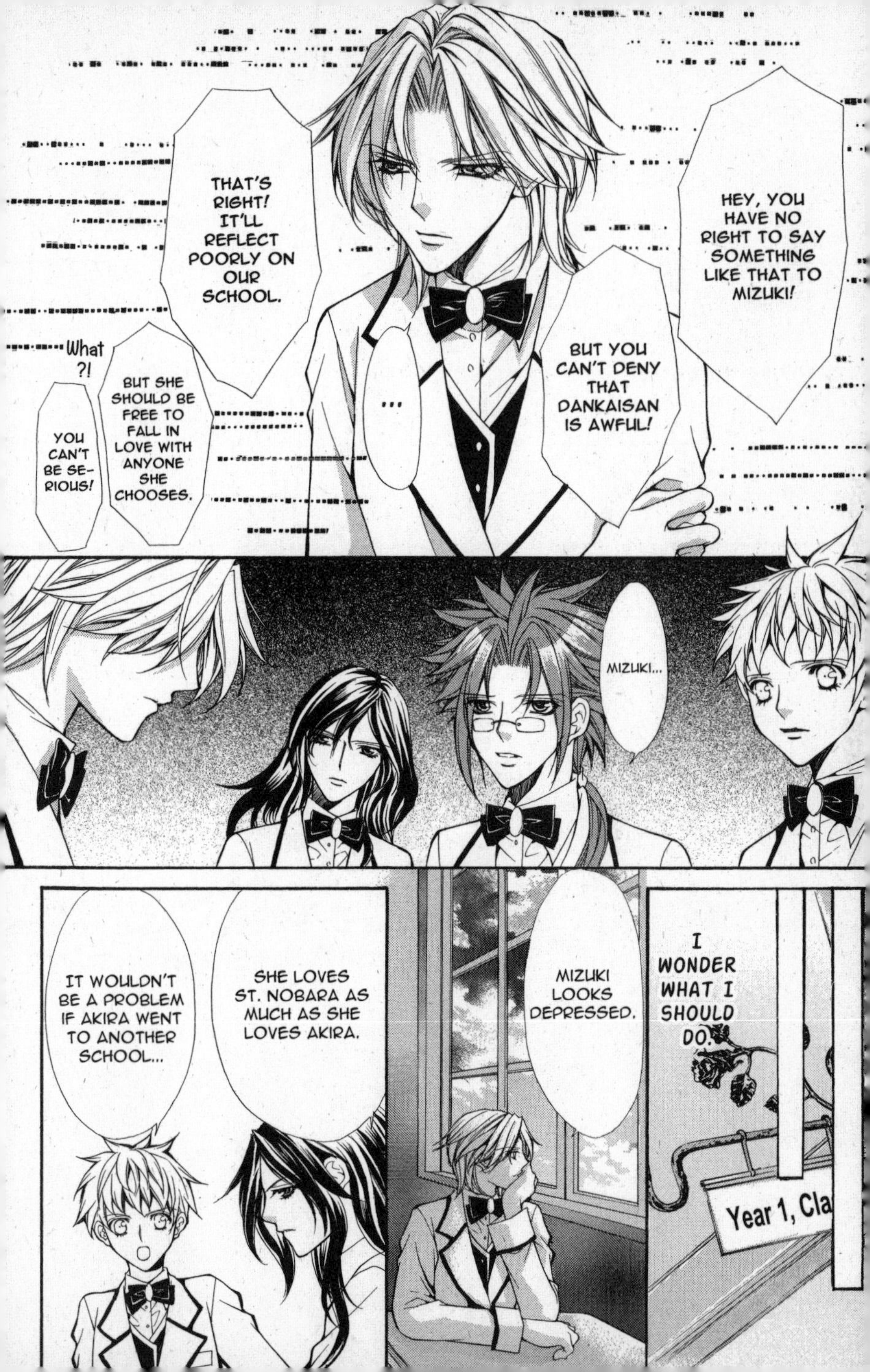
HEY, YOU HAVE NO RIGHT TO SAY SOMETHING LIKE THAT TO MIZUKI!
BUT YOU CAN'T DENY THAT DANKAISAN IS AWFUL!
...
THAT'S RIGHT! IT'LL REFLECT POORLY ON OUR SCHOOL.
BUT SHE SHOULD BE FREE TO FALL IN LOVE WITH ANYONE SHE CHOOSES.
What?!
YOU CAN'T BE SE-RIOUS!
MIZUKI...
I WONDER WHAT I SHOULD DO.
Year 1, Cla
MIZUKI LOOKS DEPRESSED.
SHE LOVES ST. NOBARA AS MUCH AS SHE LOVES AKIRA.
IT WOULDN'T BE A PROBLEM IF AKIRA WENT TO ANOTHER SCHOOL...

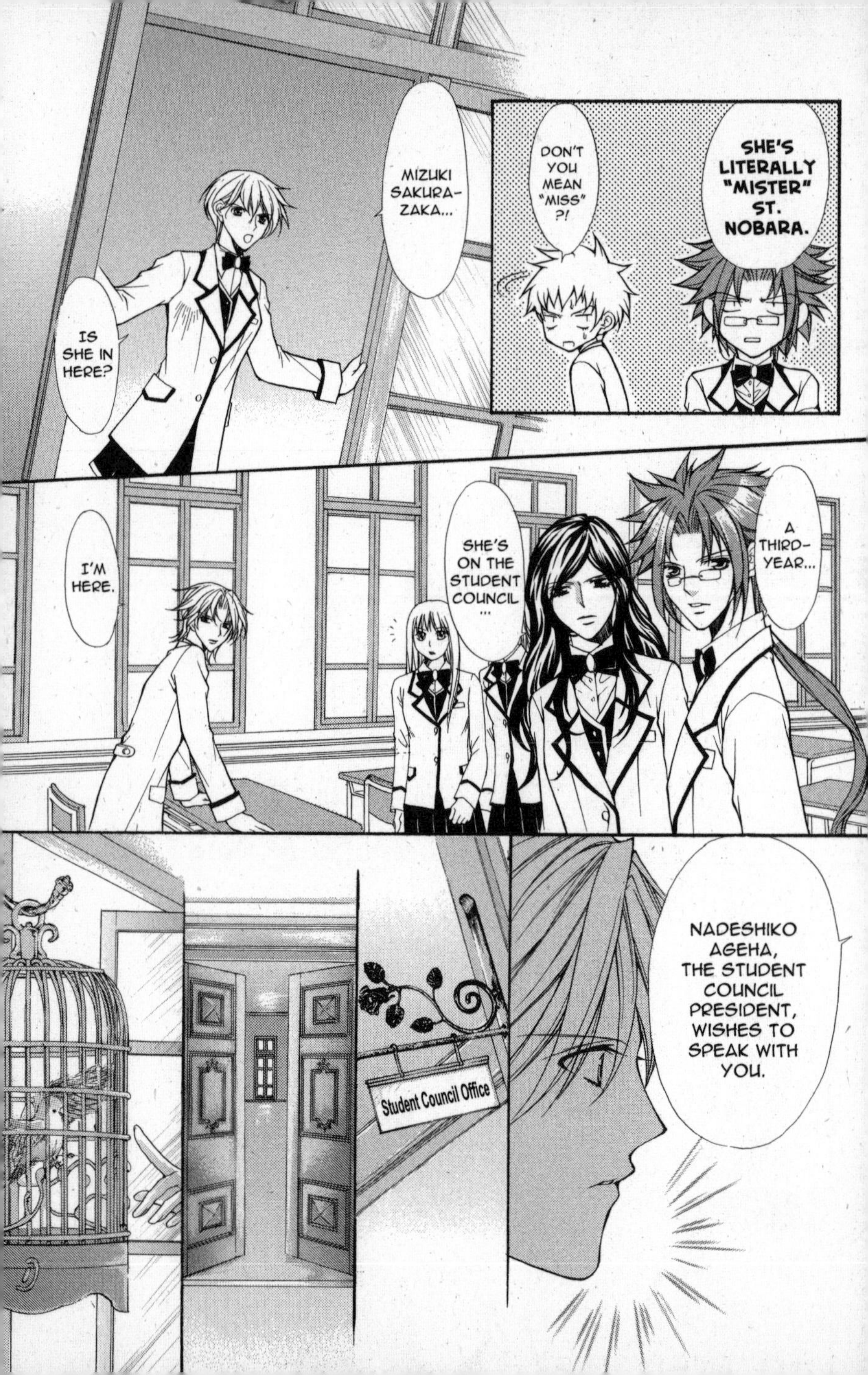
MIZUKI SAKURA-ZAKA...
IS SHE IN HERE?
SHE'S LITERALLY "MISTER" ST. NOBARA.
DON'T YOU MEAN "MISS" ?!
A THIRD-YEAR...
SHE'S ON THE STUDENT COUNCIL ...
I'M HERE.
NADESHIKO AGEHA, THE STUDENT COUNCIL PRESIDENT, WISHES TO SPEAK WITH YOU.
Student Council Office

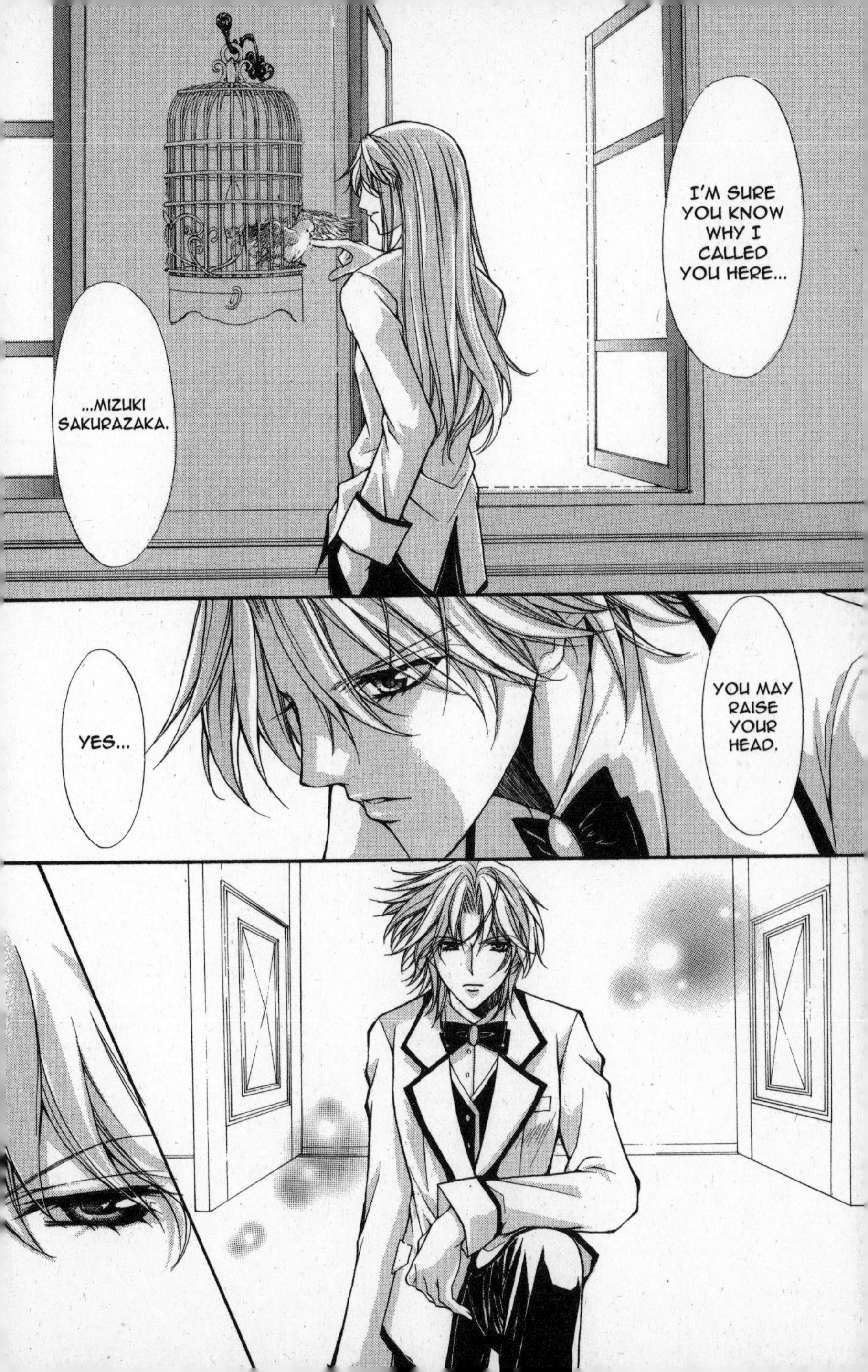
I'M SURE YOU KNOW WHY I CALLED YOU HERE...
...MIZUKI SAKURAZAKA.
YOU MAY RAISE YOUR HEAD.
YES...

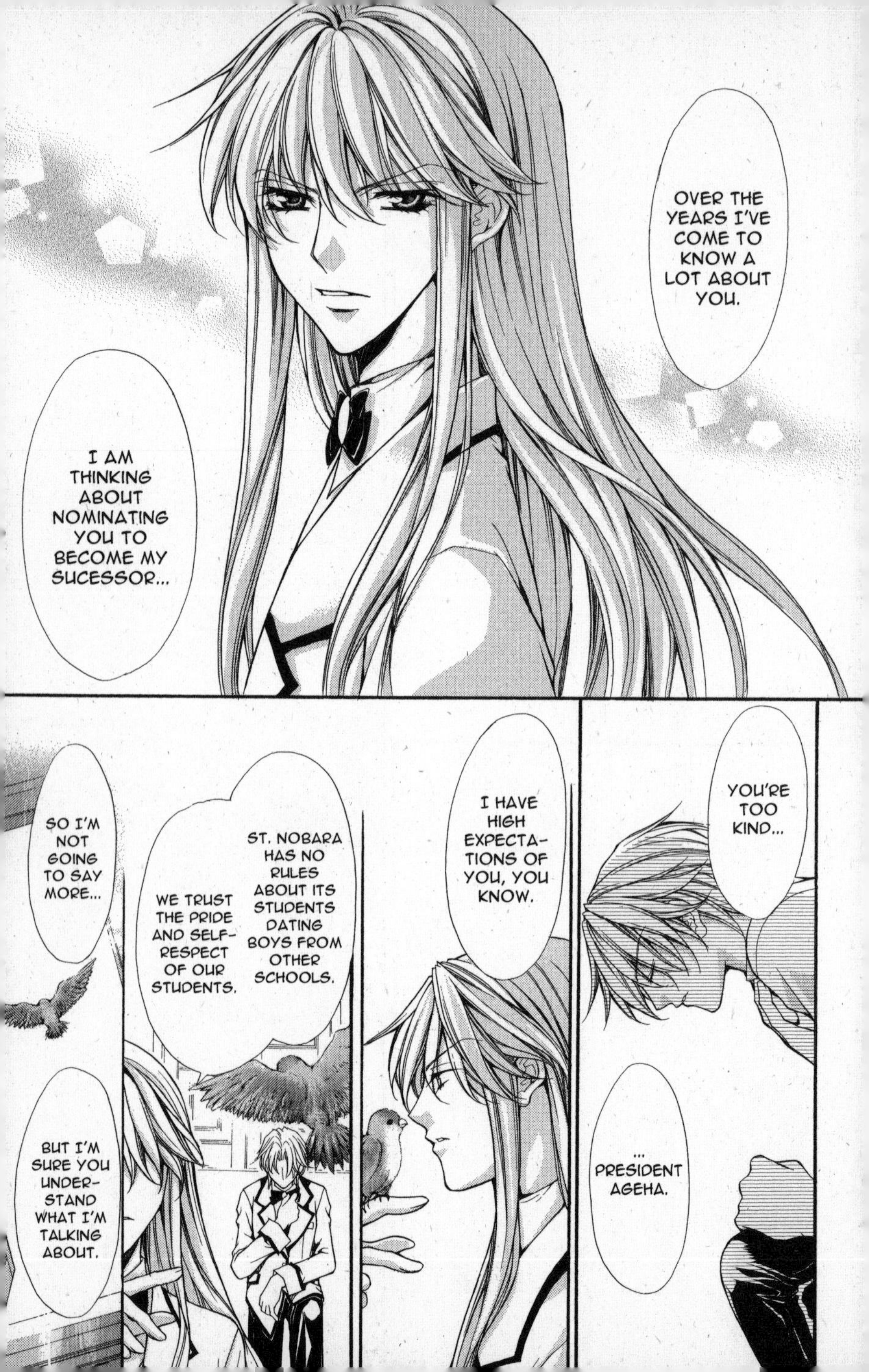
OVER THE YEARS I'VE COME TO KNOW A LOT ABOUT YOU.
I AM THINKING ABOUT NOMINATING YOU TO BECOME MY SUCESSOR...
YOU'RE TOO KIND...
... PRESIDENT AGEHA.
I HAVE HIGH EXPECTATIONS OF YOU, YOU KNOW.
ST. NOBARA HAS NO RULES ABOUT ITS STUDENTS DATING BOYS FROM OTHER SCHOOLS.
WE TRUST THE PRIDE AND SELF-RESPECT OF OUR STUDENTS.
SO I'M NOT GOING TO SAY MORE...
BUT I'M SURE YOU UNDERSTAND WHAT I'M TALKING ABOUT.

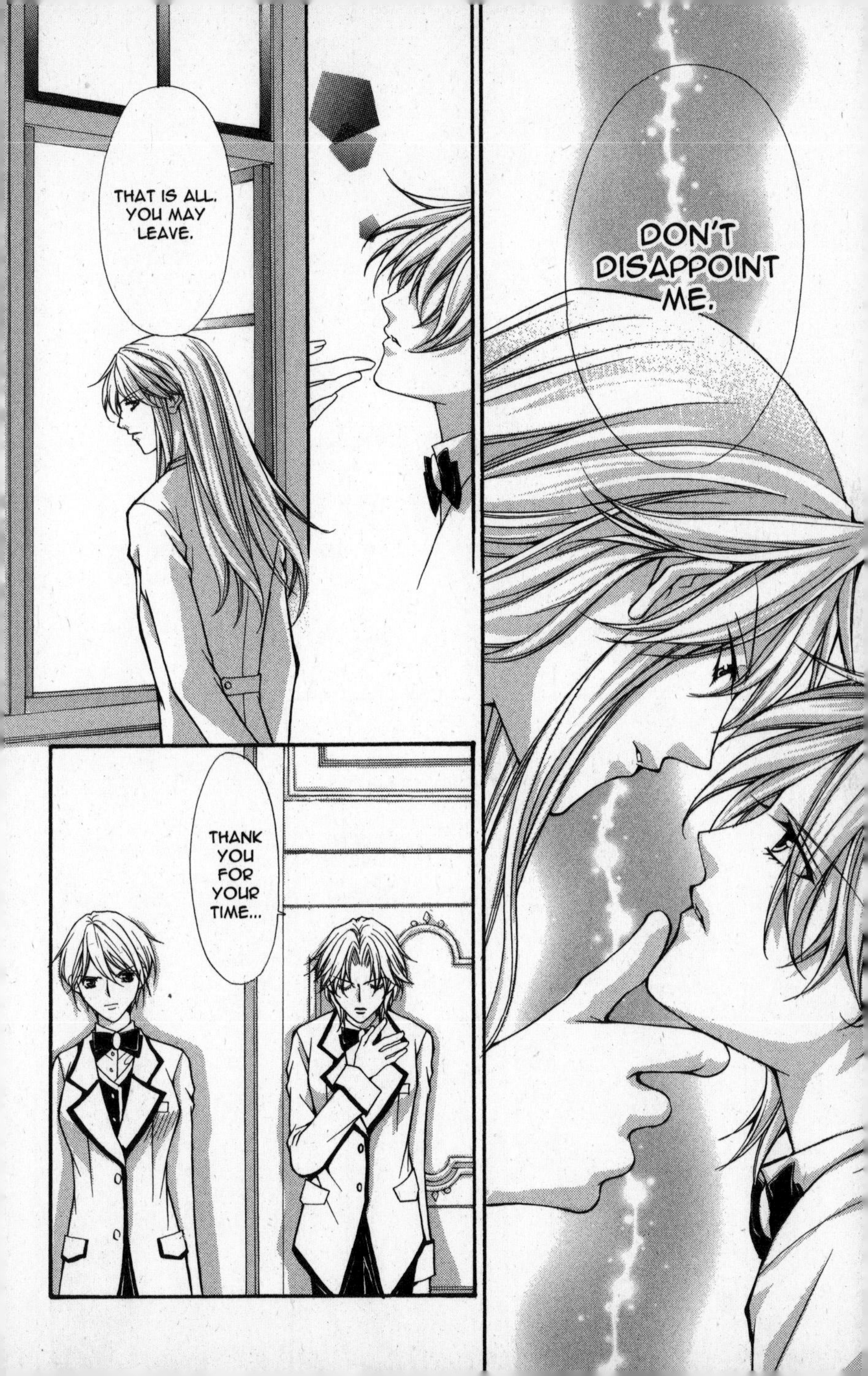
DON'T DISAPPOINT ME.
THAT IS ALL. YOU MAY LEAVE.
THANK YOU FOR YOUR TIME...

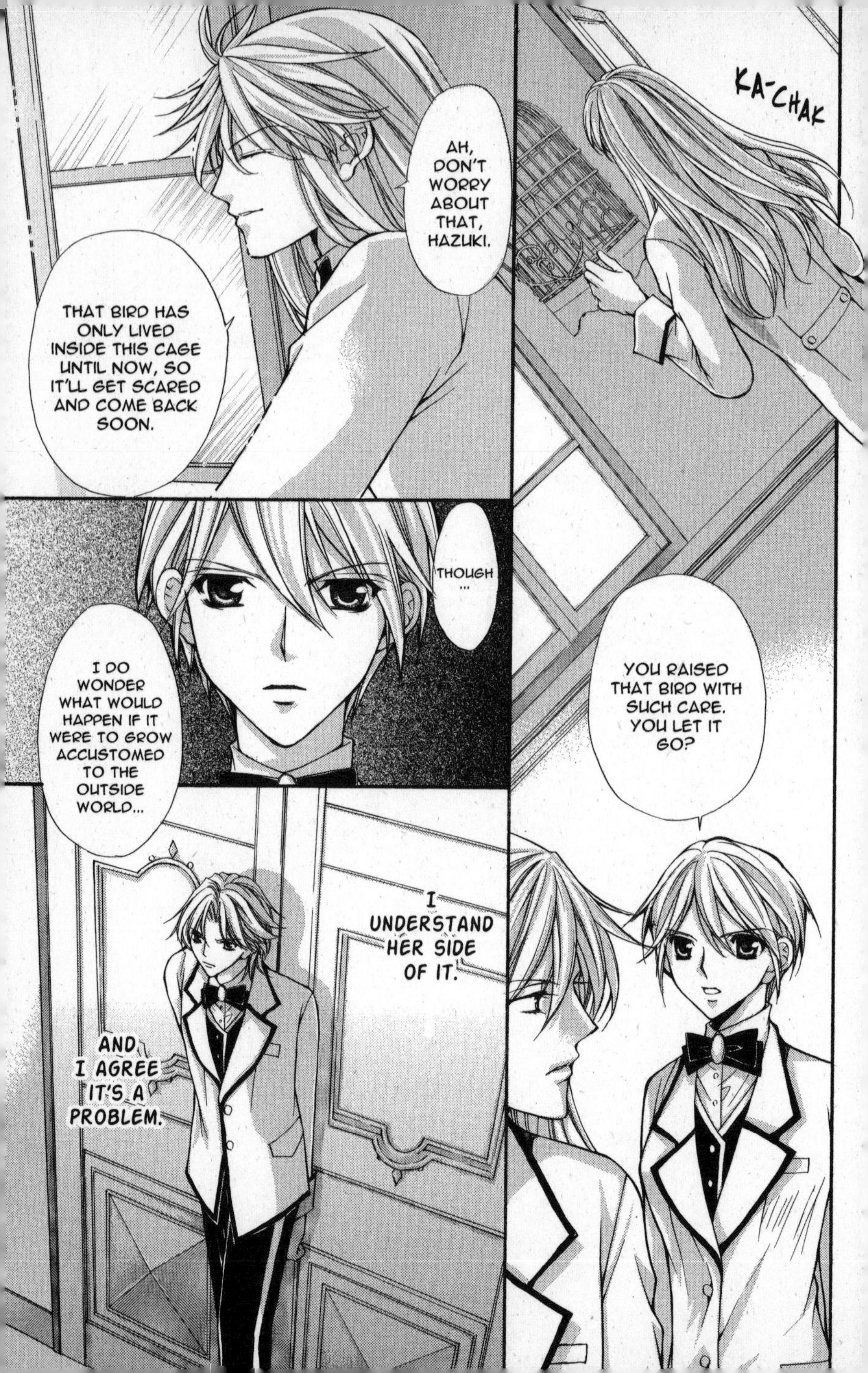
KA-CHAK
AH, DON'T WORRY ABOUT THAT, HAZUKI.
THAT BIRD HAS ONLY LIVED INSIDE THIS CAGE UNTIL NOW, SO IT'LL GET SCARED AND COME BACK SOON.
YOU RAISED THAT BIRD WITH SUCH CARE. YOU LET IT GO?
THOUGH...
I DO WONDER WHAT WOULD HAPPEN IF IT WERE TO GROW ACCUSTOMED TO THE OUTSIDE WORLD...
I UNDERSTAND HER SIDE OF IT.
AND I AGREE IT'S A PROBLEM.

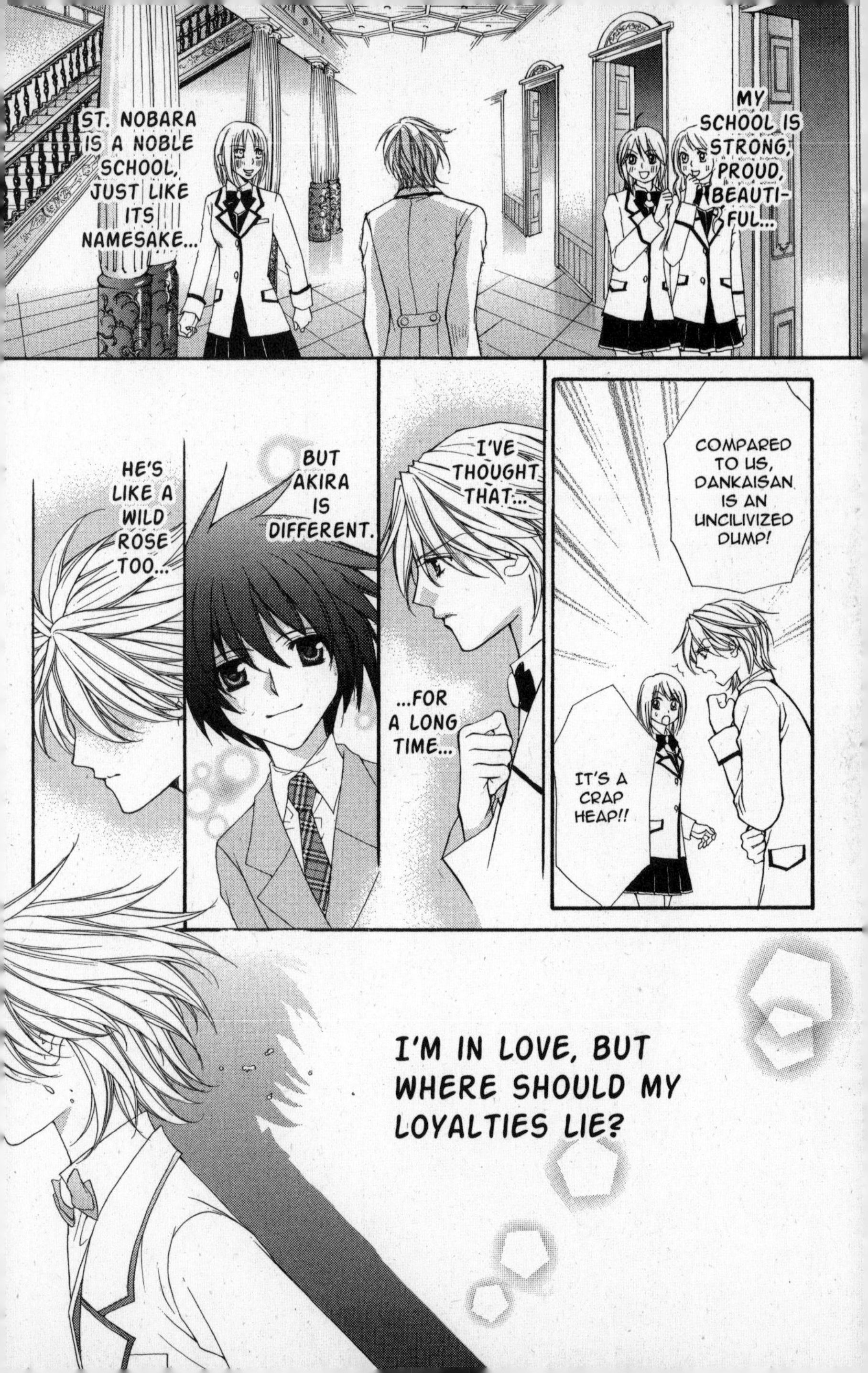
MY SCHOOL IS STRONG, PROUD, BEAUTI-FUL...
ST. NOBARA IS A NOBLE SCHOOL, JUST LIKE ITS NAMESAKE...
COMPARED TO US, DANKAISAN IS AN UNCILIVIZED DUMP!
IT'S A CRAP HEAP!!
I'VE THOUGHT THAT...
...FOR A LONG TIME...
BUT AKIRA IS DIFFERENT.
HE'S LIKE A WILD ROSE TOO...
I'M IN LOVE, BUT WHERE SHOULD MY LOYALTIES LIE?

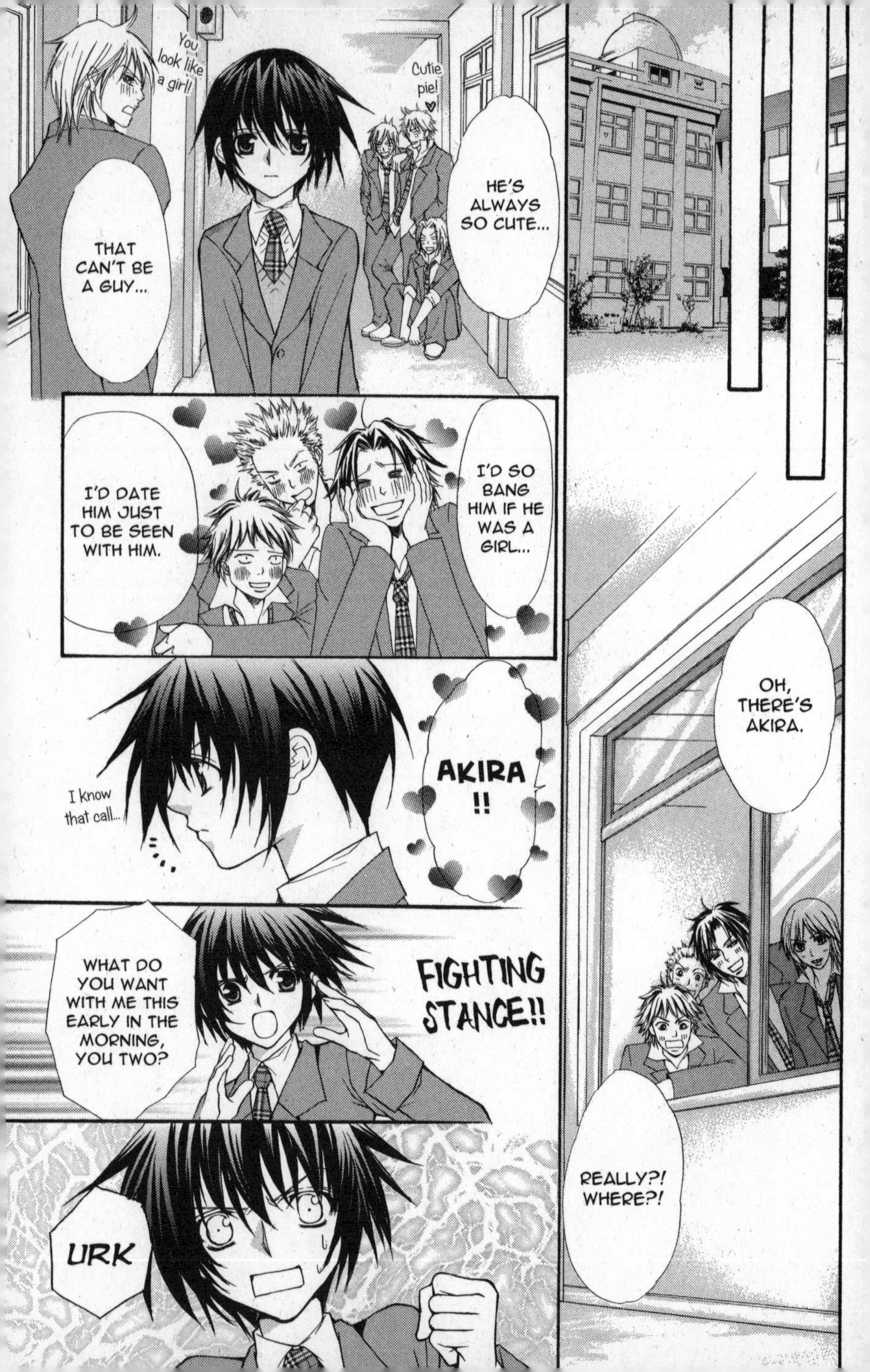
OH, THERE'S AKIRA.
REALLY?! WHERE?!
Cutie pie!
HE'S ALWAYS SO CUTE...
You look like a girl!
THAT CAN'T BE A GUY...
I'D SO BANG HIM IF HE WAS A GIRL...
I'D DATE HIM JUST TO BE SEEN WITH HIM.
AKIRA !!
I know that call...
FIGHTING STANCE!!
WHAT DO YOU WANT WITH ME THIS EARLY IN THE MORNING, YOU TWO?
URK

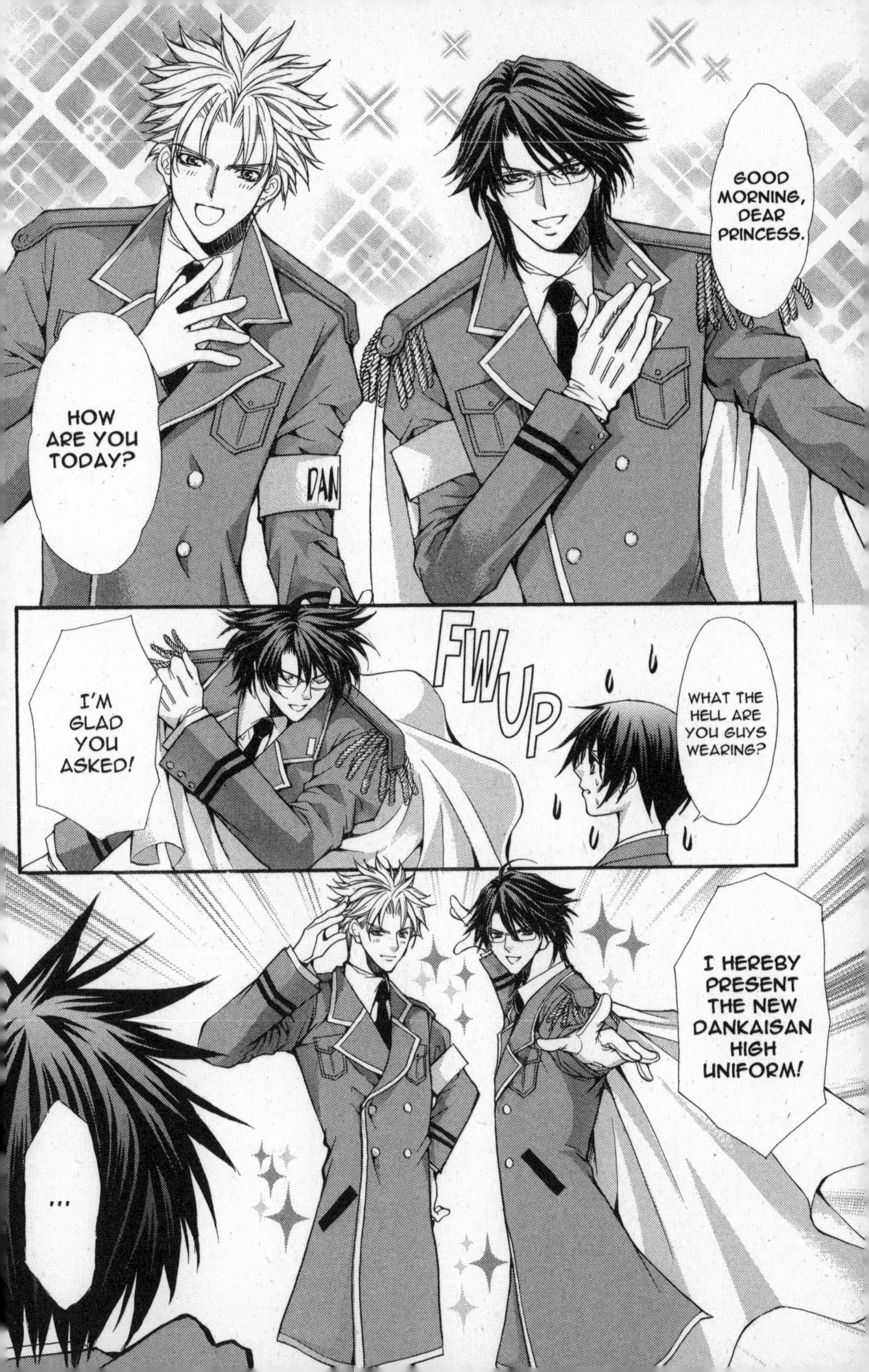
GOOD MORNING, DEAR PRINCESS.
HOW ARE YOU TODAY?
DAN
WHAT THE HELL ARE YOU GUYS WEARING?
FWUP
I'M GLAD YOU ASKED!
I HEREBY PRESENT THE NEW DANKAISAN HIGH UNIFORM!
...

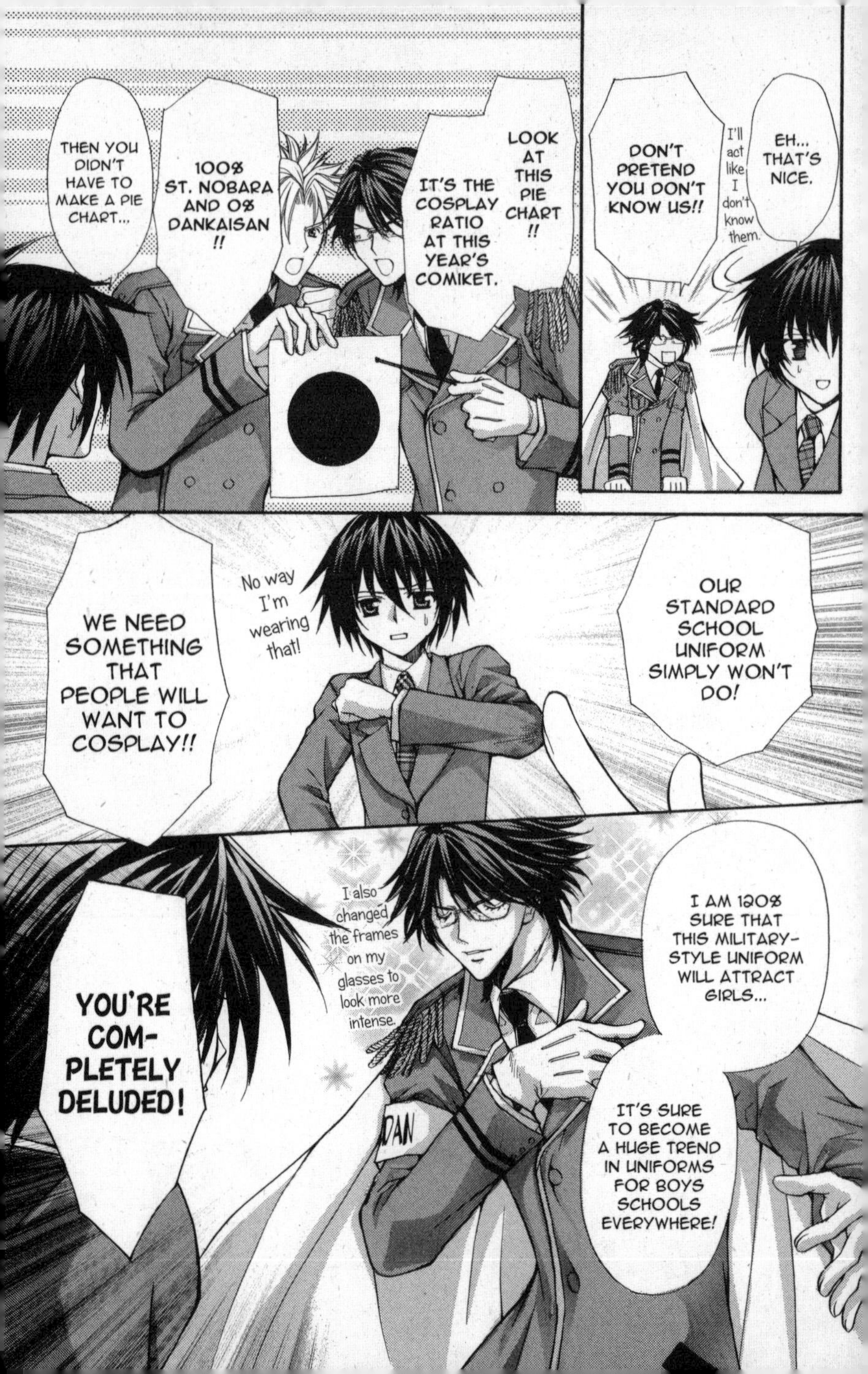
EH... THAT'S NICE.
I'll act like I don't know them.
DON'T PRETEND YOU DON'T KNOW US!!
LOOK AT THIS PIE CHART!!
IT'S THE COSPLAY RATIO AT THIS YEAR'S COMIKET.
100% ST. NOBARA AND 0% DANKAISAN!!
THEN YOU DIDN'T HAVE TO MAKE A PIE CHART...
OUR STANDARD SCHOOL UNIFORM SIMPLY WON'T DO!
No way I'm wearing that!
WE NEED SOMETHING THAT PEOPLE WILL WANT TO COSPLAY!!
I AM 120% SURE THAT THIS MILITARY-STYLE UNIFORM WILL ATTRACT GIRLS...
IT'S SURE TO BECOME A HUGE TREND IN UNIFORMS FOR BOYS SCHOOLS EVERYWHERE!
I also changed the frames on my glasses to look more intense.
YOU'RE COM-PLETELY DELUDED!

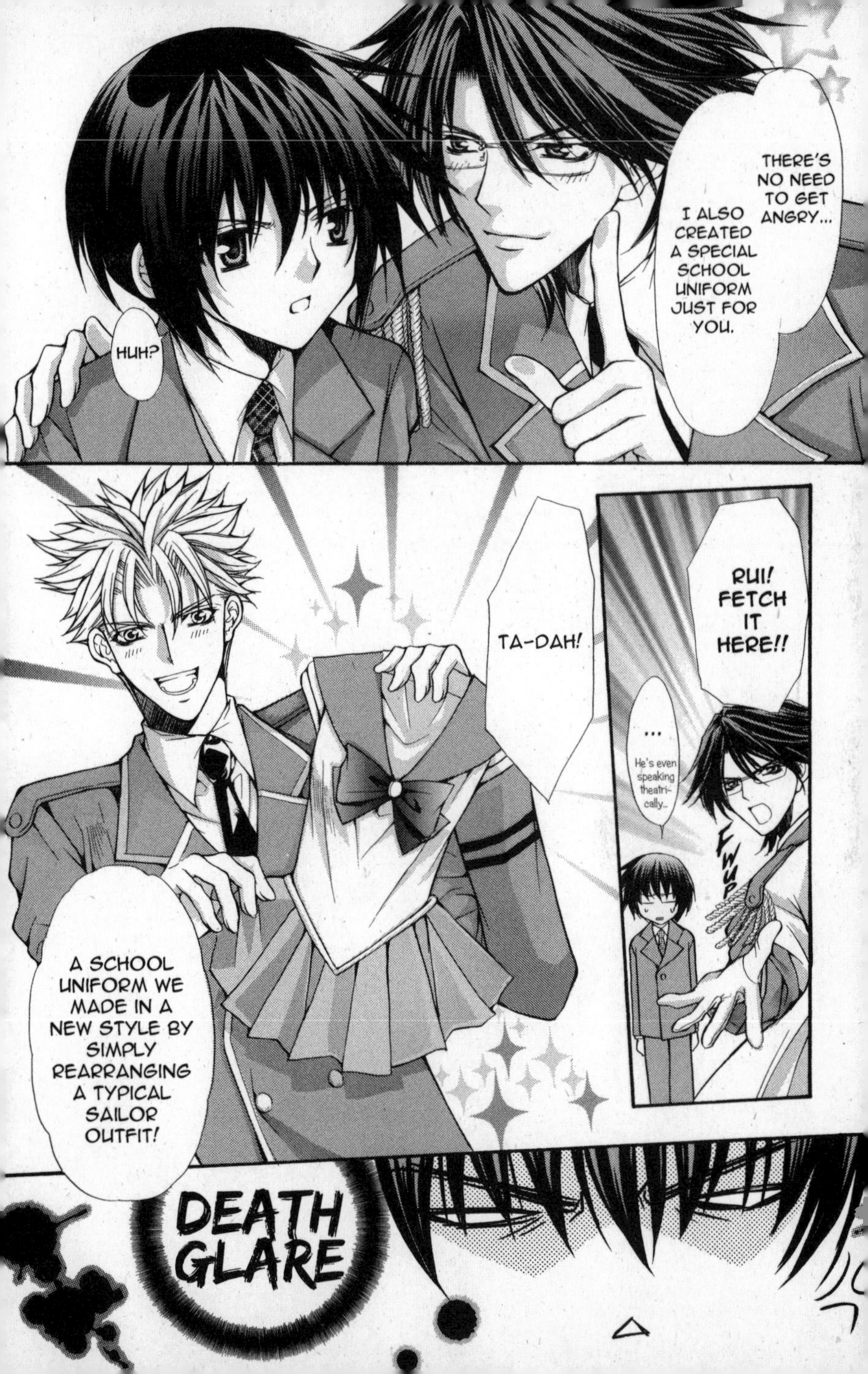
THERE'S NO NEED TO GET ANGRY...
I ALSO CREATED A SPECIAL SCHOOL UNIFORM JUST FOR YOU.
HUH?
RUI! FETCH IT HERE!!
...
He's even speaking theatri-cally...
FWUP
TA-DAH!
A SCHOOL UNIFORM WE MADE IN A NEW STYLE BY SIMPLY REARRANGING A TYPICAL SAILOR OUTFIT!
DEATH GLARE

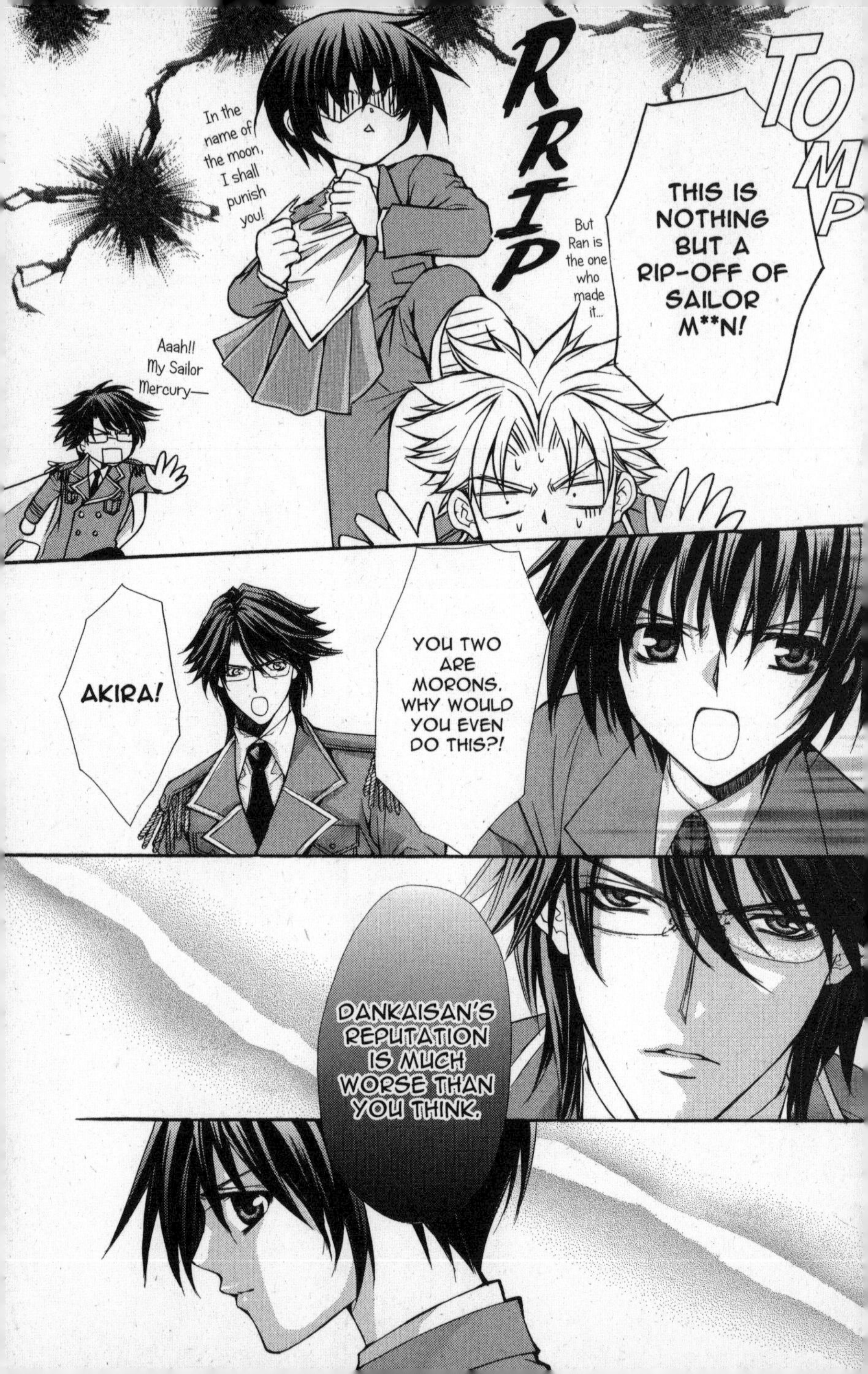
TOMP
THIS IS NOTHING BUT A RIP-OFF OF SAILOR M**N!
RRIP
But Ran is the one who made it...
In the name of the moon, I shall punish you!
Aaah!! My Sailor Mercury—
YOU TWO ARE MORONS. WHY WOULD YOU EVEN DO THIS?!
AKIRA!
DANKAISAN'S REPUTATION IS MUCH WORSE THAN YOU THINK.

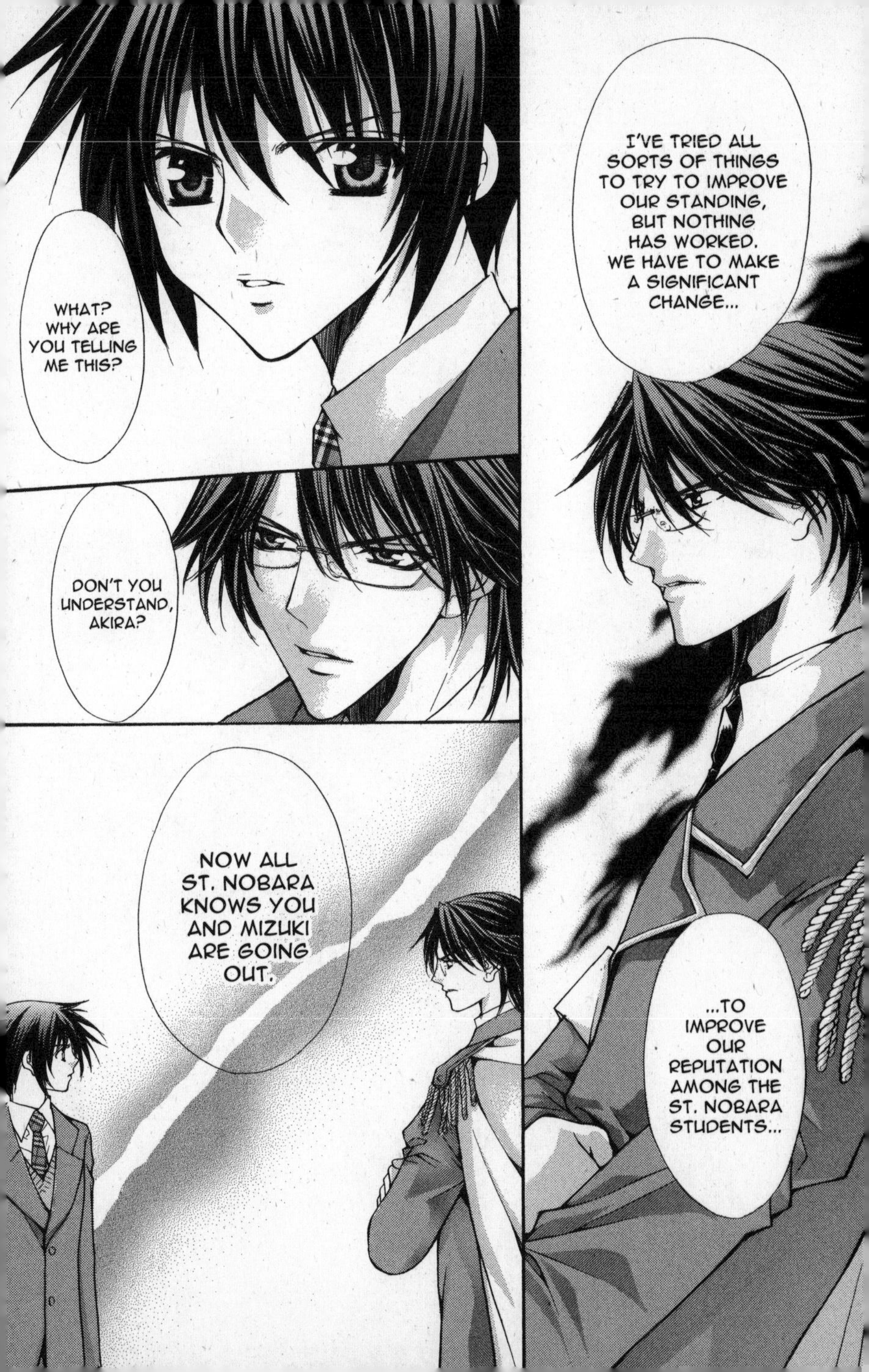
I'VE TRIED ALL SORTS OF THINGS TO TRY TO IMPROVE OUR STANDING, BUT NOTHING HAS WORKED. WE HAVE TO MAKE A SIGNIFICANT CHANGE...
...TO IMPROVE OUR REPUTATION AMONG THE ST. NOBARA STUDENTS...
WHAT? WHY ARE YOU TELLING ME THIS?
DON'T YOU UNDERSTAND, AKIRA?
NOW ALL ST. NOBARA KNOWS YOU AND MIZUKI ARE GOING OUT.

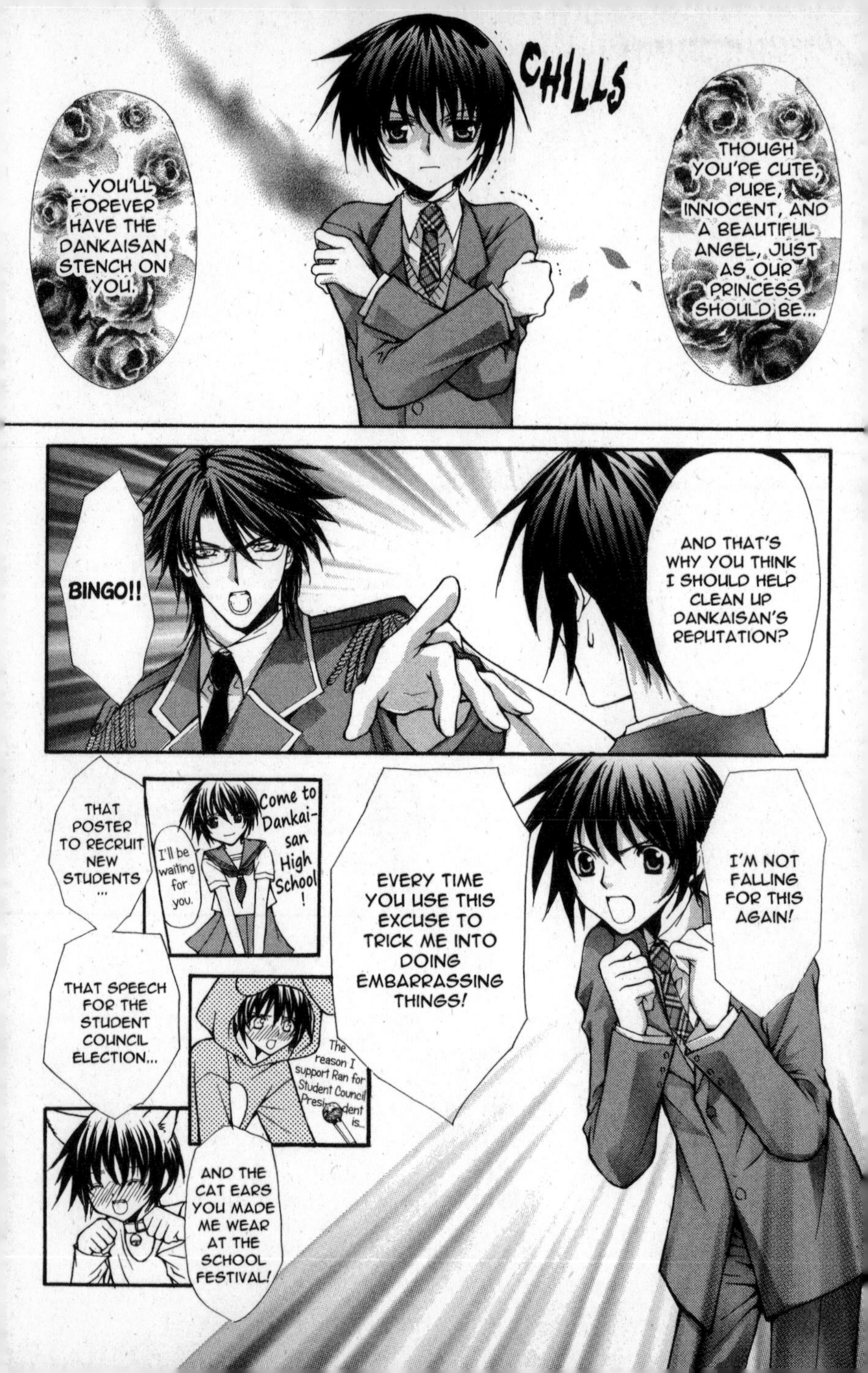
THOUGH YOU'RE CUTE, PURE, INNOCENT, AND A BEAUTIFUL ANGEL, JUST AS OUR PRINCESS SHOULD BE...
CHILLS
...YOU'LL FOREVER HAVE THE DANKAISAN STENCH ON YOU.
AND THAT'S WHY YOU THINK I SHOULD HELP CLEAN UP DANKAISAN'S REPUTATION?
BINGO!!
I'M NOT FALLING FOR THIS AGAIN!
EVERY TIME YOU USE THIS EXCUSE TO TRICK ME INTO DOING EMBARRASSING THINGS!
THAT POSTER TO RECRUIT NEW STUDENTS ...
Come to Dankai-san High School!
I'll be waiting for you.
THAT SPEECH FOR THE STUDENT COUNCIL ELECTION...
The reason I support Ran for Student Council President is...
AND THE CAT EARS YOU MADE ME WEAR AT THE SCHOOL FESTIVAL!

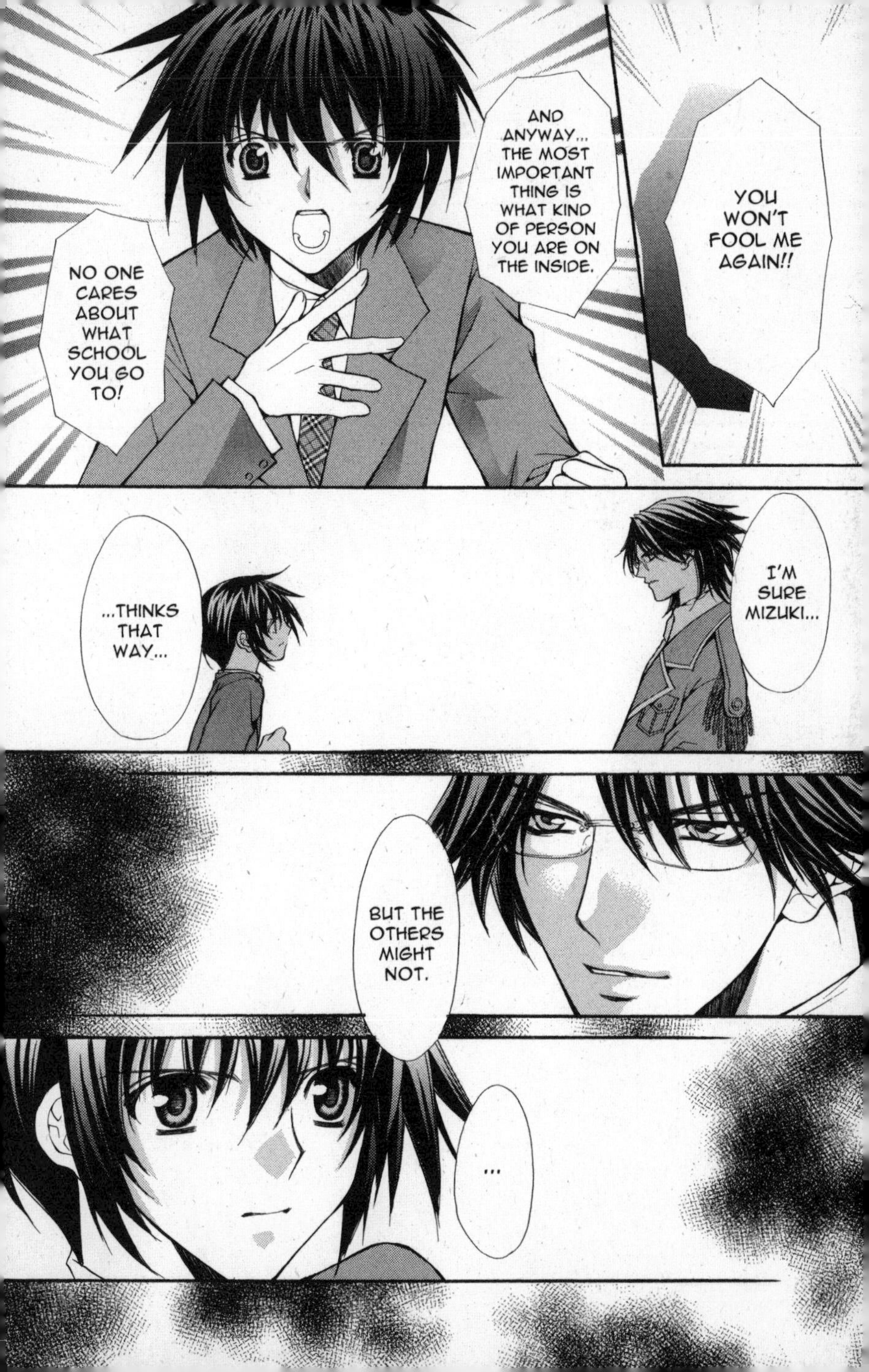
YOU WON'T FOOL ME AGAIN!!
AND ANYWAY... THE MOST IMPORTANT THING IS WHAT KIND OF PERSON YOU ARE ON THE INSIDE.
NO ONE CARES ABOUT WHAT SCHOOL YOU GO TO!
I'M SURE MIZUKI...
...THINKS THAT WAY...
BUT THE OTHERS MIGHT NOT.
...

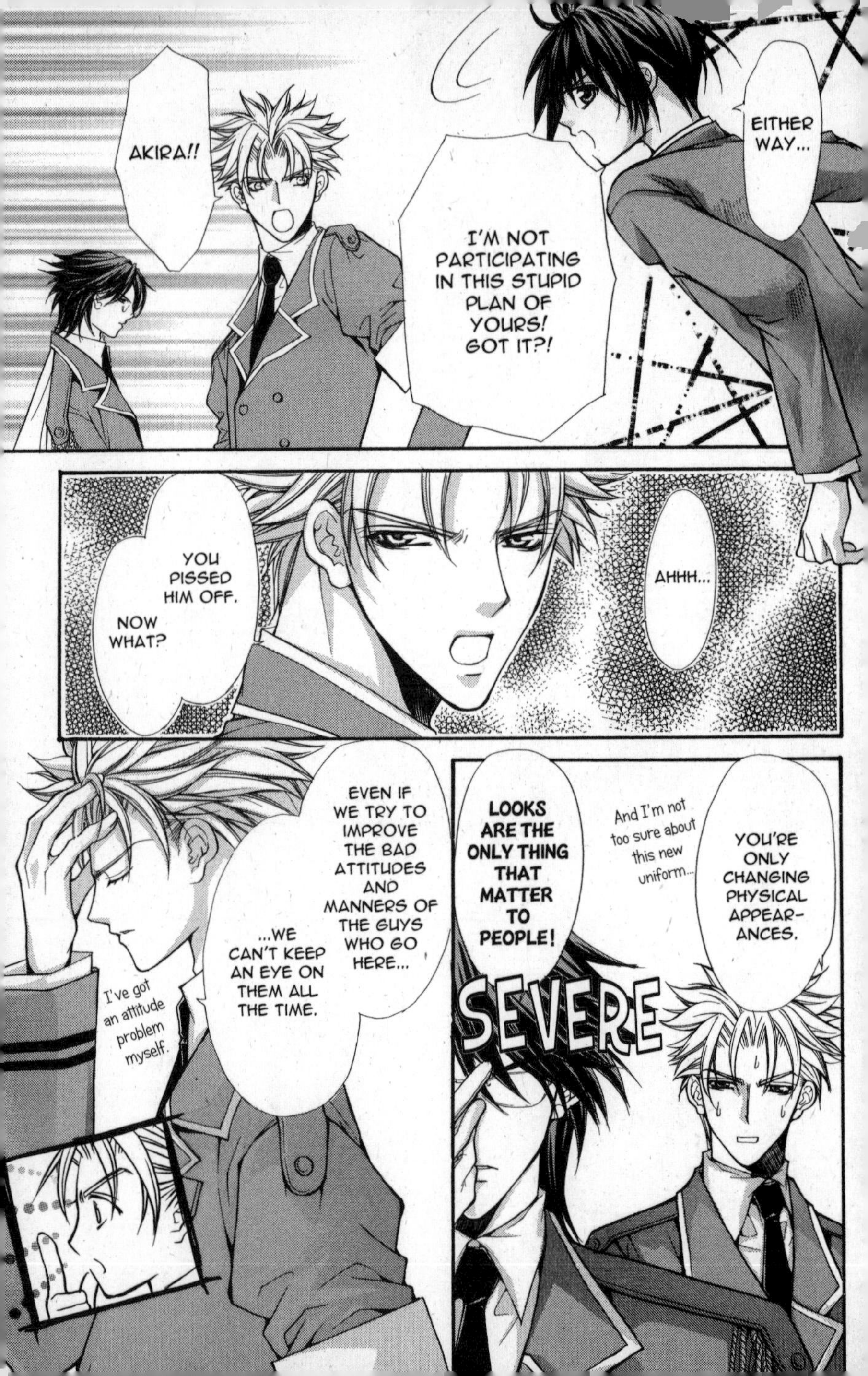
EITHER WAY...
I'M NOT PARTICIPATING IN THIS STUPID PLAN OF YOURS! GOT IT?!
AKIRA!!
AHHH...
YOU PISSED HIM OFF.
NOW WHAT?
YOU'RE ONLY CHANGING PHYSICAL APPEARANCES.
And I'm not too sure about this new uniform...
LOOKS ARE THE ONLY THING THAT MATTER TO PEOPLE!
SEVERE
EVEN IF WE TRY TO IMPROVE THE BAD ATTITUDES AND MANNERS OF THE GUYS WHO GO HERE...
...WE CAN'T KEEP AN EYE ON THEM ALL THE TIME.
I've got an attitude problem myself.

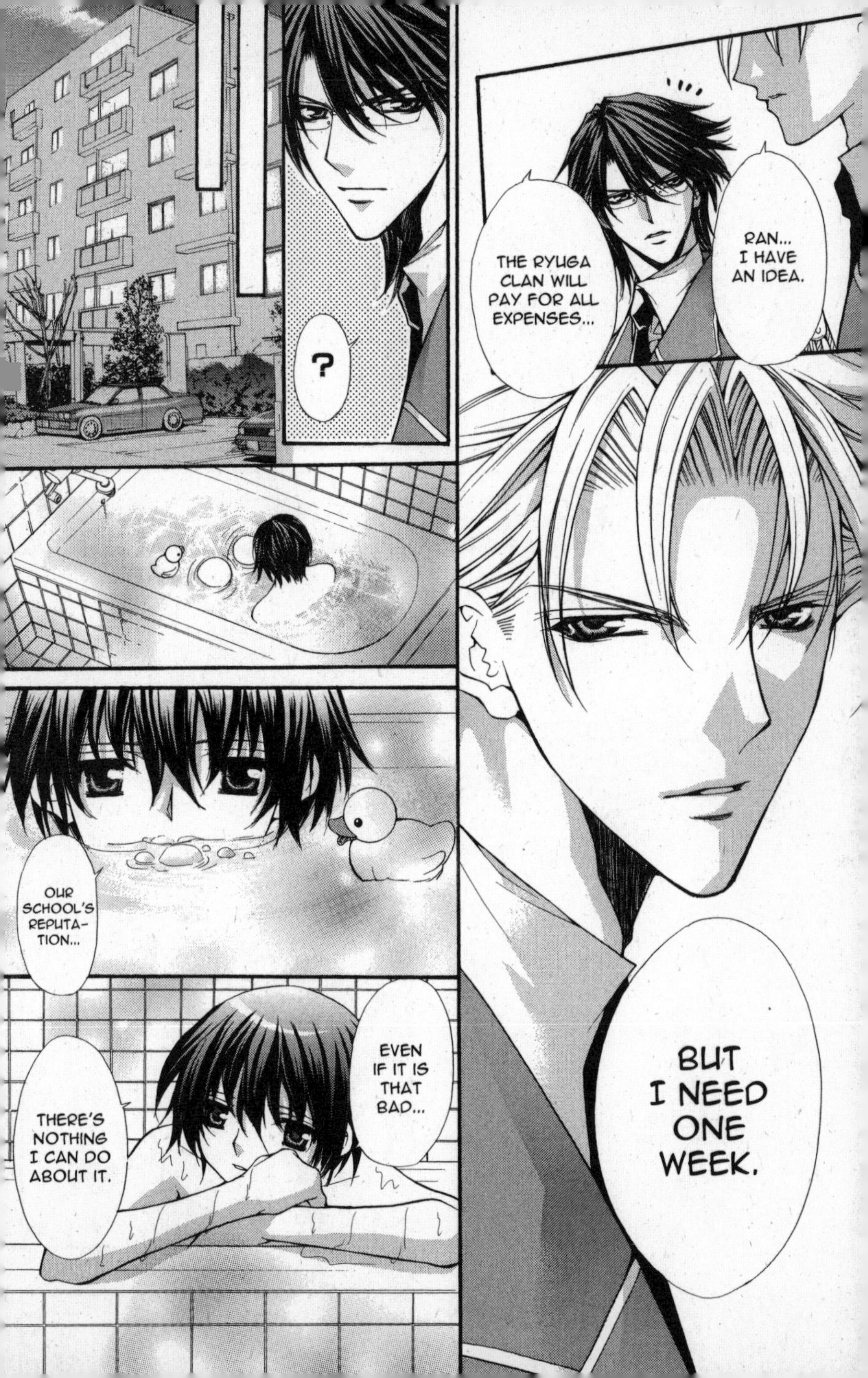
RAN... I HAVE AN IDEA.
THE RYUGA CLAN WILL PAY FOR ALL EXPENSES...
BUT I NEED ONE WEEK.
?
OUR SCHOOL'S REPUTATION...
EVEN IF IT IS THAT BAD...
THERE'S NOTHING I CAN DO ABOUT IT.

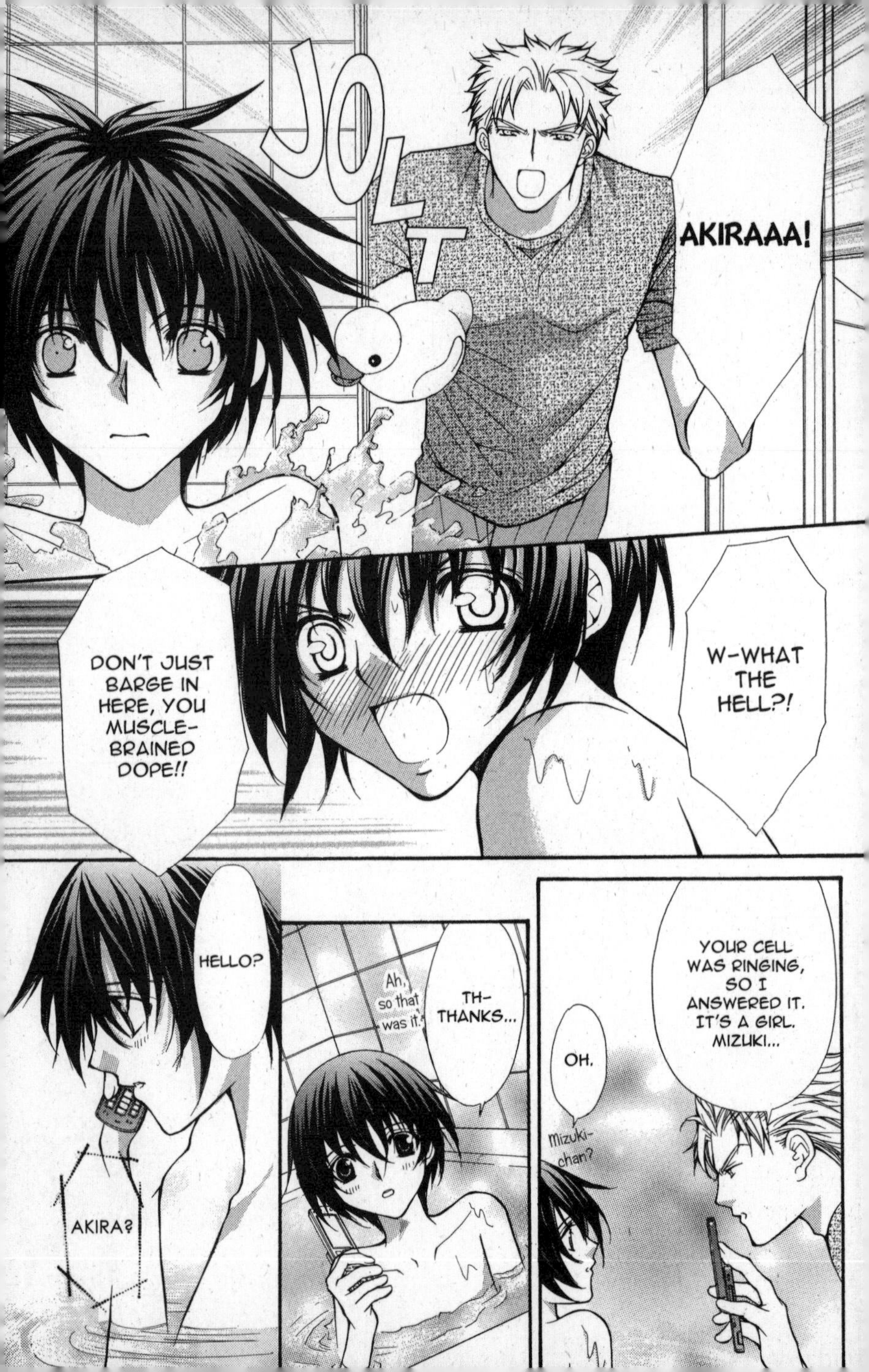
AKIRAAA!
JOLT
W-WHAT THE HELL?!
DON'T JUST BARGE IN HERE, YOU MUSCLE-BRAINED DOPE!!
YOUR CELL WAS RINGING, SO I ANSWERED IT. IT'S A GIRL. MIZUKI...
OH.
Mizuki-chan?
TH-THANKS...
Ah, so that was it.
HELLO?
AKIRA?

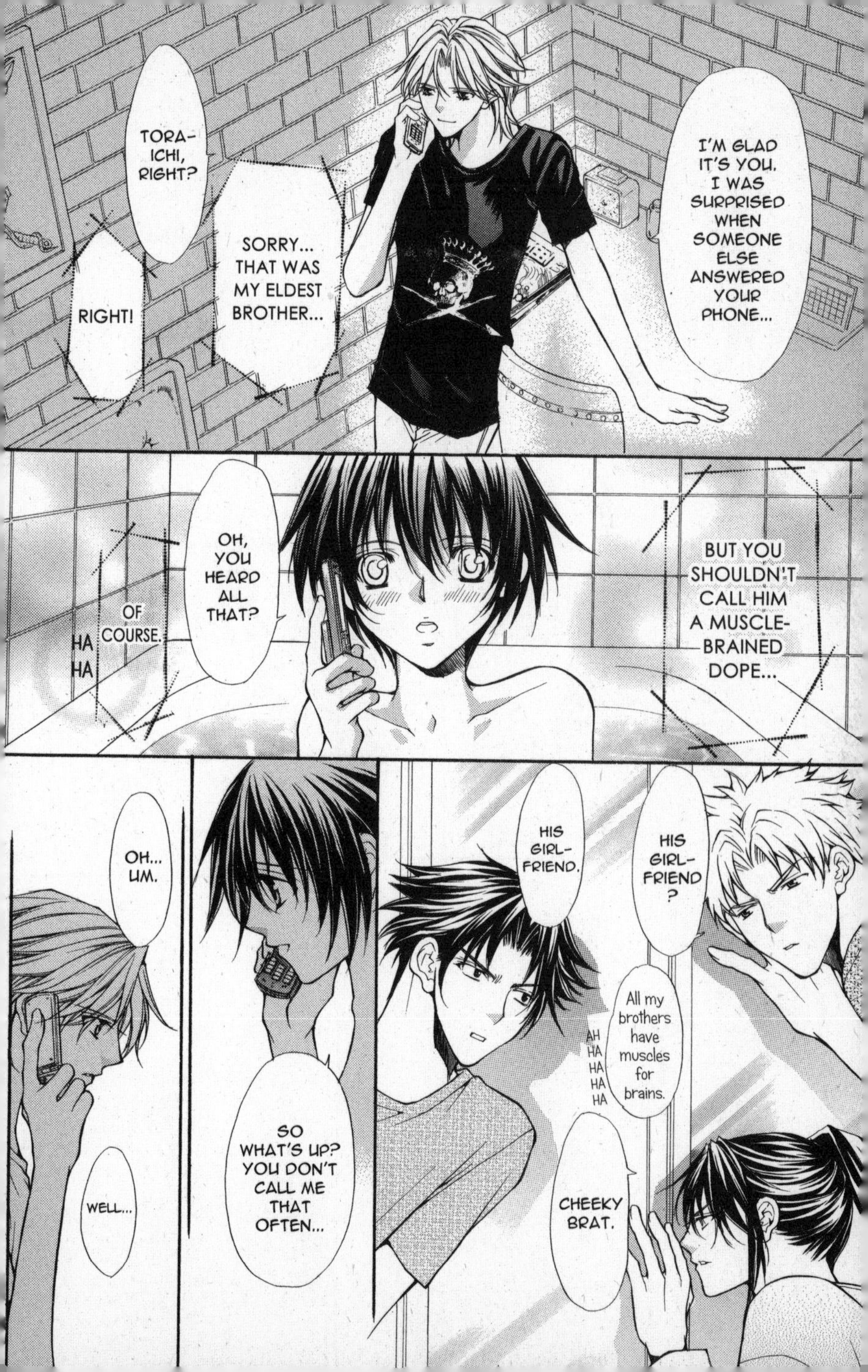
I'M GLAD IT'S YOU. I WAS SURPRISED WHEN SOMEONE ELSE ANSWERED YOUR PHONE...
SORRY... THAT WAS MY ELDEST BROTHER...
TORA-ICHI, RIGHT?
RIGHT!
BUT YOU SHOULDN'T CALL HIM A MUSCLE-BRAINED DOPE...
OH, YOU HEARD ALL THAT?
OF COURSE.
HA HA
HIS GIRL-FRIEND?
HIS GIRL-FRIEND.
All my brothers have muscles for brains.
AH HA HA HA HA HA
CHEEKY BRAT.
SO WHAT'S UP? YOU DON'T CALL ME THAT OFTEN...
OH... UM.
WELL...

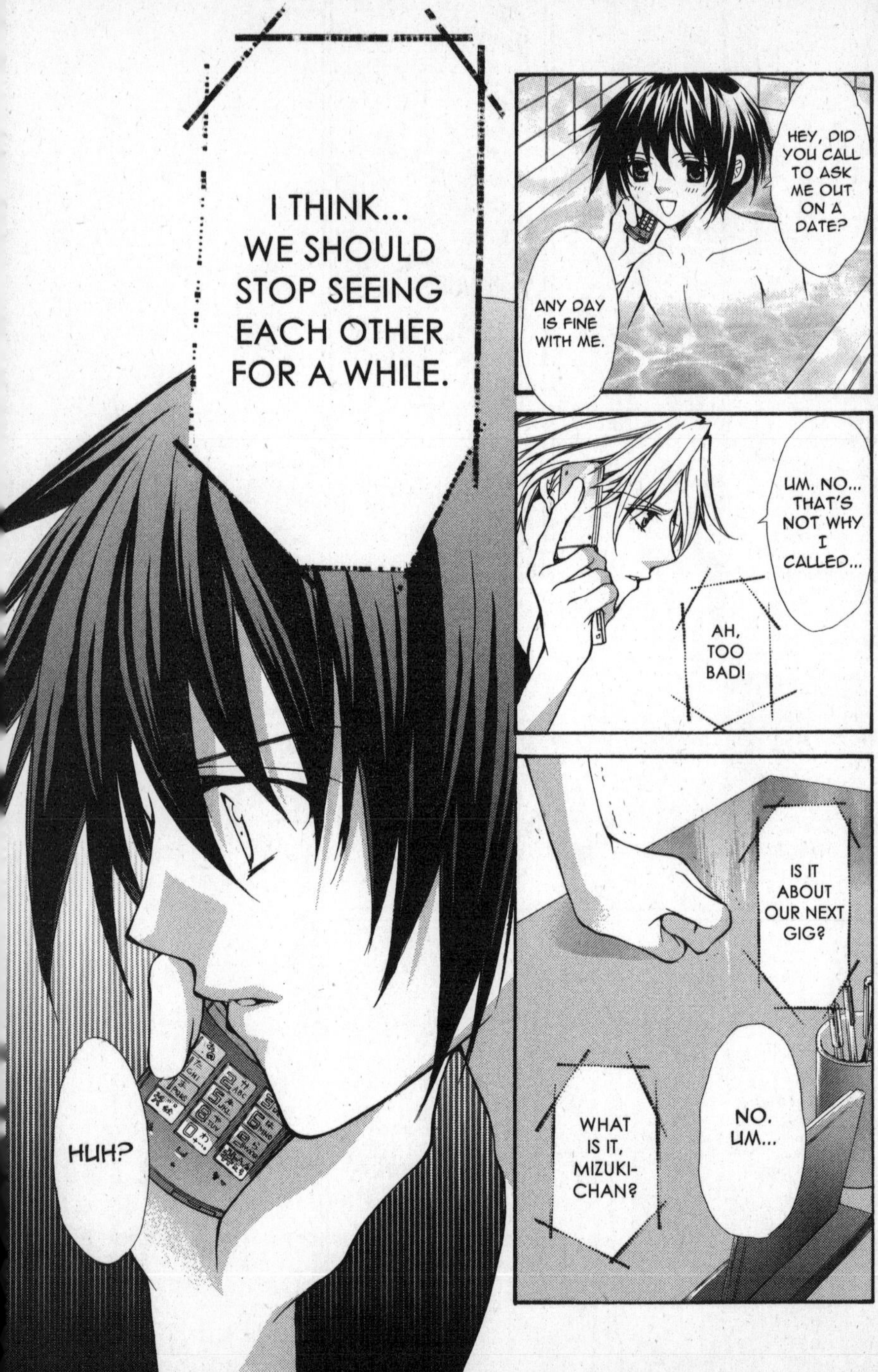
HEY, DID YOU CALL TO ASK ME OUT ON A DATE?
ANY DAY IS FINE WITH ME.
UM. NO... THAT'S NOT WHY I CALLED...
AH, TOO BAD!
IS IT ABOUT OUR NEXT GIG?
NO. UM...
WHAT IS IT, MIZUKI-CHAN?
I THINK... WE SHOULD STOP SEEING EACH OTHER FOR A WHILE.
HUH?

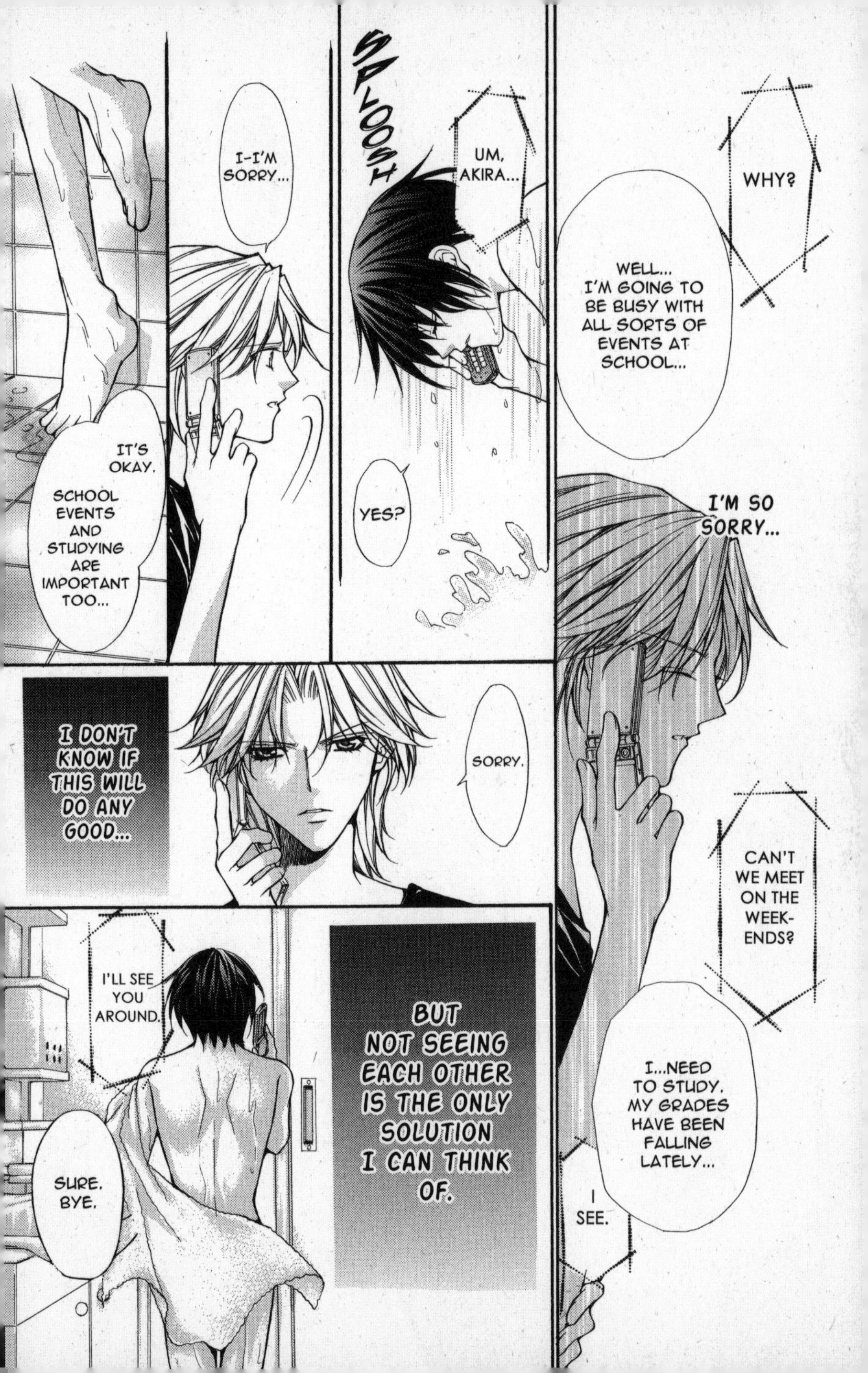
WHY?
WELL... I'M GOING TO BE BUSY WITH ALL SORTS OF EVENTS AT SCHOOL...
SPLOOSH
UM, AKIRA...
YES?
I-I'M SORRY...
IT'S OKAY.
SCHOOL EVENTS AND STUDYING ARE IMPORTANT TOO...
I'M SO SORRY...
CAN'T WE MEET ON THE WEEK-ENDS?
I...NEED TO STUDY. MY GRADES HAVE BEEN FALLING LATELY...
I SEE.
SORRY.
I DON'T KNOW IF THIS WILL DO ANY GOOD...
I'LL SEE YOU AROUND.
BUT NOT SEEING EACH OTHER IS THE ONLY SOLUTION I CAN THINK OF.
SURE. BYE.

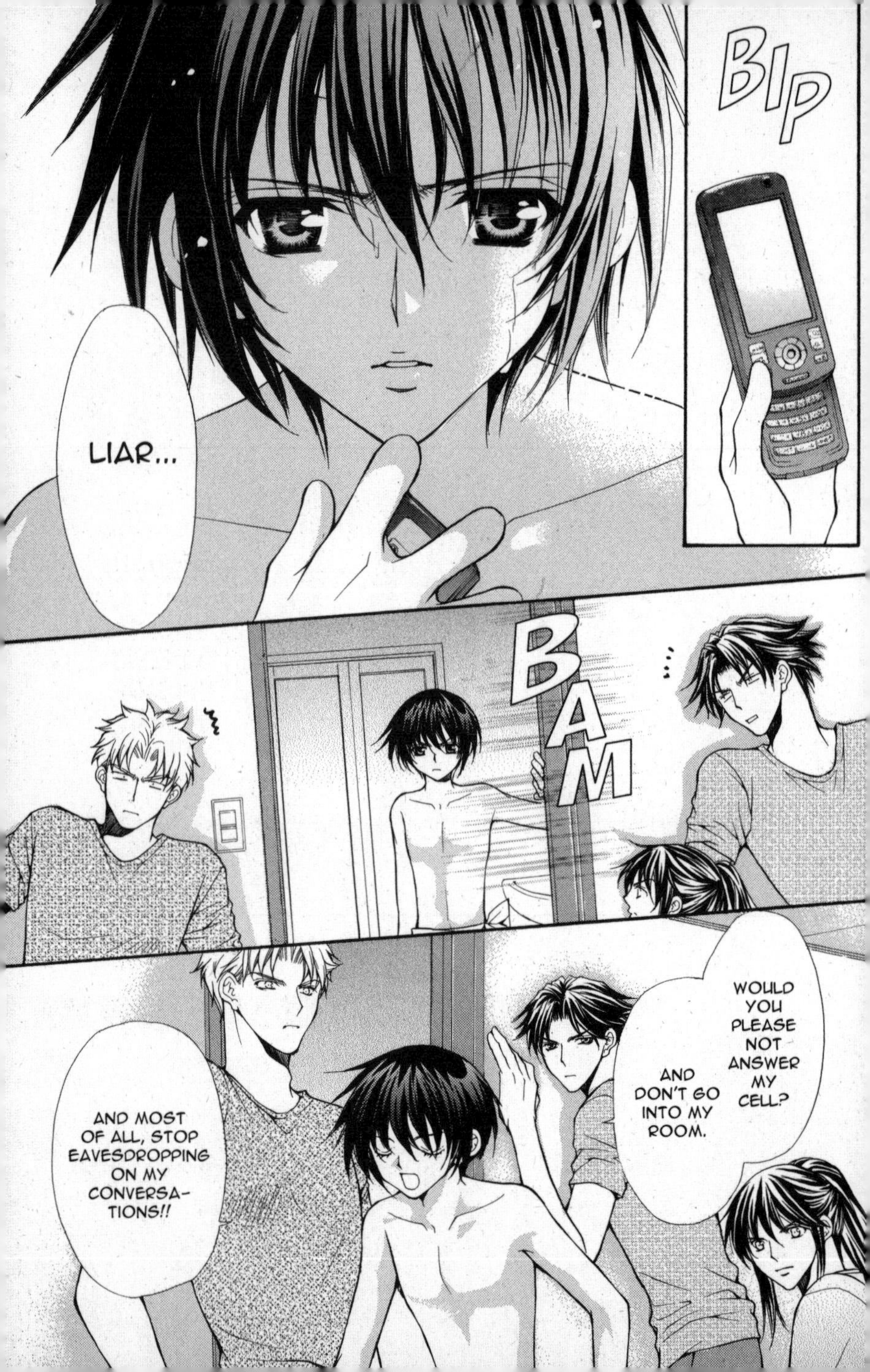
BIP
LIAR...
BAM
WOULD YOU PLEASE NOT ANSWER MY CELL?
AND DON'T GO INTO MY ROOM.
AND MOST OF ALL, STOP EAVESDROPPING ON MY CONVERSATIONS!!

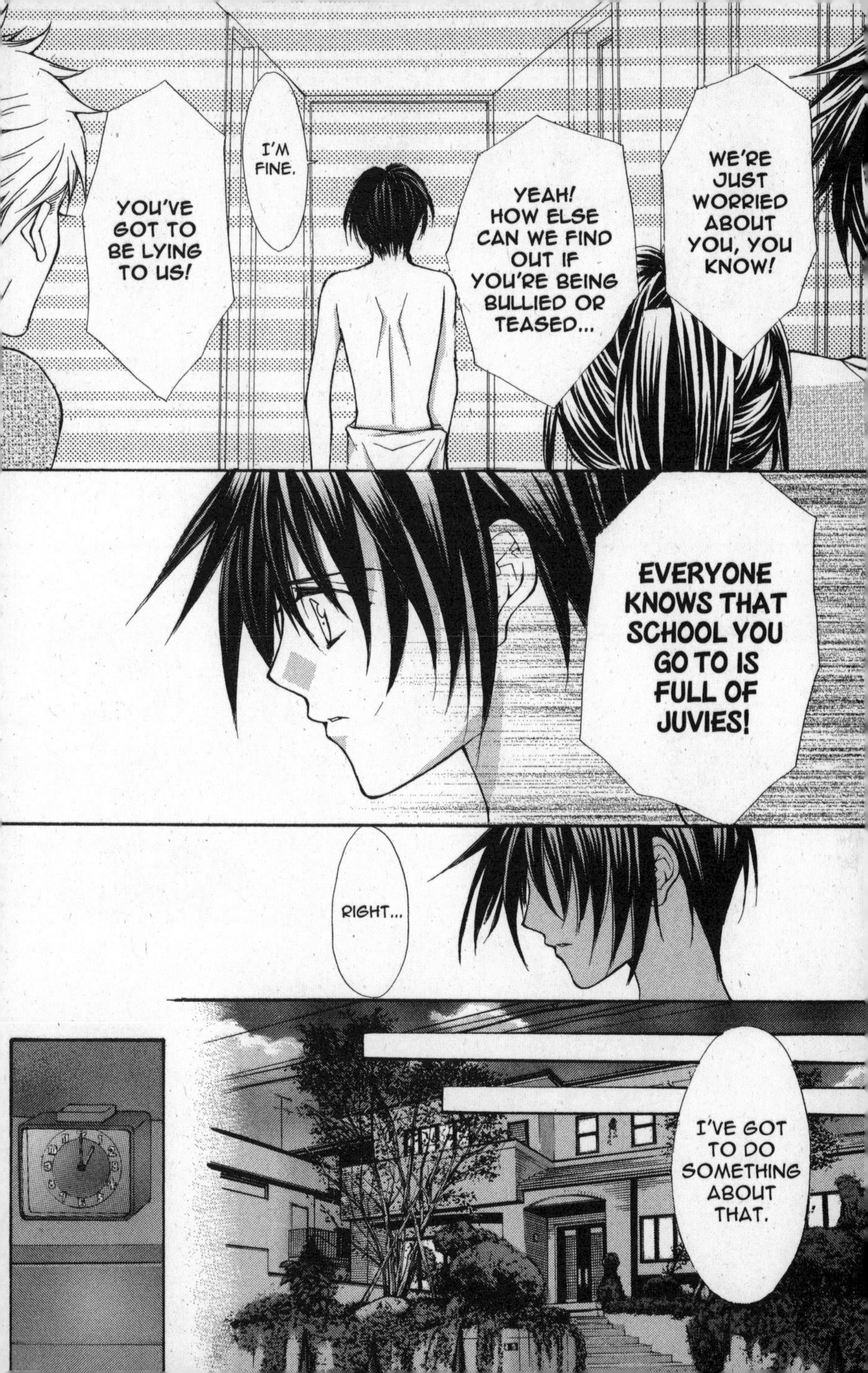
WE'RE JUST WORRIED ABOUT YOU, YOU KNOW!
YEAH! HOW ELSE CAN WE FIND OUT IF YOU'RE BEING BULLIED OR TEASED...
I'M FINE.
YOU'VE GOT TO BE LYING TO US!
EVERYONE KNOWS THAT SCHOOL YOU GO TO IS FULL OF JUVIES!
RIGHT...
I'VE GOT TO DO SOMETHING ABOUT THAT.

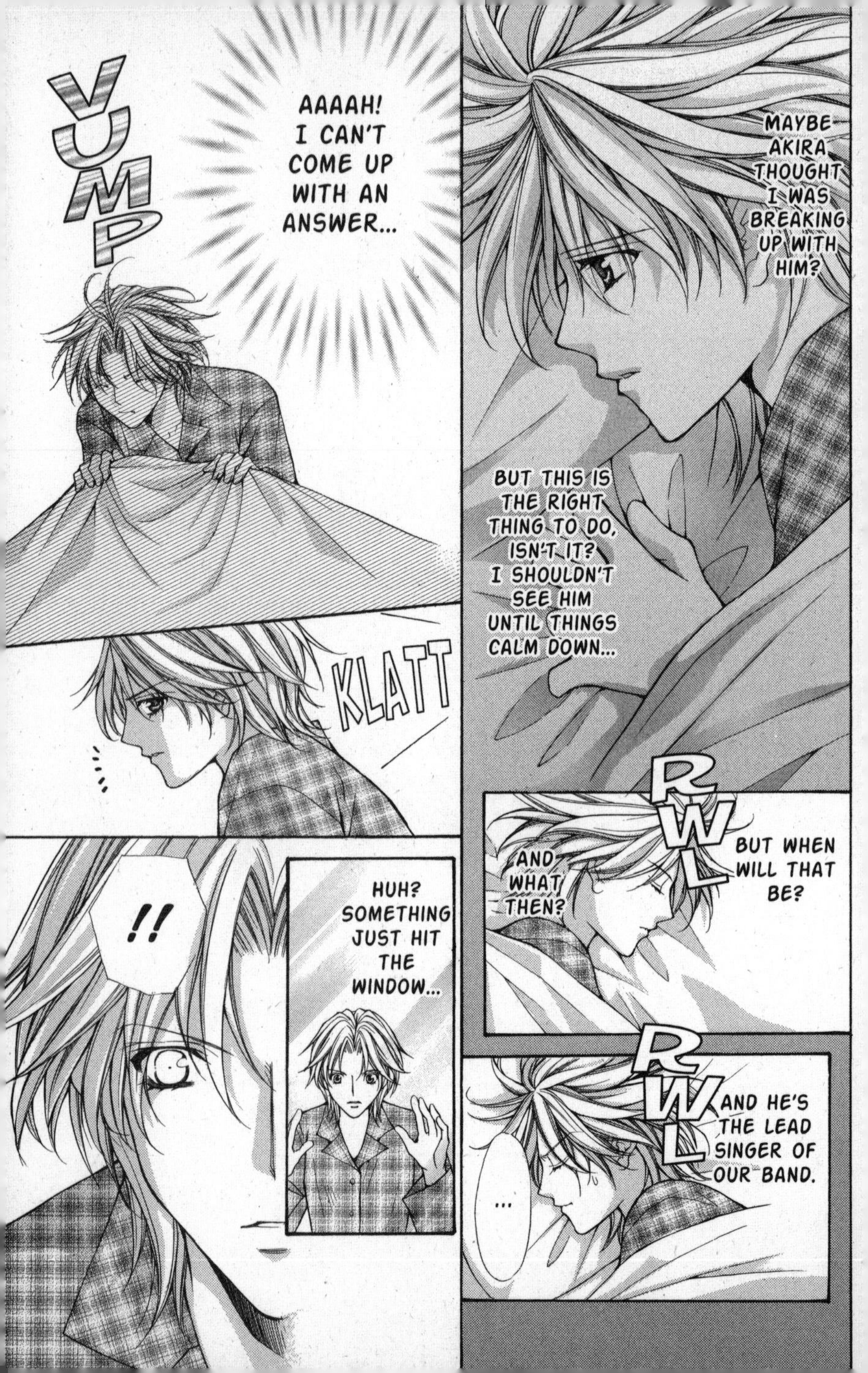
MAYBE AKIRA THOUGHT I WAS BREAKING UP WITH HIM?
BUT THIS IS THE RIGHT THING TO DO, ISN'T IT? I SHOULDN'T SEE HIM UNTIL THINGS CALM DOWN...
RWL
BUT WHEN WILL THAT BE?
AND WHAT THEN?
RWL
AND HE'S THE LEAD SINGER OF OUR BAND.
...
AAAAH! I CAN'T COME UP WITH AN ANSWER...
VUMP
KLATT
...
HUH? SOMETHING JUST HIT THE WINDOW...
!!

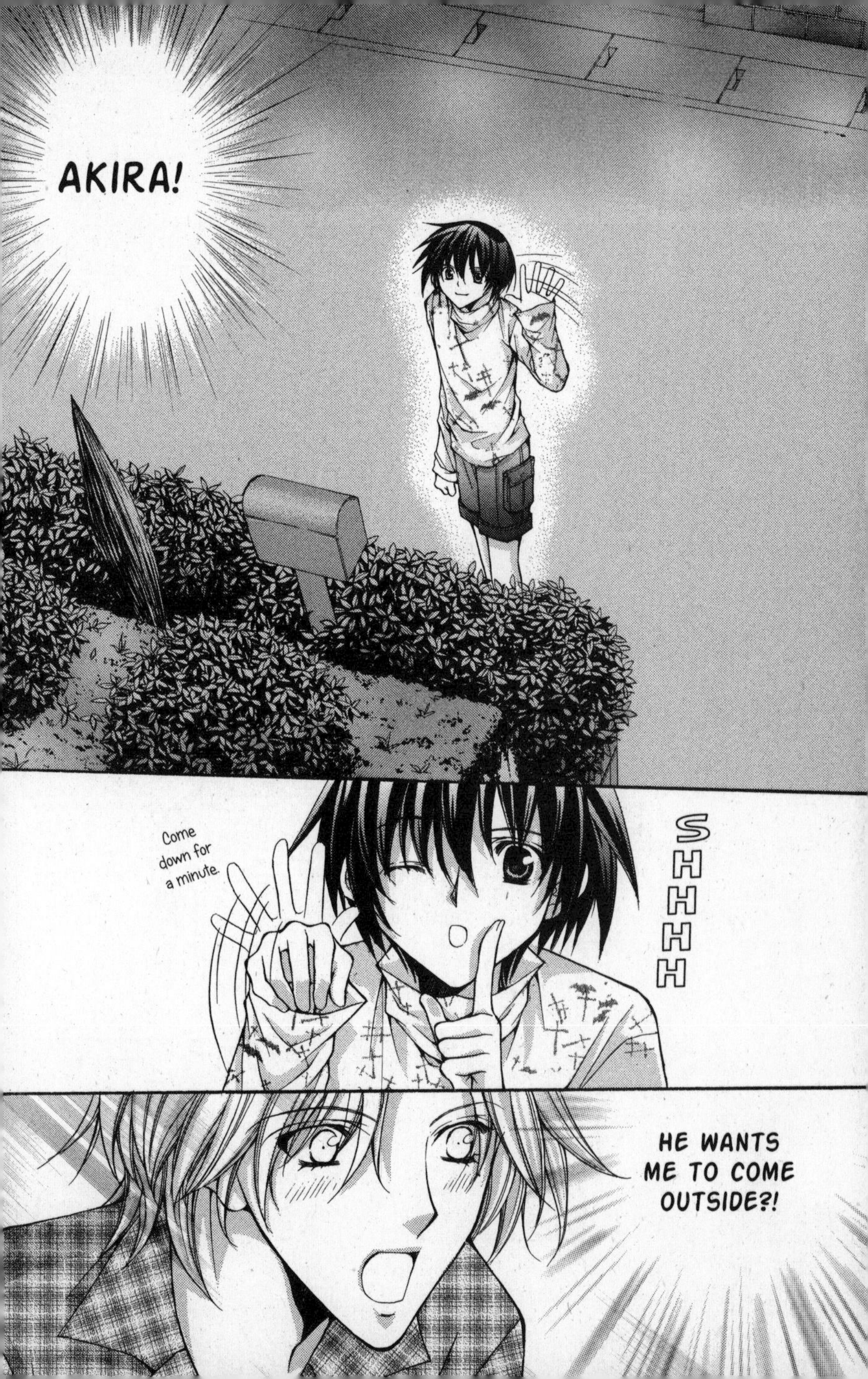
AKIRA!
SHHHH
Come down for a minute.
HE WANTS ME TO COME OUTSIDE?!

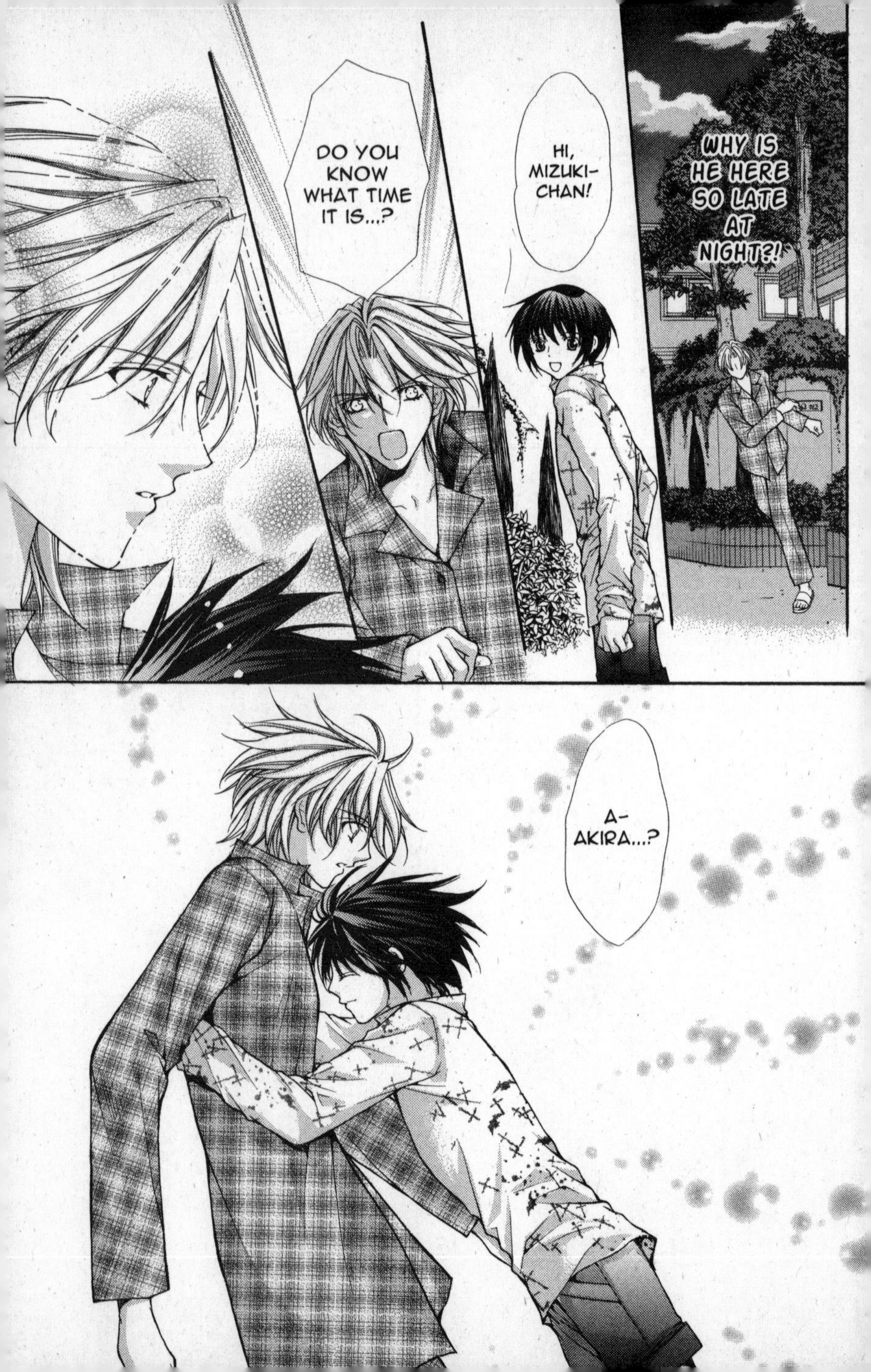
WHY IS HE HERE SO LATE AT NIGHT?!
HI, MIZUKI-CHAN!
DO YOU KNOW WHAT TIME IT IS...?
A-AKIRA...?

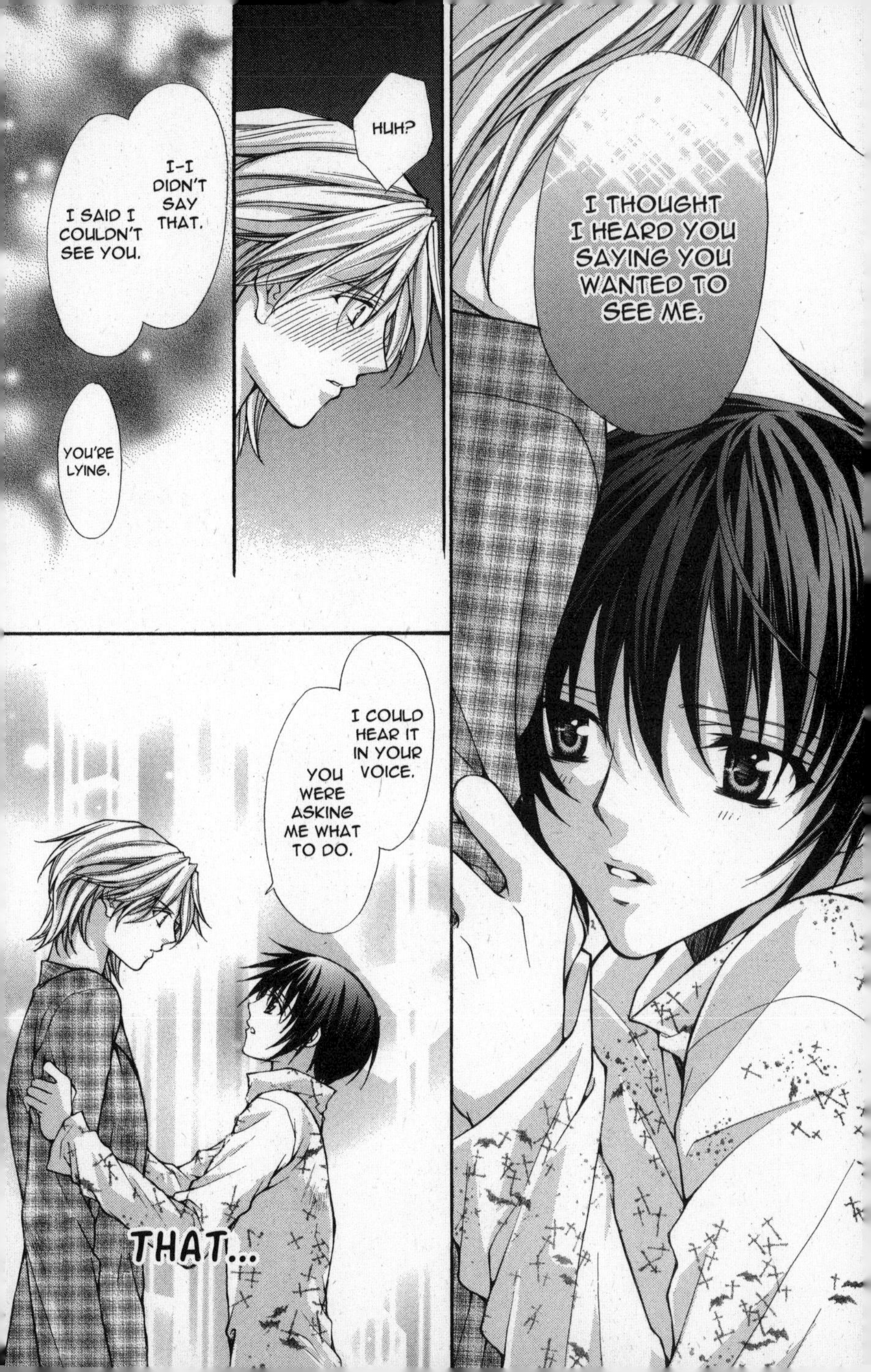
I THOUGHT I HEARD YOU SAYING YOU WANTED TO SEE ME.
HUH?
I-I DIDN'T SAY THAT.
I SAID I COULDN'T SEE YOU.
YOU'RE LYING.
I COULD HEAR IT IN YOUR VOICE.
YOU WERE ASKING ME WHAT TO DO.
THAT...

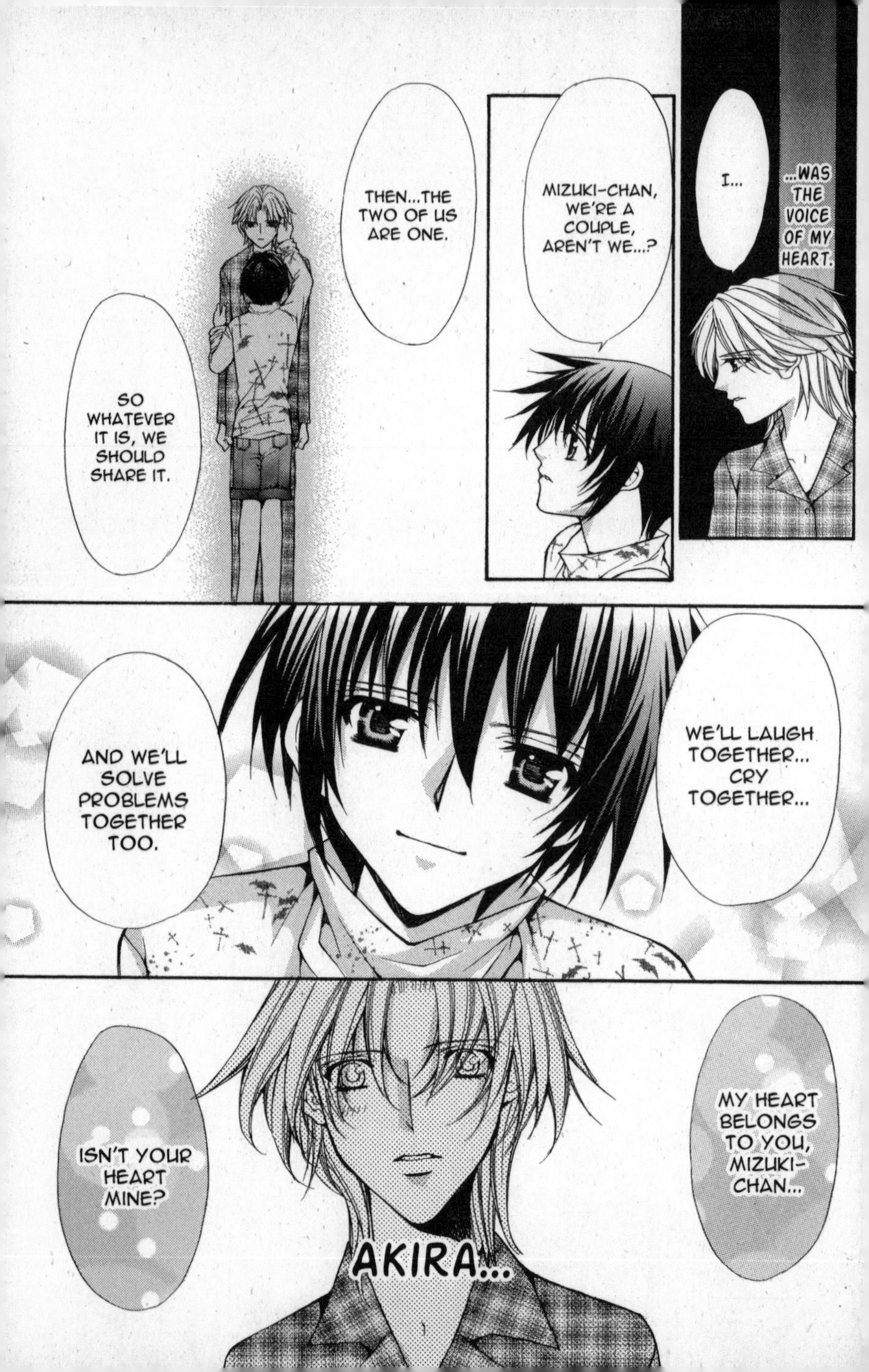
I...
...WAS THE VOICE OF MY HEART.
MIZUKI-CHAN, WE'RE A COUPLE, AREN'T WE...?
THEN...THE TWO OF US ARE ONE.
SO WHATEVER IT IS, WE SHOULD SHARE IT.
WE'LL LAUGH TOGETHER... CRY TOGETHER...
AND WE'LL SOLVE PROBLEMS TOGETHER TOO.
MY HEART BELONGS TO YOU, MIZUKI-CHAN...
AKIRA...
ISN'T YOUR HEART MINE?

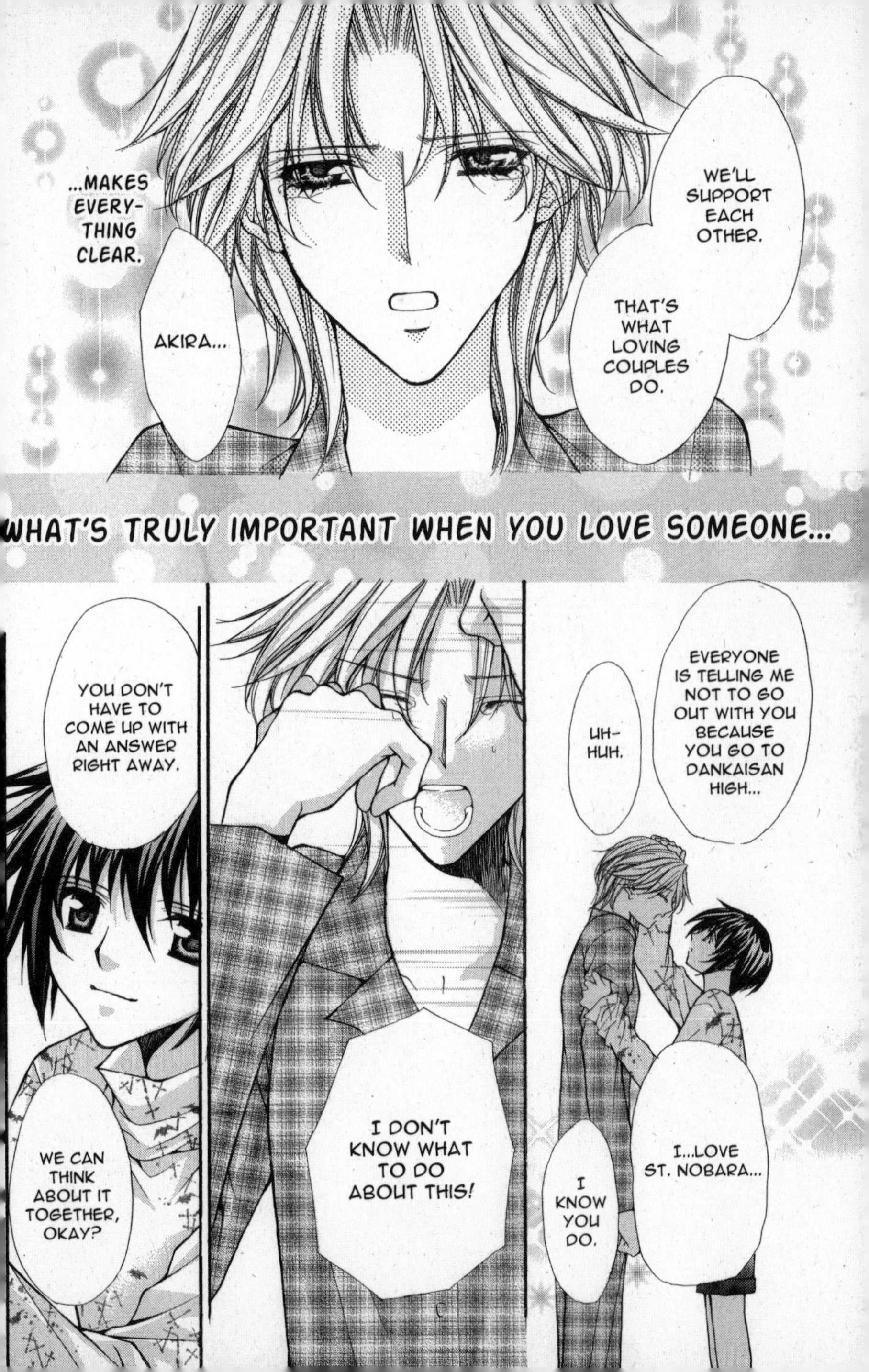
WE'LL SUPPORT EACH OTHER.
THAT'S WHAT LOVING COUPLES DO.
AKIRA...
...MAKES EVERYTHING CLEAR.
WHAT'S TRULY IMPORTANT WHEN YOU LOVE SOMEONE...
EVERYONE IS TELLING ME NOT TO GO OUT WITH YOU BECAUSE YOU GO TO DANKAISAN HIGH...
UH-HUH.
I...LOVE ST. NOBARA...
I KNOW YOU DO.
I DON'T KNOW WHAT TO DO ABOUT THIS!
YOU DON'T HAVE TO COME UP WITH AN ANSWER RIGHT AWAY.
WE CAN THINK ABOUT IT TOGETHER, OKAY?

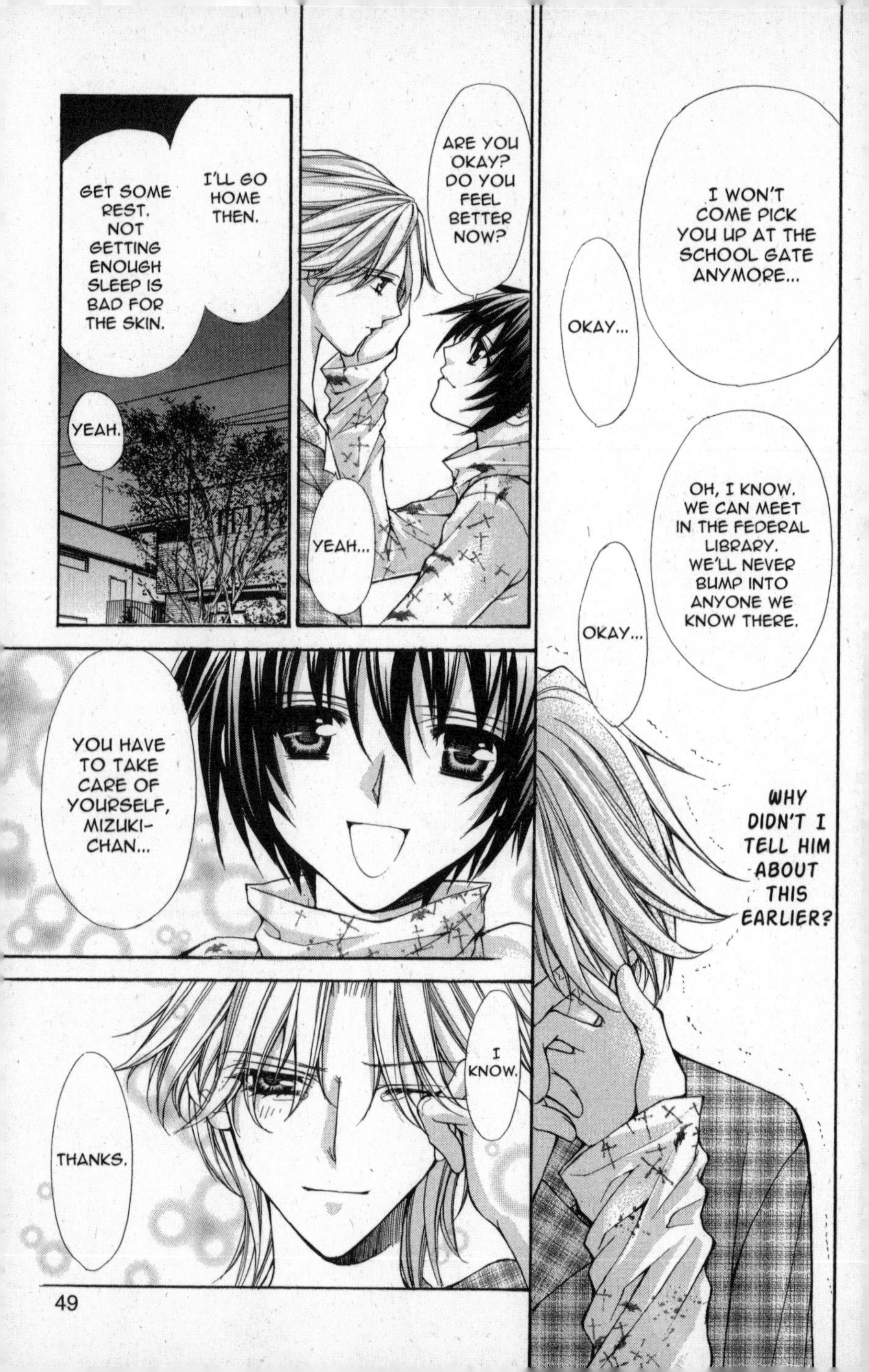
I WON'T COME PICK YOU UP AT THE SCHOOL GATE ANYMORE...
OKAY...
OH, I KNOW. WE CAN MEET IN THE FEDERAL LIBRARY. WE'LL NEVER BUMP INTO ANYONE WE KNOW THERE.
OKAY...
WHY DIDN'T I TELL HIM ABOUT THIS EARLIER?
ARE YOU OKAY? DO YOU FEEL BETTER NOW?
YEAH...
I'LL GO HOME THEN.
GET SOME REST. NOT GETTING ENOUGH SLEEP IS BAD FOR THE SKIN.
YEAH.
YOU HAVE TO TAKE CARE OF YOURSELF, MIZUKI-CHAN...
I KNOW.
THANKS.

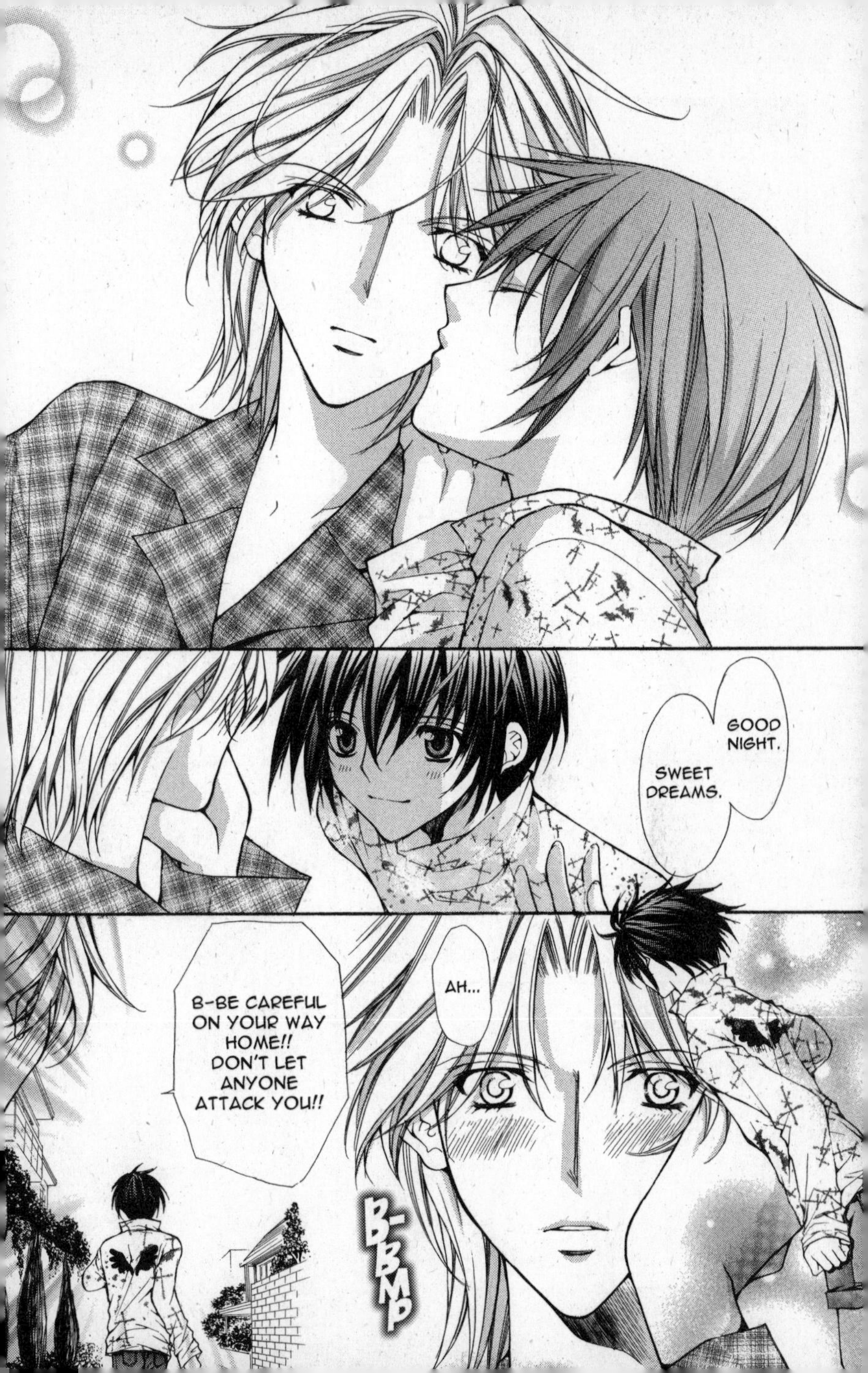
GOOD NIGHT. SWEET DREAMS.
AH...
B-BMP
B-BE CAREFUL ON YOUR WAY HOME!! DON'T LET ANYONE ATTACK YOU!!

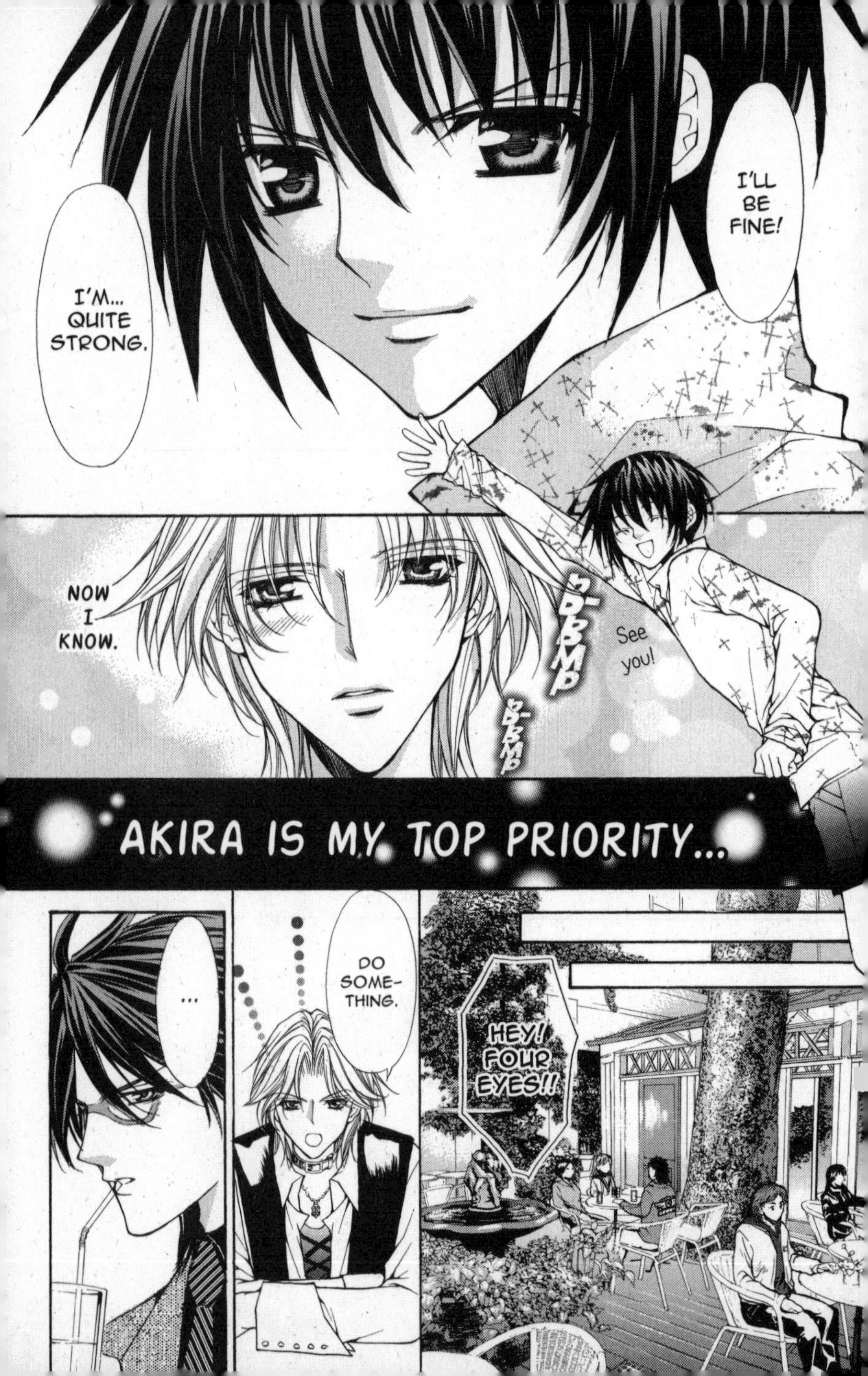
I'LL BE FINE!
I'M... QUITE STRONG.
See you!
NOW I KNOW.
AKIRA IS MY TOP PRIORITY...
HEY! FOUR EYES!!
DO SOME-THING.
...

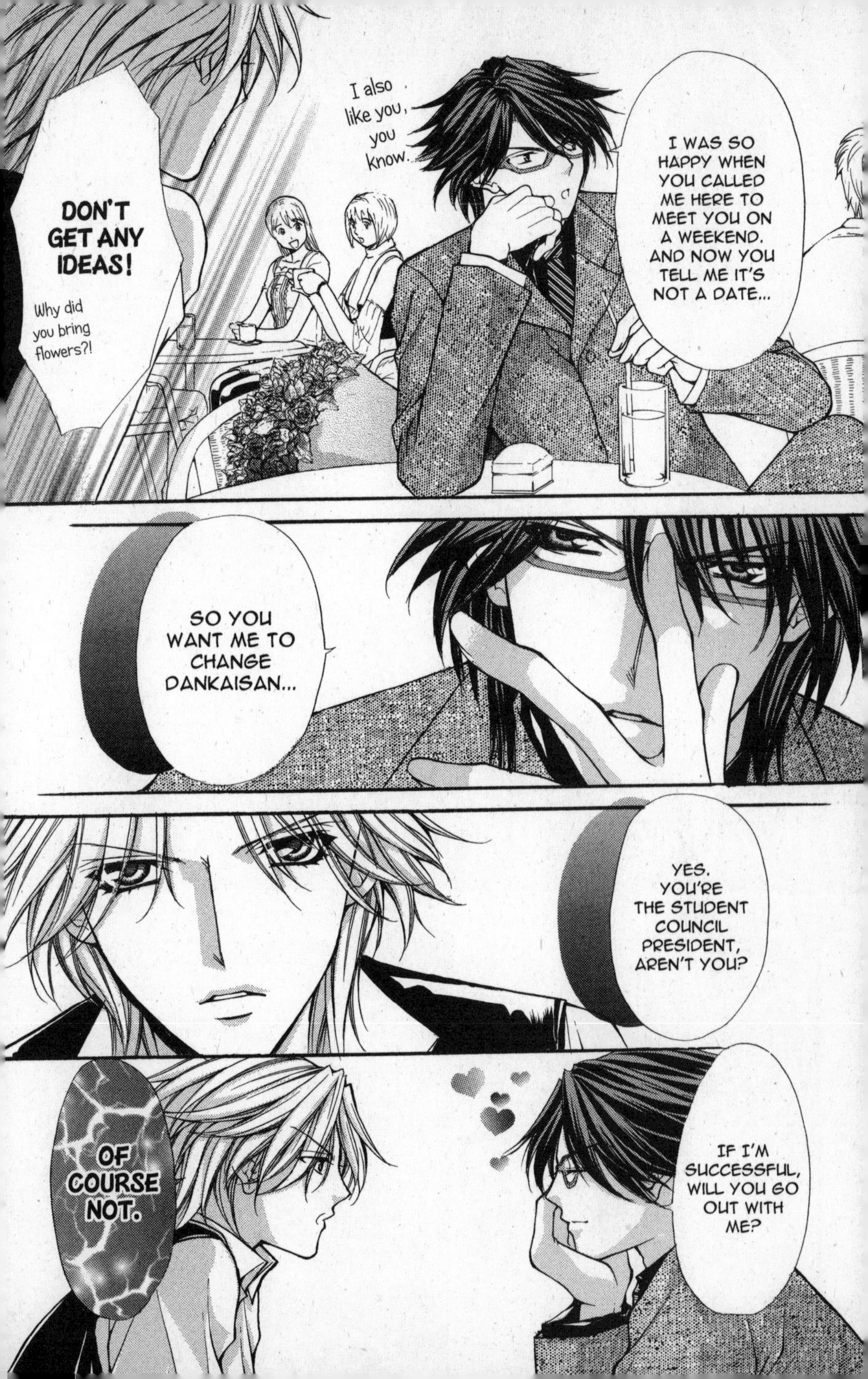
I WAS SO HAPPY WHEN YOU CALLED ME HERE TO MEET YOU ON A WEEKEND. AND NOW YOU TELL ME IT'S NOT A DATE...
I also like you, you know.
DON'T GET ANY IDEAS!
Why did you bring flowers?!
SO YOU WANT ME TO CHANGE DANKAISAN...
YES. YOU'RE THE STUDENT COUNCIL PRESIDENT, AREN'T YOU?
IF I'M SUCCESSFUL, WILL YOU GO OUT WITH ME?
OF COURSE NOT.

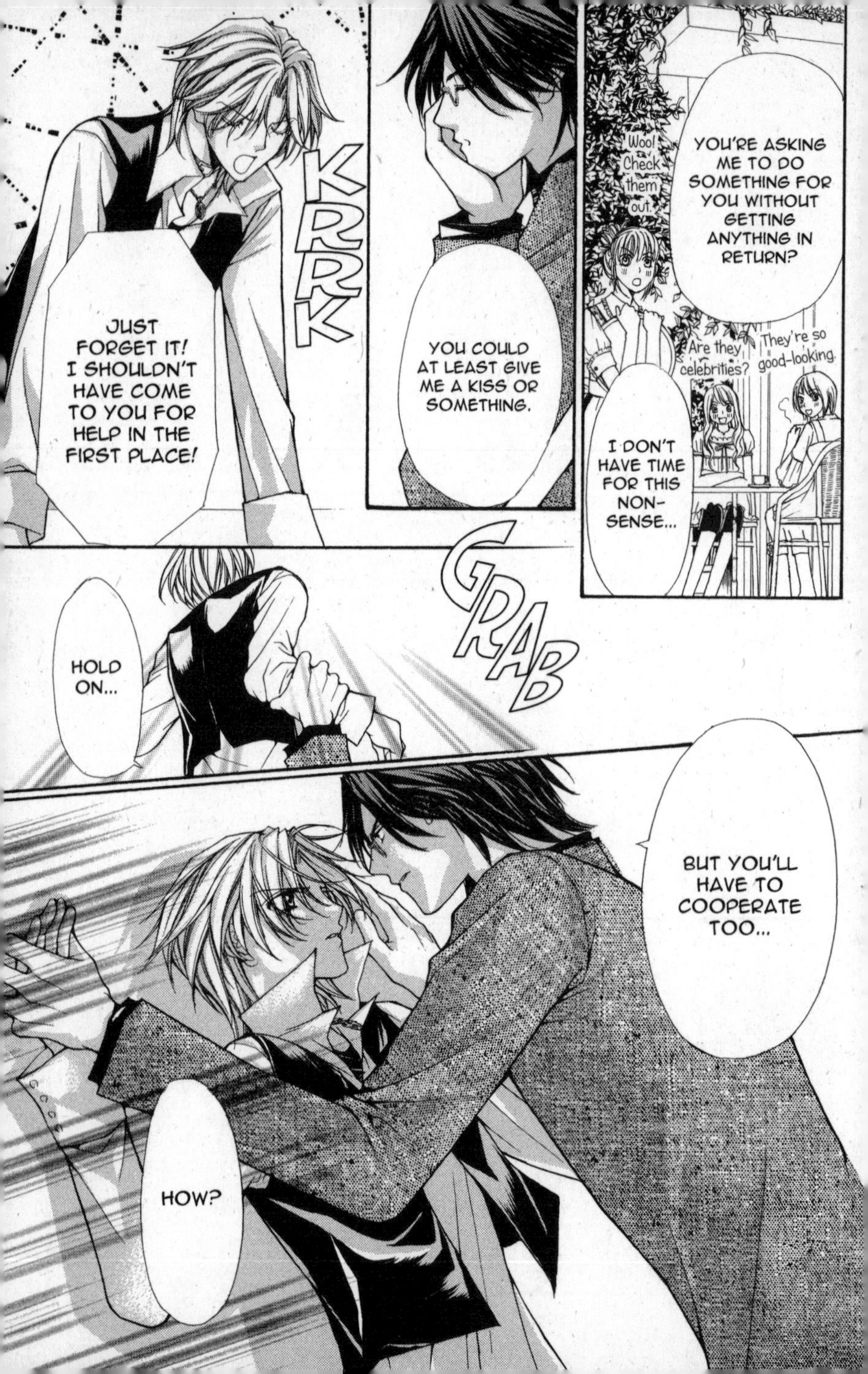
YOU'RE ASKING ME TO DO SOMETHING FOR YOU WITHOUT GETTING ANYTHING IN RETURN?
Woo! Check them out.
They're so good-looking.
Are they celebrities?
I DON'T HAVE TIME FOR THIS NON-SENSE...
YOU COULD AT LEAST GIVE ME A KISS OR SOMETHING.
KRRK
JUST FORGET IT! I SHOULDN'T HAVE COME TO YOU FOR HELP IN THE FIRST PLACE!
GRAB
HOLD ON...
BUT YOU'LL HAVE TO COOPERATE TOO...
HOW?

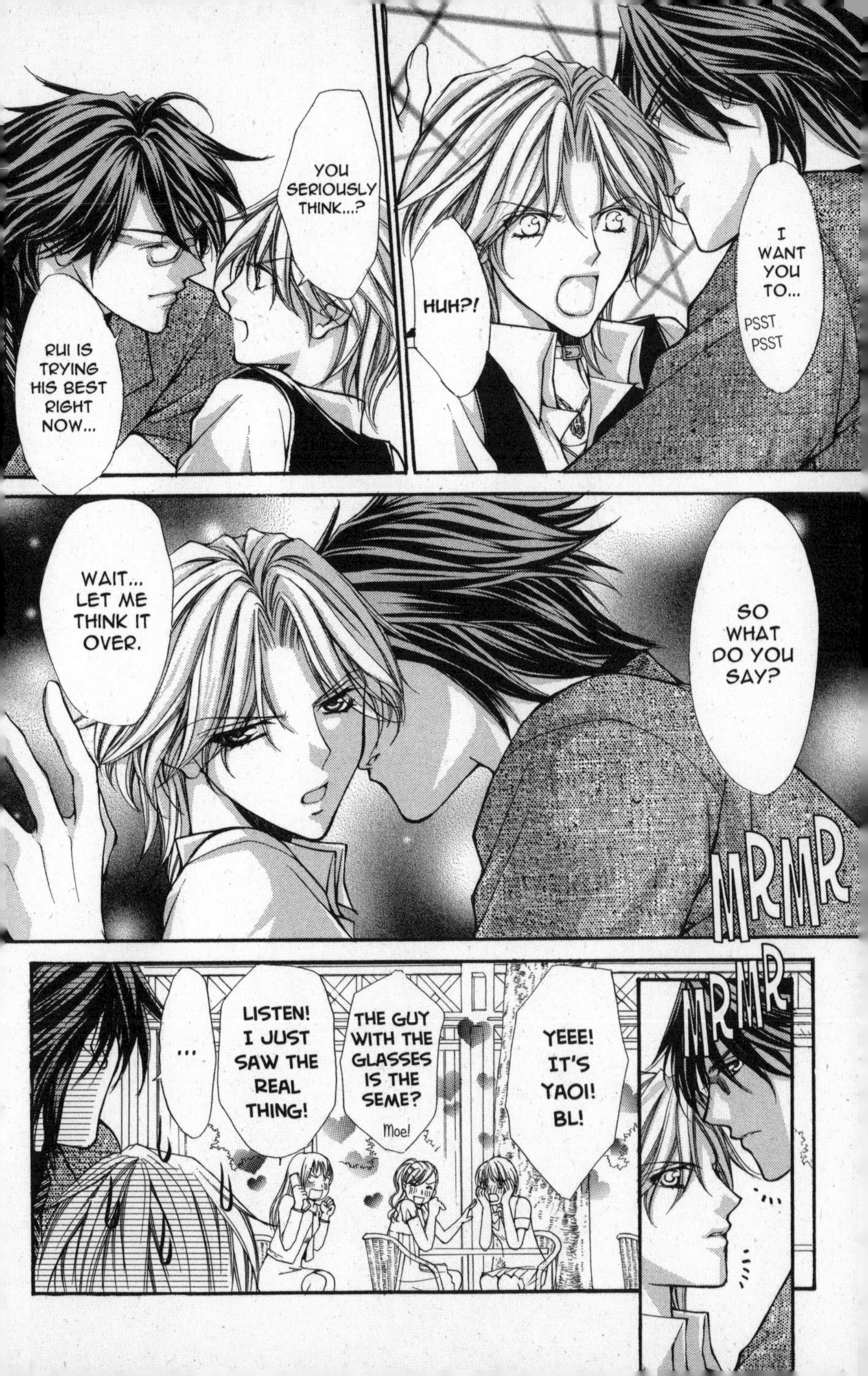
I WANT YOU TO...
PSST PSST
HUH?!
YOU SERIOUSLY THINK...?
RUI IS TRYING HIS BEST RIGHT NOW...
SO WHAT DO YOU SAY?
MRMR
WAIT... LET ME THINK IT OVER.
MRMR
YEEE! IT'S YAOI! BL!
THE GUY WITH THE GLASSES IS THE SEME?
Moe!
LISTEN! I JUST SAW THE REAL THING!
...

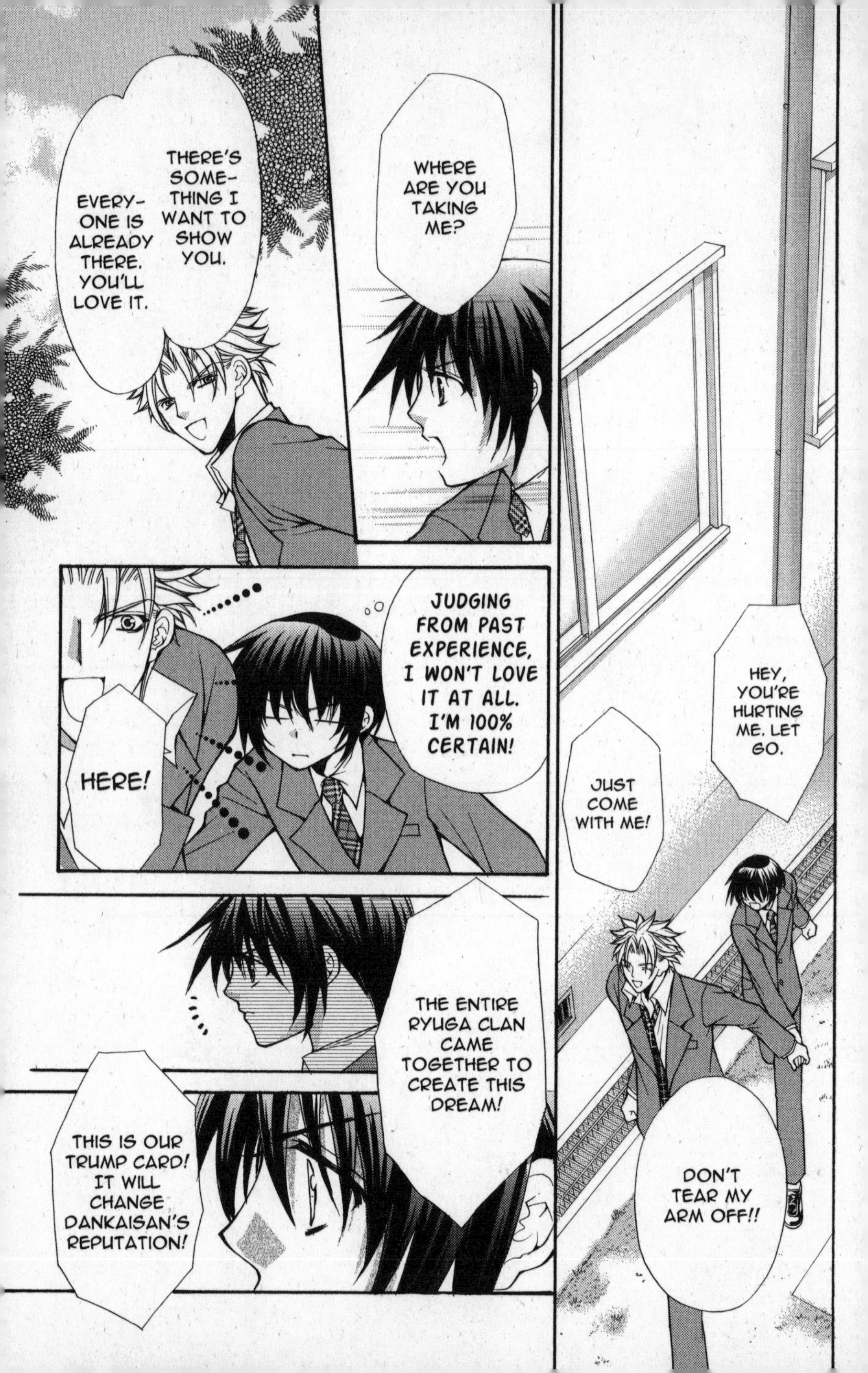
HEY, YOU'RE HURTING ME. LET GO.
JUST COME WITH ME!
DON'T TEAR MY ARM OFF!!
WHERE ARE YOU TAKING ME?
THERE'S SOME-THING I WANT TO SHOW YOU.
EVERY-ONE IS ALREADY THERE. YOU'LL LOVE IT.
JUDGING FROM PAST EXPERIENCE, I WON'T LOVE IT AT ALL. I'M 100% CERTAIN!
HERE!
THE ENTIRE RYUGA CLAN CAME TOGETHER TO CREATE THIS DREAM!
THIS IS OUR TRUMP CARD! IT WILL CHANGE DANKAISAN'S REPUTATION!

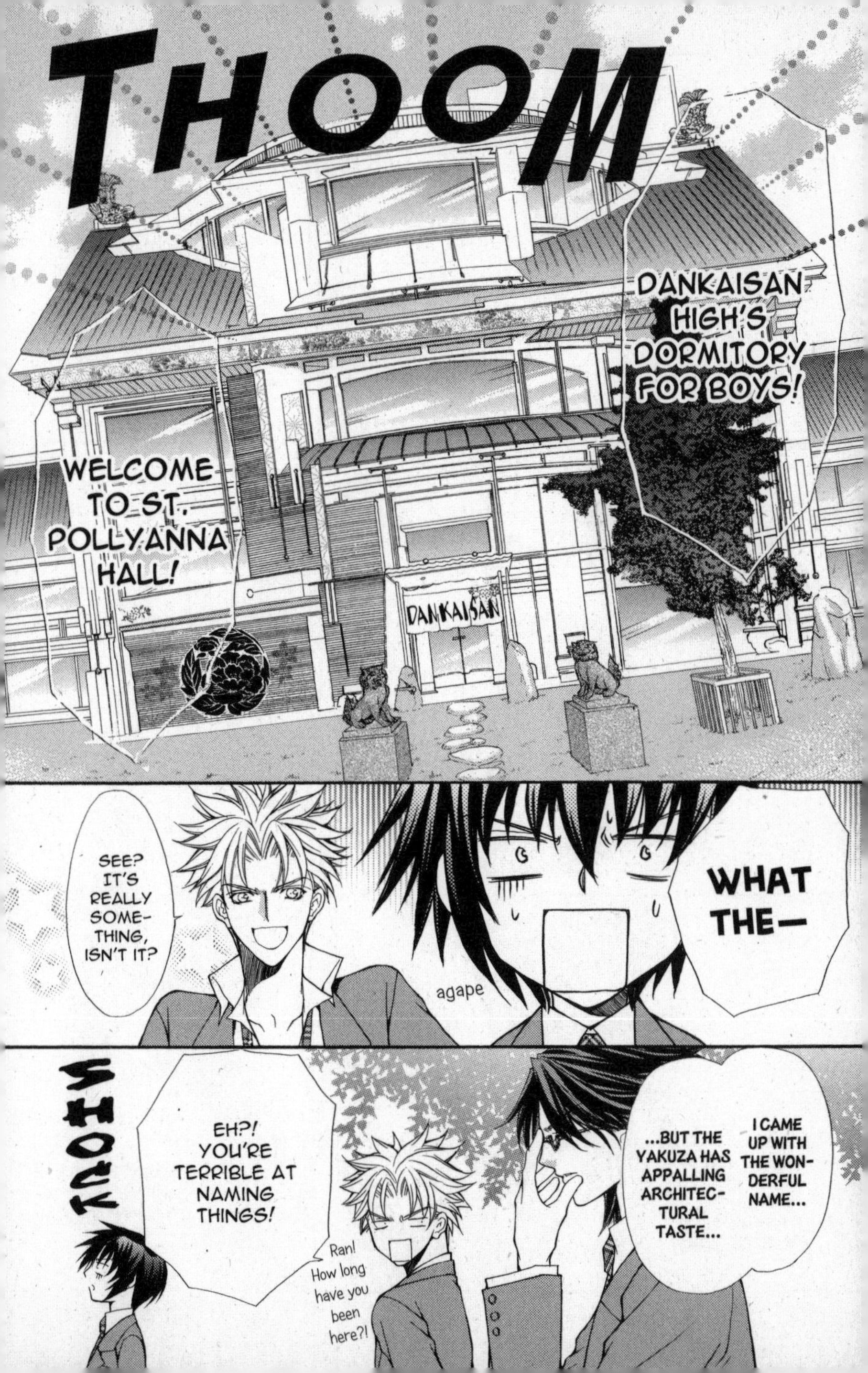
THOOM
DANKAISAN HIGH'S DORMITORY FOR BOYS!
WELCOME TO ST. POLLYANNA HALL!
DANKAISAN
WHAT THE—
agape
SEE? IT'S REALLY SOMETHING, ISN'T IT?
I CAME UP WITH THE WONDERFUL NAME...
...BUT THE YAKUZA HAS APPALLING ARCHITECTURAL TASTE...
EH?! YOU'RE TERRIBLE AT NAMING THINGS!
SHOUT
Ran! How long have you been here?!

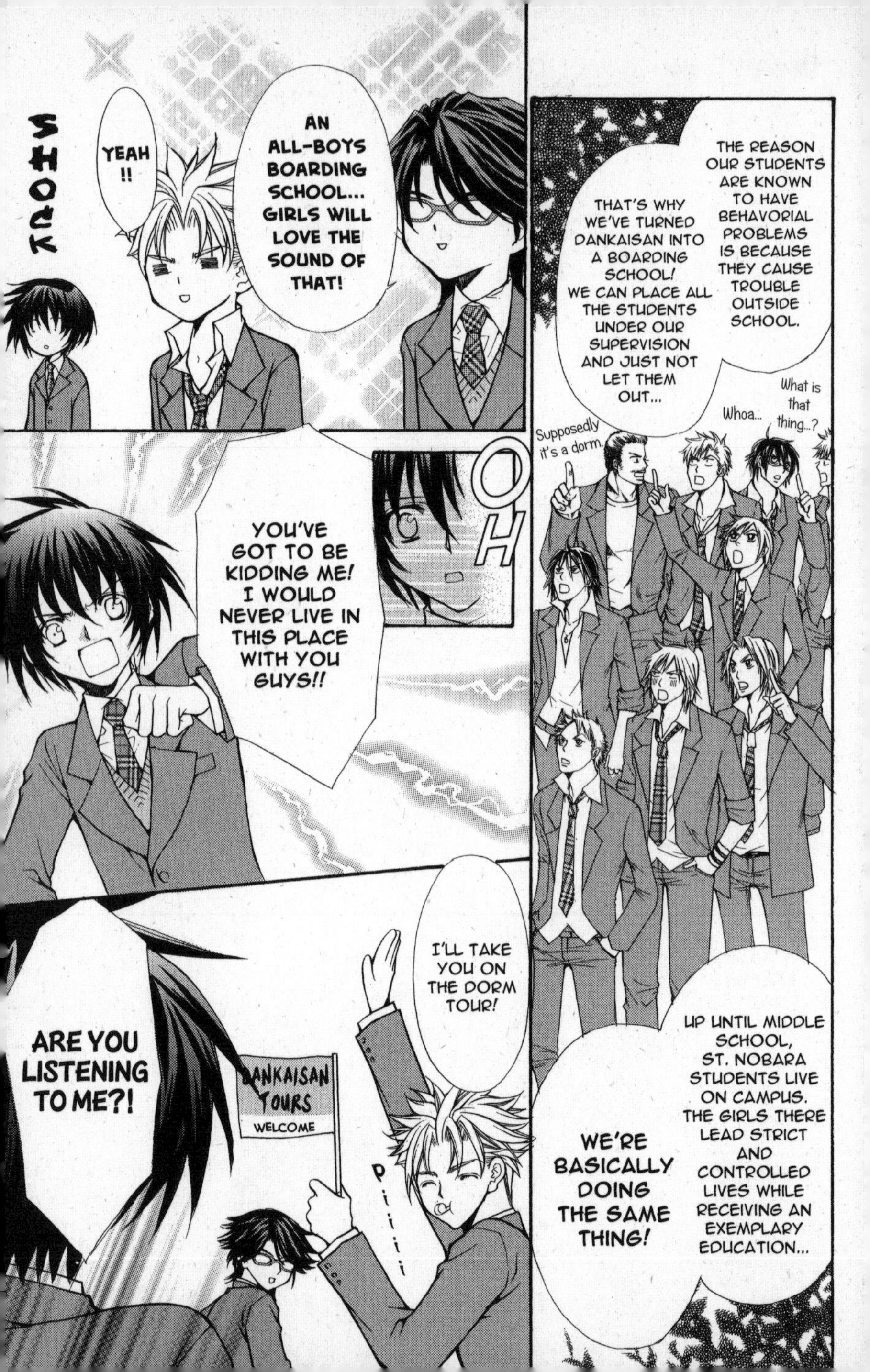
THE REASON OUR STUDENTS ARE KNOWN TO HAVE BEHAVORIAL PROBLEMS IS BECAUSE THEY CAUSE TROUBLE OUTSIDE SCHOOL.
THAT'S WHY WE'VE TURNED DANKAISAN INTO A BOARDING SCHOOL! WE CAN PLACE ALL THE STUDENTS UNDER OUR SUPERVISION AND JUST NOT LET THEM OUT...
What is that thing...?
Whoa...
Supposedly it's a dorm.
UP UNTIL MIDDLE SCHOOL, ST. NOBARA STUDENTS LIVE ON CAMPUS. THE GIRLS THERE LEAD STRICT AND CONTROLLED LIVES WHILE RECEIVING AN EXEMPLARY EDUCATION...
WE'RE BASICALLY DOING THE SAME THING!
AN ALL-BOYS BOARDING SCHOOL... GIRLS WILL LOVE THE SOUND OF THAT!
YEAH !!
SHOCK
OH
YOU'VE GOT TO BE KIDDING ME! I WOULD NEVER LIVE IN THIS PLACE WITH YOU GUYS!!
I'LL TAKE YOU ON THE DORM TOUR!
DANKAISAN TOURS
WELCOME
P......
ARE YOU LISTENING TO ME?!

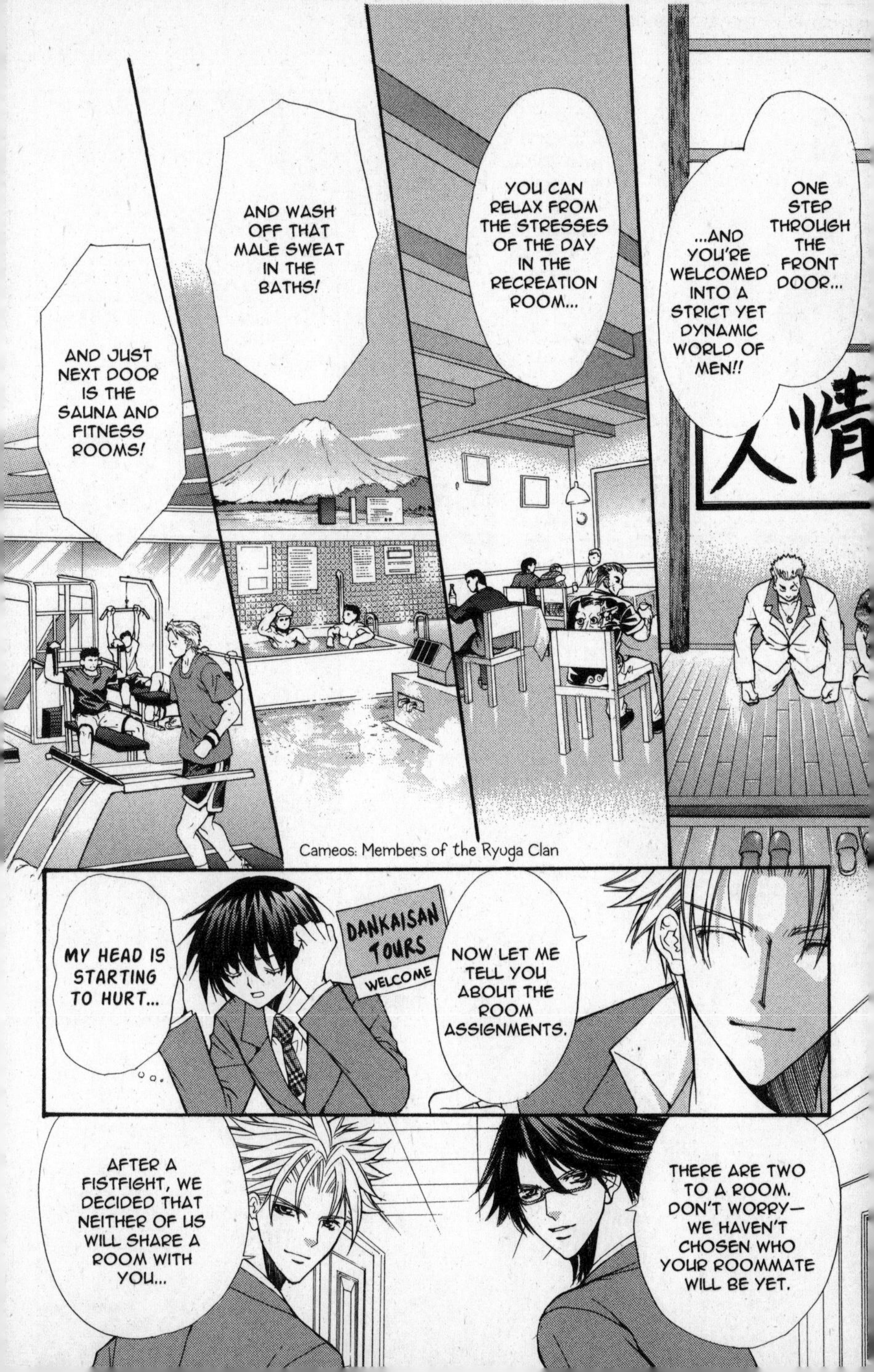
ONE STEP THROUGH THE FRONT DOOR...
...AND YOU'RE WELCOMED INTO A STRICT YET DYNAMIC WORLD OF MEN!!
人情
YOU CAN RELAX FROM THE STRESSES OF THE DAY IN THE RECREATION ROOM...
AND WASH OFF THAT MALE SWEAT IN THE BATHS!
AND JUST NEXT DOOR IS THE SAUNA AND FITNESS ROOMS!
Cameos: Members of the Ryuga Clan
NOW LET ME TELL YOU ABOUT THE ROOM ASSIGNMENTS.
DANKAISAN TOURS
WELCOME
MY HEAD IS STARTING TO HURT...
THERE ARE TWO TO A ROOM. DON'T WORRY—WE HAVEN'T CHOSEN WHO YOUR ROOMMATE WILL BE YET.
AFTER A FISTFIGHT, WE DECIDED THAT NEITHER OF US WILL SHARE A ROOM WITH YOU...

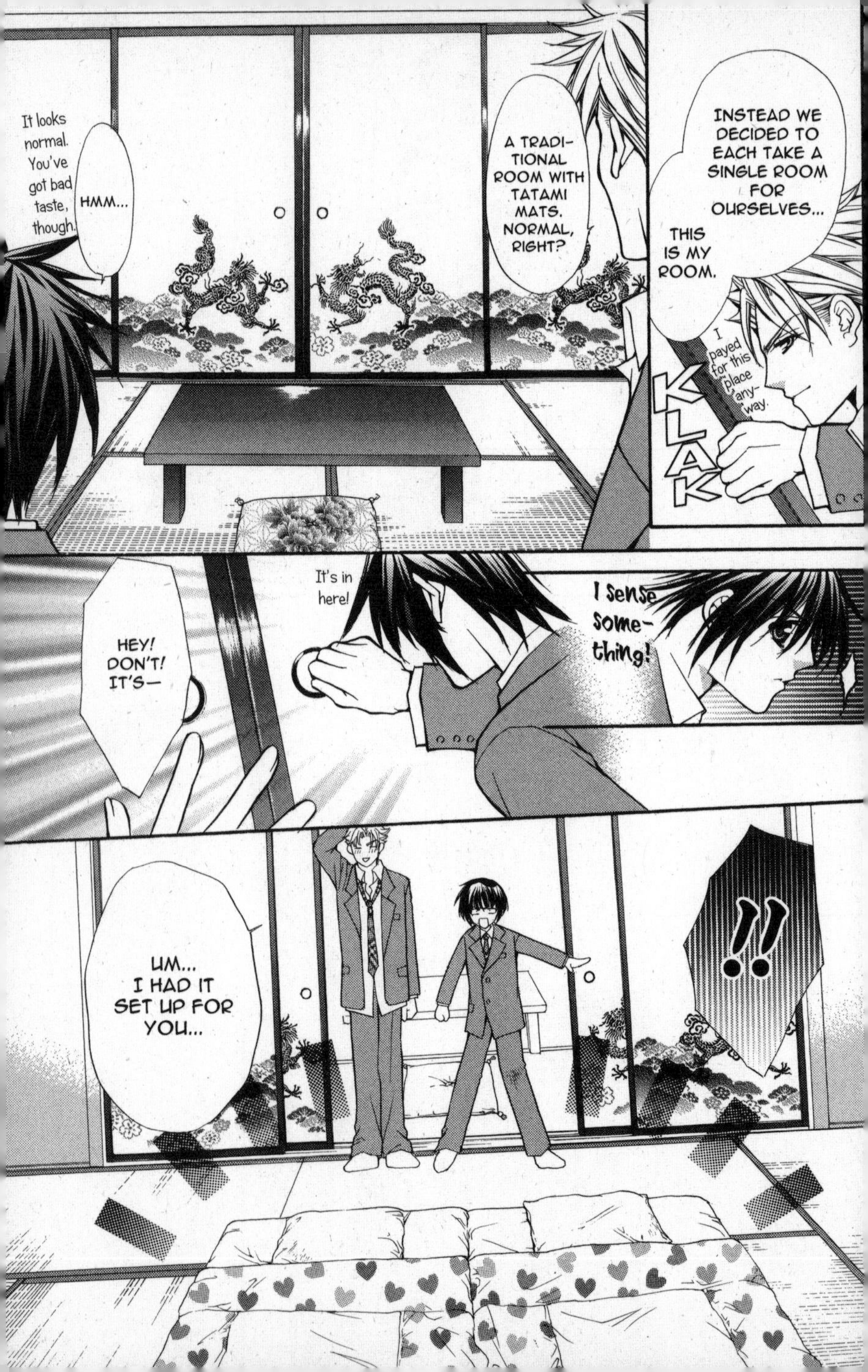
INSTEAD WE DECIDED TO EACH TAKE A SINGLE ROOM FOR OURSELVES...
THIS IS MY ROOM.
I payed for this place any-way.
KLLAK
A TRADI-TIONAL ROOM WITH TATAMI MATS. NORMAL, RIGHT?
HMM...
It looks normal. You've got bad taste, though.
I sense some-thing!
It's in here!
HEY! DON'T! IT'S—
!!
UM... I HAD IT SET UP FOR YOU...

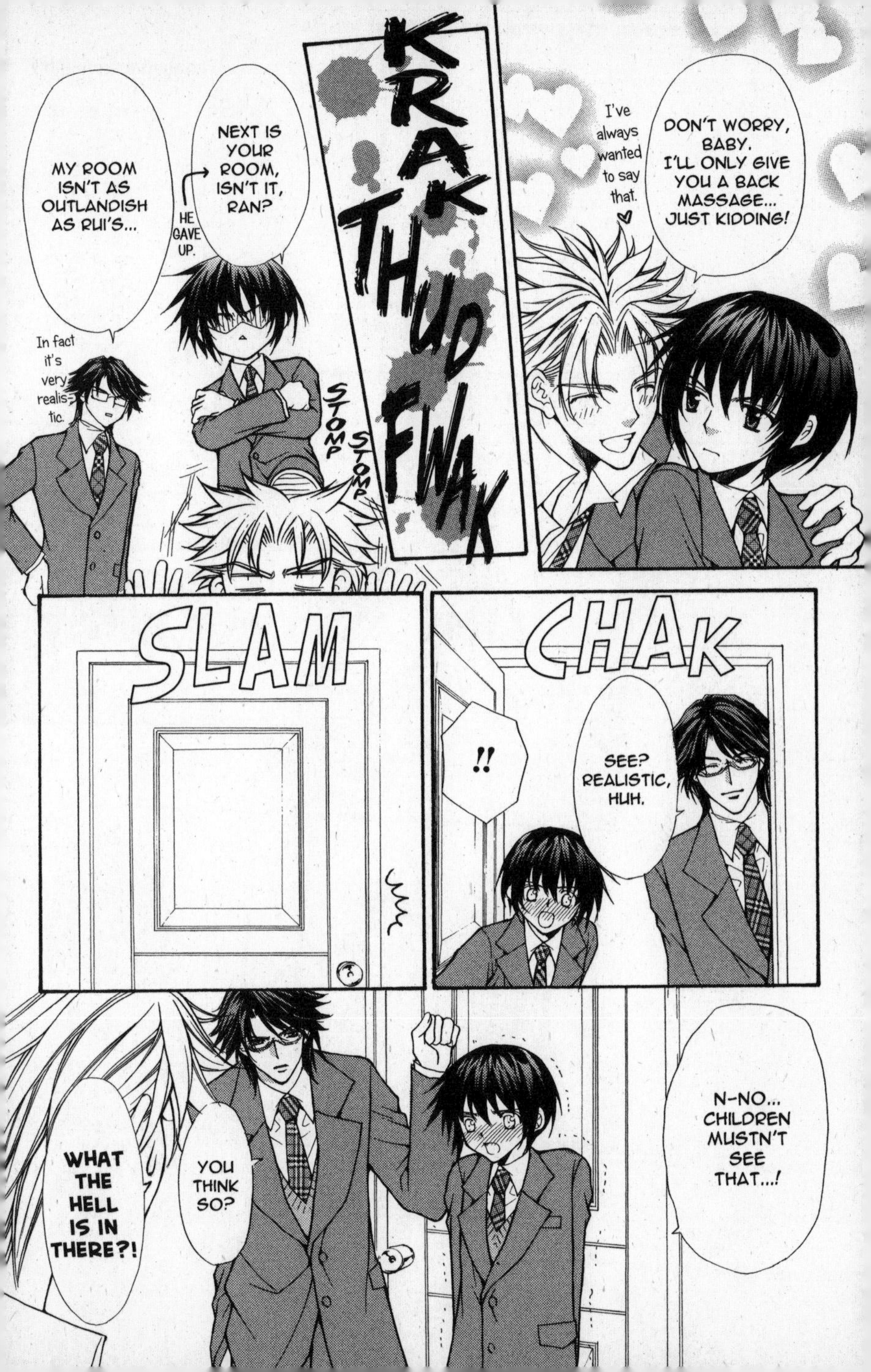
DON'T WORRY, BABY. I'LL ONLY GIVE YOU A BACK MASSAGE... JUST KIDDING!
I've always wanted to say that.
KRAK THUD FWAK
NEXT IS YOUR ROOM, ISN'T IT, RAN?
HE GAVE UP.
MY ROOM ISN'T AS OUTLANDISH AS RUI'S...
In fact it's very realistic.
STOMP STOMP
CHAK
!!
SEE? REALISTIC, HUH.
SLAM
N-NO... CHILDREN MUSTN'T SEE THAT...!
YOU THINK SO?
WHAT THE HELL IS IN THERE?!

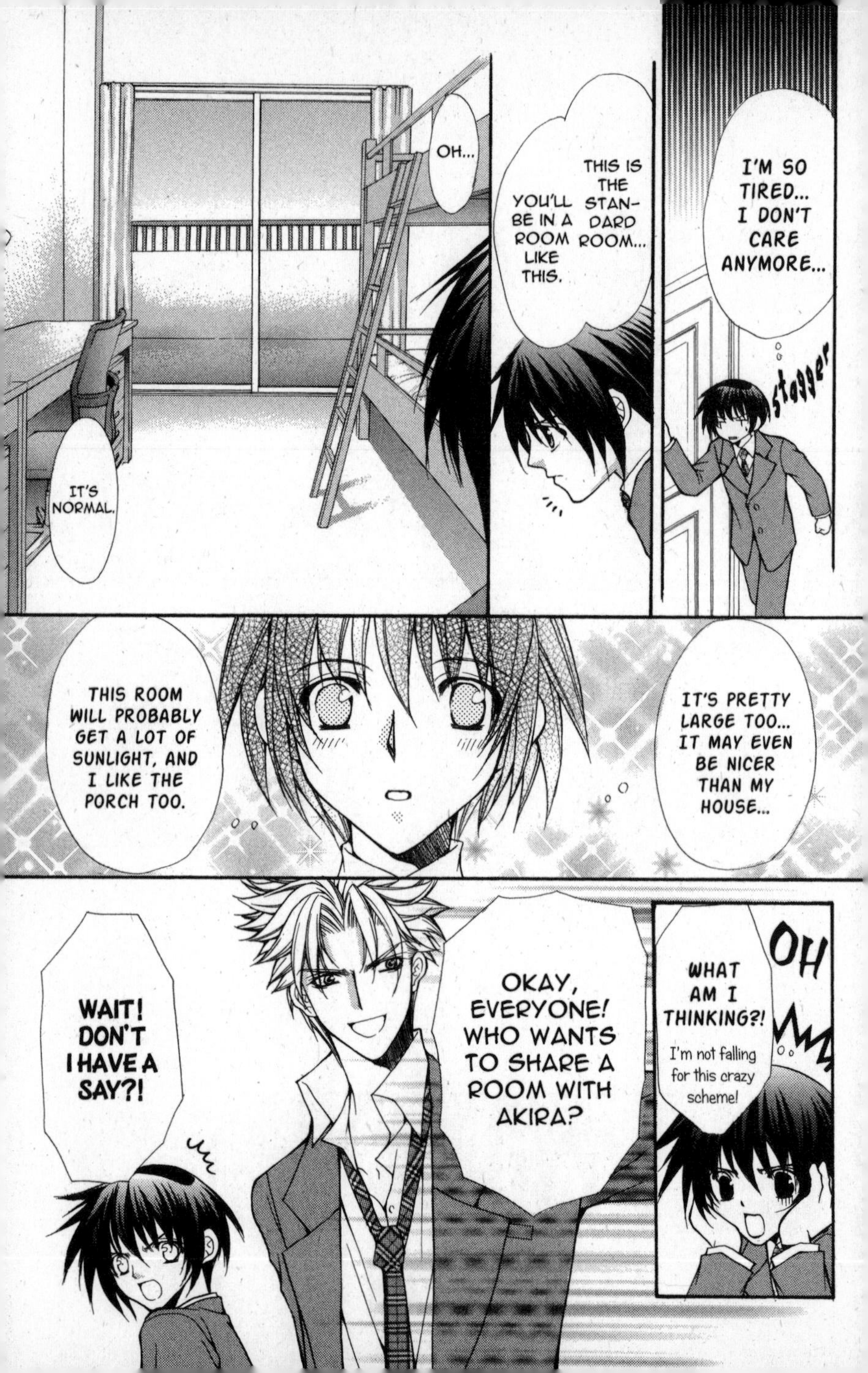
I'M SO TIRED... I DON'T CARE ANYMORE...
stagger
THIS IS THE STAN-DARD ROOM...
YOU'LL BE IN A ROOM LIKE THIS.
OH...
IT'S NORMAL.
IT'S PRETTY LARGE TOO... IT MAY EVEN BE NICER THAN MY HOUSE...
THIS ROOM WILL PROBABLY GET A LOT OF SUNLIGHT, AND I LIKE THE PORCH TOO.
OH
WHAT AM I THINKING?!
I'm not falling for this crazy scheme!
OKAY, EVERYONE! WHO WANTS TO SHARE A ROOM WITH AKIRA?
WAIT! DON'T I HAVE A SAY?!

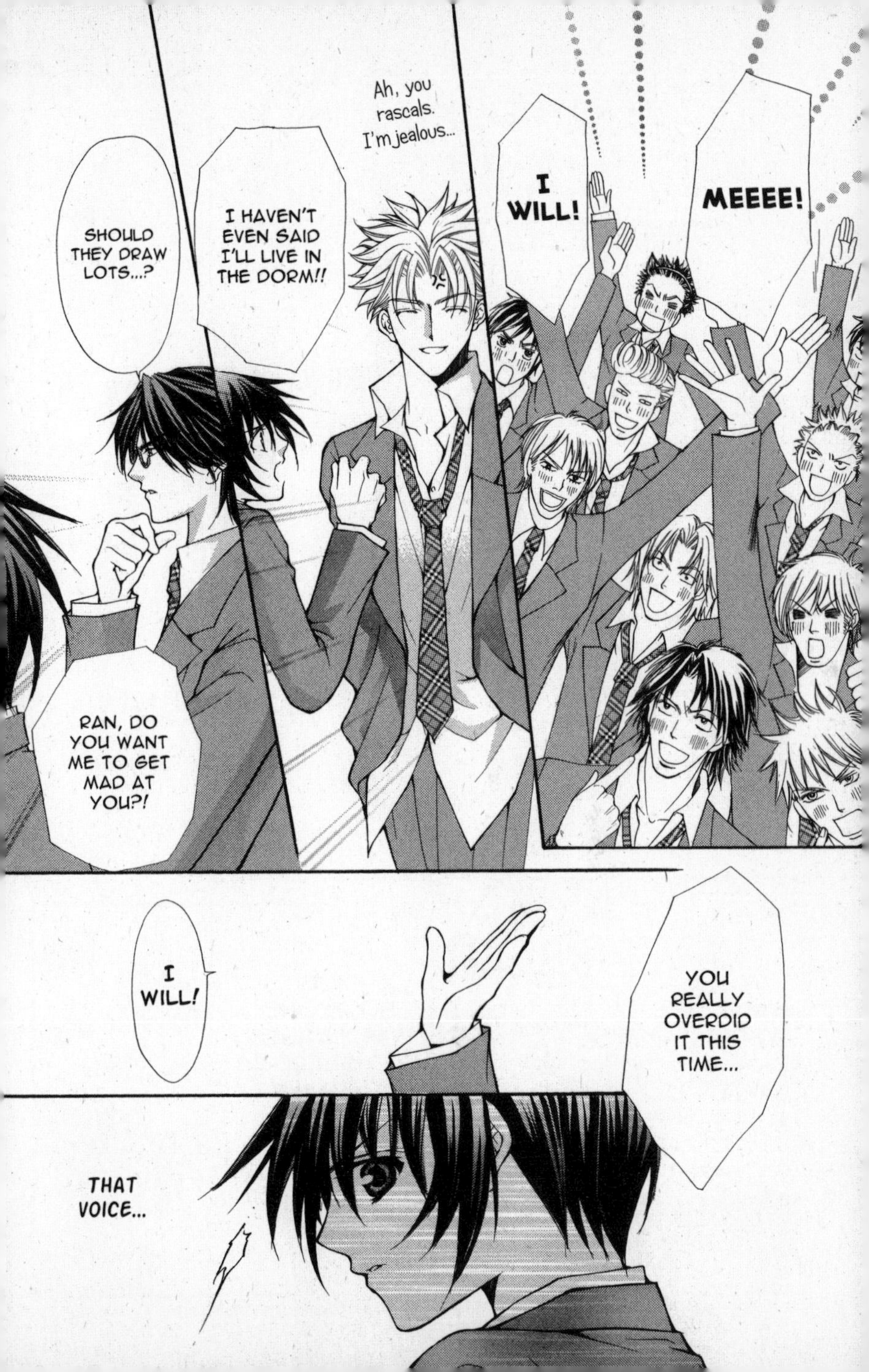
MEEEE!
I WILL!
Ah, you rascals. I'm jealous...
I HAVEN'T EVEN SAID I'LL LIVE IN THE DORM!!
SHOULD THEY DRAW LOTS...?
RAN, DO YOU WANT ME TO GET MAD AT YOU?!
YOU REALLY OVERDID IT THIS TIME...
I WILL!
THAT VOICE...

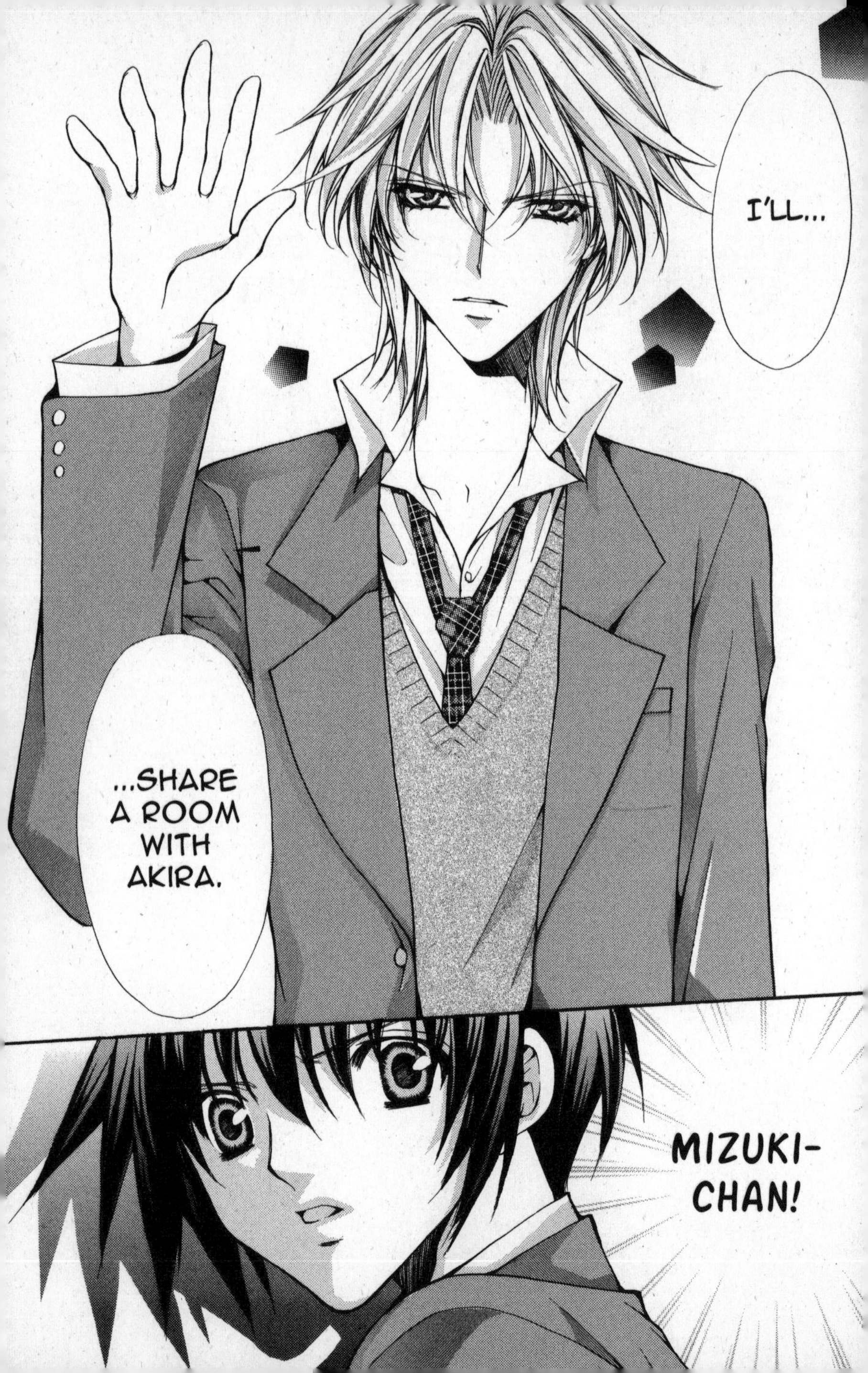
I'LL...
...SHARE A ROOM WITH AKIRA.
MIZUKI-CHAN!

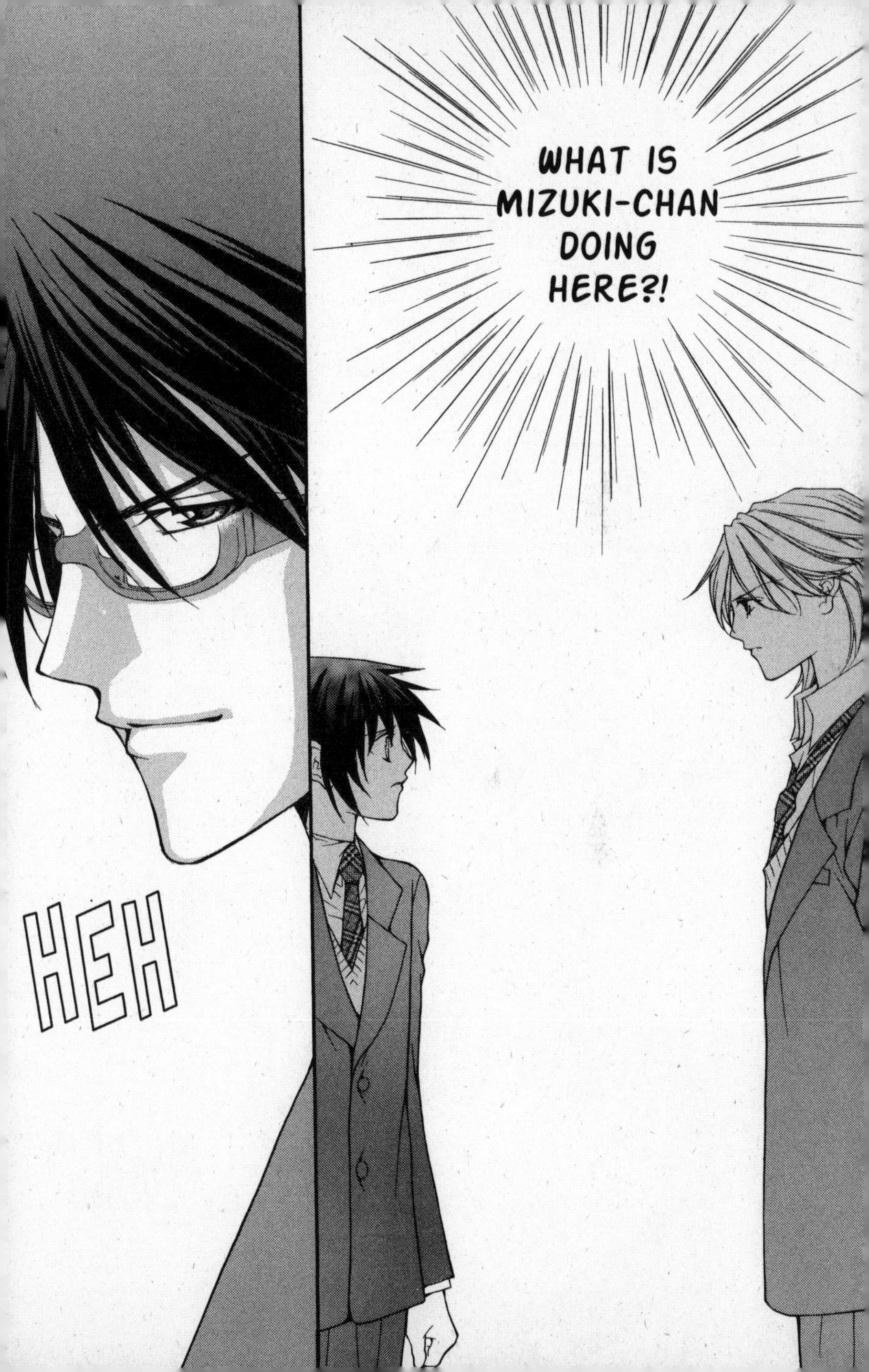
WHAT IS MIZUKI-CHAN DOING HERE?!
HEH

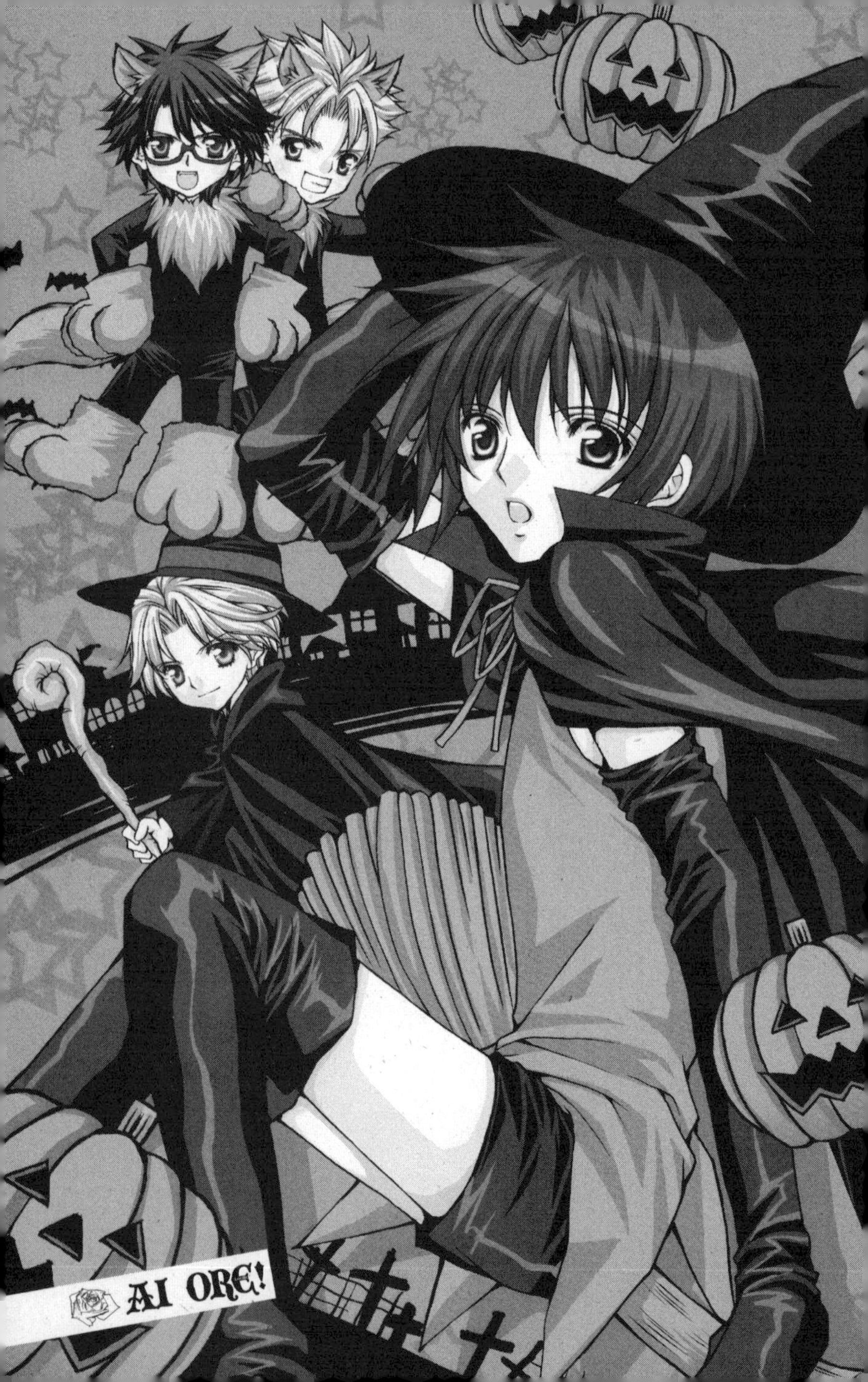
AI ORE!

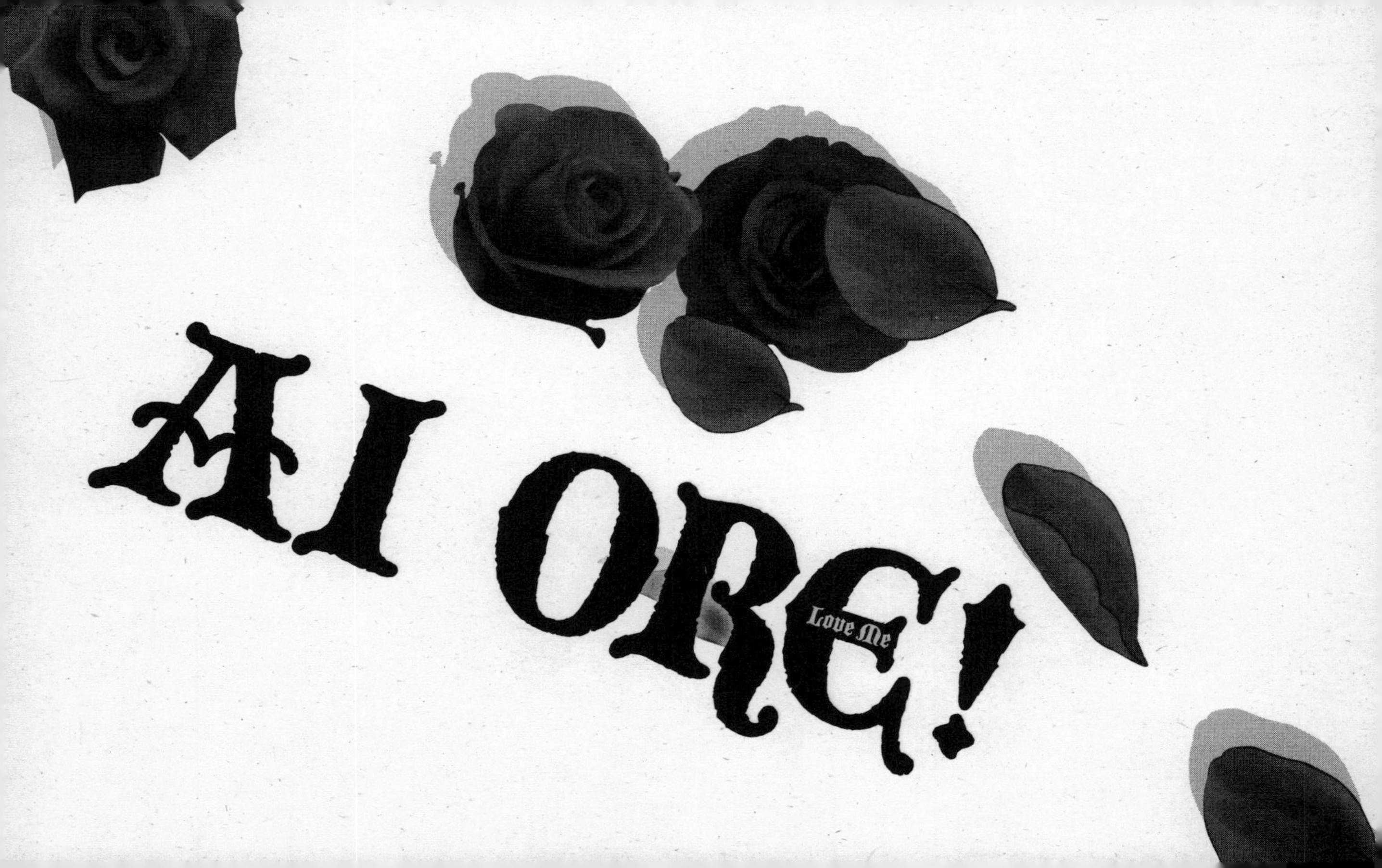
AI ORE!
Love Me

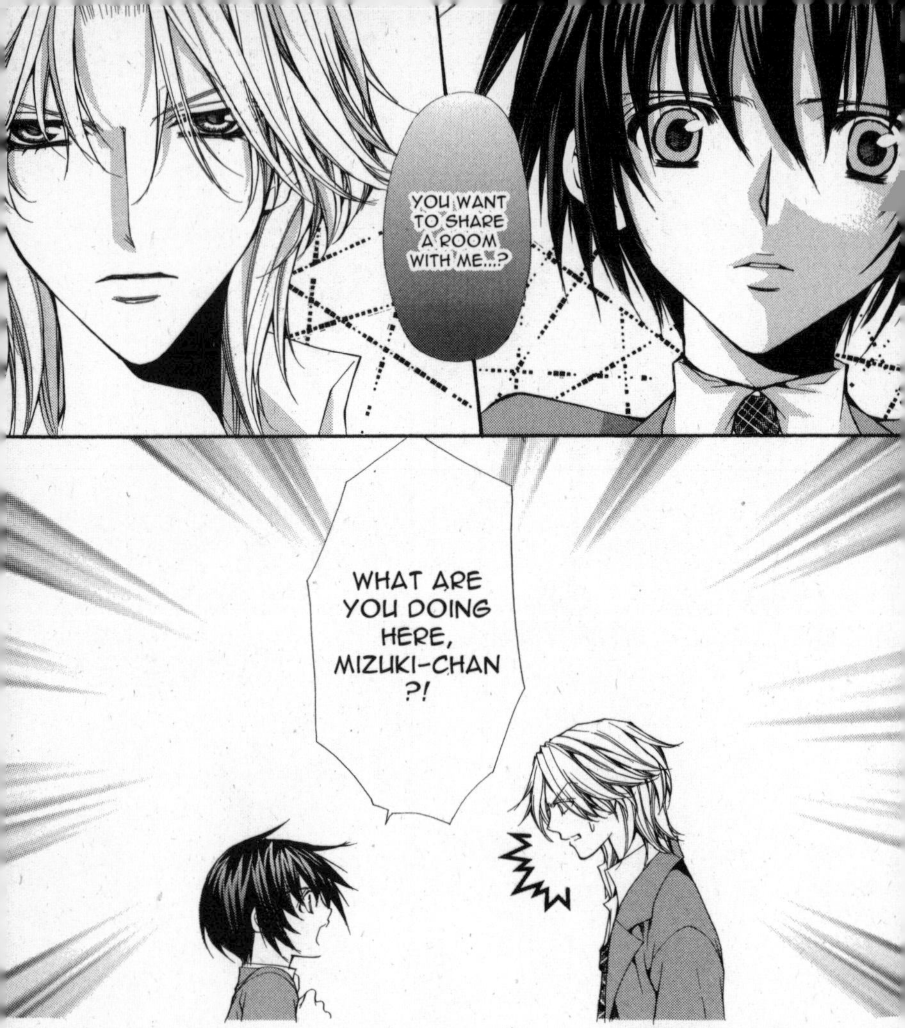
YOU WANT TO SHARE A ROOM WITH ME...?
WHAT ARE YOU DOING HERE, MIZUKI-CHAN?!

How do you do! I'm Mayu Shinjo.

This volume of *Ai Ore!* is finally out!
A lot of things happened to me, but I've come this far, and I'm beyond words. I'm very happy I've been able to deliver this to the people who were waiting for it.
I would like to dedicate this book to everyone who loves *Ai Ore!* and has supported this series. Thank you very much!

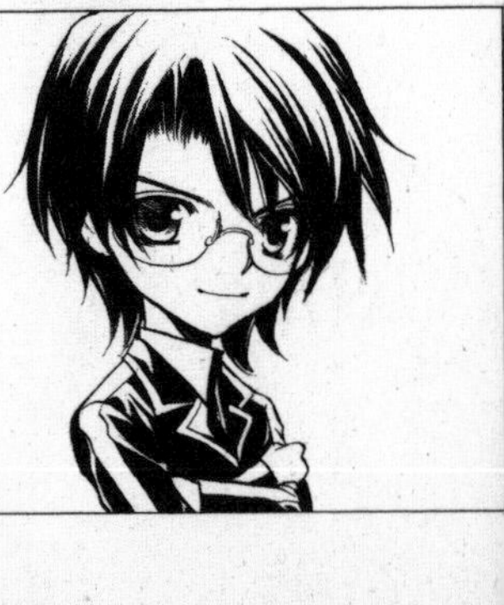

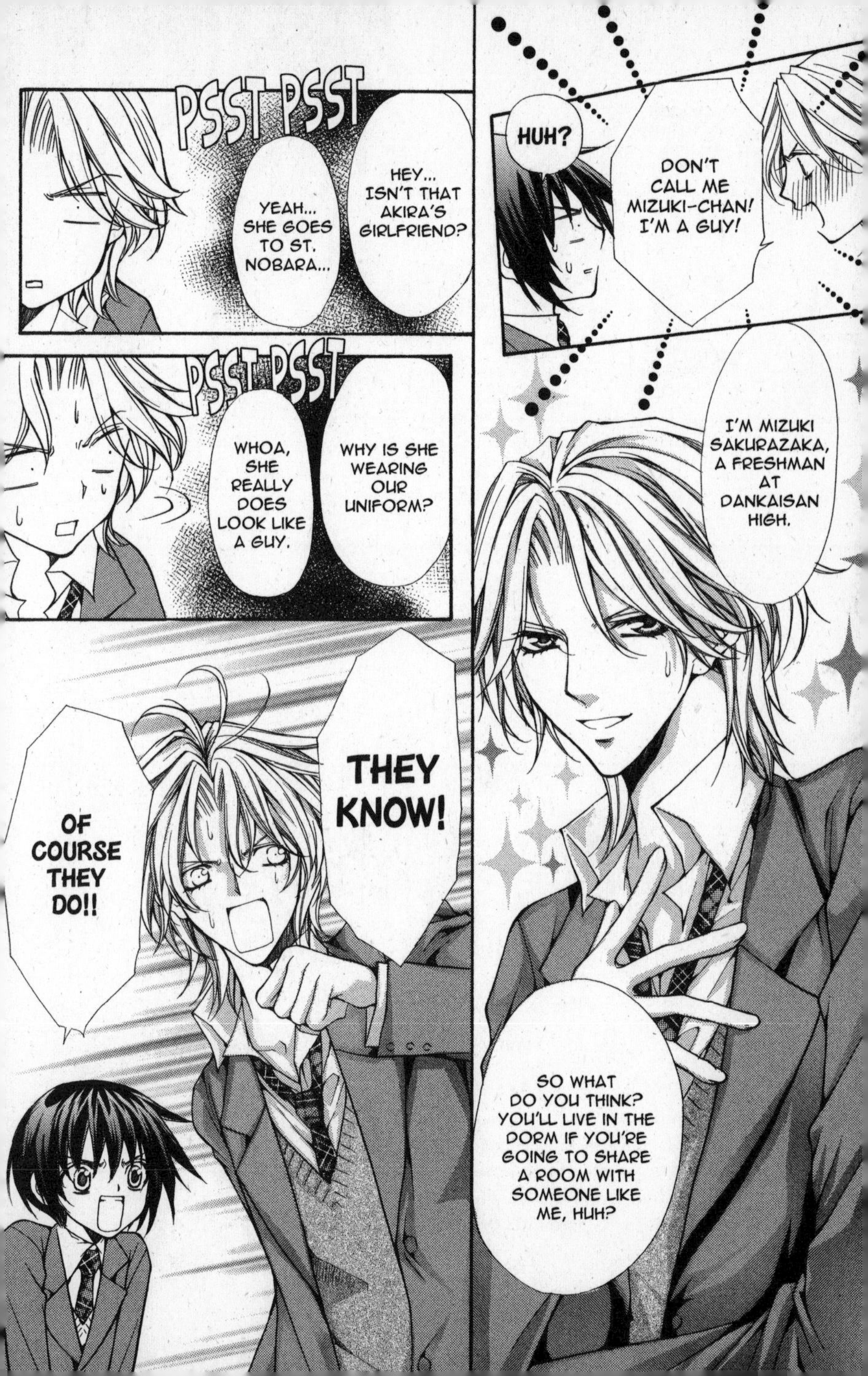
HUH?
DON'T CALL ME MIZUKI-CHAN! I'M A GUY!
I'M MIZUKI SAKURAZAKA, A FRESHMAN AT DANKAISAN HIGH.
SO WHAT DO YOU THINK? YOU'LL LIVE IN THE DORM IF YOU'RE GOING TO SHARE A ROOM WITH SOMEONE LIKE ME, HUH?
PSST PSST
HEY... ISN'T THAT AKIRA'S GIRLFRIEND?
YEAH... SHE GOES TO ST. NOBARA...
PSST PSST
WHY IS SHE WEARING OUR UNIFORM?
WHOA, SHE REALLY DOES LOOK LIKE A GUY.
THEY KNOW!
OF COURSE THEY DO!!

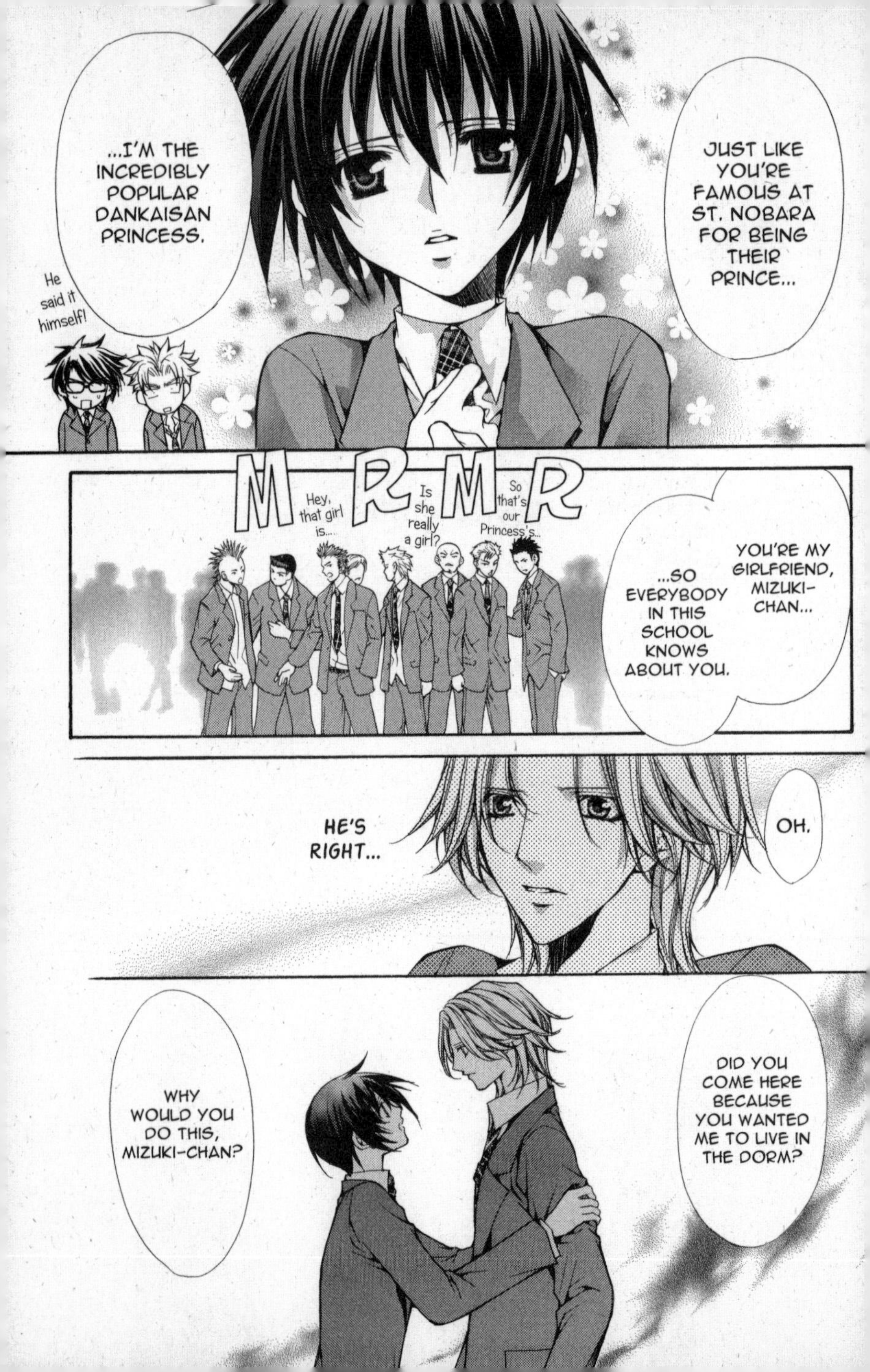
JUST LIKE YOU'RE FAMOUS AT ST. NOBARA FOR BEING THEIR PRINCE...
...I'M THE INCREDIBLY POPULAR DANKAISAN PRINCESS.
He said it himself!
YOU'RE MY GIRLFRIEND, MIZUKI-CHAN...
...SO EVERYBODY IN THIS SCHOOL KNOWS ABOUT YOU.
MRMR
So that's our Princess's...
Is she really a girl?
Hey, that girl is...
OH.
HE'S RIGHT...
DID YOU COME HERE BECAUSE YOU WANTED ME TO LIVE IN THE DORM?
WHY WOULD YOU DO THIS, MIZUKI-CHAN?

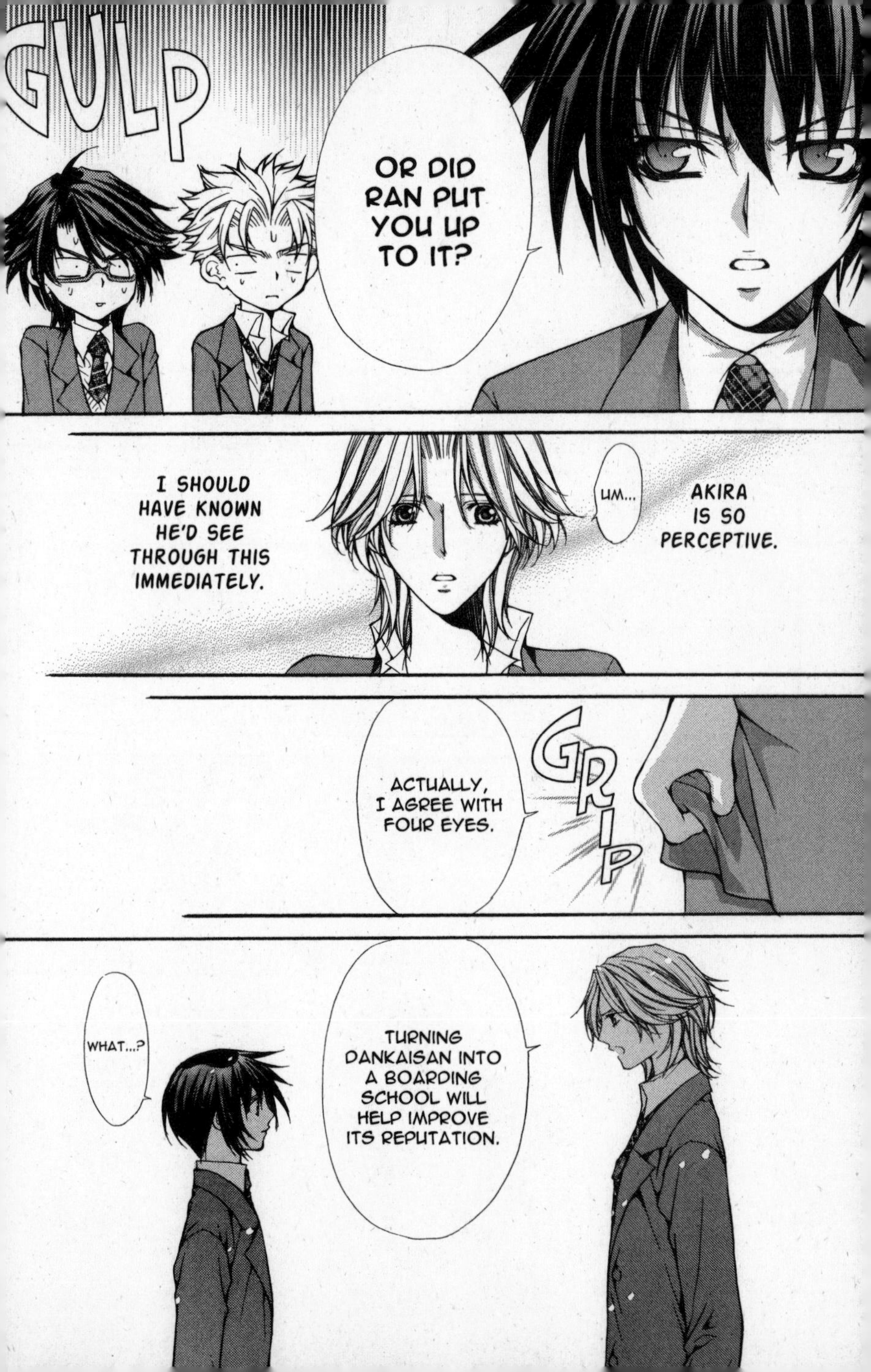
OR DID RAN PUT YOU UP TO IT?
GULP
AKIRA IS SO PERCEPTIVE.
UM...
I SHOULD HAVE KNOWN HE'D SEE THROUGH THIS IMMEDIATELY.
GRIP
ACTUALLY, I AGREE WITH FOUR EYES.
TURNING DANKAISAN INTO A BOARDING SCHOOL WILL HELP IMPROVE ITS REPUTATION.
WHAT...?

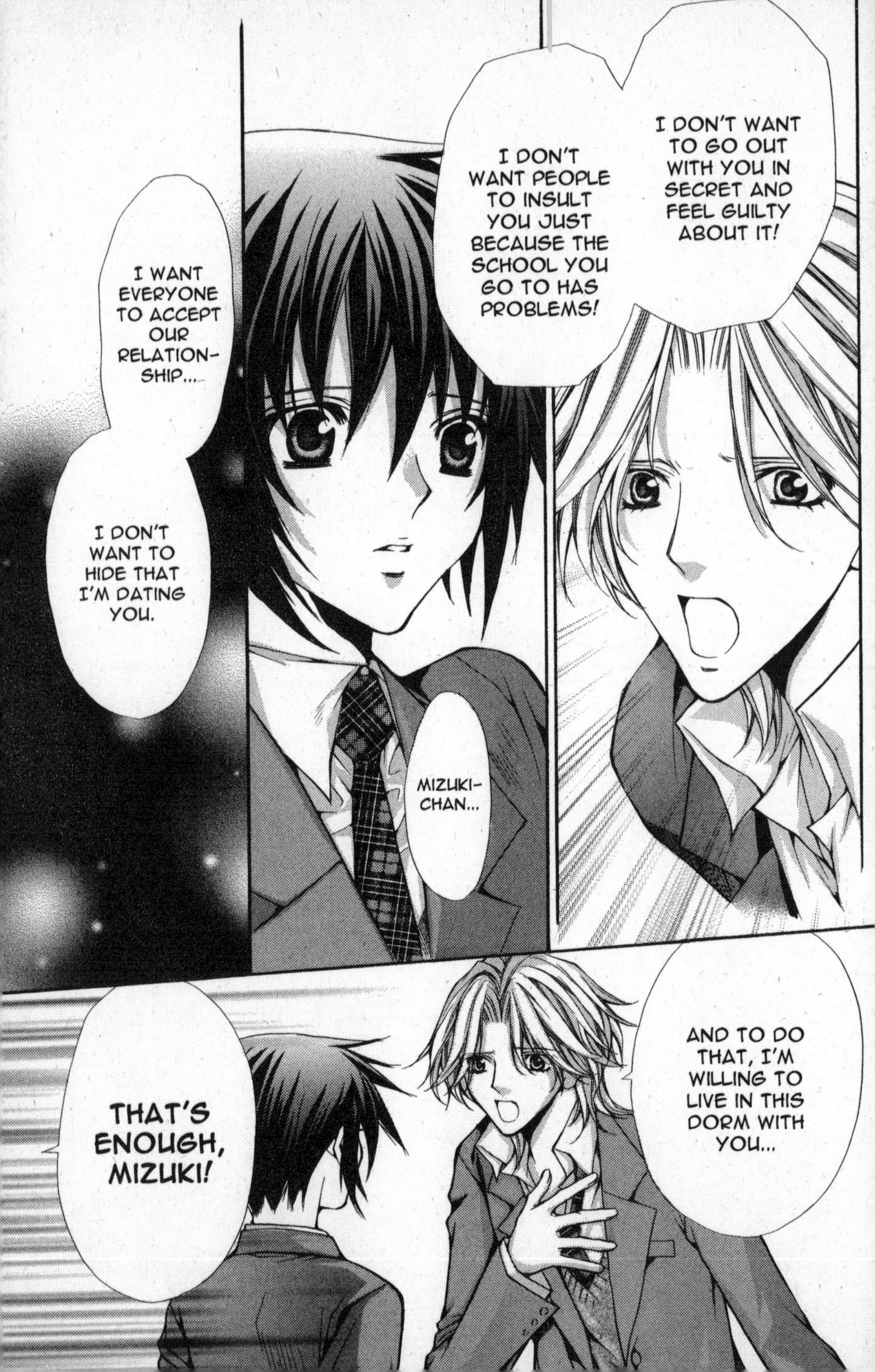
I DON'T WANT TO GO OUT WITH YOU IN SECRET AND FEEL GUILTY ABOUT IT!
I DON'T WANT PEOPLE TO INSULT YOU JUST BECAUSE THE SCHOOL YOU GO TO HAS PROBLEMS!
MIZUKI-CHAN...
I WANT EVERYONE TO ACCEPT OUR RELATION-SHIP...
I DON'T WANT TO HIDE THAT I'M DATING YOU.
AND TO DO THAT, I'M WILLING TO LIVE IN THIS DORM WITH YOU...
THAT'S ENOUGH, MIZUKI!

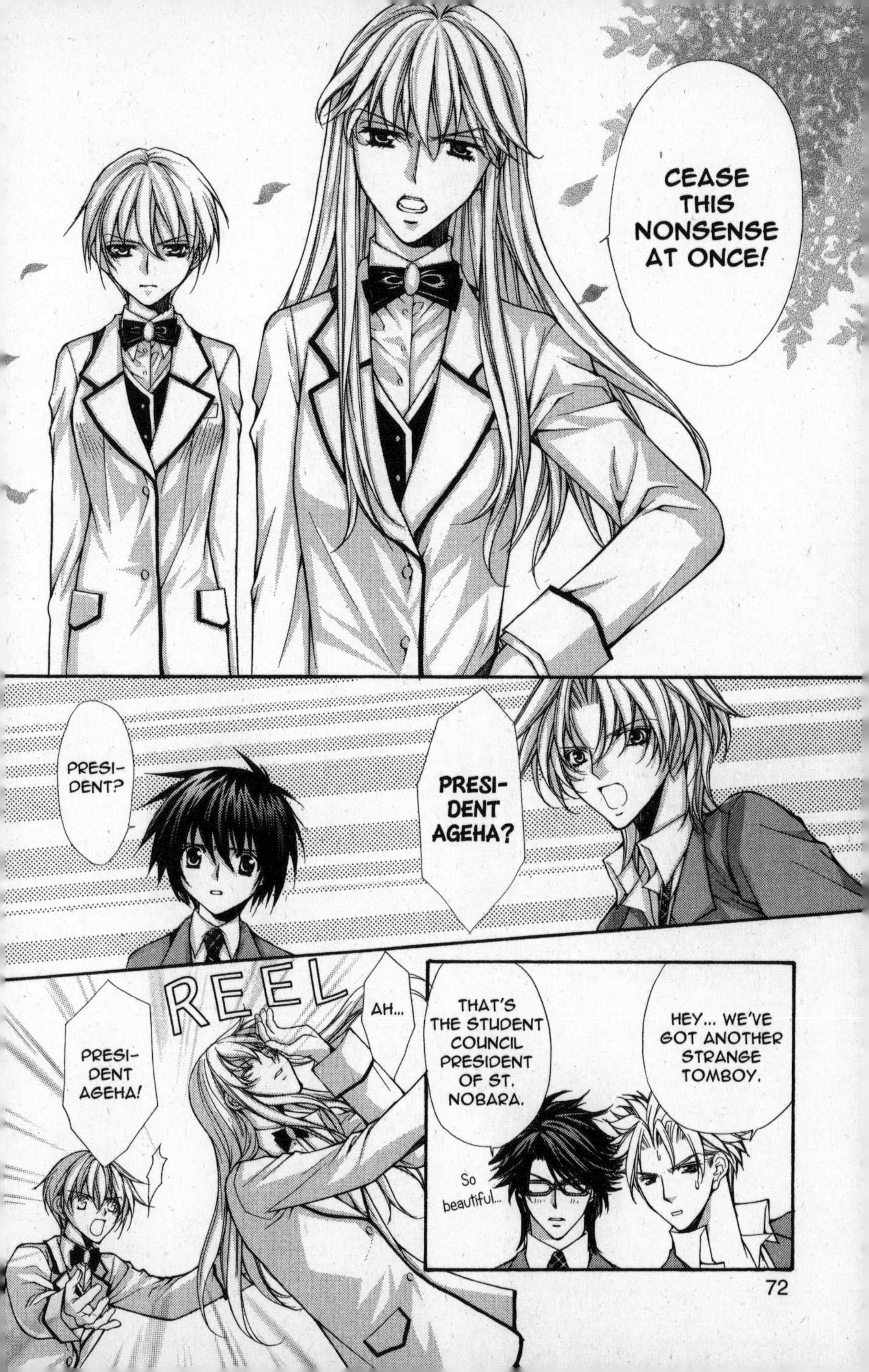
CEASE THIS NONSENSE AT ONCE!
PRESI-DENT AGEHA?
PRESI-DENT?
HEY... WE'VE GOT ANOTHER STRANGE TOMBOY.
THAT'S THE STUDENT COUNCIL PRESIDENT OF ST. NOBARA.
So beautiful...
AH...
REEL
PRESI-DENT AGEHA!

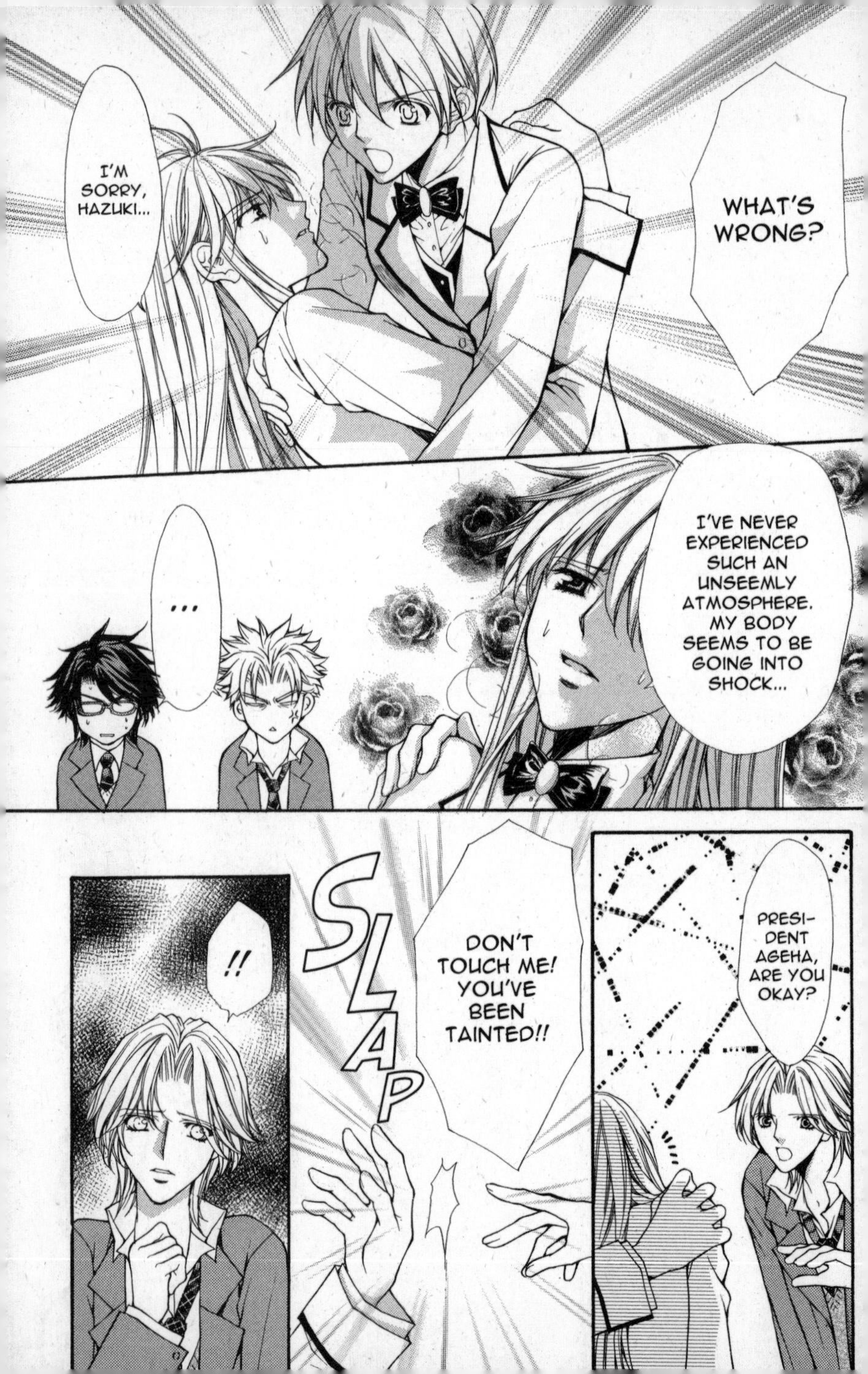
WHAT'S WRONG?
I'M SORRY, HAZUKI...
I'VE NEVER EXPERIENCED SUCH AN UNSEEMLY ATMOSPHERE. MY BODY SEEMS TO BE GOING INTO SHOCK...
...
PRESI-DENT AGEHA, ARE YOU OKAY?
DON'T TOUCH ME! YOU'VE BEEN TAINTED!!
SLAP
!!

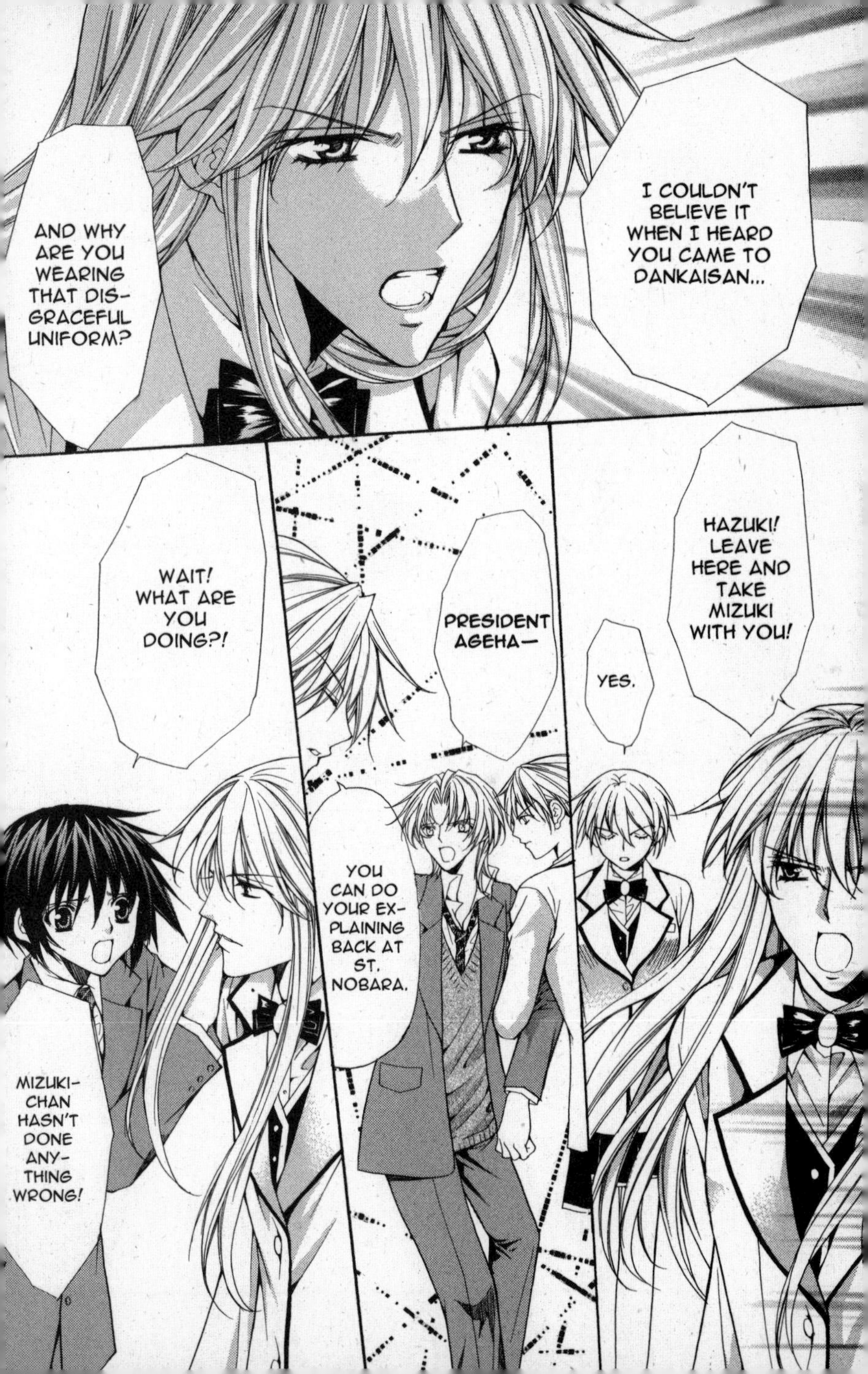
I COULDN'T BELIEVE IT WHEN I HEARD YOU CAME TO DANKAISAN...
AND WHY ARE YOU WEARING THAT DISGRACEFUL UNIFORM?
HAZUKI! LEAVE HERE AND TAKE MIZUKI WITH YOU!
YES.
PRESIDENT AGEHA—
YOU CAN DO YOUR EXPLAINING BACK AT ST. NOBARA.
WAIT! WHAT ARE YOU DOING?!
MIZUKI-CHAN HASN'T DONE ANYTHING WRONG!

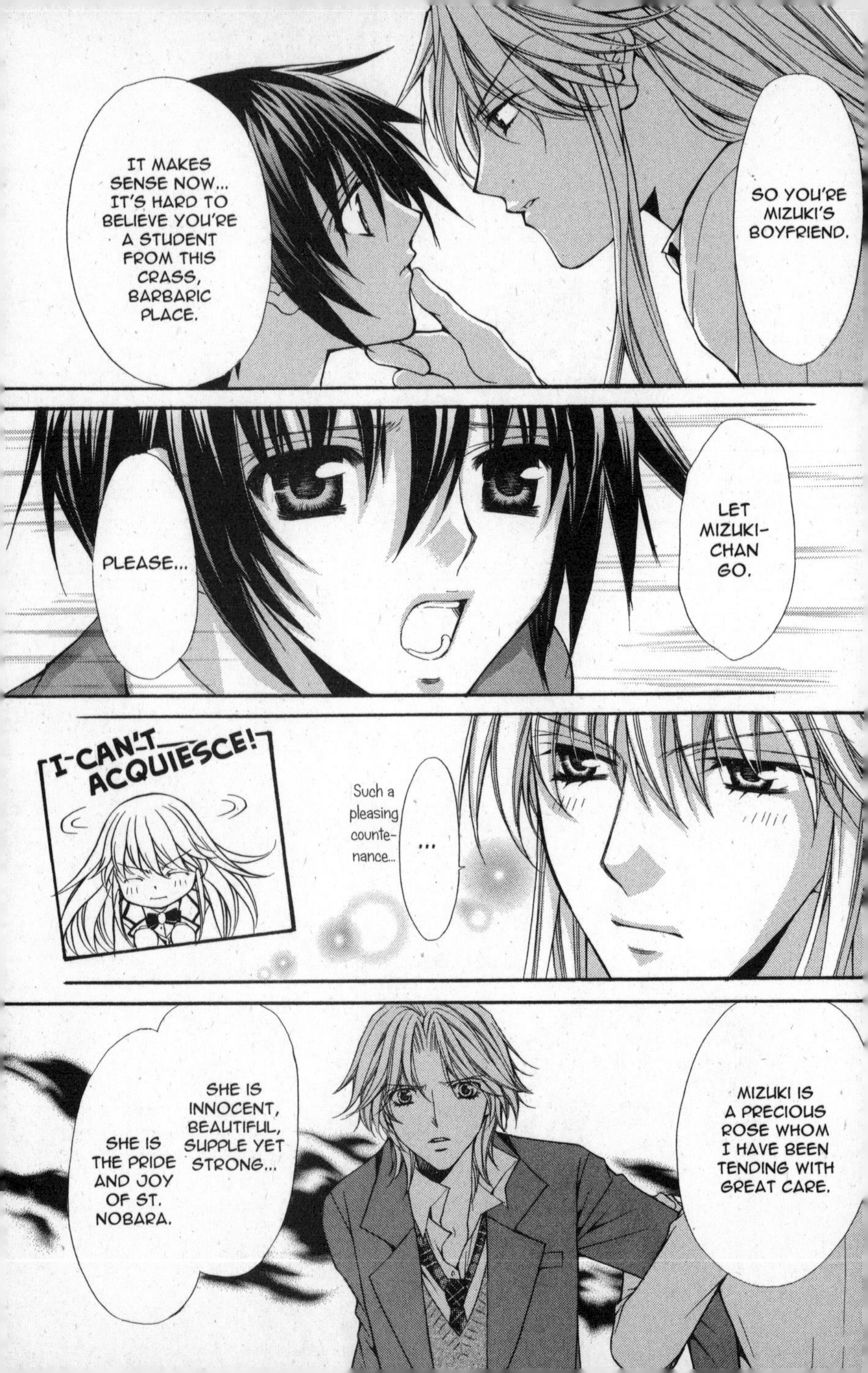
SO YOU'RE MIZUKI'S BOYFRIEND.
IT MAKES SENSE NOW... IT'S HARD TO BELIEVE YOU'RE A STUDENT FROM THIS CRASS, BARBARIC PLACE.
LET MIZUKI-CHAN GO.
PLEASE...
...
Such a pleasing countenance...
I-CAN'T ACQUIESCE!
MIZUKI IS A PRECIOUS ROSE WHOM I HAVE BEEN TENDING WITH GREAT CARE.
SHE IS INNOCENT, BEAUTIFUL, SUPPLE YET STRONG...
SHE IS THE PRIDE AND JOY OF ST. NOBARA.

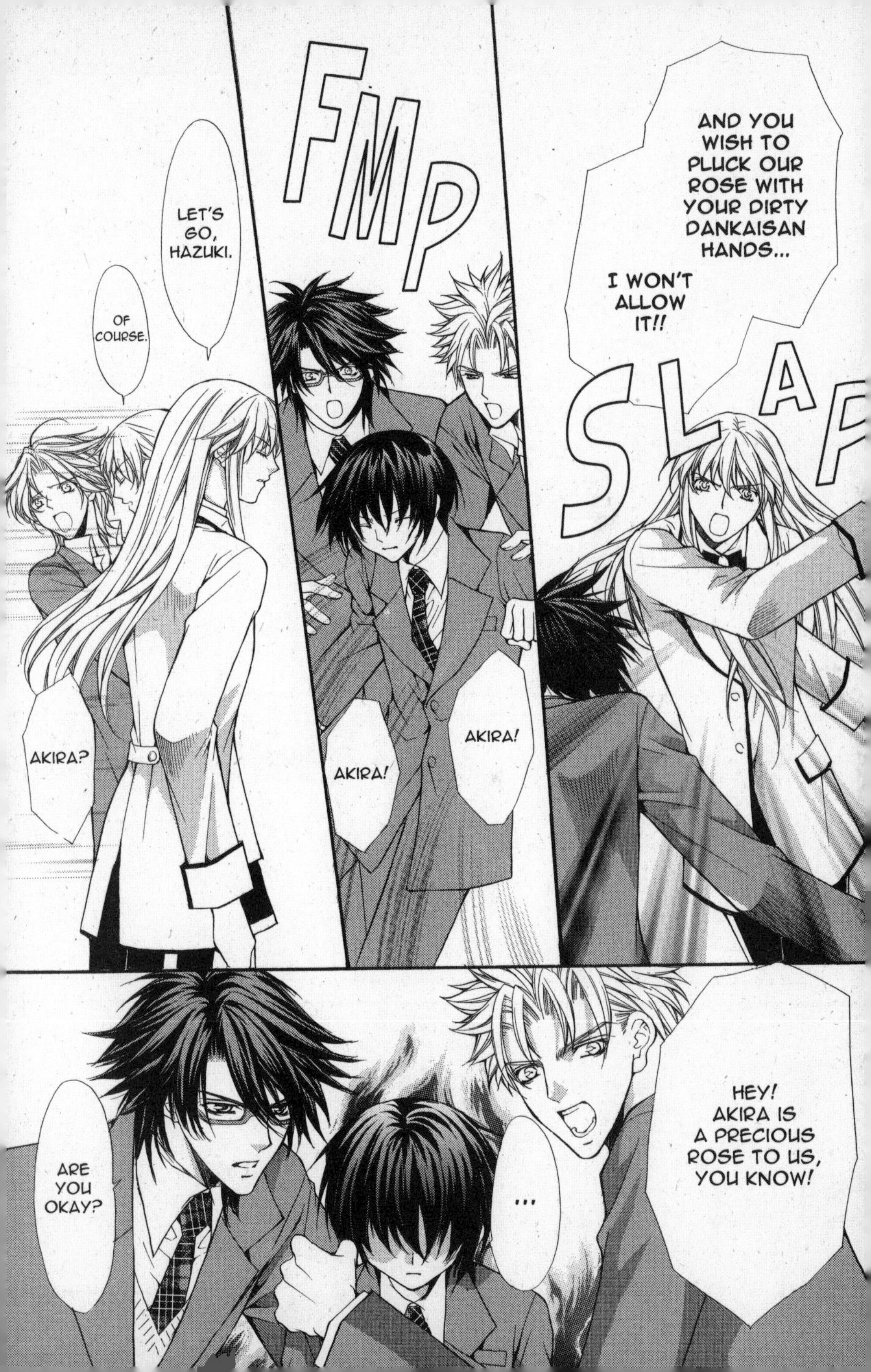
AND YOU WISH TO PLUCK OUR ROSE WITH YOUR DIRTY DANKAISAN HANDS...
I WON'T ALLOW IT!!
SLAP
FMP
AKIRA!
AKIRA!
LET'S GO, HAZUKI.
OF COURSE.
AKIRA?
HEY! AKIRA IS A PRECIOUS ROSE TO US, YOU KNOW!
...
ARE YOU OKAY?

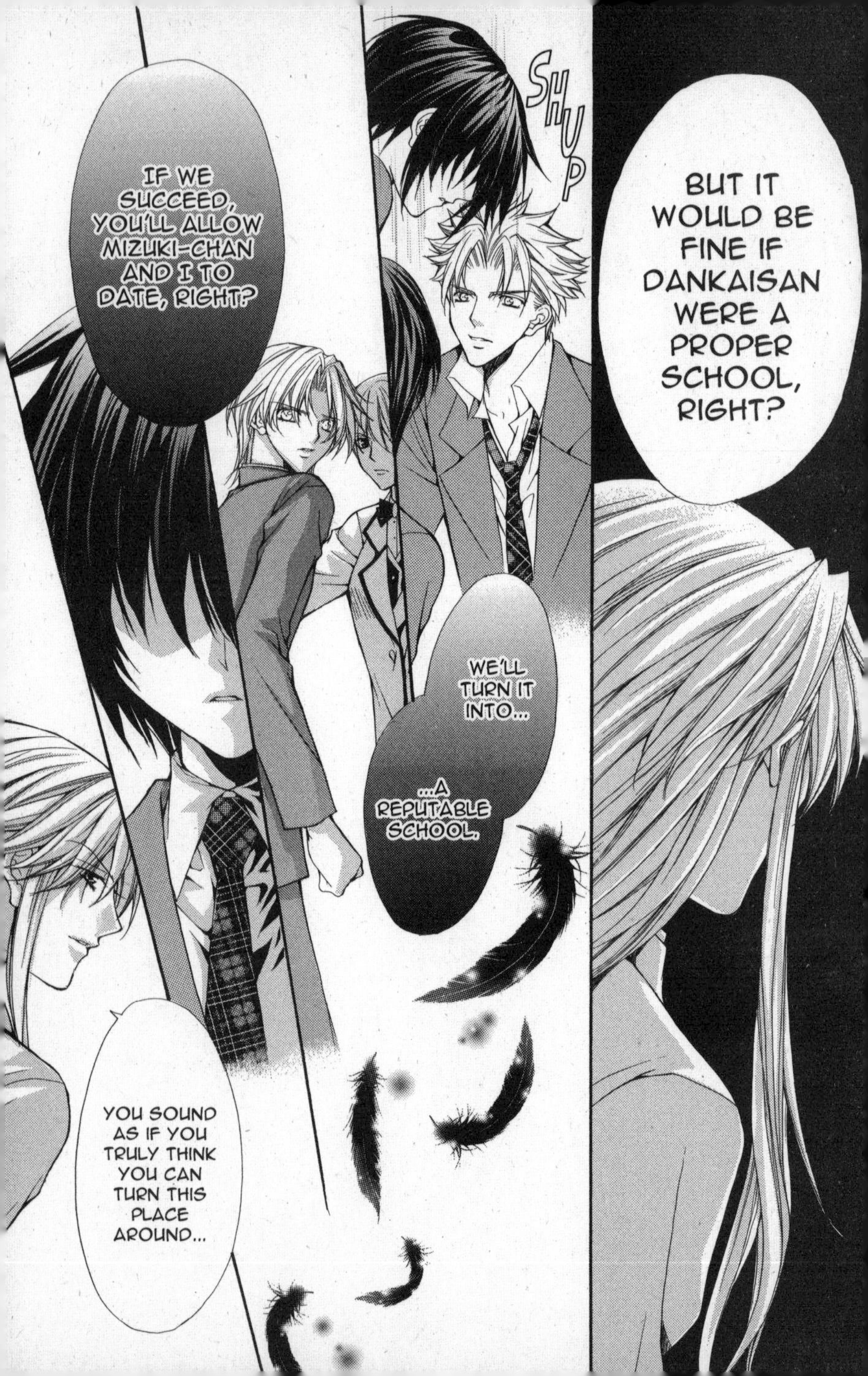
BUT IT WOULD BE FINE IF DANKAISAN WERE A PROPER SCHOOL, RIGHT?
SHUP
IF WE SUCCEED, YOU'LL ALLOW MIZUKI-CHAN AND I TO DATE, RIGHT?
WE'LL TURN IT INTO...
...A REPUTABLE SCHOOL.
YOU SOUND AS IF YOU TRULY THINK YOU CAN TURN THIS PLACE AROUND...

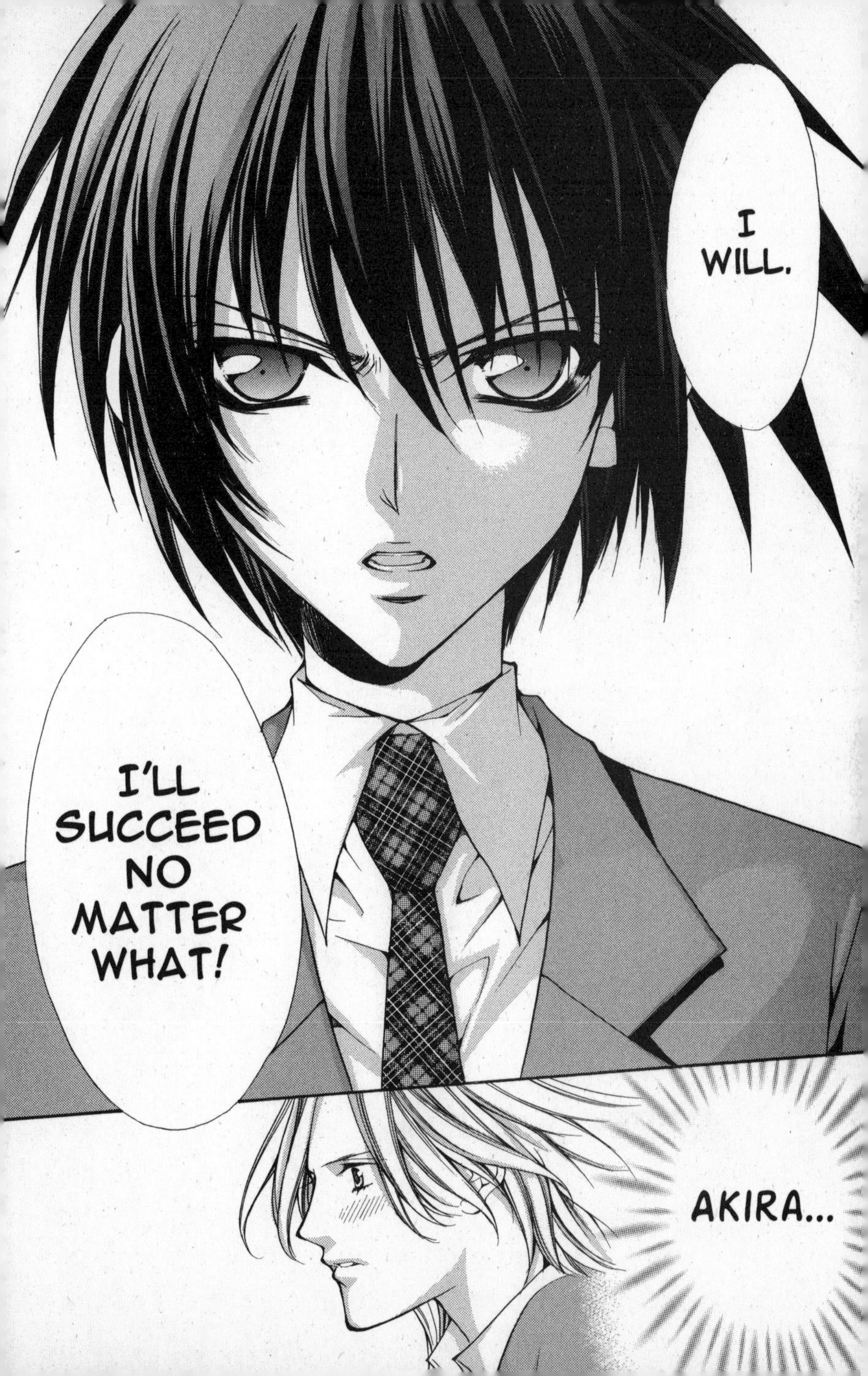
I WILL.
I'LL SUCCEED NO MATTER WHAT!
AKIRA...

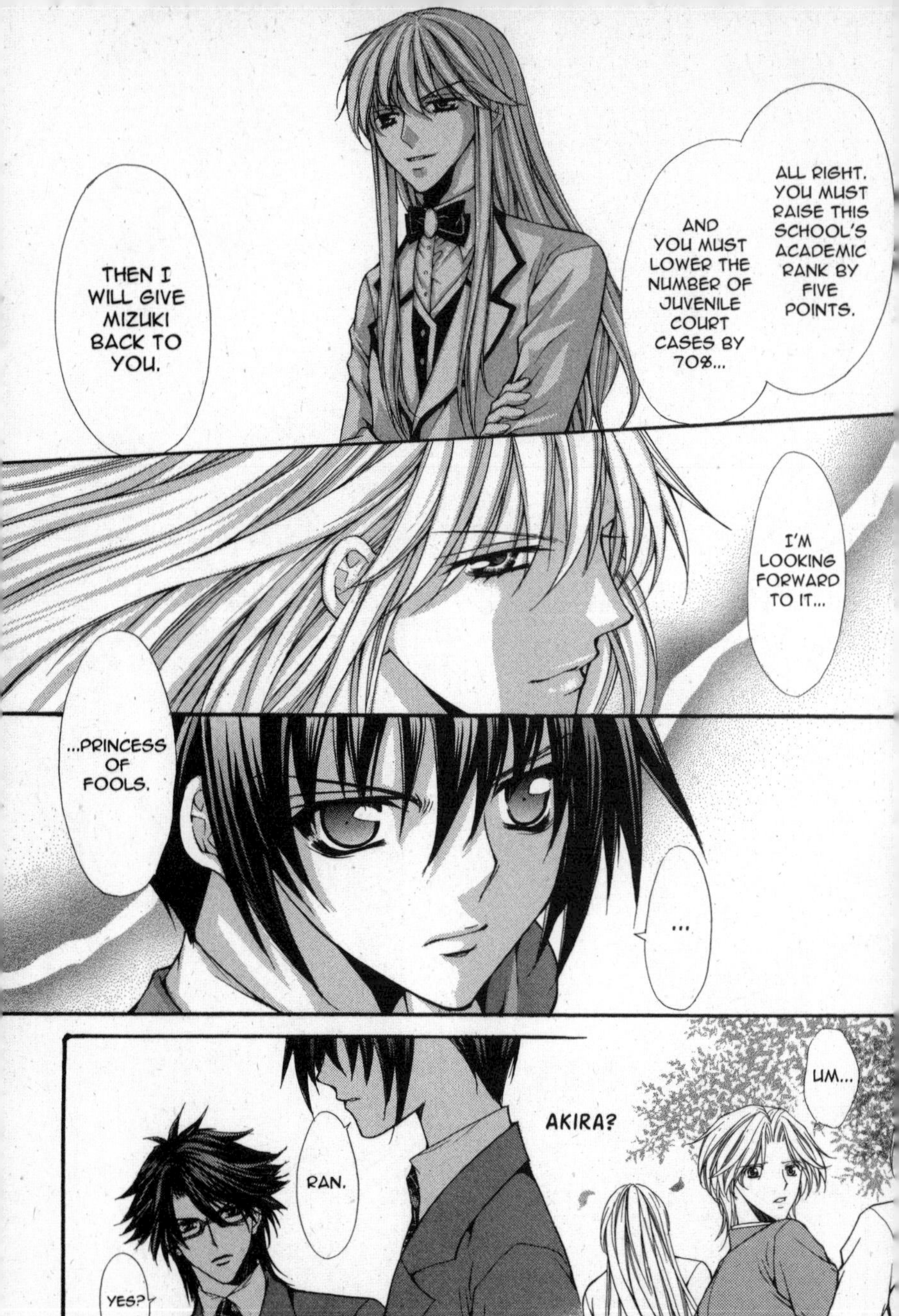
ALL RIGHT. YOU MUST RAISE THIS SCHOOL'S ACADEMIC RANK BY FIVE POINTS.
AND YOU MUST LOWER THE NUMBER OF JUVENILE COURT CASES BY 70%...
THEN I WILL GIVE MIZUKI BACK TO YOU.
I'M LOOKING FORWARD TO IT...
...PRINCESS OF FOOLS.
...
UM...
AKIRA?
RAN.
YES?

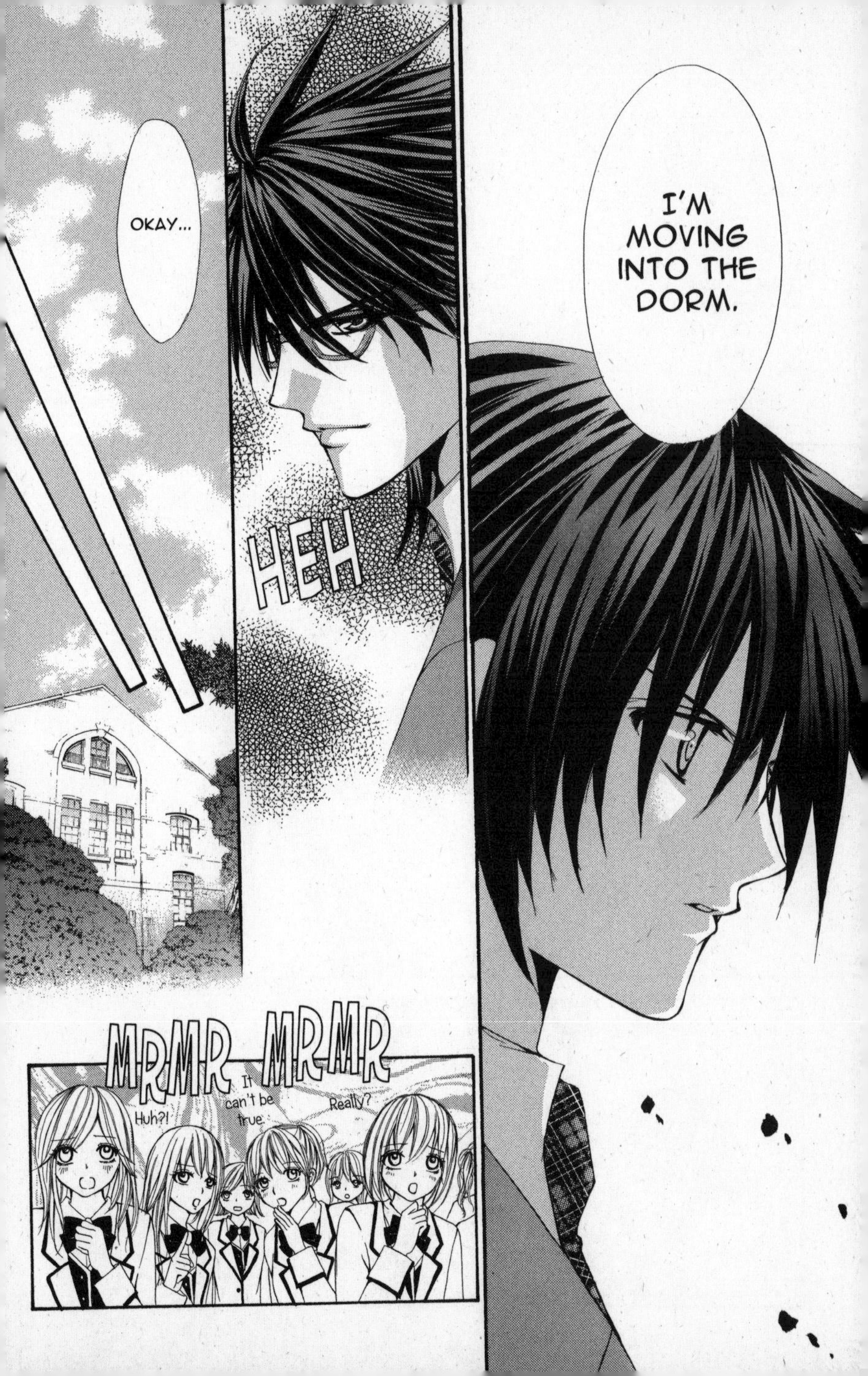
I'M MOVING INTO THE DORM.
HEH
OKAY...
MRMR MRMR
Really?
It can't be true.
Huh?!

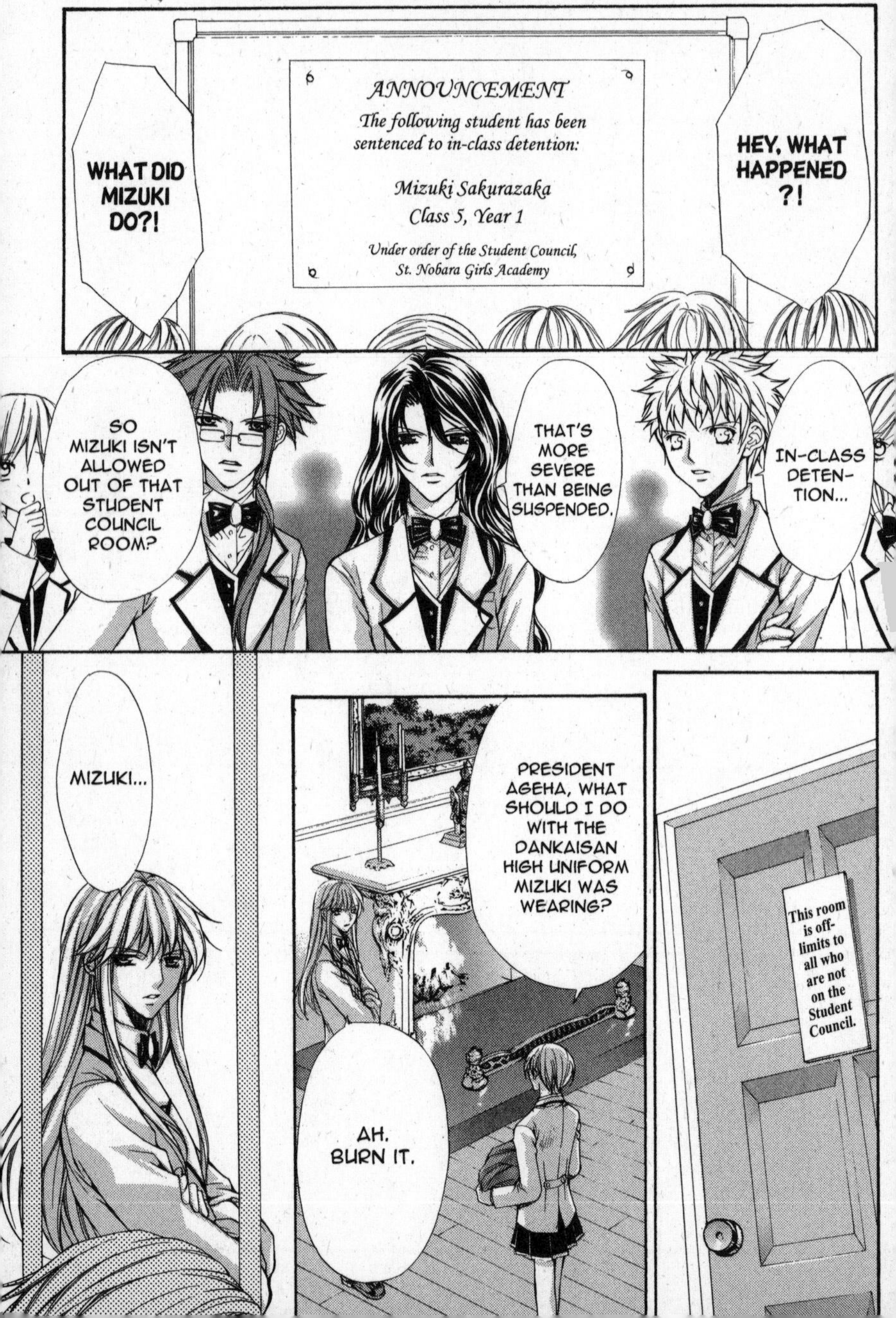
HEY, WHAT HAPPENED?!
ANNOUNCEMENT
The following student has been sentenced to in-class detention:
Mizuki Sakurazaka
Class 5, Year 1
Under order of the Student Council, St. Nobara Girls Academy
WHAT DID MIZUKI DO?!
IN-CLASS DETENTION...
THAT'S MORE SEVERE THAN BEING SUSPENDED.
SO MIZUKI ISN'T ALLOWED OUT OF THAT STUDENT COUNCIL ROOM?
This room is off-limits to all who are not on the Student Council.
PRESIDENT AGEHA, WHAT SHOULD I DO WITH THE DANKAISAN HIGH UNIFORM MIZUKI WAS WEARING?
AH. BURN IT.
MIZUKI...

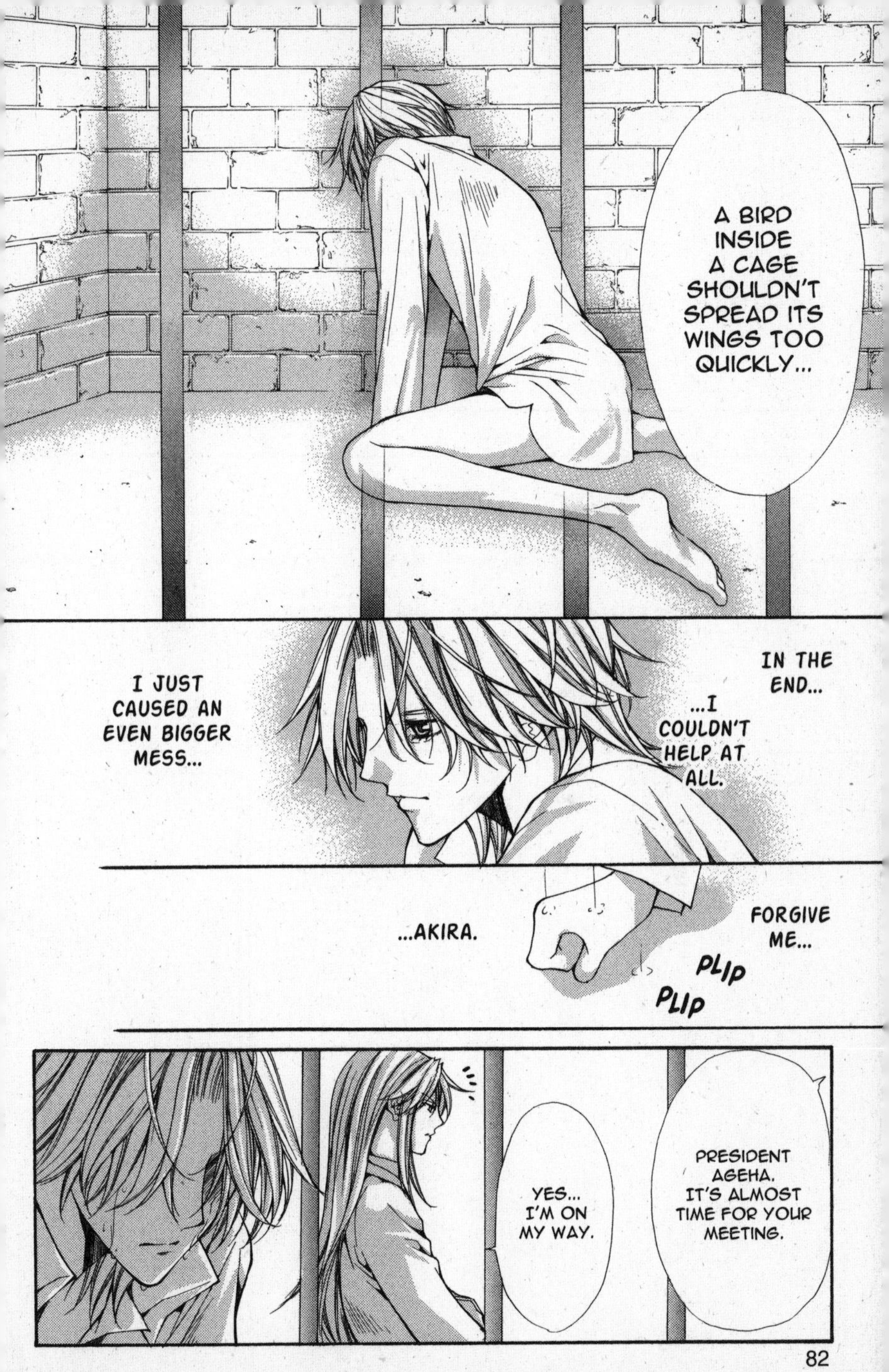
A BIRD INSIDE A CAGE SHOULDN'T SPREAD ITS WINGS TOO QUICKLY...
IN THE END...
...I COULDN'T HELP AT ALL.
I JUST CAUSED AN EVEN BIGGER MESS...
FORGIVE ME...
PLIP
PLIP
...AKIRA.
PRESIDENT AGEHA. IT'S ALMOST TIME FOR YOUR MEETING.
YES... I'M ON MY WAY.

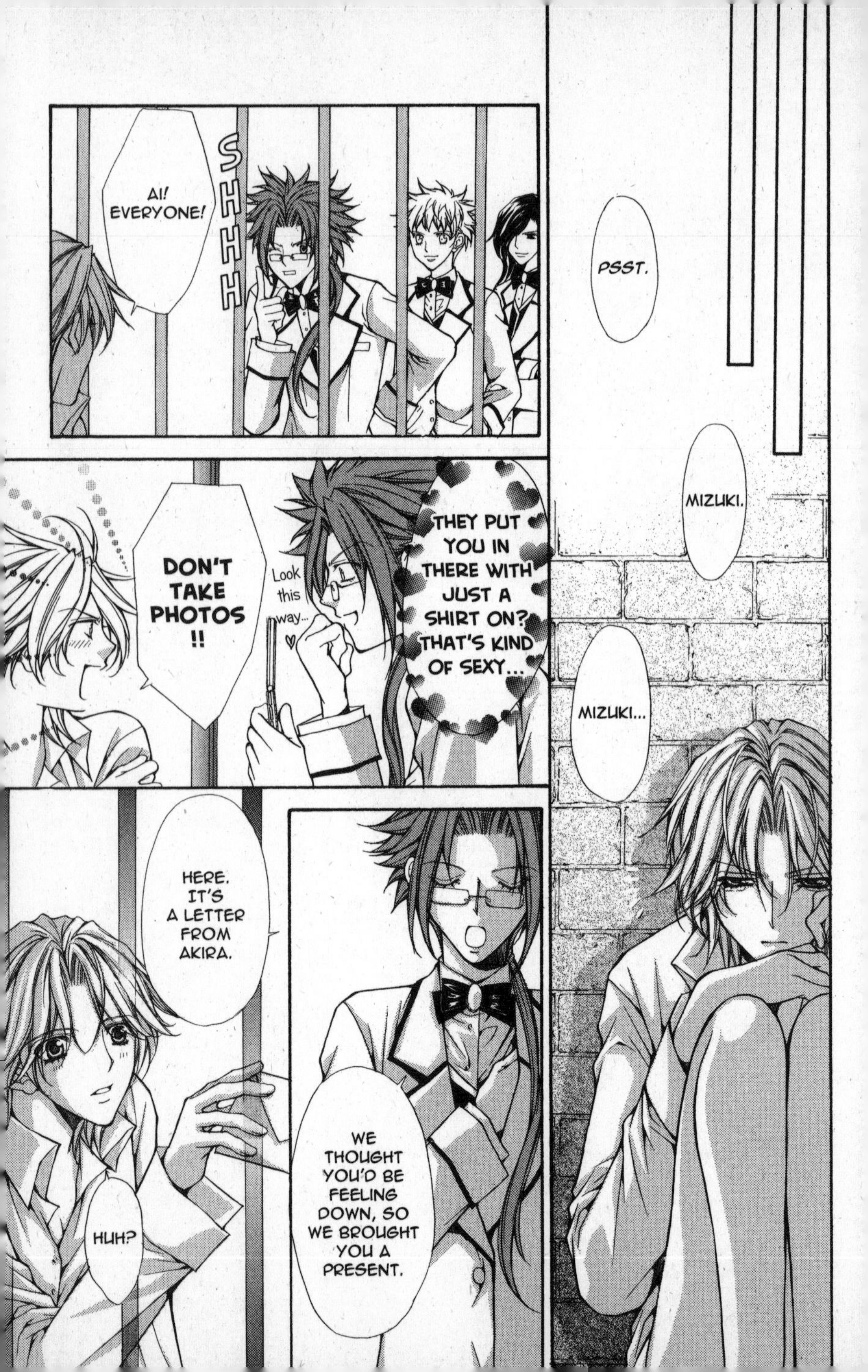
PSST.
MIZUKI.
MIZUKI...
AI! EVERYONE!
SHHHH
THEY PUT YOU IN THERE WITH JUST A SHIRT ON? THAT'S KIND OF SEXY...
Look this way... ♥
DON'T TAKE PHOTOS !!
WE THOUGHT YOU'D BE FEELING DOWN, SO WE BROUGHT YOU A PRESENT.
HERE. IT'S A LETTER FROM AKIRA.
HUH?

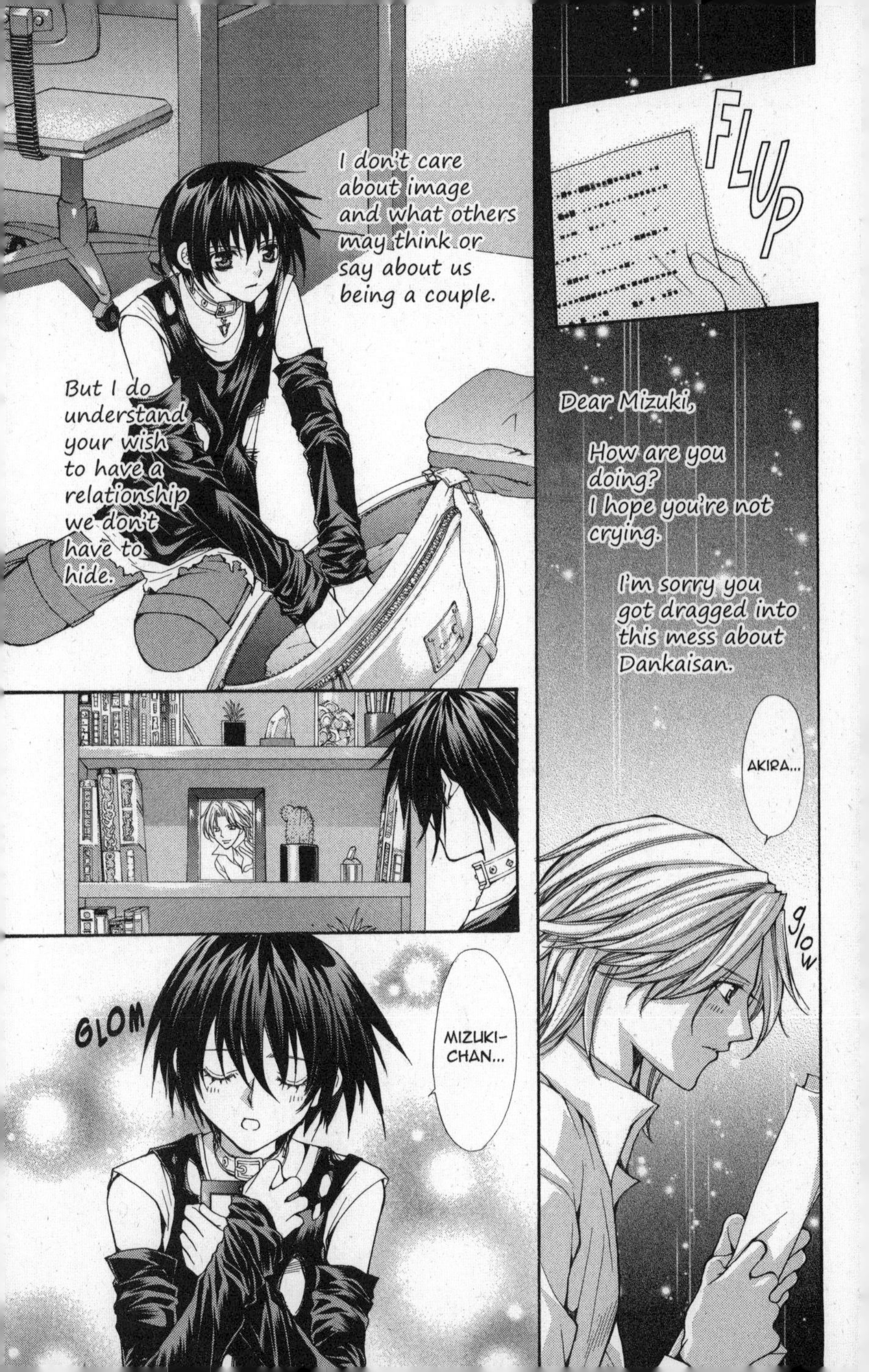
FLUP
Dear Mizuki,
How are you doing?
I hope you're not crying.
I'm sorry you got dragged into this mess about Dankaisan.
AKIRA...
glow
I don't care about image and what others may think or say about us being a couple.
But I do understand your wish to have a relationship we don't have to hide.
GLOM
MIZUKI-CHAN...

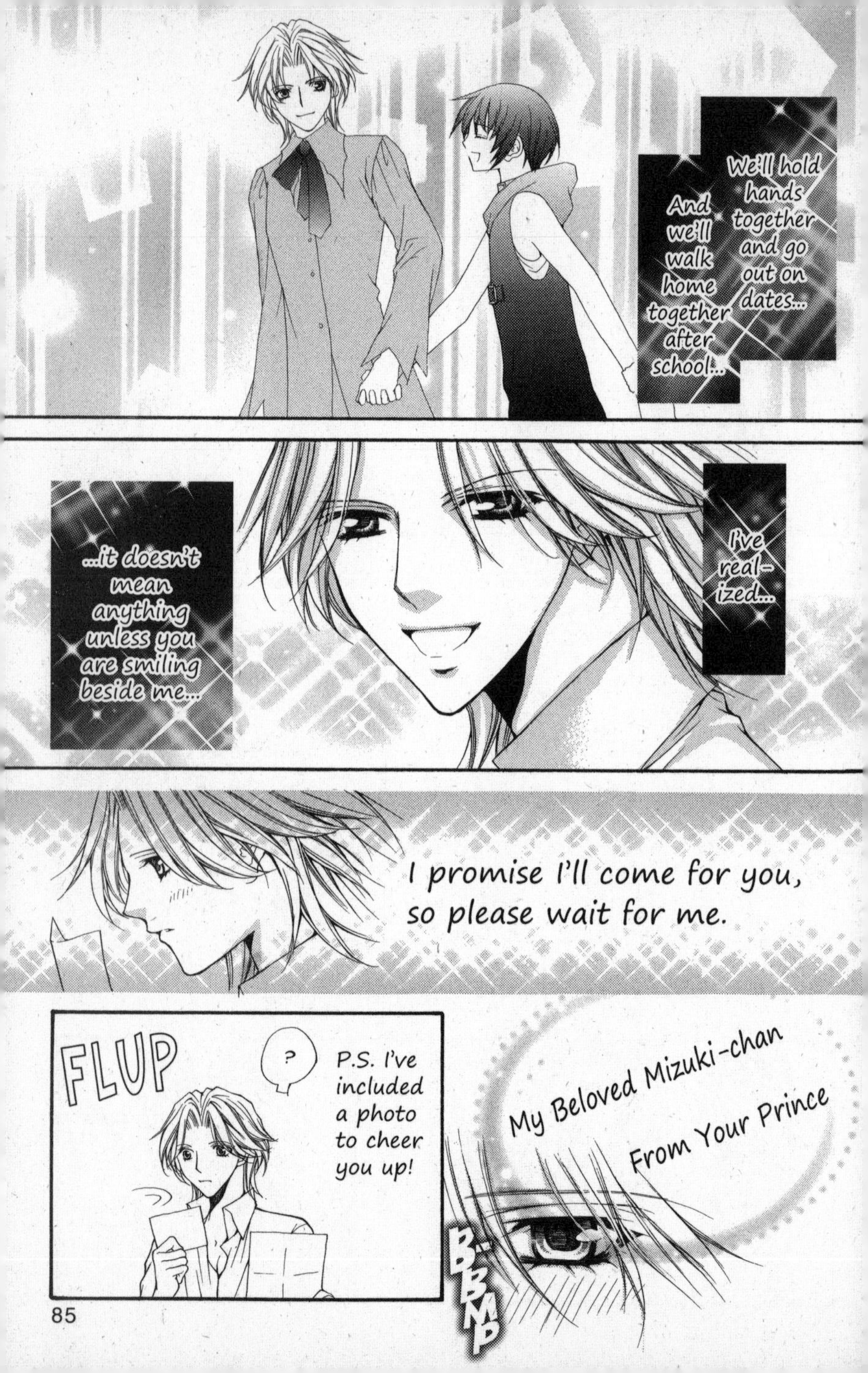
We'll hold hands together and go out on dates...
And we'll walk home together after school...
I've real-ized...
...it doesn't mean anything unless you are smiling beside me...
I promise I'll come for you, so please wait for me.
My Beloved Mizuki-chan
From Your Prince
B-BMP
?
P.S. I've included a photo to cheer you up!
FLUP

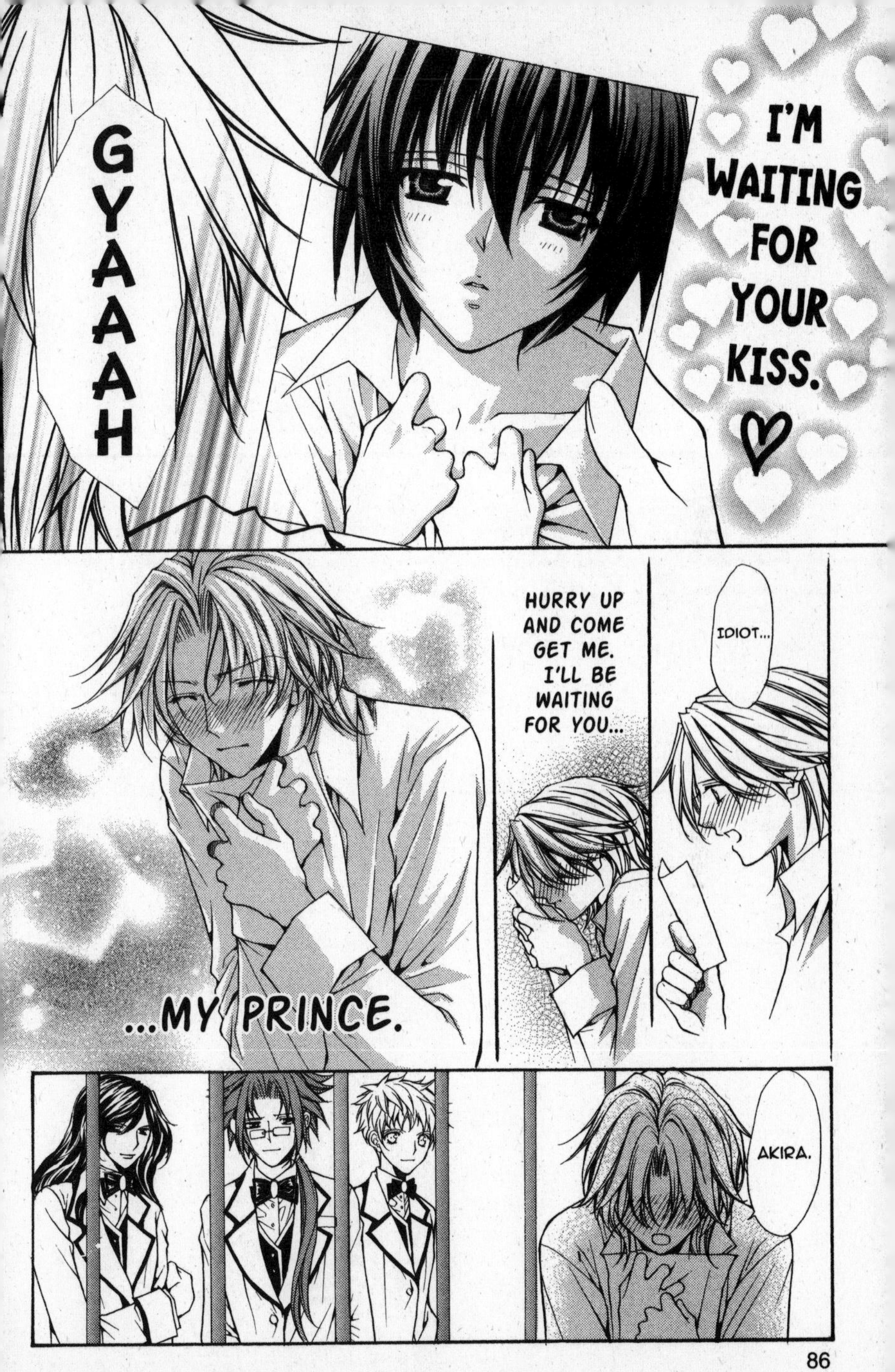
I'M WAITING FOR YOUR KISS. ♥
GYAAAH
IDIOT...
HURRY UP AND COME GET ME. I'LL BE WAITING FOR YOU...
...MY PRINCE.
AKIRA.

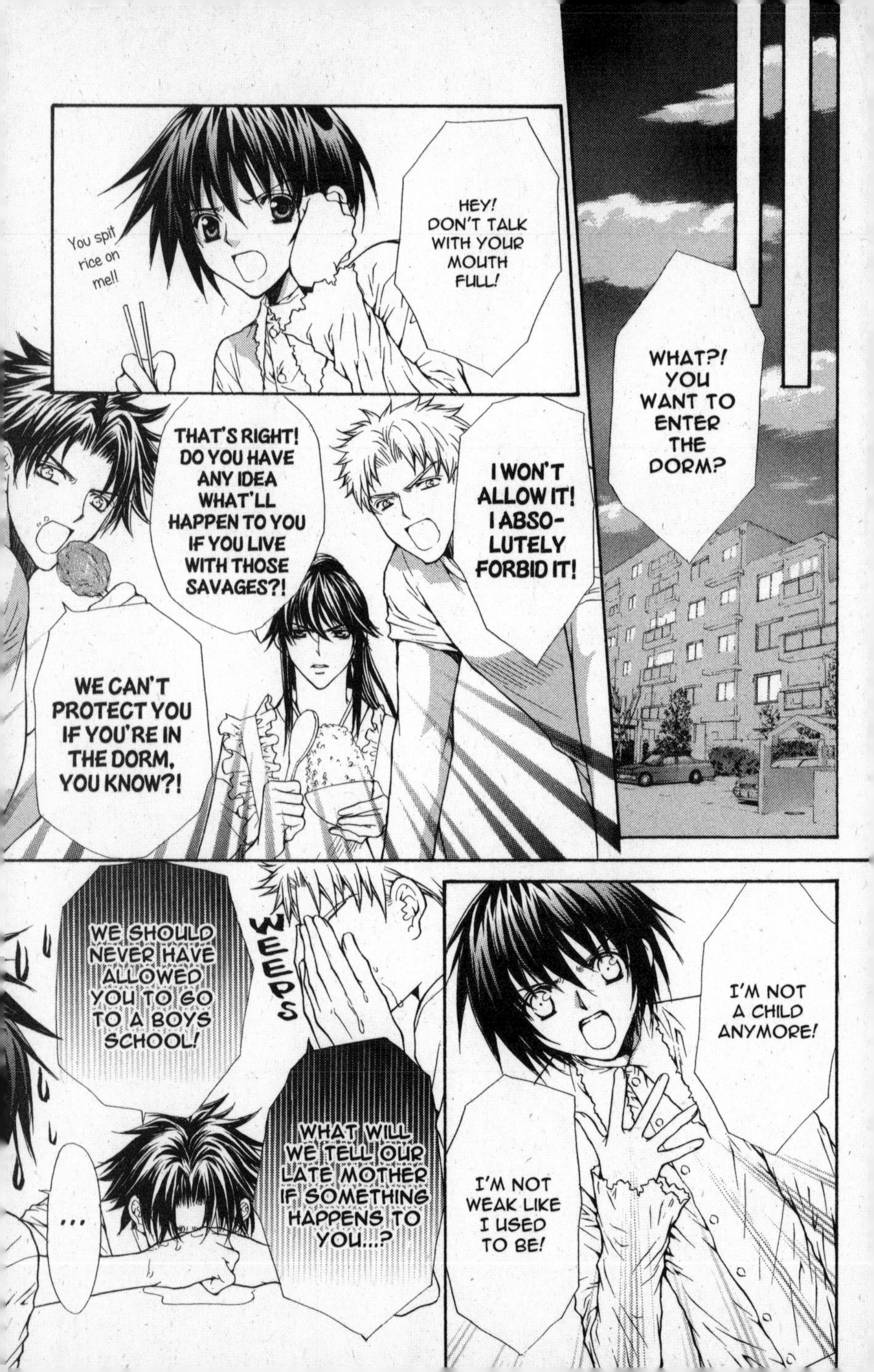
WHAT?! YOU WANT TO ENTER THE DORM?
HEY! DON'T TALK WITH YOUR MOUTH FULL!
You spit rice on me!!
I WON'T ALLOW IT! I ABSOLUTELY FORBID IT!
THAT'S RIGHT! DO YOU HAVE ANY IDEA WHAT'LL HAPPEN TO YOU IF YOU LIVE WITH THOSE SAVAGES?!
WE CAN'T PROTECT YOU IF YOU'RE IN THE DORM, YOU KNOW?!
I'M NOT A CHILD ANYMORE!
I'M NOT WEAK LIKE I USED TO BE!
WEEPS
WE SHOULD NEVER HAVE ALLOWED YOU TO GO TO A BOYS SCHOOL!
WHAT WILL WE TELL OUR LATE MOTHER IF SOMETHING HAPPENS TO YOU...?
...

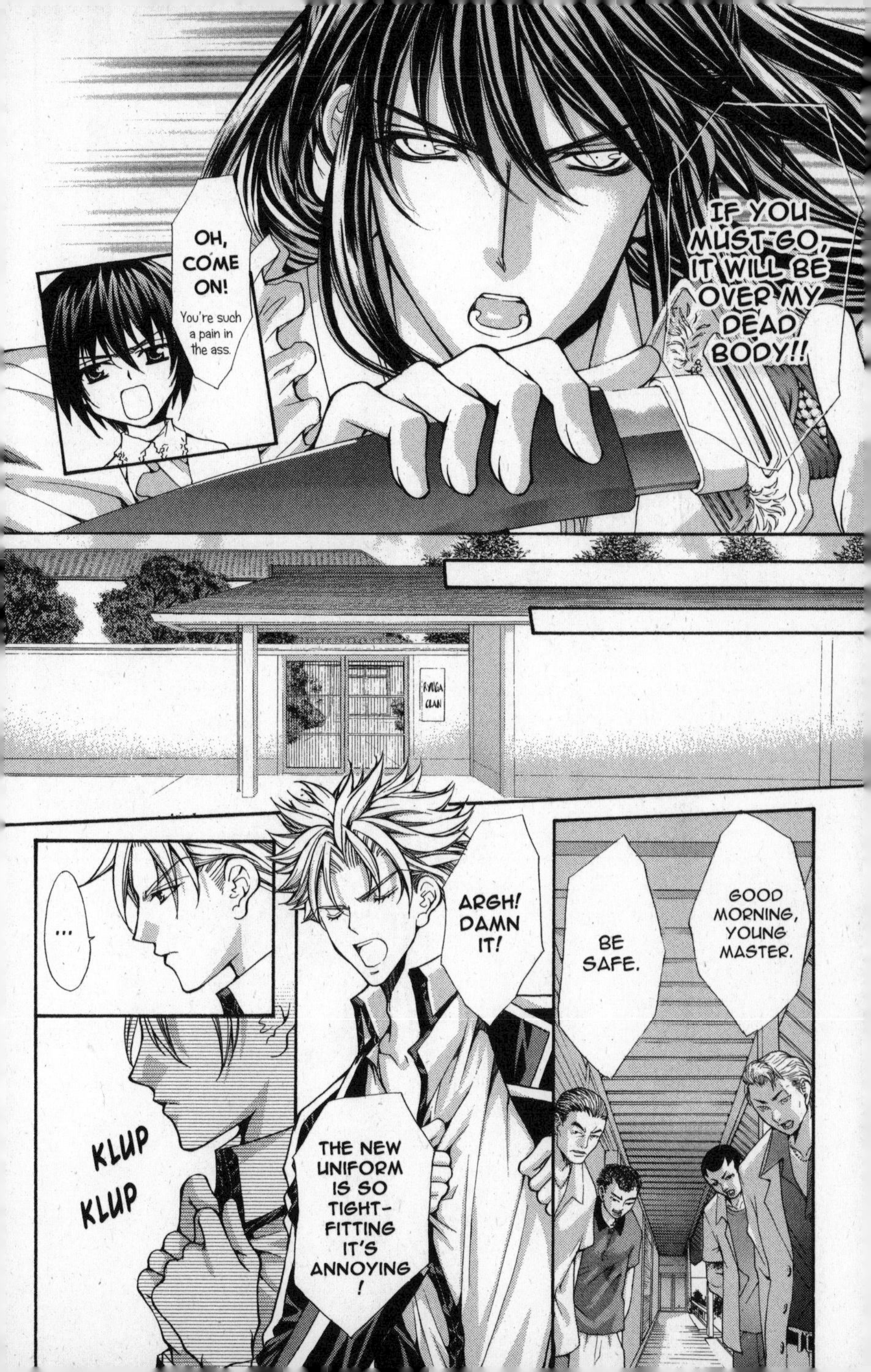
IF YOU MUST GO, IT WILL BE OVER MY DEAD BODY!!
OH, COME ON!
You're such a pain in the ass.
RYUGA CLAN
GOOD MORNING, YOUNG MASTER.
BE SAFE.
ARGH! DAMN IT!
THE NEW UNIFORM IS SO TIGHT-FITTING IT'S ANNOYING!
...
KLUP KLUP

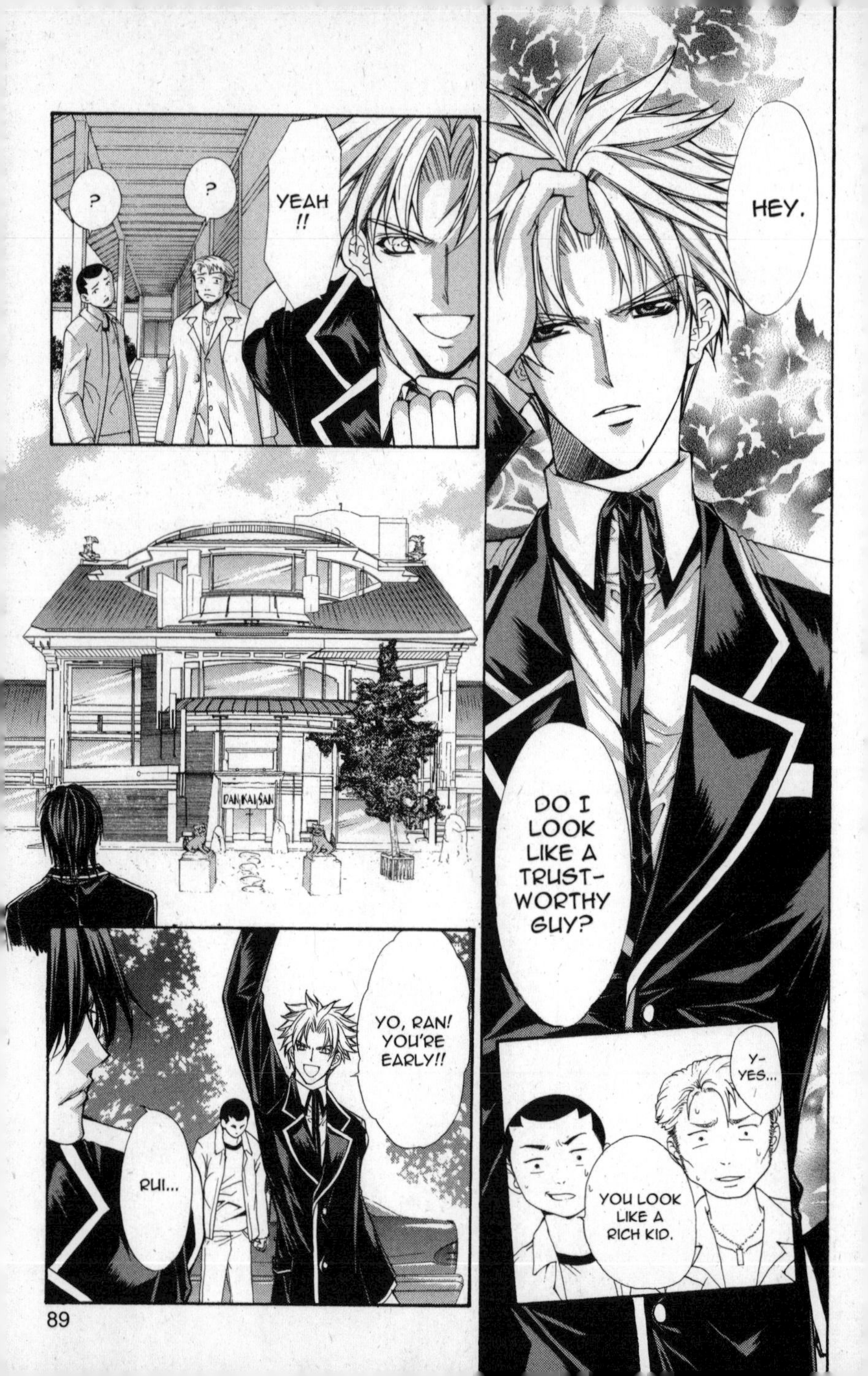
HEY.
DO I LOOK LIKE A TRUST-WORTHY GUY?
Y-YES...
YOU LOOK LIKE A RICH KID.
YEAH !!
?
?
DANKAISAN
YO, RAN! YOU'RE EARLY!!
RUI...

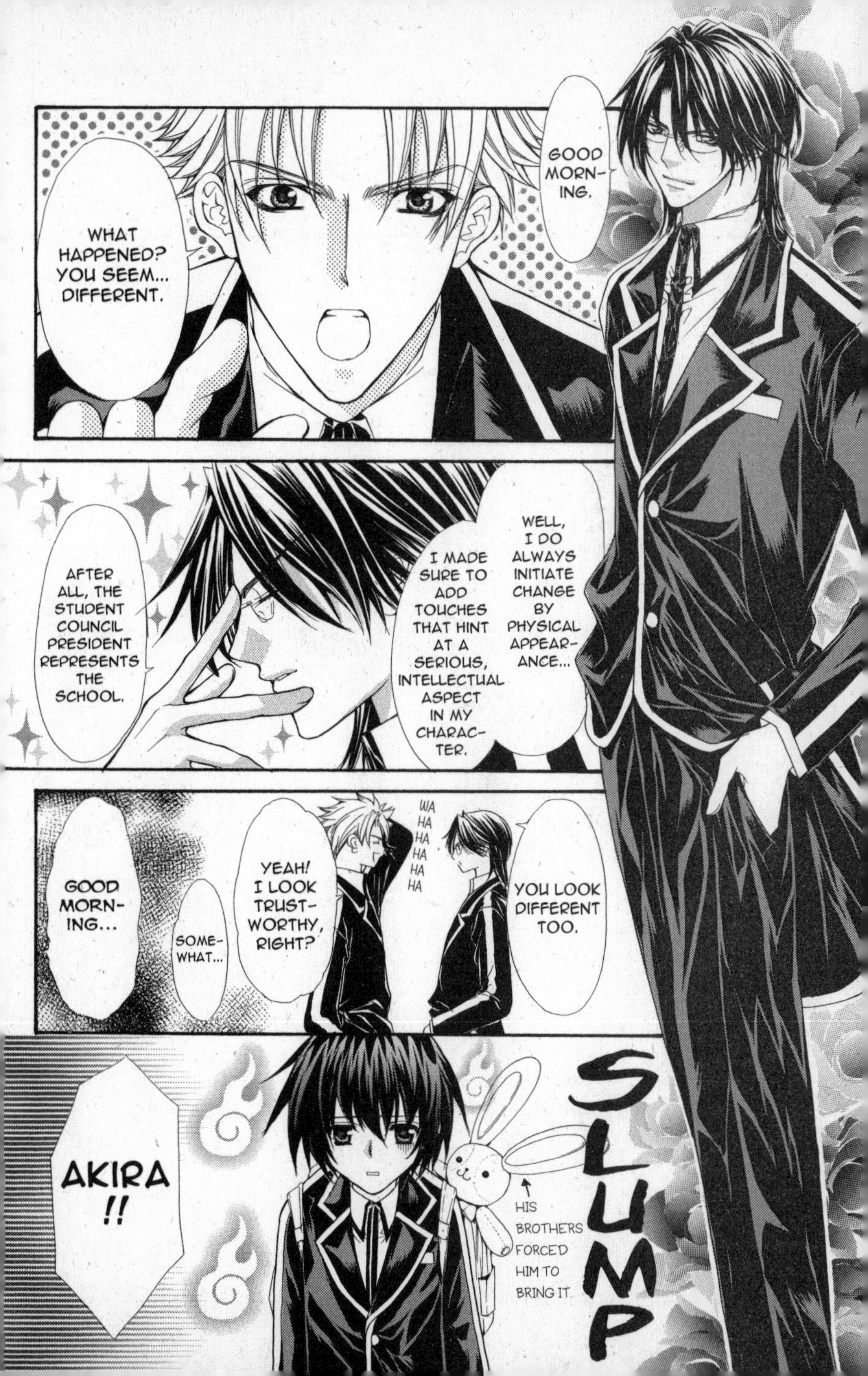
GOOD MORNING.
WHAT HAPPENED? YOU SEEM... DIFFERENT.
WELL, I DO ALWAYS INITIATE CHANGE BY PHYSICAL APPEARANCE...
I MADE SURE TO ADD TOUCHES THAT HINT AT A SERIOUS, INTELLECTUAL ASPECT IN MY CHARACTER.
AFTER ALL, THE STUDENT COUNCIL PRESIDENT REPRESENTS THE SCHOOL.
YOU LOOK DIFFERENT TOO.
WA HA HA HA HA HA HA
YEAH! I LOOK TRUSTWORTHY, RIGHT?
SOME-WHAT...
GOOD MORNING...
SLUMP
HIS BROTHERS FORCED HIM TO BRING IT.
AKIRA !!

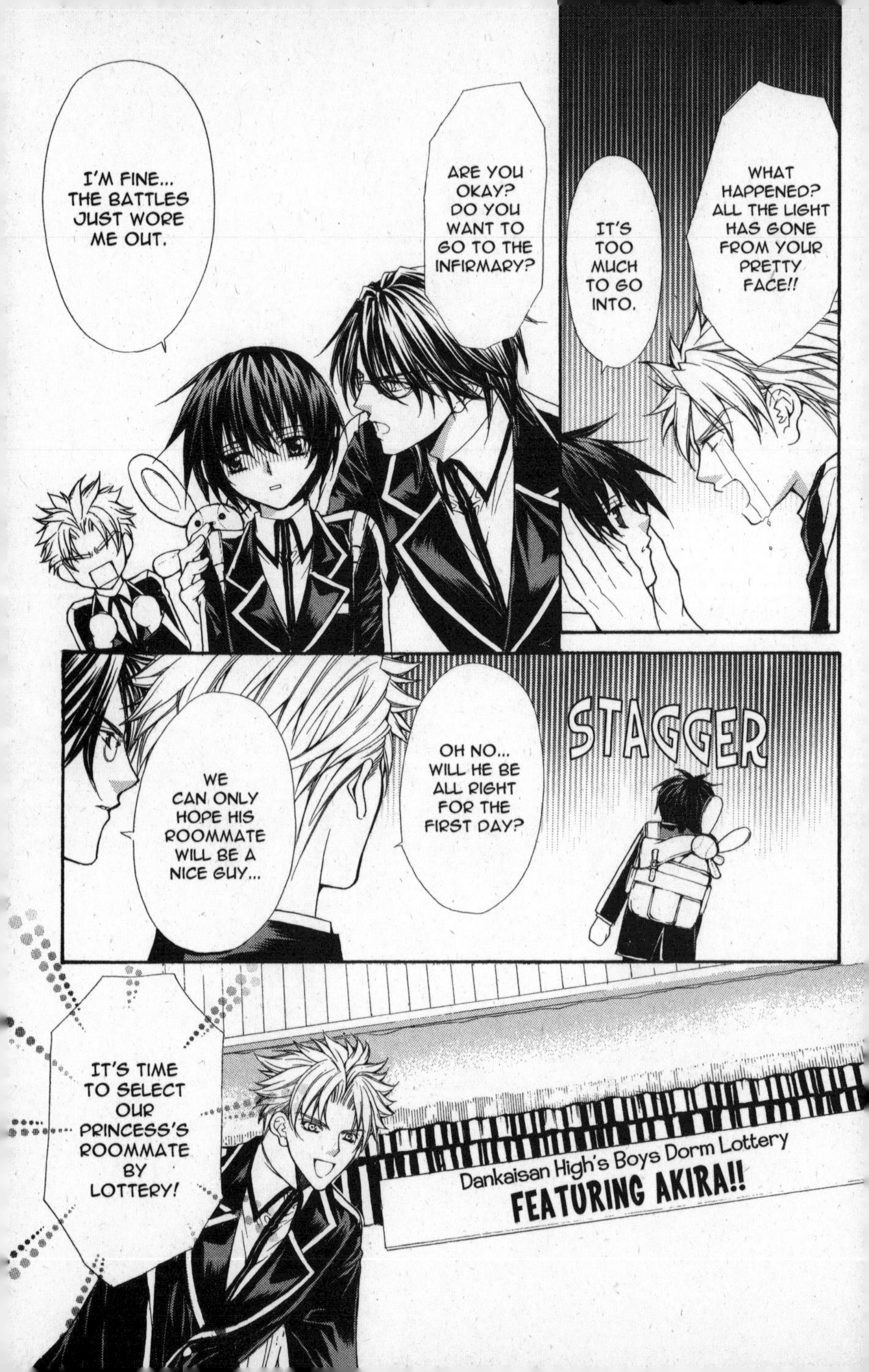
WHAT HAPPENED? ALL THE LIGHT HAS GONE FROM YOUR PRETTY FACE!!
IT'S TOO MUCH TO GO INTO.
ARE YOU OKAY? DO YOU WANT TO GO TO THE INFIRMARY?
I'M FINE... THE BATTLES JUST WORE ME OUT.
STAGGER
OH NO... WILL HE BE ALL RIGHT FOR THE FIRST DAY?
WE CAN ONLY HOPE HIS ROOMMATE WILL BE A NICE GUY...
Dankaisan High's Boys Dorm Lottery
FEATURING AKIRA!!
IT'S TIME TO SELECT OUR PRINCESS'S ROOMMATE BY LOTTERY!

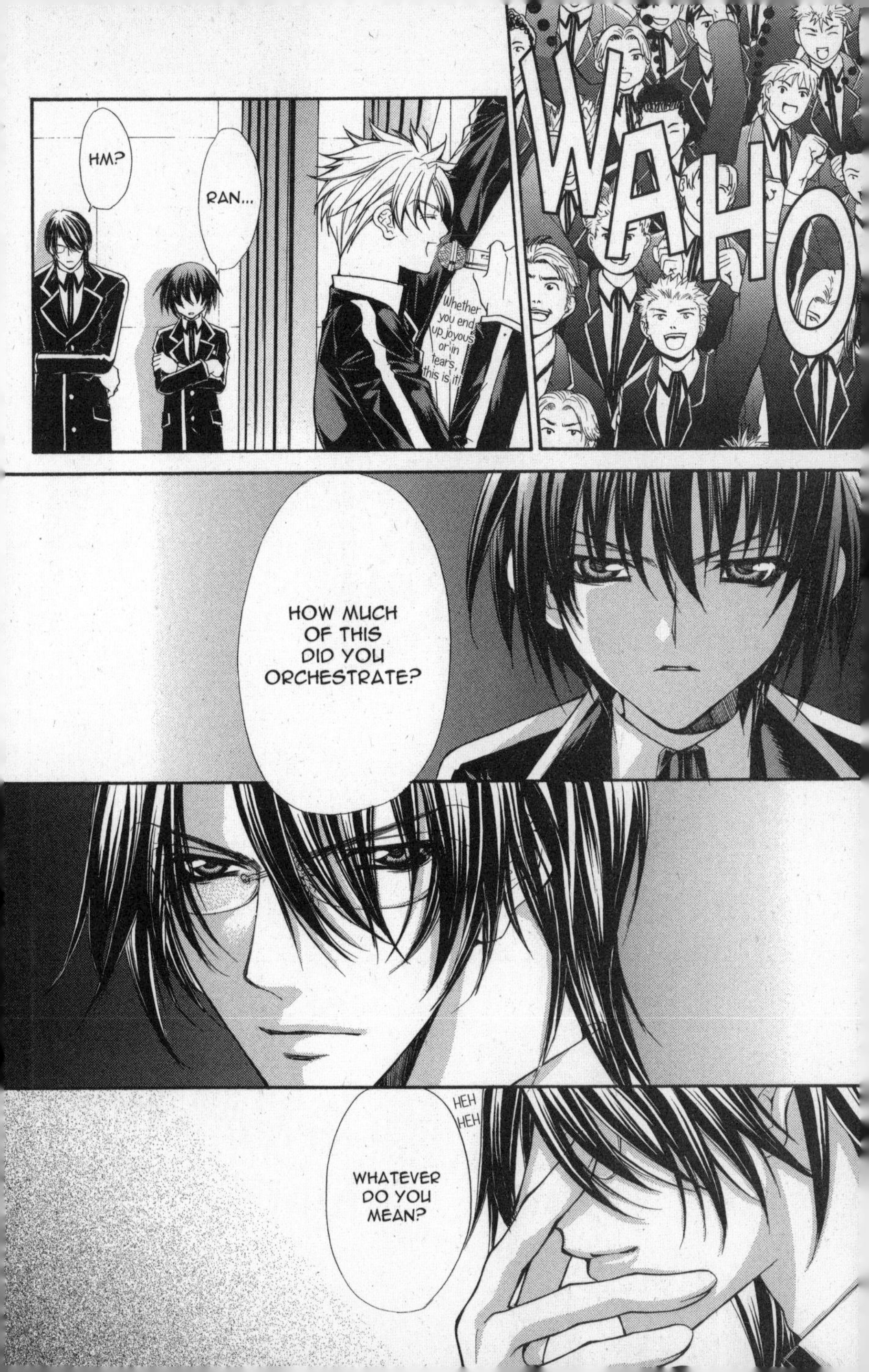
WAHO
Whether you end up joyous or in tears, this is it!
RAN...
HM?
HOW MUCH OF THIS DID YOU ORCHESTRATE?
HEH HEH
WHATEVER DO YOU MEAN?

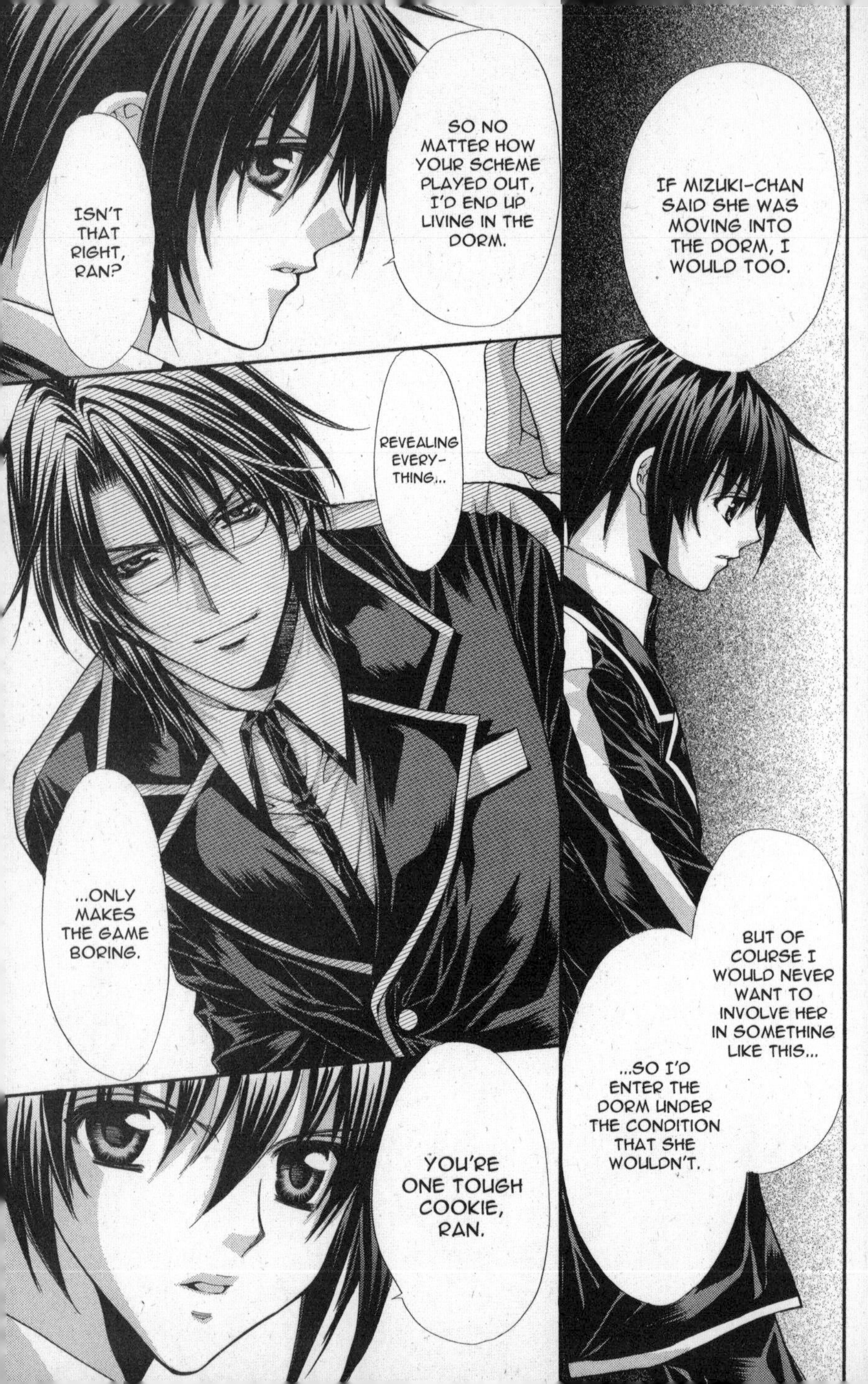
IF MIZUKI-CHAN SAID SHE WAS MOVING INTO THE DORM, I WOULD TOO.
BUT OF COURSE I WOULD NEVER WANT TO INVOLVE HER IN SOMETHING LIKE THIS...
...SO I'D ENTER THE DORM UNDER THE CONDITION THAT SHE WOULDN'T.
SO NO MATTER HOW YOUR SCHEME PLAYED OUT, I'D END UP LIVING IN THE DORM.
ISN'T THAT RIGHT, RAN?
REVEALING EVERY-THING...
...ONLY MAKES THE GAME BORING.
YOU'RE ONE TOUGH COOKIE, RAN.

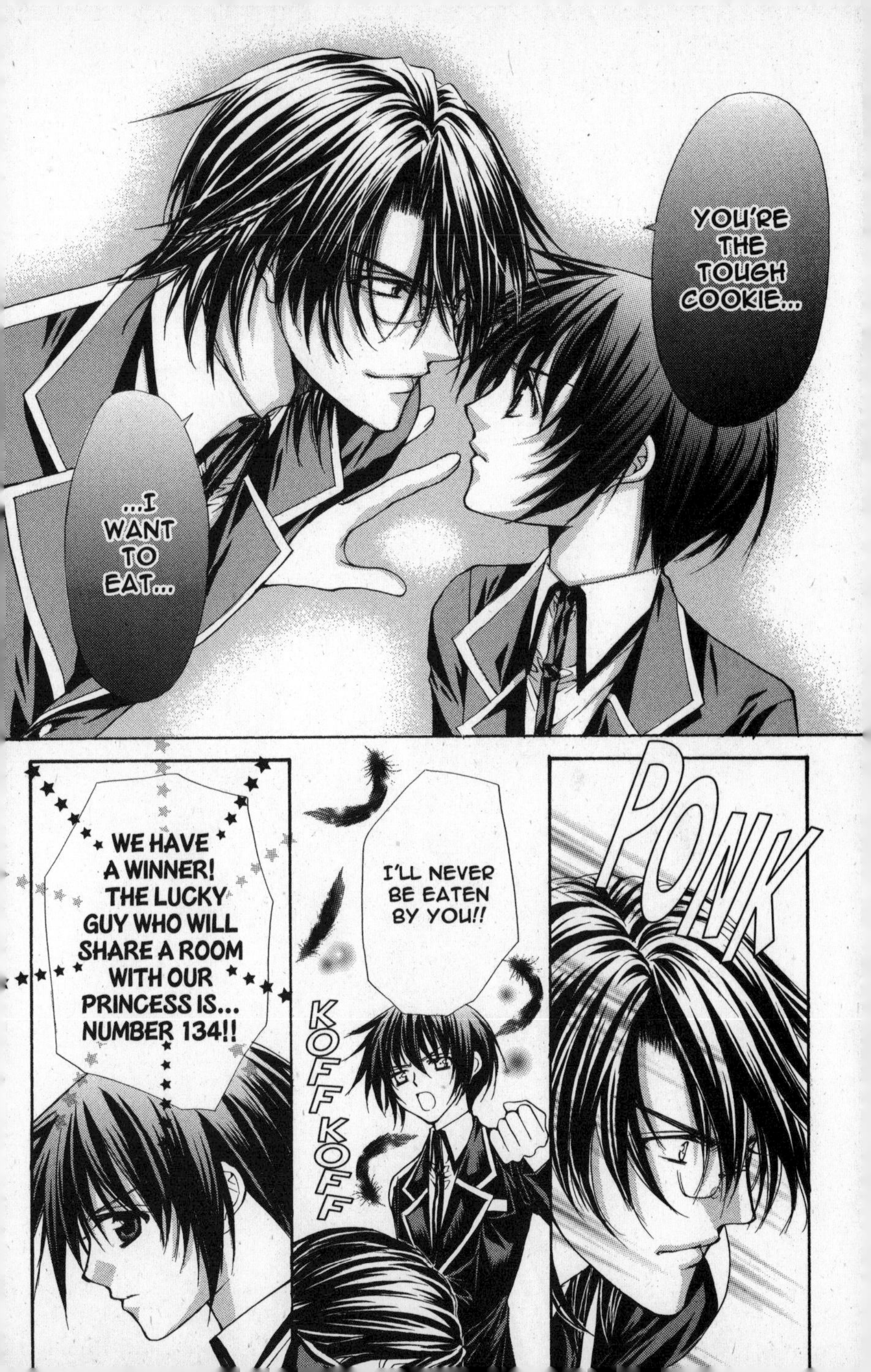
YOU'RE THE TOUGH COOKIE...
...I WANT TO EAT...
PONK
I'LL NEVER BE EATEN BY YOU!!
KOFF KOFF
WE HAVE A WINNER! THE LUCKY GUY WHO WILL SHARE A ROOM WITH OUR PRINCESS IS... NUMBER 134!!

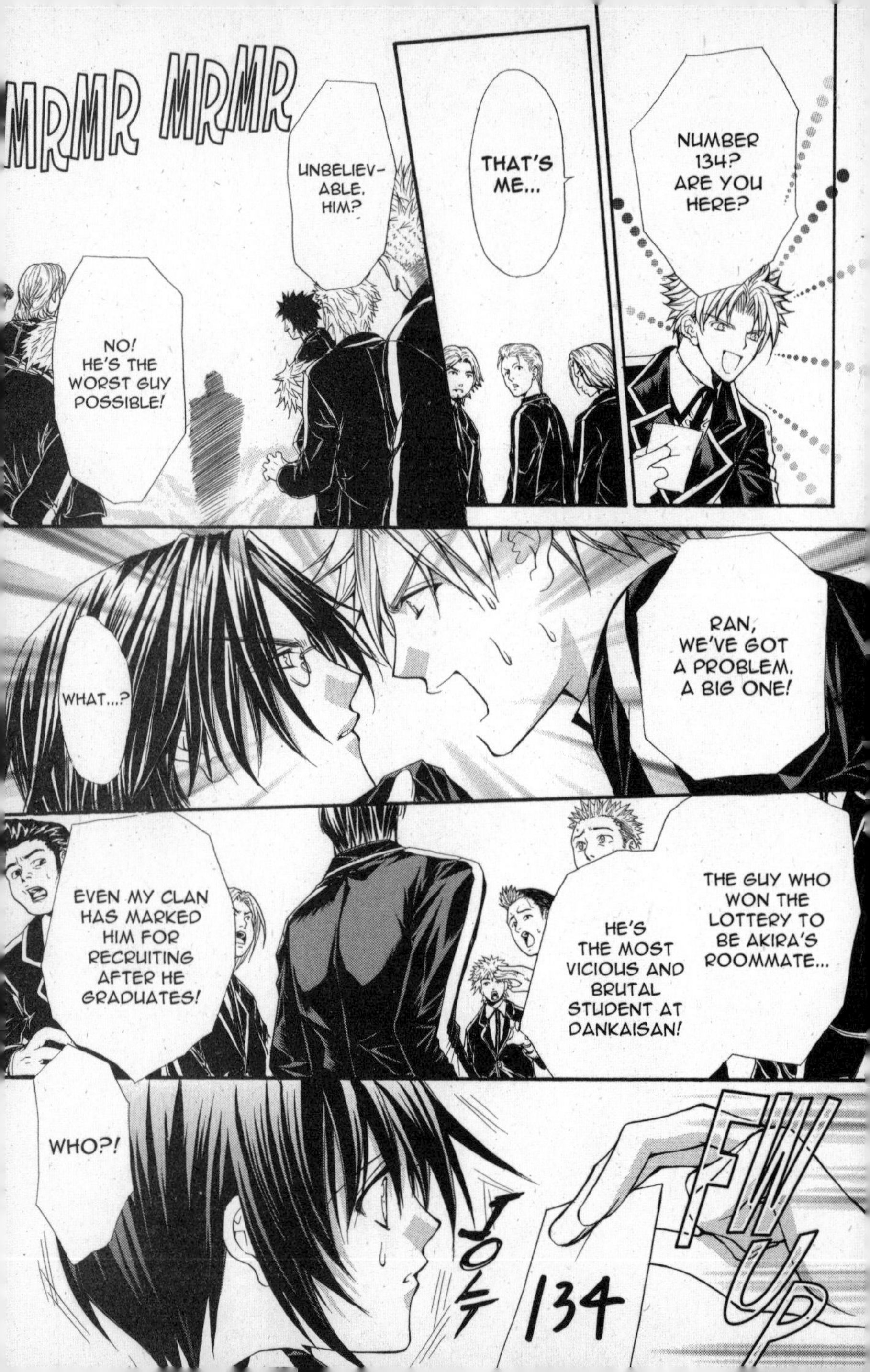
NUMBER 134? ARE YOU HERE?
THAT'S ME...
MRMR MRMR
UNBELIEV-ABLE. HIM?
NO! HE'S THE WORST GUY POSSIBLE!
RAN, WE'VE GOT A PROBLEM. A BIG ONE!
WHAT...?
THE GUY WHO WON THE LOTTERY TO BE AKIRA'S ROOMMATE...
HE'S THE MOST VICIOUS AND BRUTAL STUDENT AT DANKAISAN!
EVEN MY CLAN HAS MARKED HIM FOR RECRUITING AFTER HE GRADUATES!
FWUP
134
JOLT
WHO?!

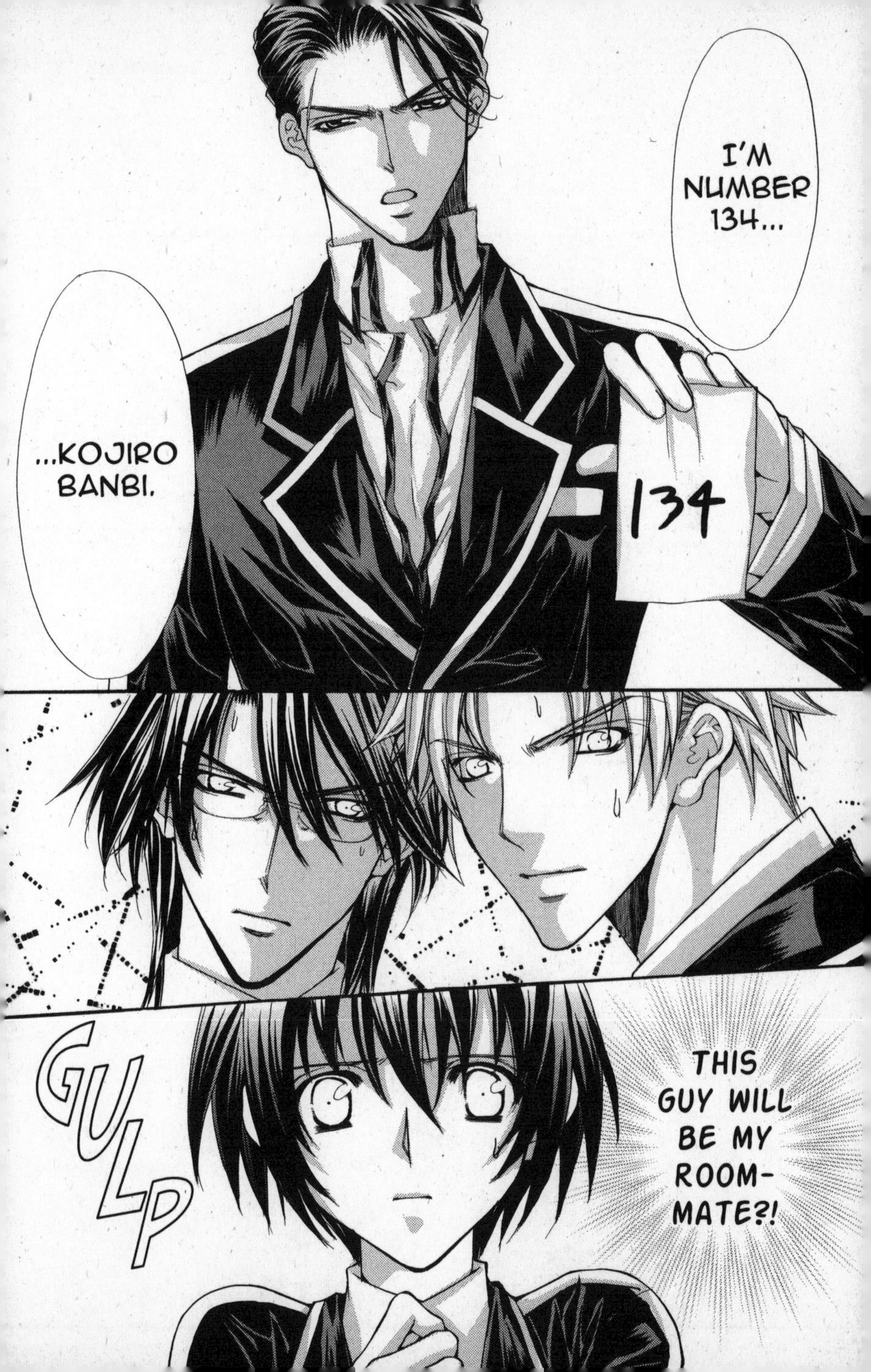
I'M NUMBER 134...
134
...KOJIRO BANBI.
THIS GUY WILL BE MY ROOM-MATE?!
GULP

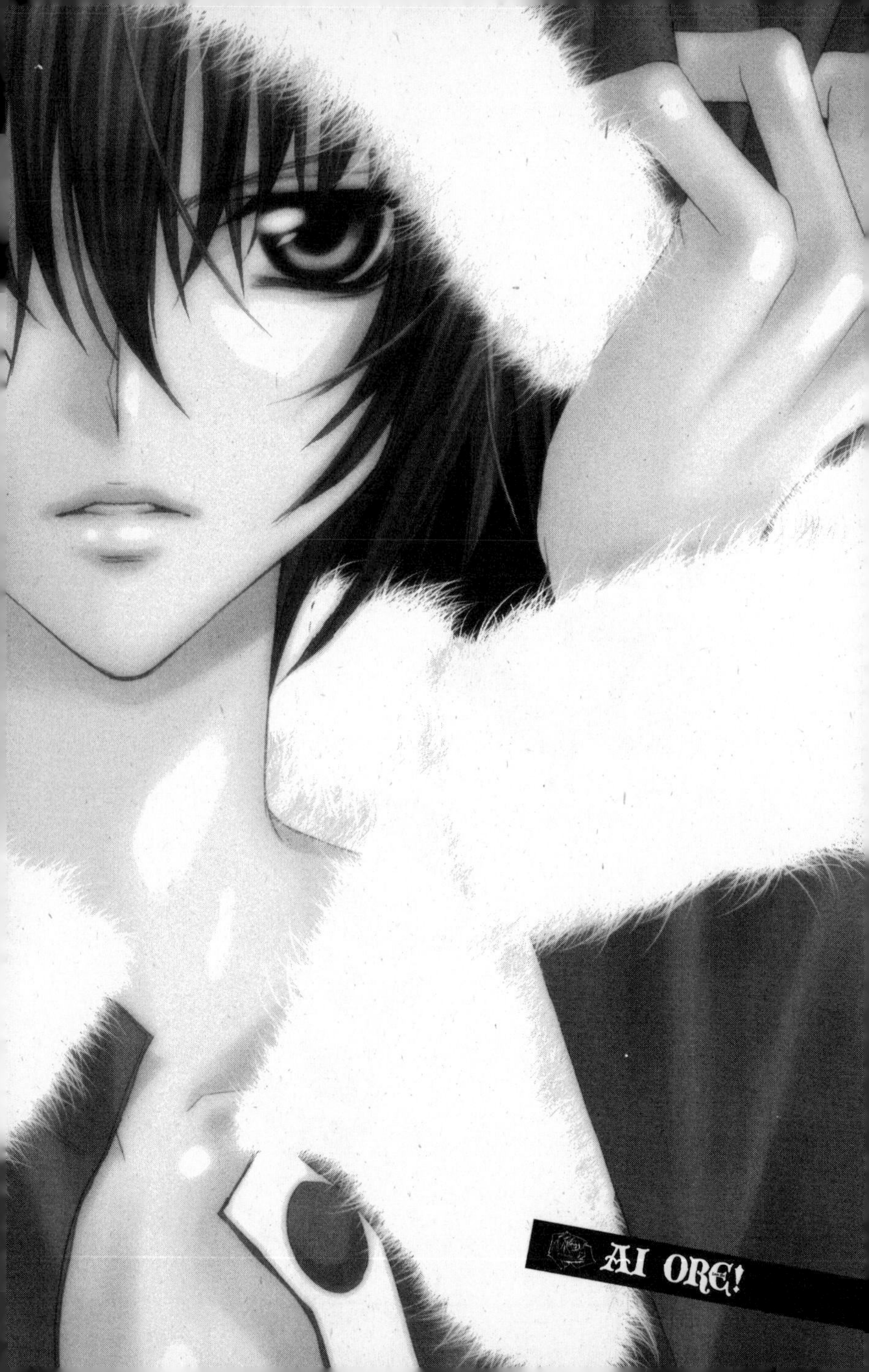
AI ORE!

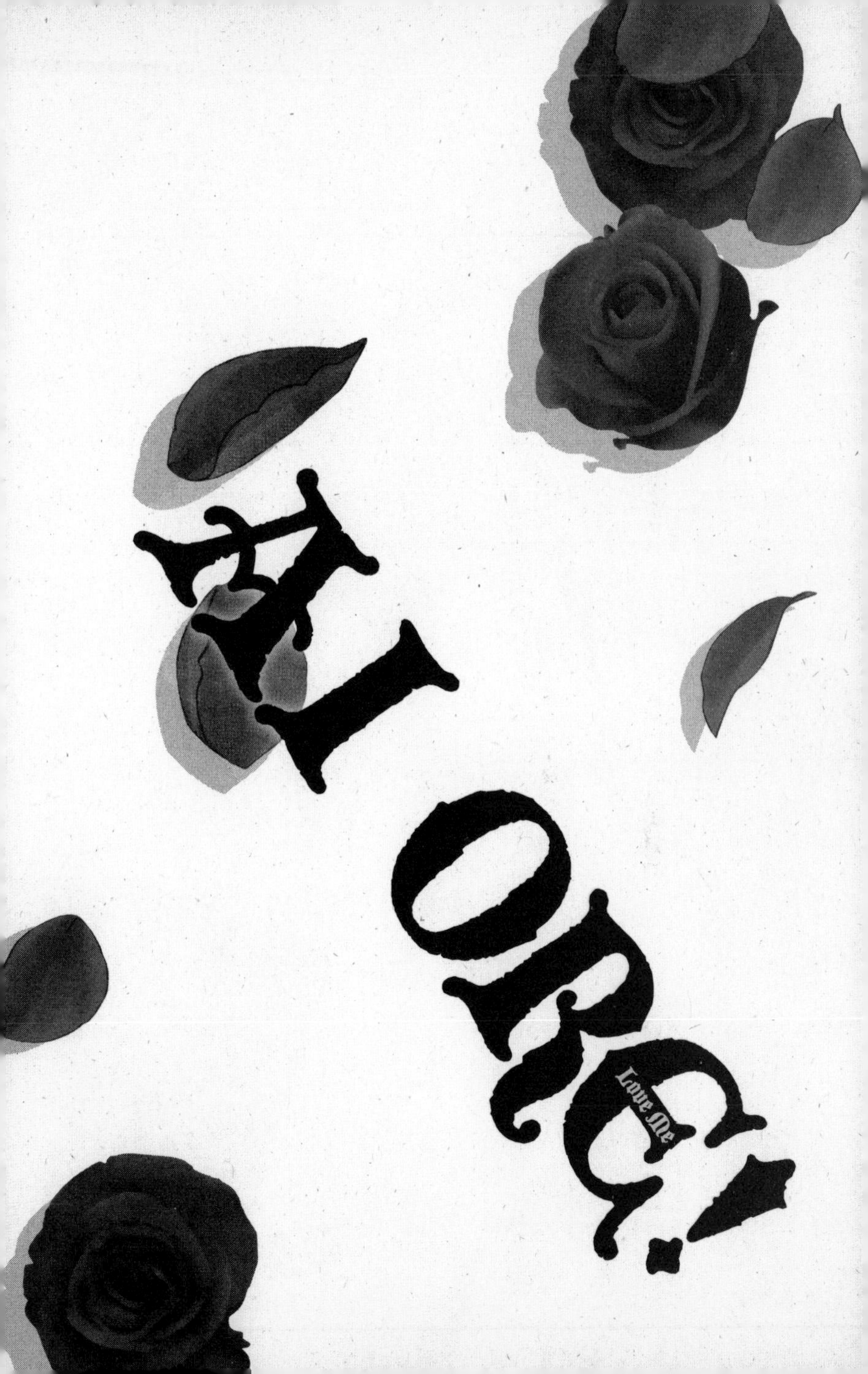
AI ORE!
Love Me

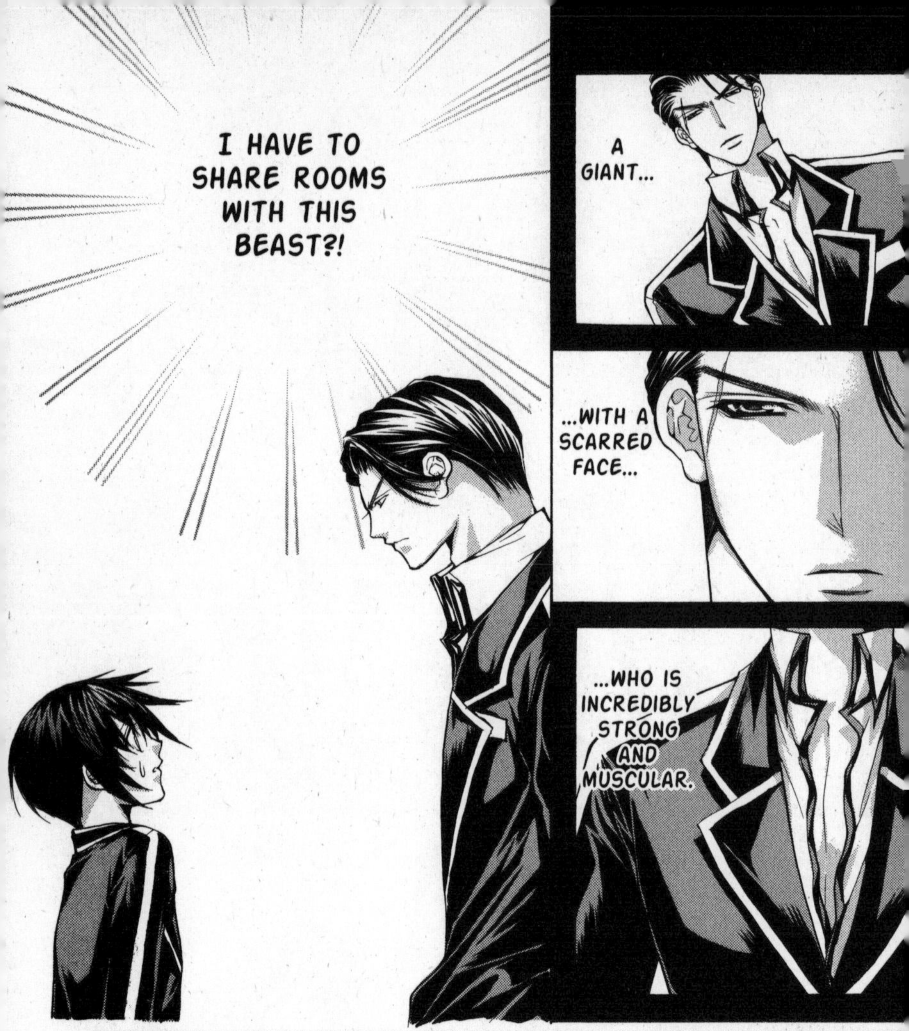
A GIANT...
...WITH A SCARRED FACE...
...WHO IS INCREDIBLY STRONG AND MUSCULAR.
I HAVE TO SHARE ROOMS WITH THIS BEAST?!

About Akira

I don't think there are any other characters who have received the same amount of love I've given to Akira.
He has so many delicious settings and untold stories. There are stories I want to publish somewhere when I get the chance, and some that will never be public. (laugh)
When I ask everyone which they prefer, Pure Akira or Dark Akira, most of them say Dark Akira.
But I think Dark Akira's presence can only be possible with the existence of Pure Akira.

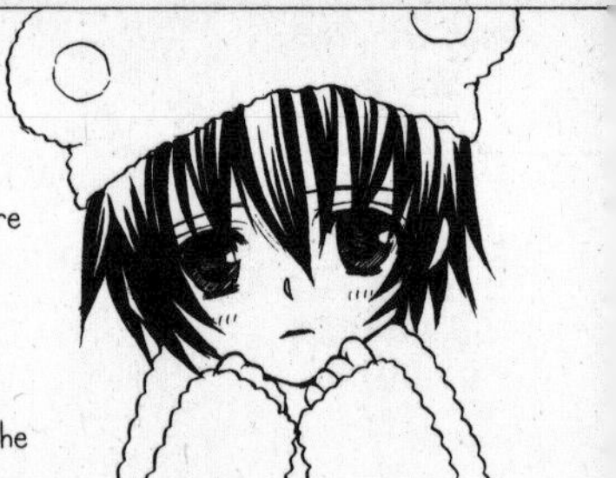

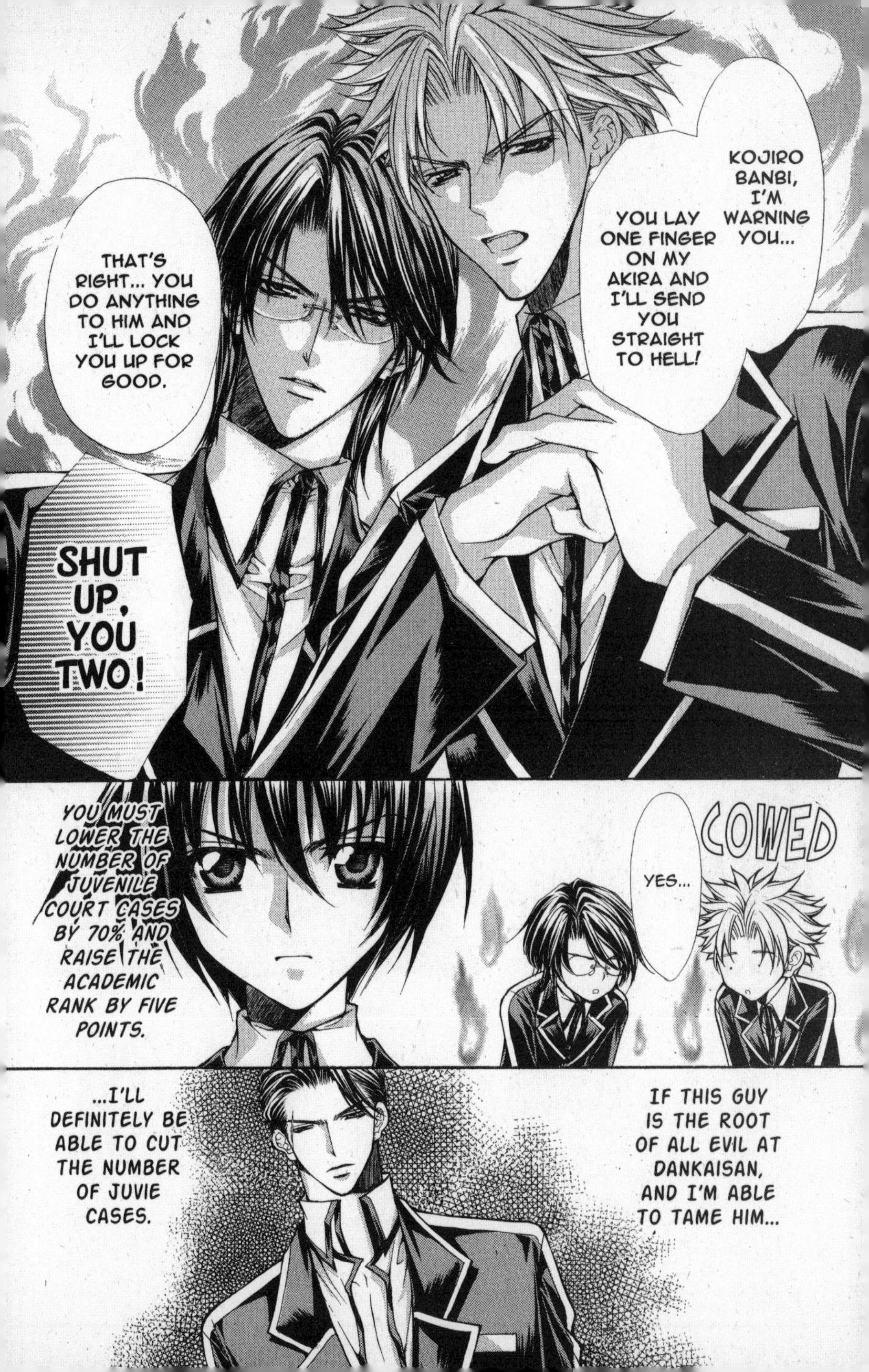
KOJIRO BANBI, I'M WARNING YOU...
YOU LAY ONE FINGER ON MY AKIRA AND I'LL SEND YOU STRAIGHT TO HELL!
THAT'S RIGHT... YOU DO ANYTHING TO HIM AND I'LL LOCK YOU UP FOR GOOD.
SHUT UP, YOU TWO!
COWED
YES...
YOU MUST LOWER THE NUMBER OF JUVENILE COURT CASES BY 70% AND RAISE THE ACADEMIC RANK BY FIVE POINTS.
IF THIS GUY IS THE ROOT OF ALL EVIL AT DANKAISAN, AND I'M ABLE TO TAME HIM...
...I'LL DEFINITELY BE ABLE TO CUT THE NUMBER OF JUVIE CASES.

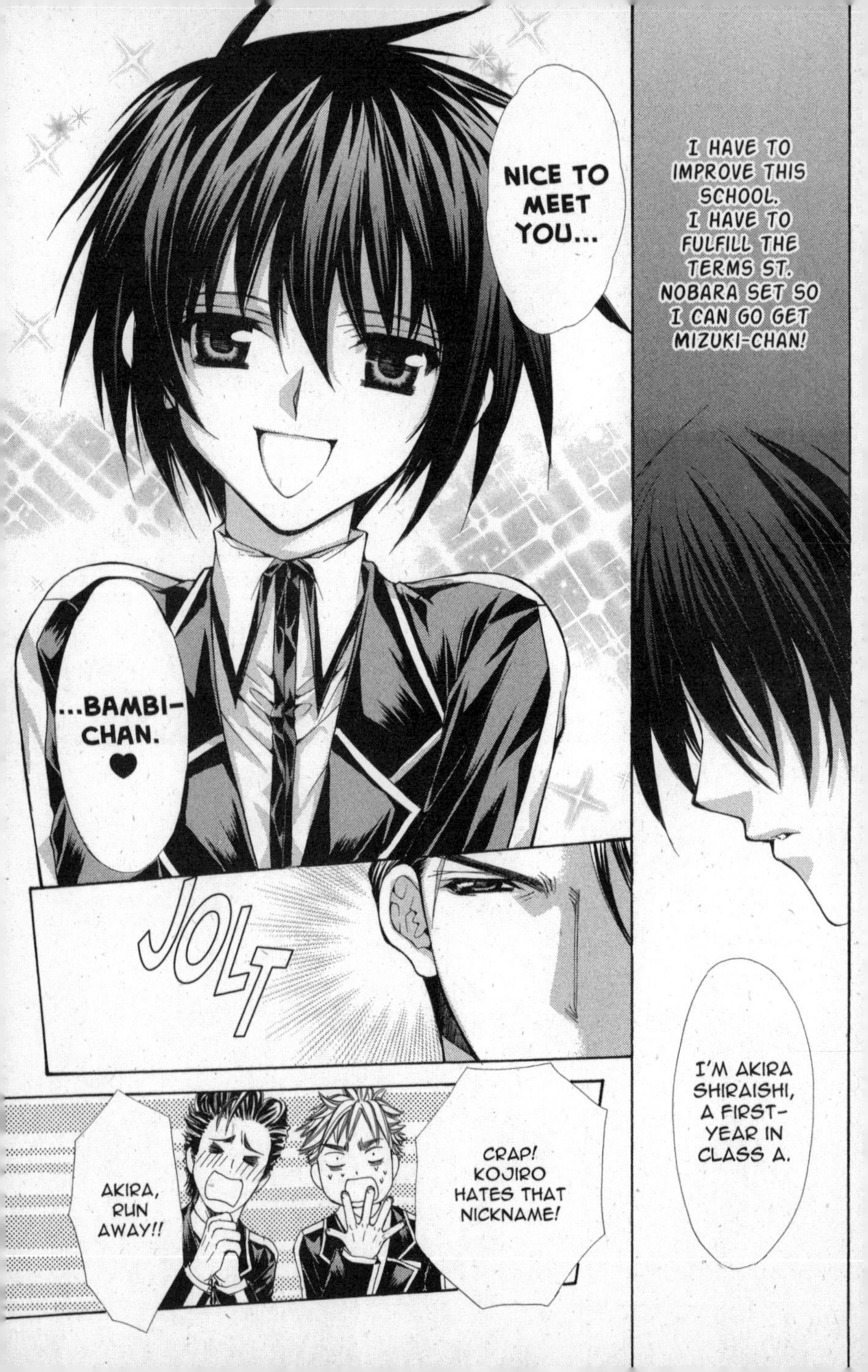
I HAVE TO IMPROVE THIS SCHOOL. I HAVE TO FULFILL THE TERMS ST. NOBARA SET SO I CAN GO GET MIZUKI-CHAN!
I'M AKIRA SHIRAISHI, A FIRST-YEAR IN CLASS A.
NICE TO MEET YOU...
...BAMBI-CHAN. ♥
JOLT
CRAP! KOJIRO HATES THAT NICKNAME!
AKIRA, RUN AWAY!!

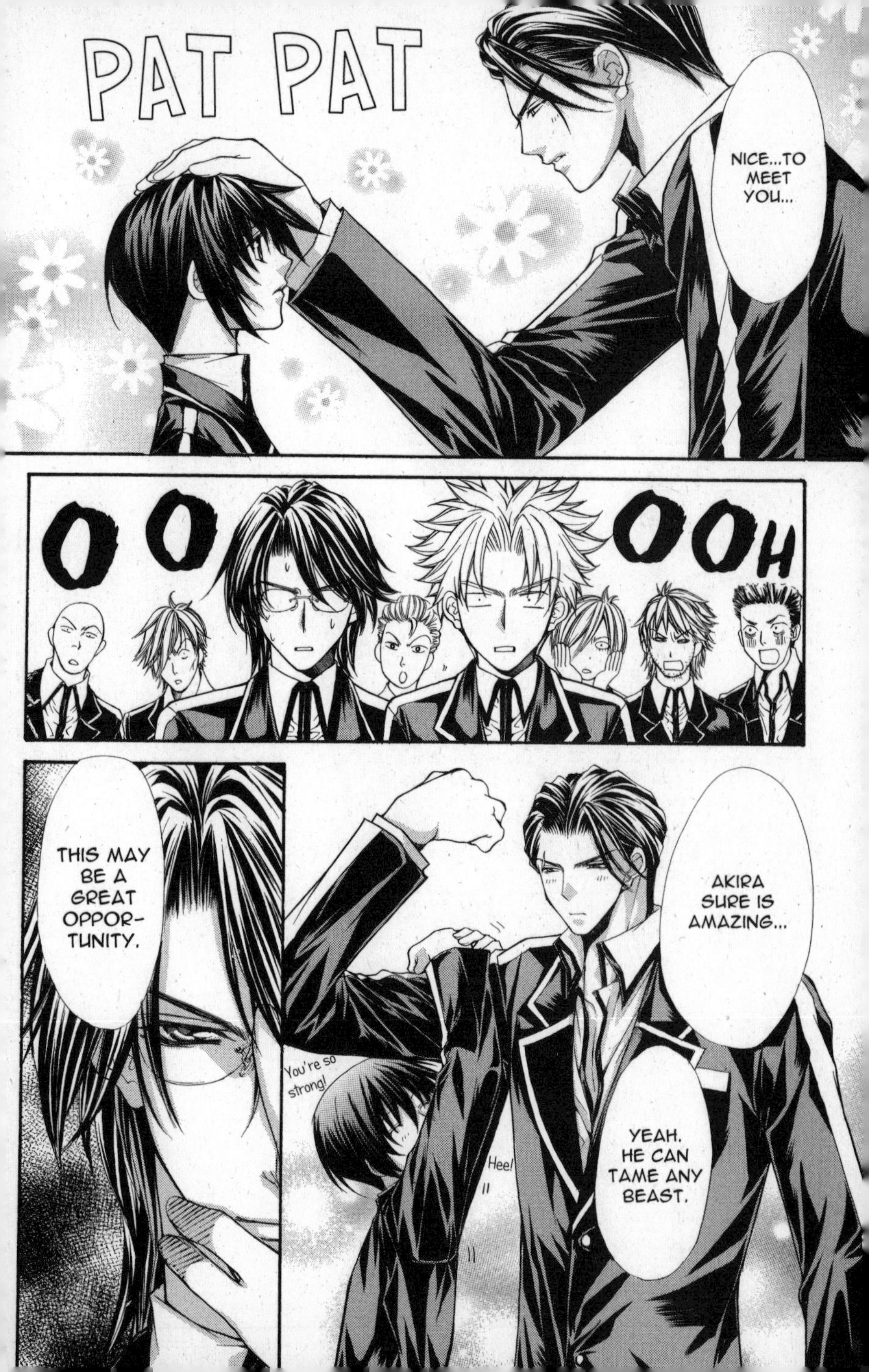
NICE...TO MEET YOU...
PAT PAT
OOOOOH
AKIRA SURE IS AMAZING...
YEAH. HE CAN TAME ANY BEAST.
You're so strong!
Hee!
THIS MAY BE A GREAT OPPOR-TUNITY.

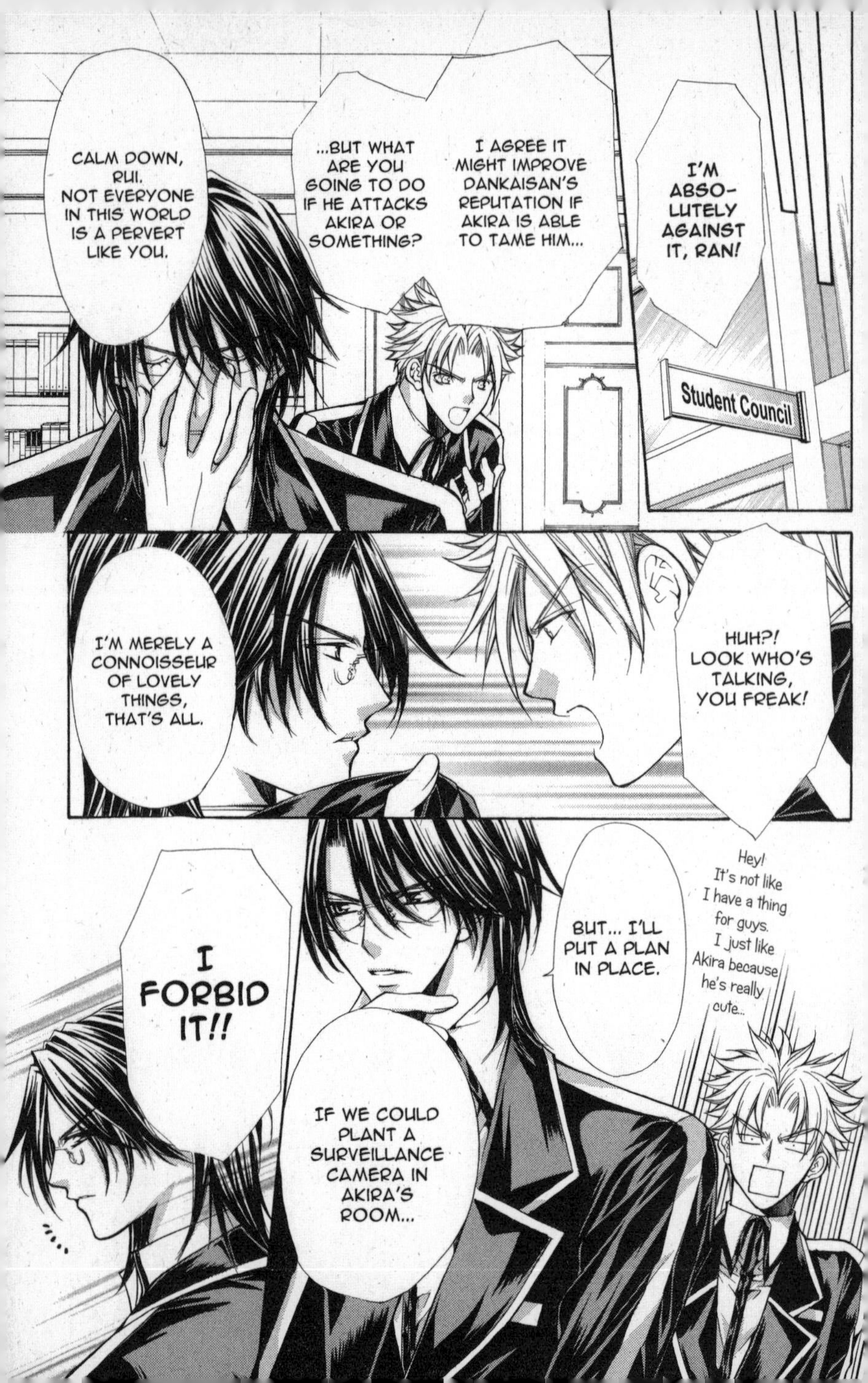
I'M ABSO-LUTELY AGAINST IT, RAN!
I AGREE IT MIGHT IMPROVE DANKAISAN'S REPUTATION IF AKIRA IS ABLE TO TAME HIM...
...BUT WHAT ARE YOU GOING TO DO IF HE ATTACKS AKIRA OR SOMETHING?
Student Council
CALM DOWN, RUI. NOT EVERYONE IN THIS WORLD IS A PERVERT LIKE YOU.
HUH?! LOOK WHO'S TALKING, YOU FREAK!
I'M MERELY A CONNOISSEUR OF LOVELY THINGS, THAT'S ALL.
Hey! It's not like I have a thing for guys. I just like Akira because he's really cute...
BUT... I'LL PUT A PLAN IN PLACE.
IF WE COULD PLANT A SURVEILLANCE CAMERA IN AKIRA'S ROOM...
I FORBID IT!!
.....

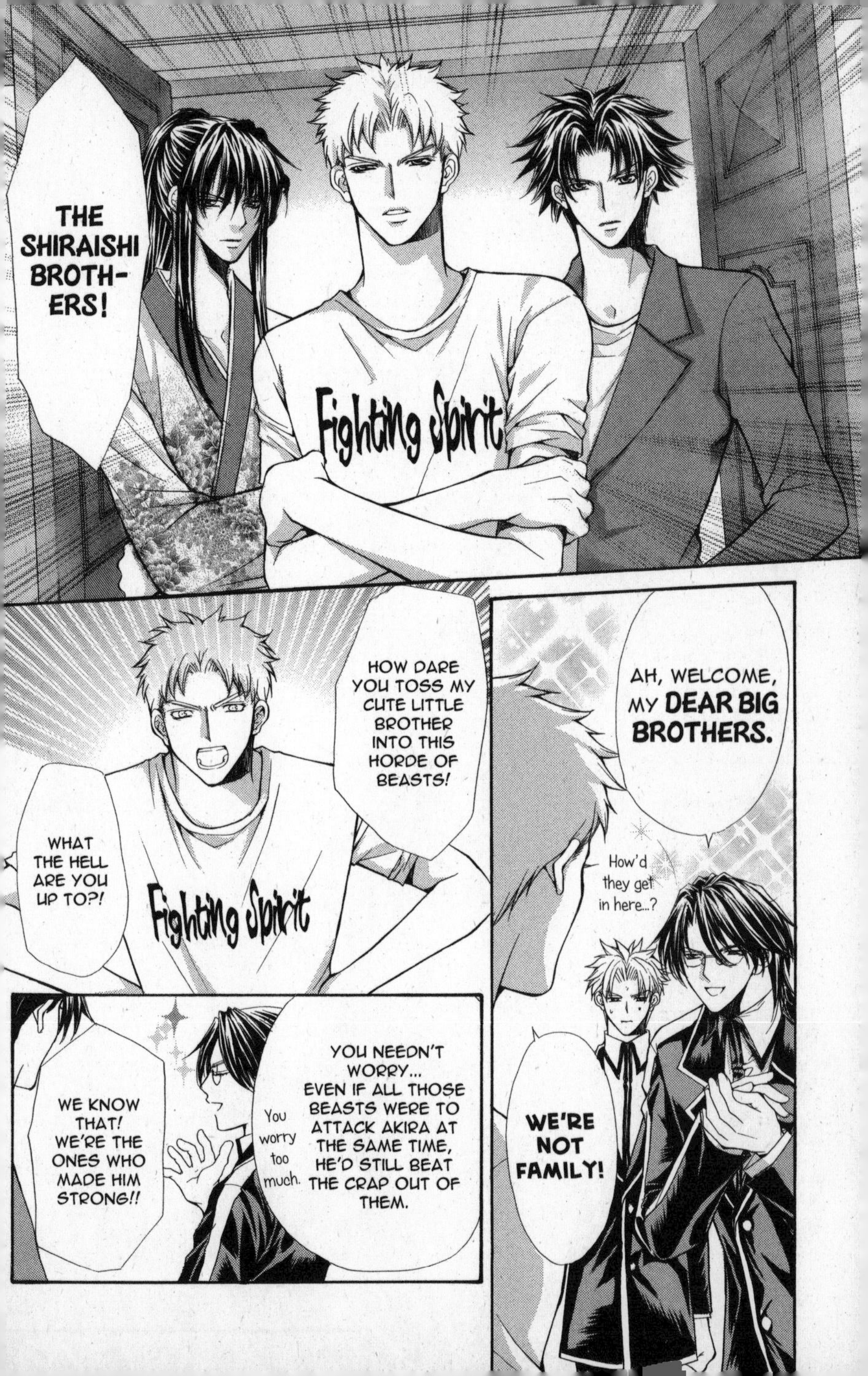
THE SHIRAISHI BROTH- ERS!
Fighting Spirit
AH, WELCOME, MY DEAR BIG BROTHERS.
How'd they get in here...?
WE'RE NOT FAMILY!
HOW DARE YOU TOSS MY CUTE LITTLE BROTHER INTO THIS HORDE OF BEASTS!
WHAT THE HELL ARE YOU UP TO?!
Fighting Spirit
YOU NEEDN'T WORRY... EVEN IF ALL THOSE BEASTS WERE TO ATTACK AKIRA AT THE SAME TIME, HE'D STILL BEAT THE CRAP OUT OF THEM.
You worry too much.
WE KNOW THAT! WE'RE THE ONES WHO MADE HIM STRONG!!

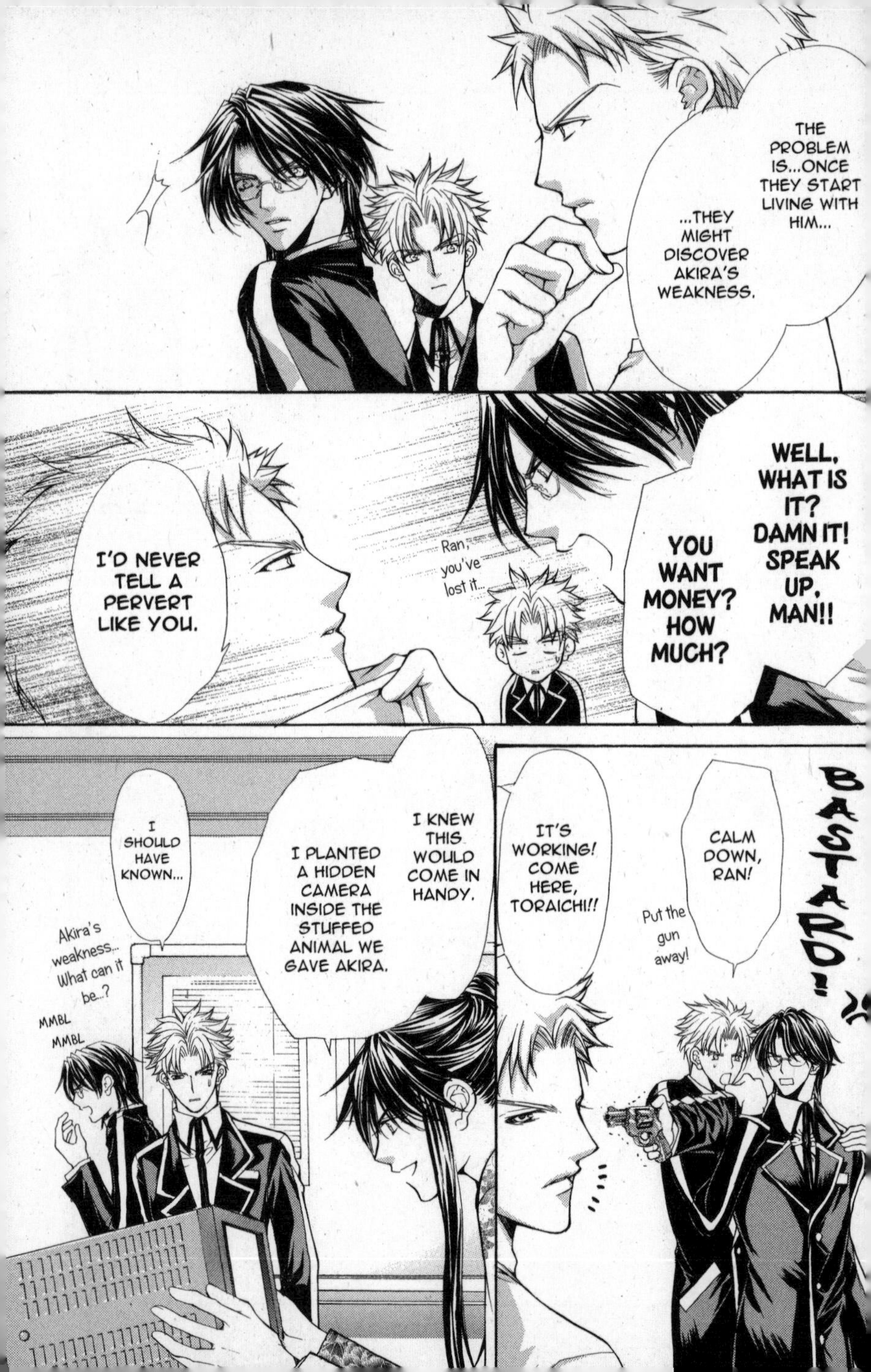
THE PROBLEM IS...ONCE THEY START LIVING WITH HIM...
...THEY MIGHT DISCOVER AKIRA'S WEAKNESS.
WELL, WHAT IS IT? DAMN IT! SPEAK UP, MAN!!
YOU WANT MONEY? HOW MUCH?
Ran, you've lost it...
I'D NEVER TELL A PERVERT LIKE YOU.
BASTARD!!
CALM DOWN, RAN!
Put the gun away!
IT'S WORKING! COME HERE, TORAICHI!!
I KNEW THIS WOULD COME IN HANDY.
I PLANTED A HIDDEN CAMERA INSIDE THE STUFFED ANIMAL WE GAVE AKIRA.
I SHOULD HAVE KNOWN...
Akira's weakness... What can it be...?
MMBL MMBL

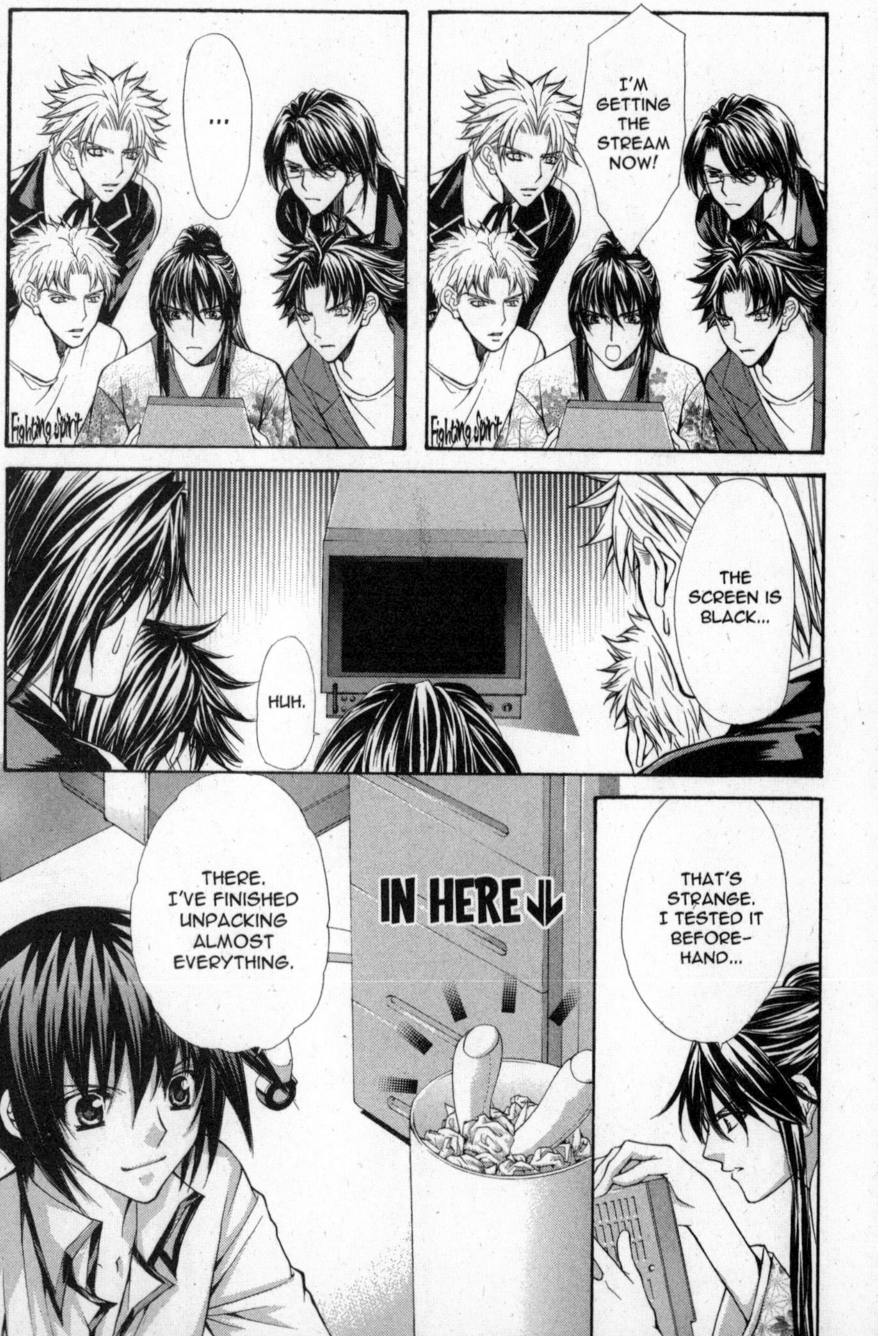
I'M GETTING THE STREAM NOW!
Fighting Spirit
...
Fighting Spirit
THE SCREEN IS BLACK...
HUH.
THAT'S STRANGE. I TESTED IT BEFORE-HAND...
THERE. I'VE FINISHED UNPACKING ALMOST EVERYTHING.
IN HERE↓

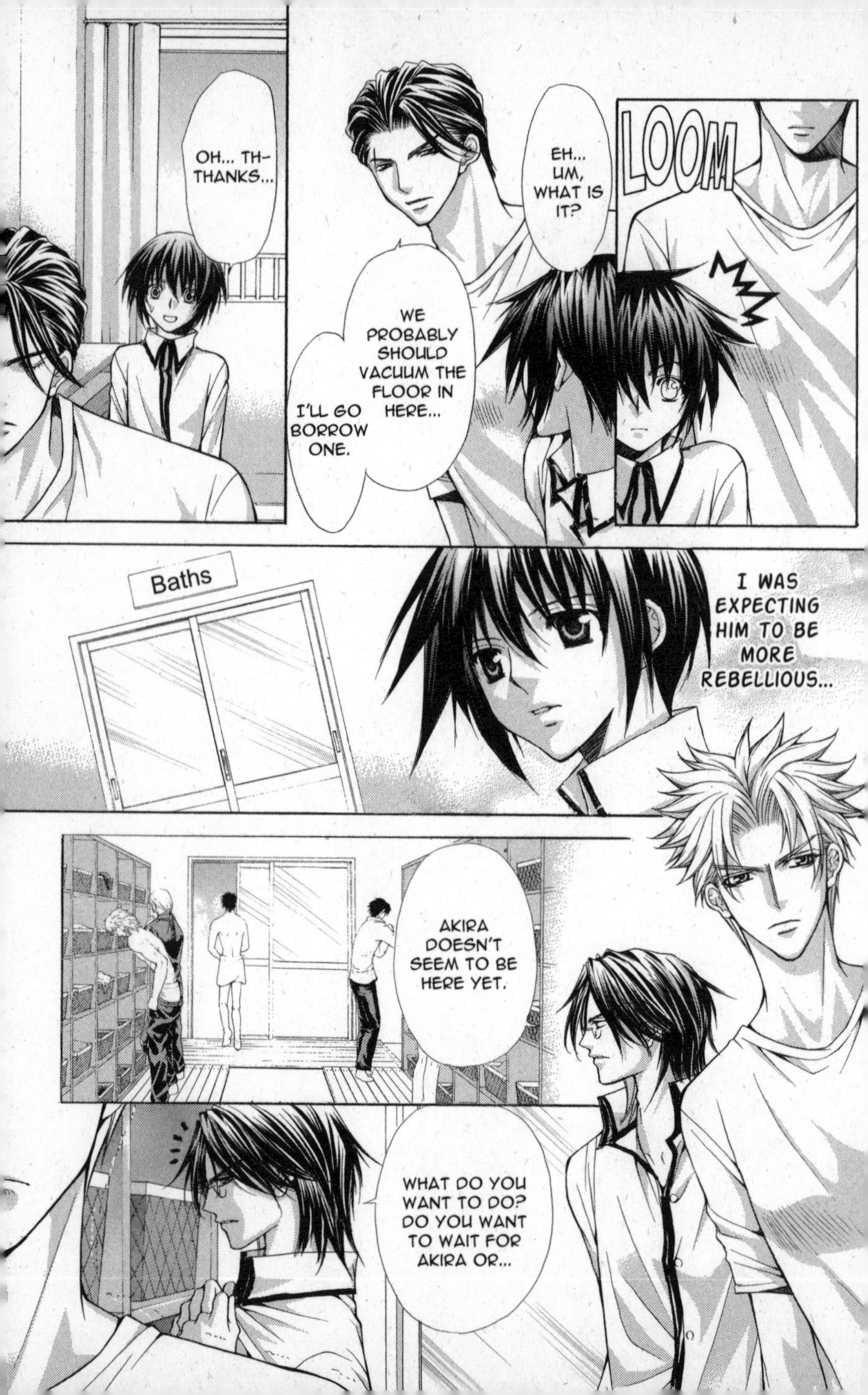
LOOM
EH... UM, WHAT IS IT?
WE PROBABLY SHOULD VACUUM THE FLOOR IN HERE...
I'LL GO BORROW ONE.
OH... TH-THANKS...
I WAS EXPECTING HIM TO BE MORE REBELLIOUS...
Baths
AKIRA DOESN'T SEEM TO BE HERE YET.
WHAT DO YOU WANT TO DO? DO YOU WANT TO WAIT FOR AKIRA OR...

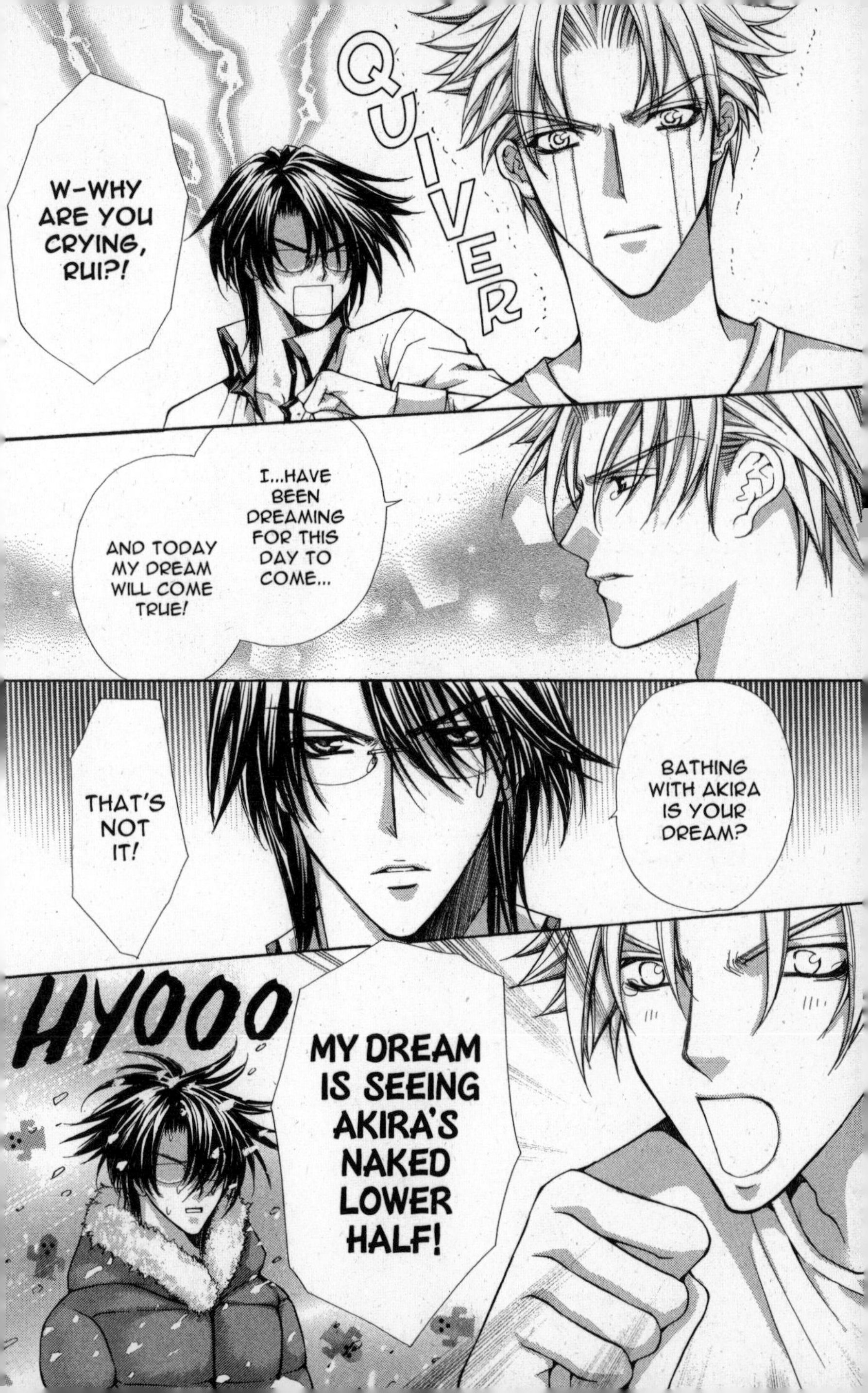
QUIVER
W-WHY ARE YOU CRYING, RUI?!
I...HAVE BEEN DREAMING FOR THIS DAY TO COME...
AND TODAY MY DREAM WILL COME TRUE!
BATHING WITH AKIRA IS YOUR DREAM?
THAT'S NOT IT!
MY DREAM IS SEEING AKIRA'S NAKED LOWER HALF!
HYOOO

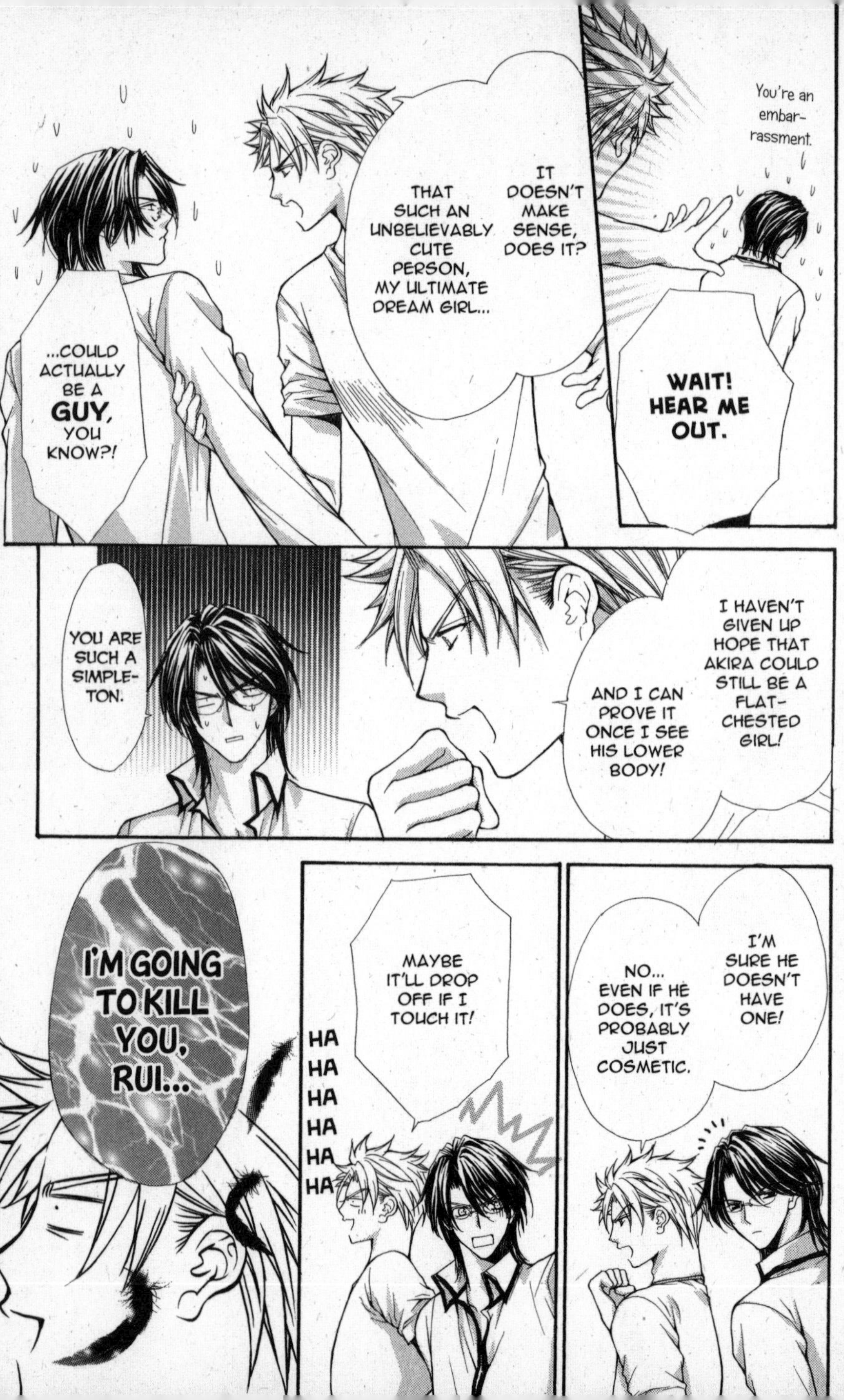
You're an embar-rassment.
WAIT! HEAR ME OUT.
IT DOESN'T MAKE SENSE, DOES IT?
THAT SUCH AN UNBELIEVABLY CUTE PERSON, MY ULTIMATE DREAM GIRL...
...COULD ACTUALLY BE A **GUY,** YOU KNOW?!
I HAVEN'T GIVEN UP HOPE THAT AKIRA COULD STILL BE A FLAT-CHESTED GIRL!
AND I CAN PROVE IT ONCE I SEE HIS LOWER BODY!
YOU ARE SUCH A SIMPLE-TON.
I'M SURE HE DOESN'T HAVE ONE!
NO... EVEN IF HE DOES, IT'S PROBABLY JUST COSMETIC.
MAYBE IT'LL DROP OFF IF I TOUCH IT!
HA HA HA HA HA HA
I'M GOING TO KILL YOU, RUI...

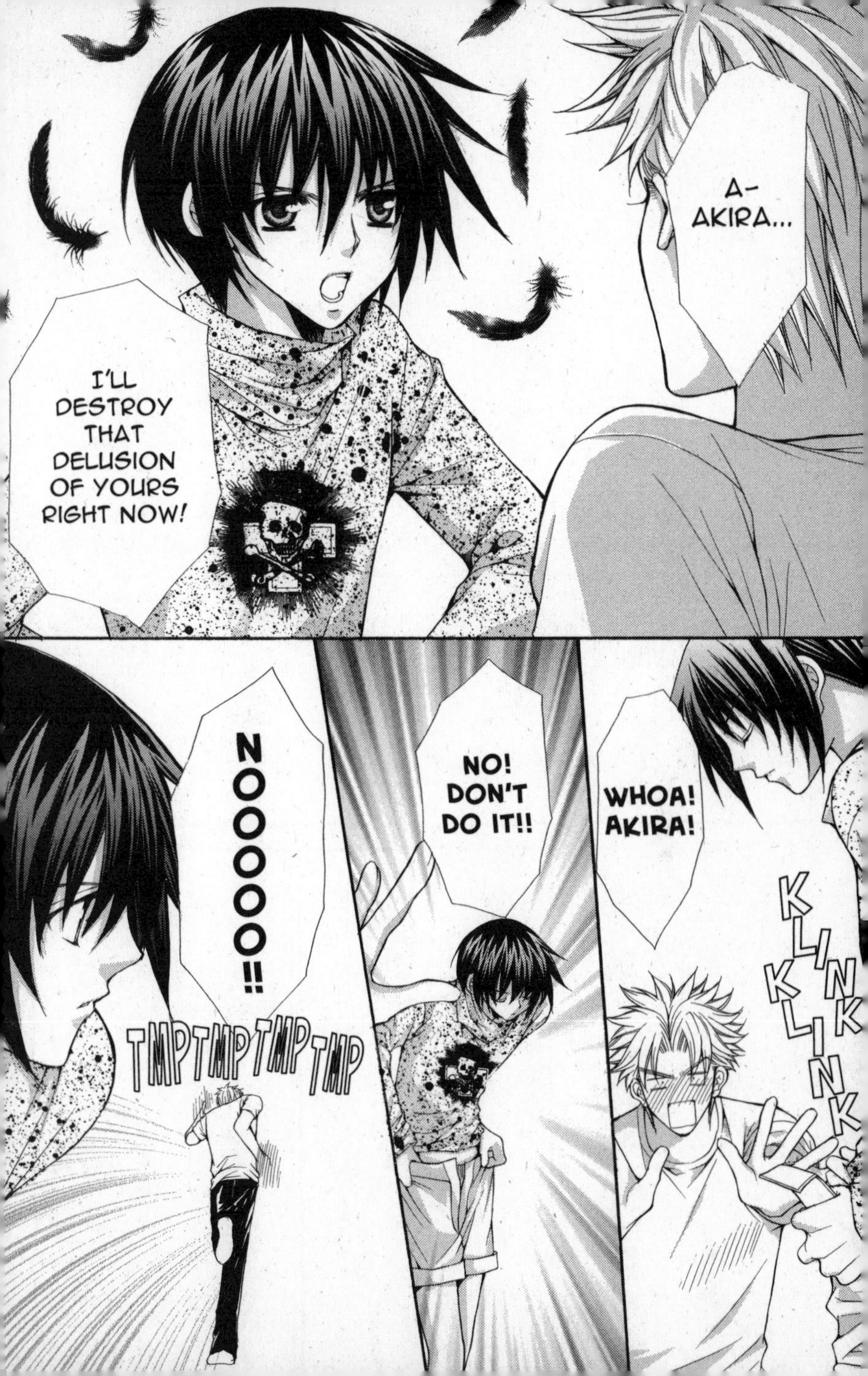
A-
AKIRA...
I'LL DESTROY THAT DELUSION OF YOURS RIGHT NOW!
WHOA! AKIRA!
KLINK
KLINK
NO! DON'T DO IT!!
NOOOOOO!!
TMPTMPTMPTMP

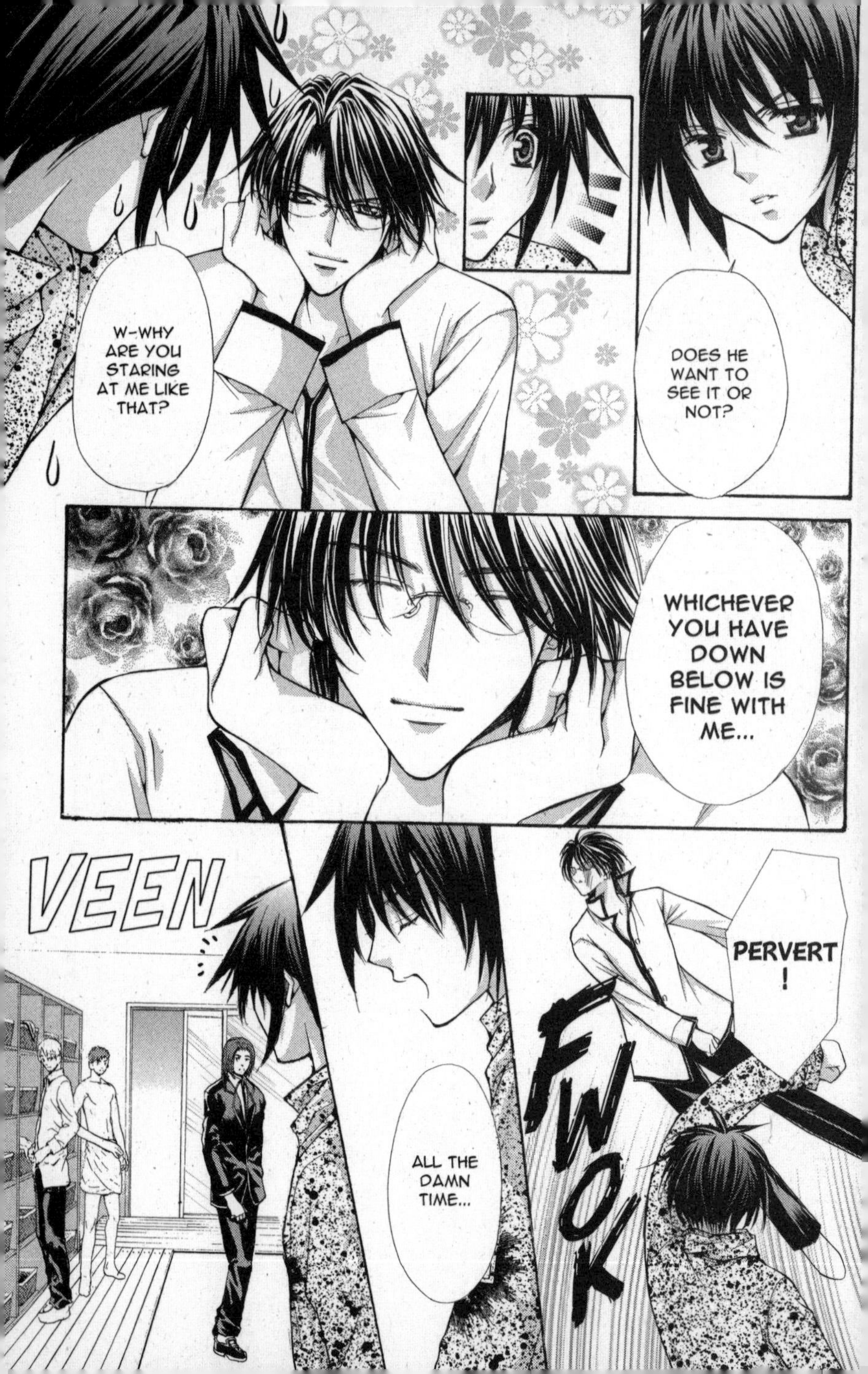
DOES HE WANT TO SEE IT OR NOT?
W-WHY ARE YOU STARING AT ME LIKE THAT?
WHICHEVER YOU HAVE DOWN BELOW IS FINE WITH ME...
PERVERT!
FWOK
ALL THE DAMN TIME...
VEEN

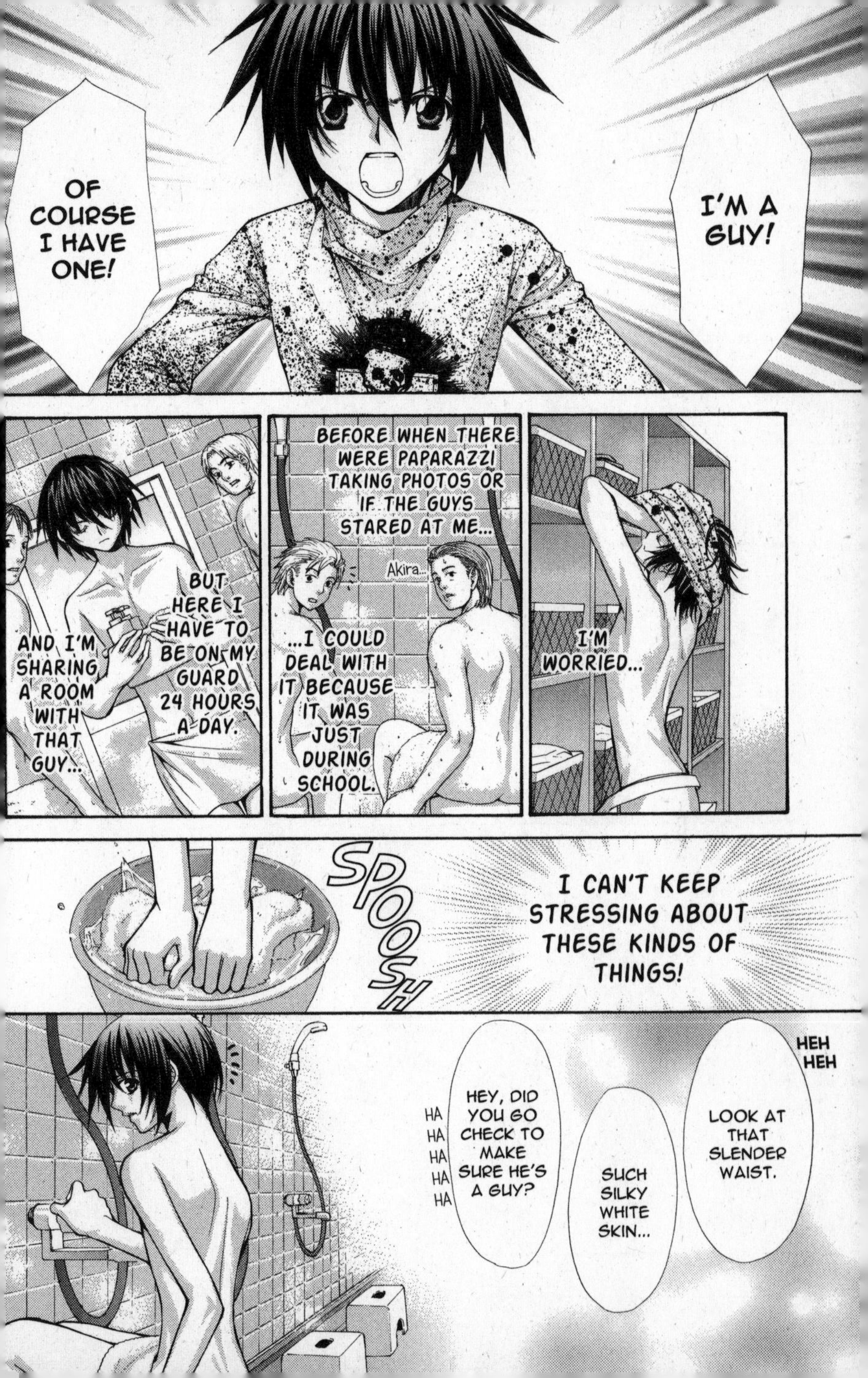
I'M A GUY!
OF COURSE I HAVE ONE!
I'M WORRIED...
BEFORE WHEN THERE WERE PAPARAZZI TAKING PHOTOS OR IF THE GUYS STARED AT ME...
Akira...
...I COULD DEAL WITH IT BECAUSE IT WAS JUST DURING SCHOOL.
BUT HERE I HAVE TO BE ON MY GUARD 24 HOURS A DAY.
AND I'M SHARING A ROOM WITH THAT GUY...
I CAN'T KEEP STRESSING ABOUT THESE KINDS OF THINGS!
SPOOSH
HEH HEH
LOOK AT THAT SLENDER WAIST.
SUCH SILKY WHITE SKIN...
HEY, DID YOU GO CHECK TO MAKE SURE HE'S A GUY?
HA HA HA HA HA

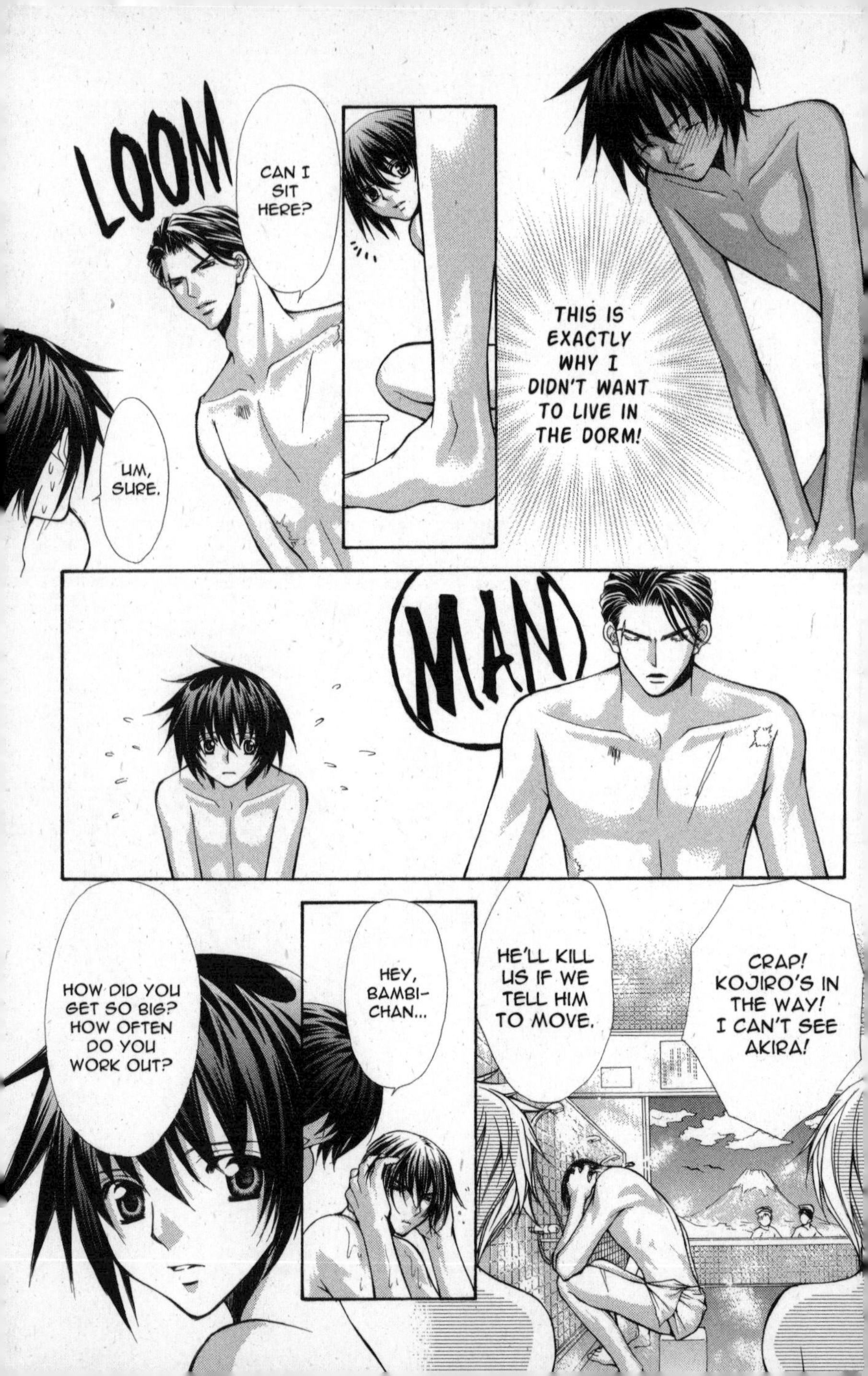
THIS IS EXACTLY WHY I DIDN'T WANT TO LIVE IN THE DORM!
LOOM
CAN I SIT HERE?
UM, SURE.
MAN
CRAP! KOJIRO'S IN THE WAY! I CAN'T SEE AKIRA!
HE'LL KILL US IF WE TELL HIM TO MOVE.
HEY, BAMBI-CHAN...
HOW DID YOU GET SO BIG? HOW OFTEN DO YOU WORK OUT?

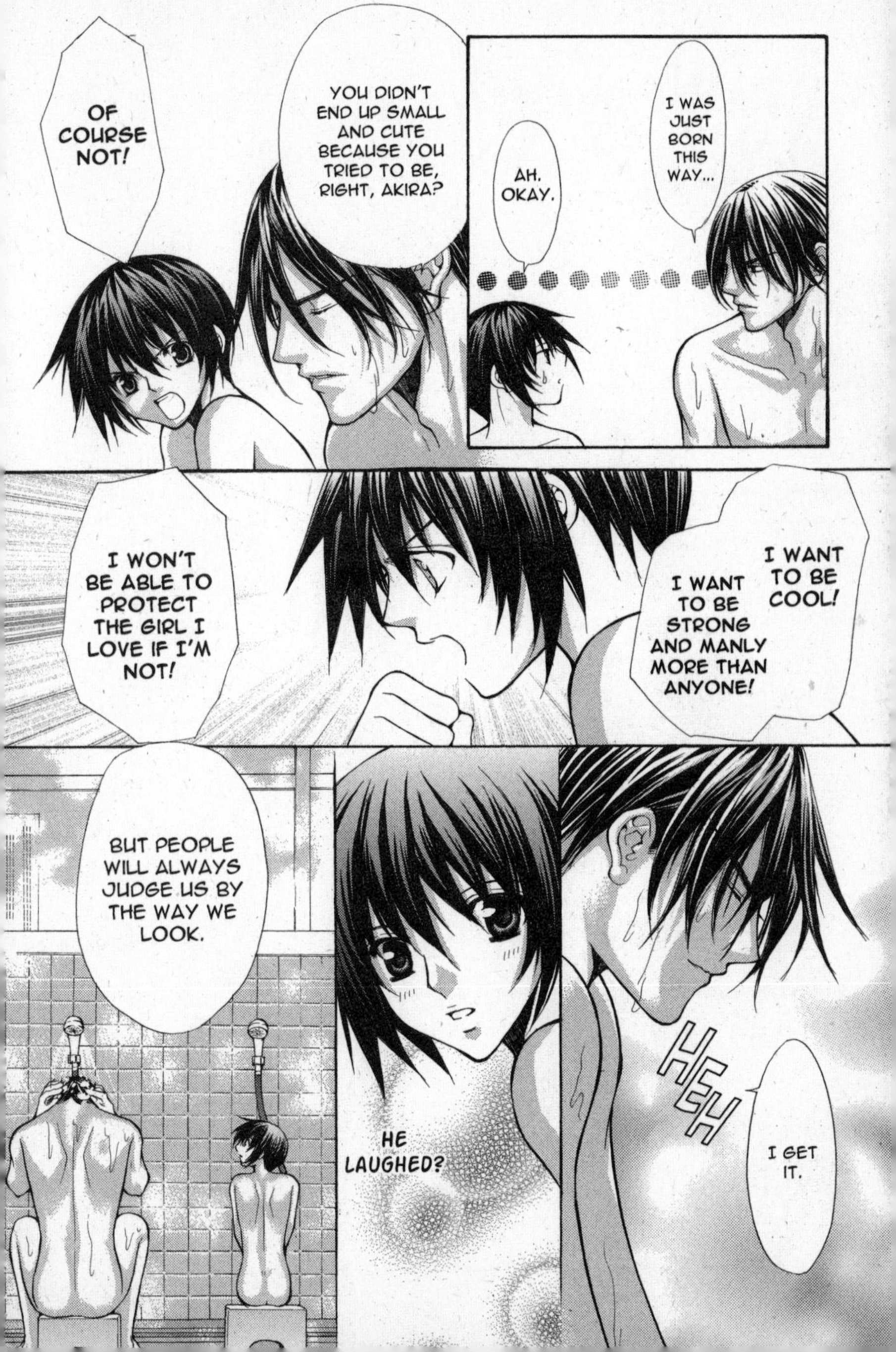
I WAS JUST BORN THIS WAY...
AH. OKAY.
YOU DIDN'T END UP SMALL AND CUTE BECAUSE YOU TRIED TO BE, RIGHT, AKIRA?
OF COURSE NOT!
I WANT TO BE COOL!
I WANT TO BE STRONG AND MANLY MORE THAN ANYONE!
I WON'T BE ABLE TO PROTECT THE GIRL I LOVE IF I'M NOT!
HEH
I GET IT.
HE LAUGHED?
BUT PEOPLE WILL ALWAYS JUDGE US BY THE WAY WE LOOK.

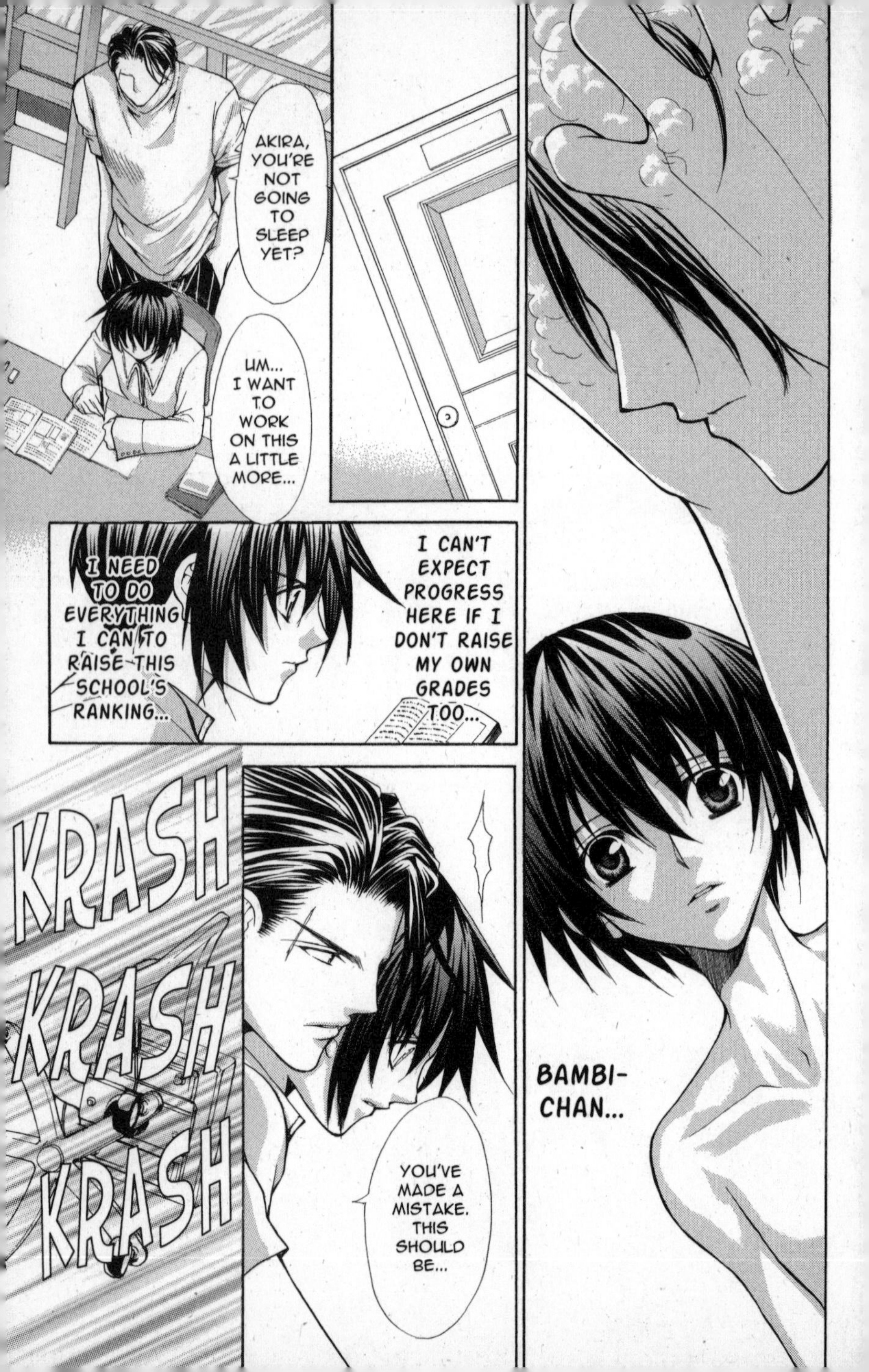
BAMBI-CHAN...
AKIRA, YOU'RE NOT GOING TO SLEEP YET?
UM... I WANT TO WORK ON THIS A LITTLE MORE...
I CAN'T EXPECT PROGRESS HERE IF I DON'T RAISE MY OWN GRADES TOO...
I NEED TO DO EVERYTHING I CAN TO RAISE THIS SCHOOL'S RANKING...
YOU'VE MADE A MISTAKE. THIS SHOULD BE...
KRASH
KRASH
KRASH

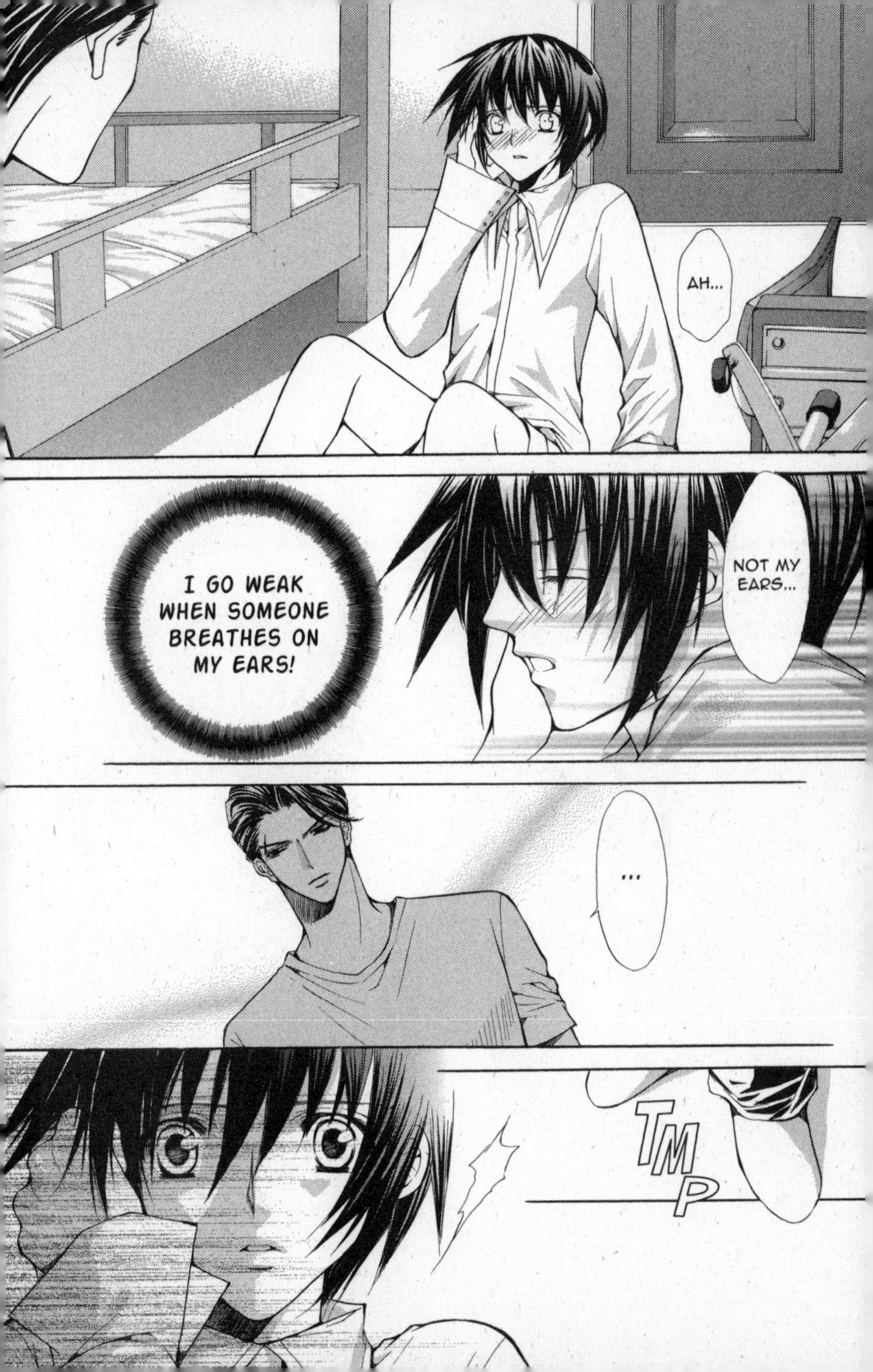
AH...
NOT MY EARS...
I GO WEAK WHEN SOMEONE BREATHES ON MY EARS!
...
TMP

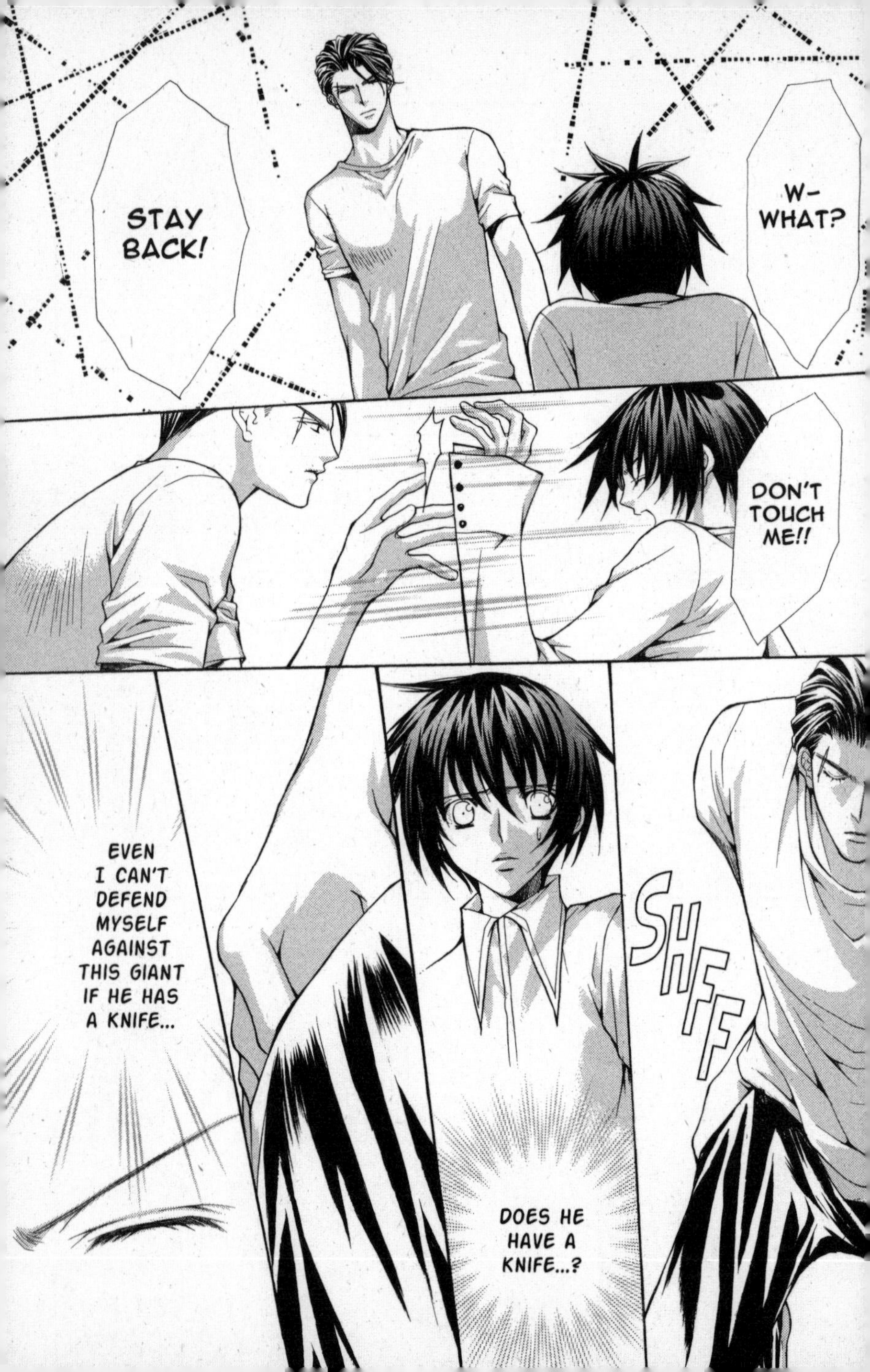
W-WHAT?
STAY BACK!
DON'T TOUCH ME!!
SHFF
DOES HE HAVE A KNIFE...?
EVEN I CAN'T DEFEND MYSELF AGAINST THIS GIANT IF HE HAS A KNIFE...

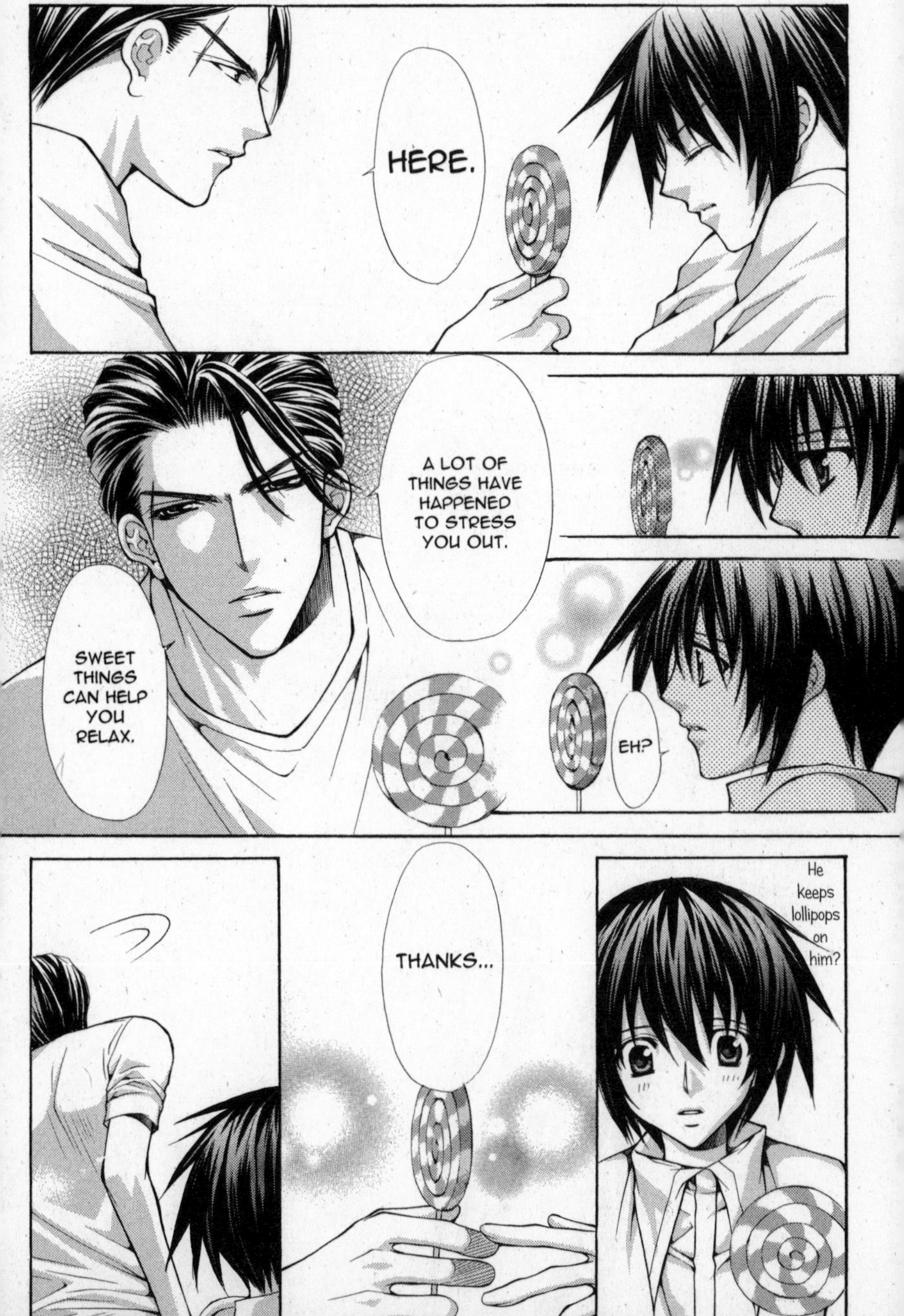
HERE.
EH?
A LOT OF THINGS HAVE HAPPENED TO STRESS YOU OUT.
SWEET THINGS CAN HELP YOU RELAX.
He keeps lollipops on him?
THANKS...

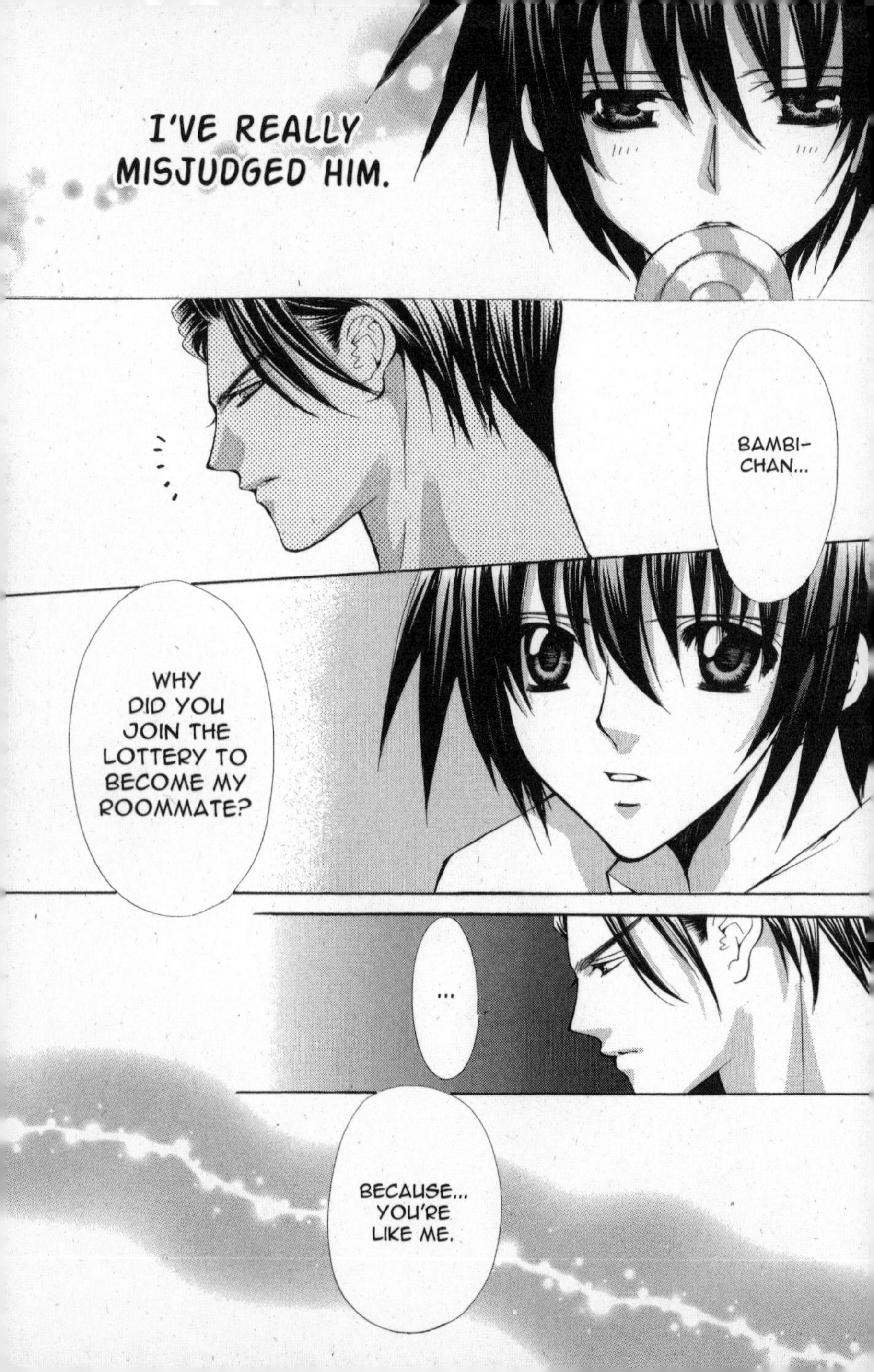
I'VE REALLY MISJUDGED HIM.
BAMBI-CHAN...
WHY DID YOU JOIN THE LOTTERY TO BECOME MY ROOMMATE?
...
BECAUSE... YOU'RE LIKE ME.

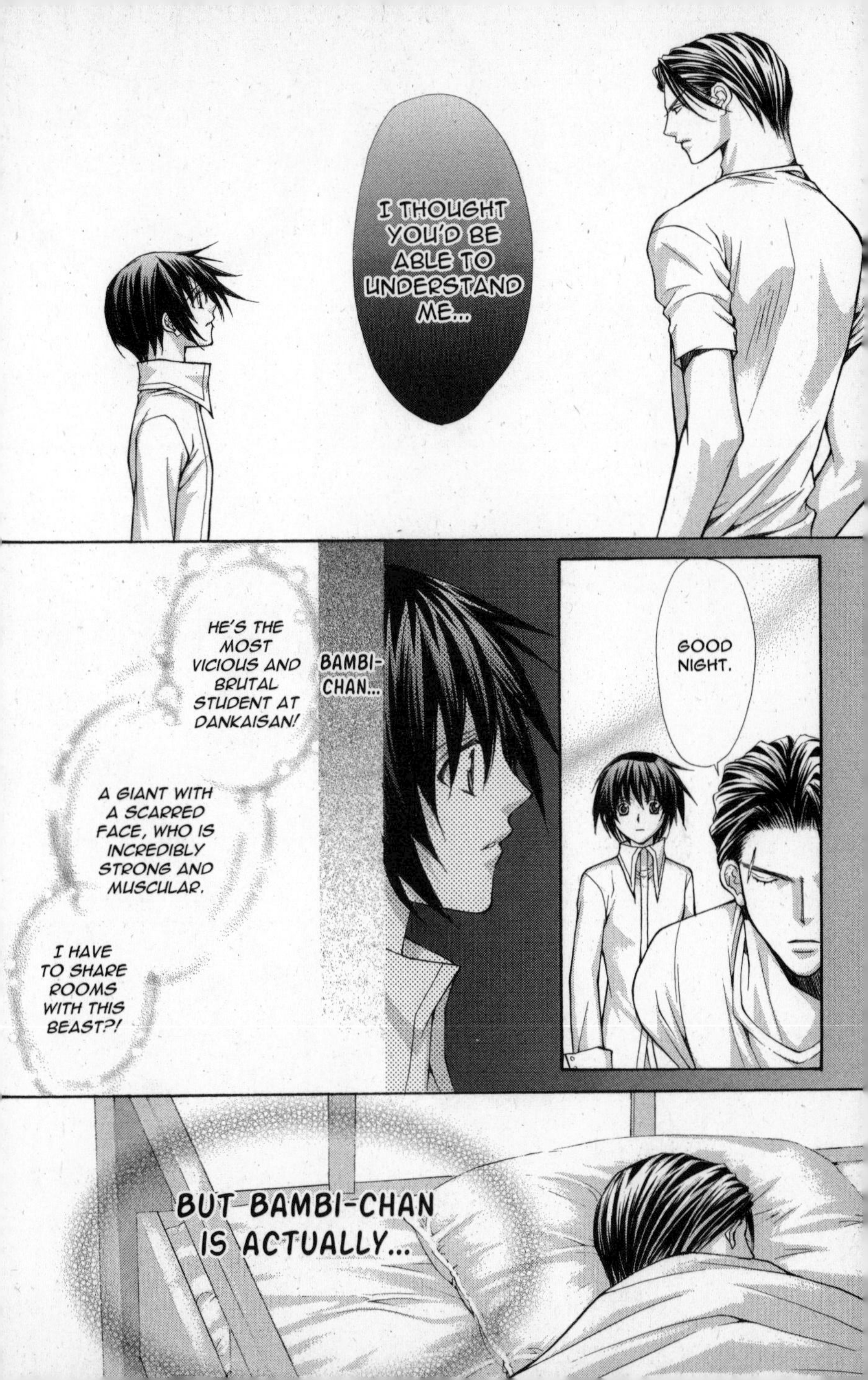
I THOUGHT YOU'D BE ABLE TO UNDERSTAND ME...
GOOD NIGHT.
BAMBI-CHAN...
HE'S THE MOST VICIOUS AND BRUTAL STUDENT AT DANKAISAN!
A GIANT WITH A SCARRED FACE, WHO IS INCREDIBLY STRONG AND MUSCULAR.
I HAVE TO SHARE ROOMS WITH THIS BEAST?!
BUT BAMBI-CHAN IS ACTUALLY...

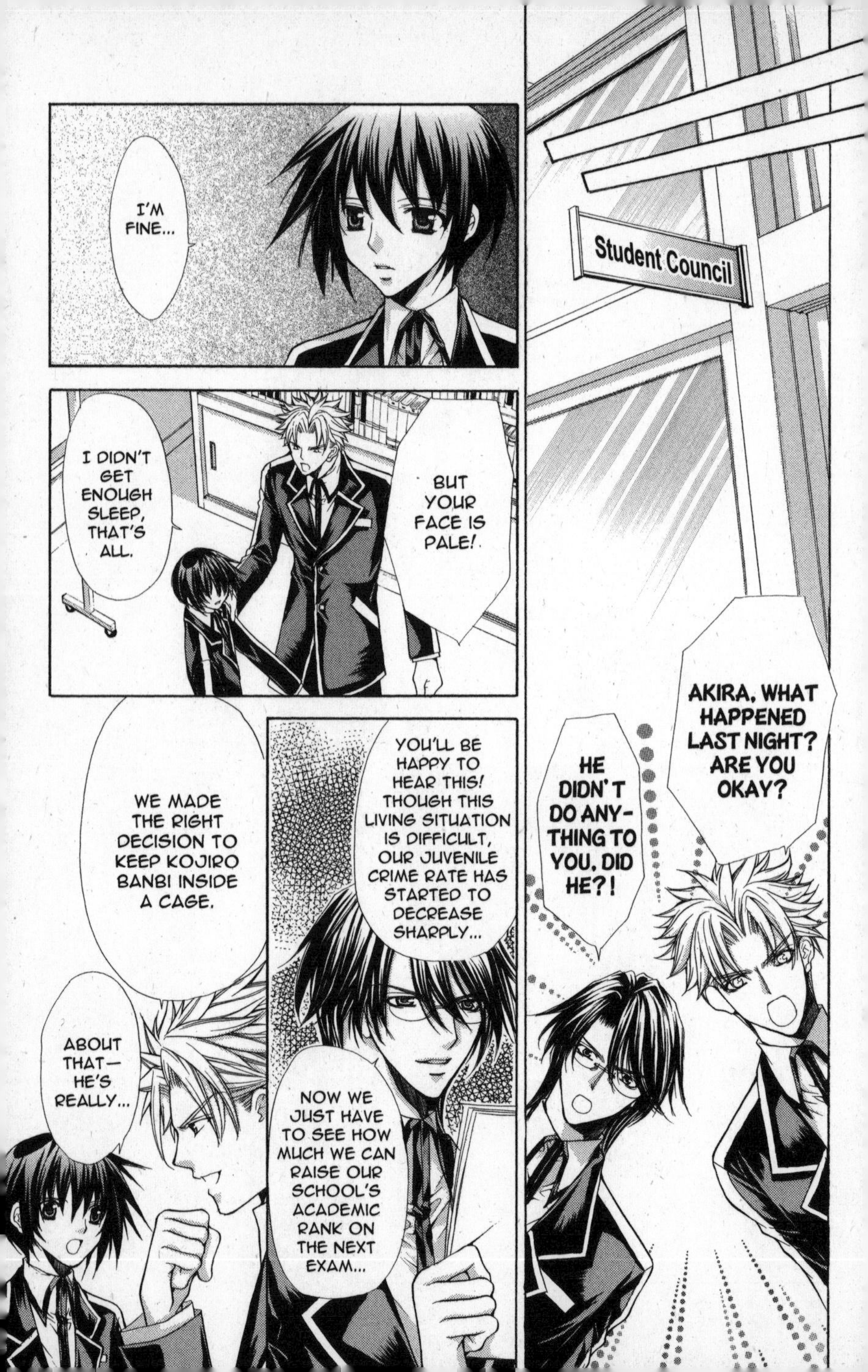
Student Council
AKIRA, WHAT HAPPENED LAST NIGHT? ARE YOU OKAY?
HE DIDN'T DO ANY-THING TO YOU, DID HE?!
I'M FINE...
BUT YOUR FACE IS PALE!
I DIDN'T GET ENOUGH SLEEP, THAT'S ALL.
YOU'LL BE HAPPY TO HEAR THIS! THOUGH THIS LIVING SITUATION IS DIFFICULT, OUR JUVENILE CRIME RATE HAS STARTED TO DECREASE SHARPLY...
NOW WE JUST HAVE TO SEE HOW MUCH WE CAN RAISE OUR SCHOOL'S ACADEMIC RANK ON THE NEXT EXAM...
WE MADE THE RIGHT DECISION TO KEEP KOJIRO BANBI INSIDE A CAGE.
ABOUT THAT— HE'S REALLY...

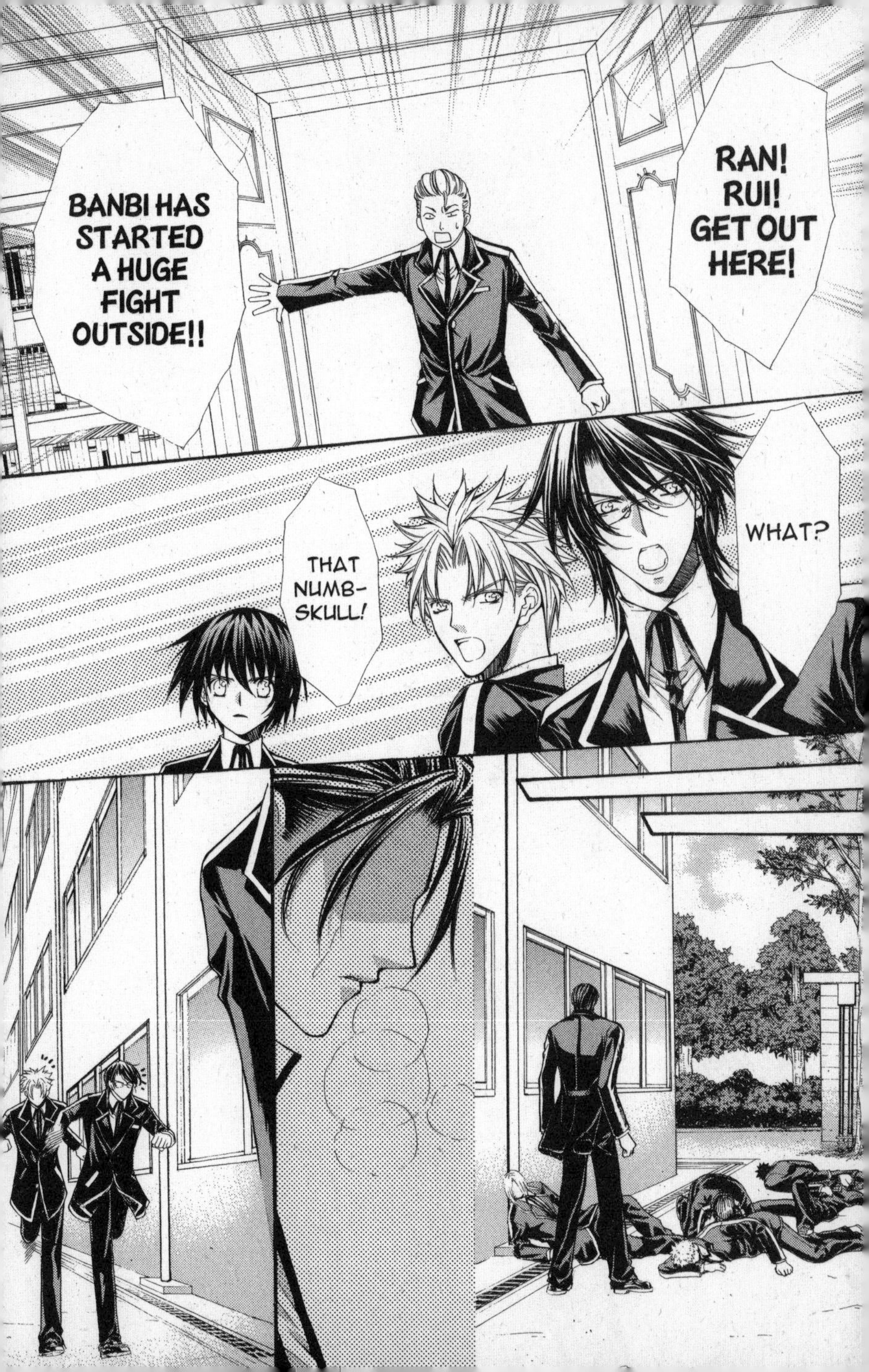
RAN! RUI! GET OUT HERE!
BANBI HAS STARTED A HUGE FIGHT OUTSIDE!!
WHAT?
THAT NUMB-SKULL!

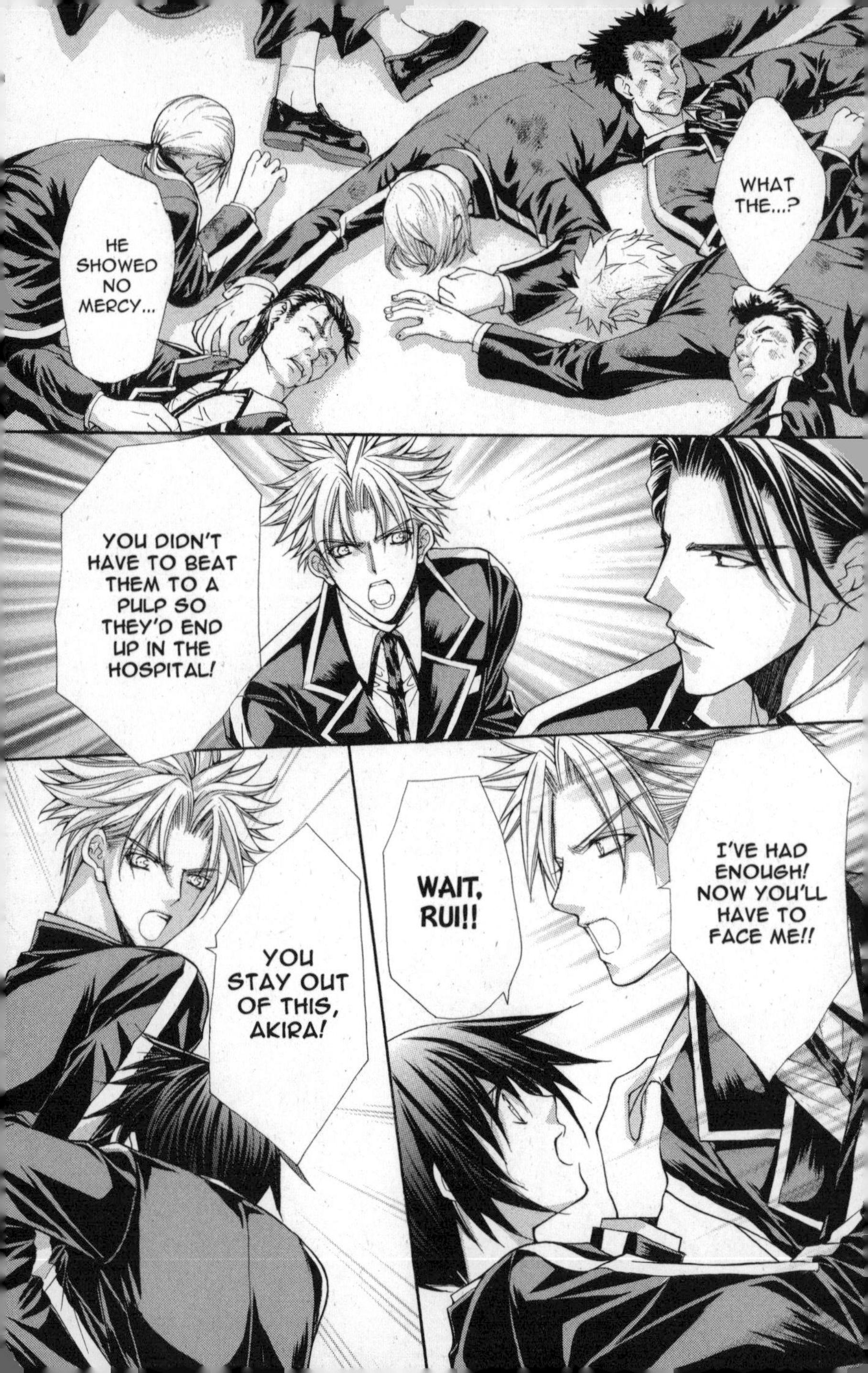
WHAT THE...?
HE SHOWED NO MERCY...
YOU DIDN'T HAVE TO BEAT THEM TO A PULP SO THEY'D END UP IN THE HOSPITAL!
I'VE HAD ENOUGH! NOW YOU'LL HAVE TO FACE ME!!
WAIT, RUI!!
YOU STAY OUT OF THIS, AKIRA!

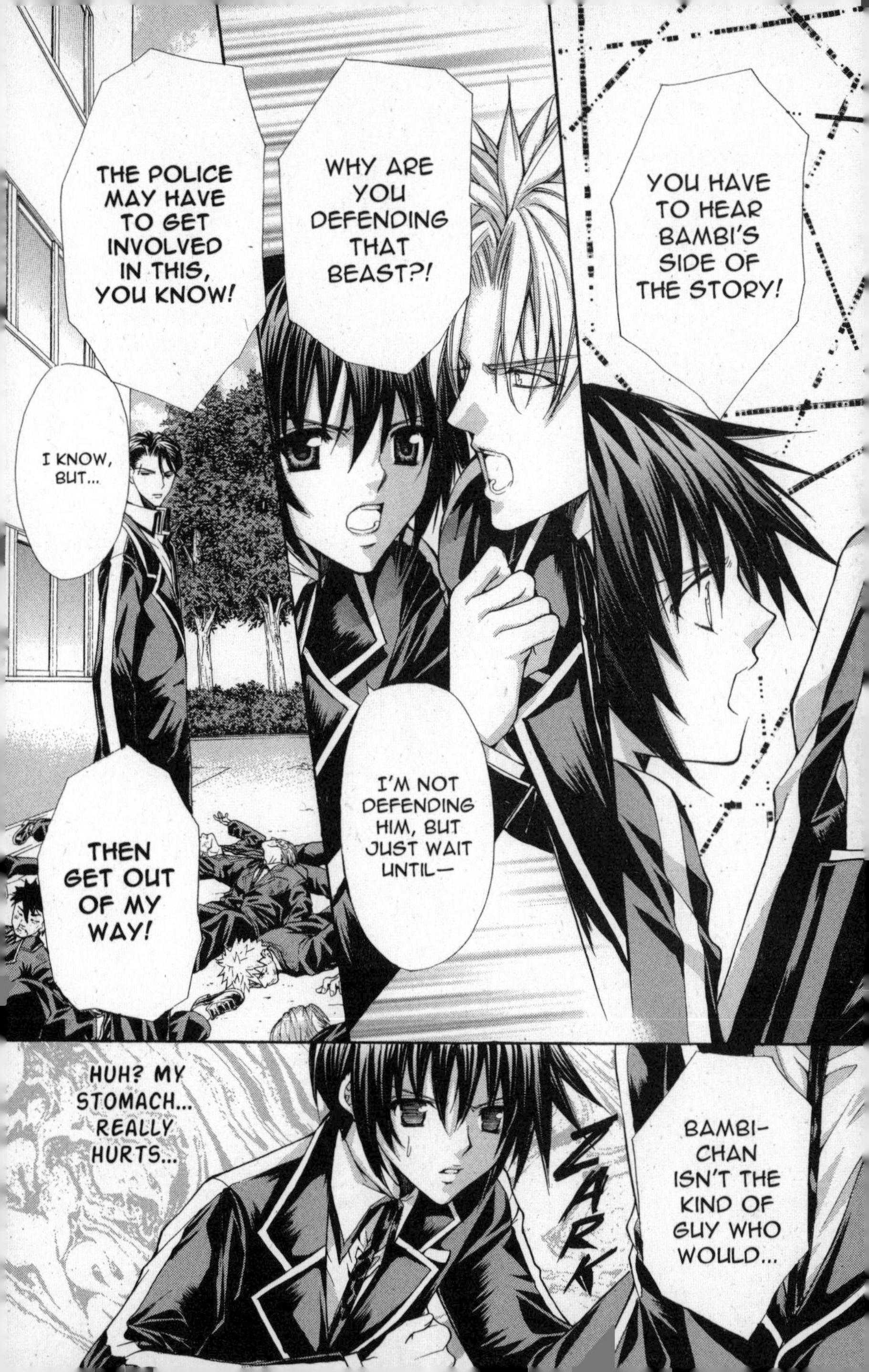
YOU HAVE TO HEAR BAMBI'S SIDE OF THE STORY!
WHY ARE YOU DEFENDING THAT BEAST?!
I'M NOT DEFENDING HIM, BUT JUST WAIT UNTIL—
THE POLICE MAY HAVE TO GET INVOLVED IN THIS, YOU KNOW!
I KNOW, BUT...
THEN GET OUT OF MY WAY!
BAMBI-CHAN ISN'T THE KIND OF GUY WHO WOULD...
ZARK
HUH? MY STOMACH... REALLY HURTS...

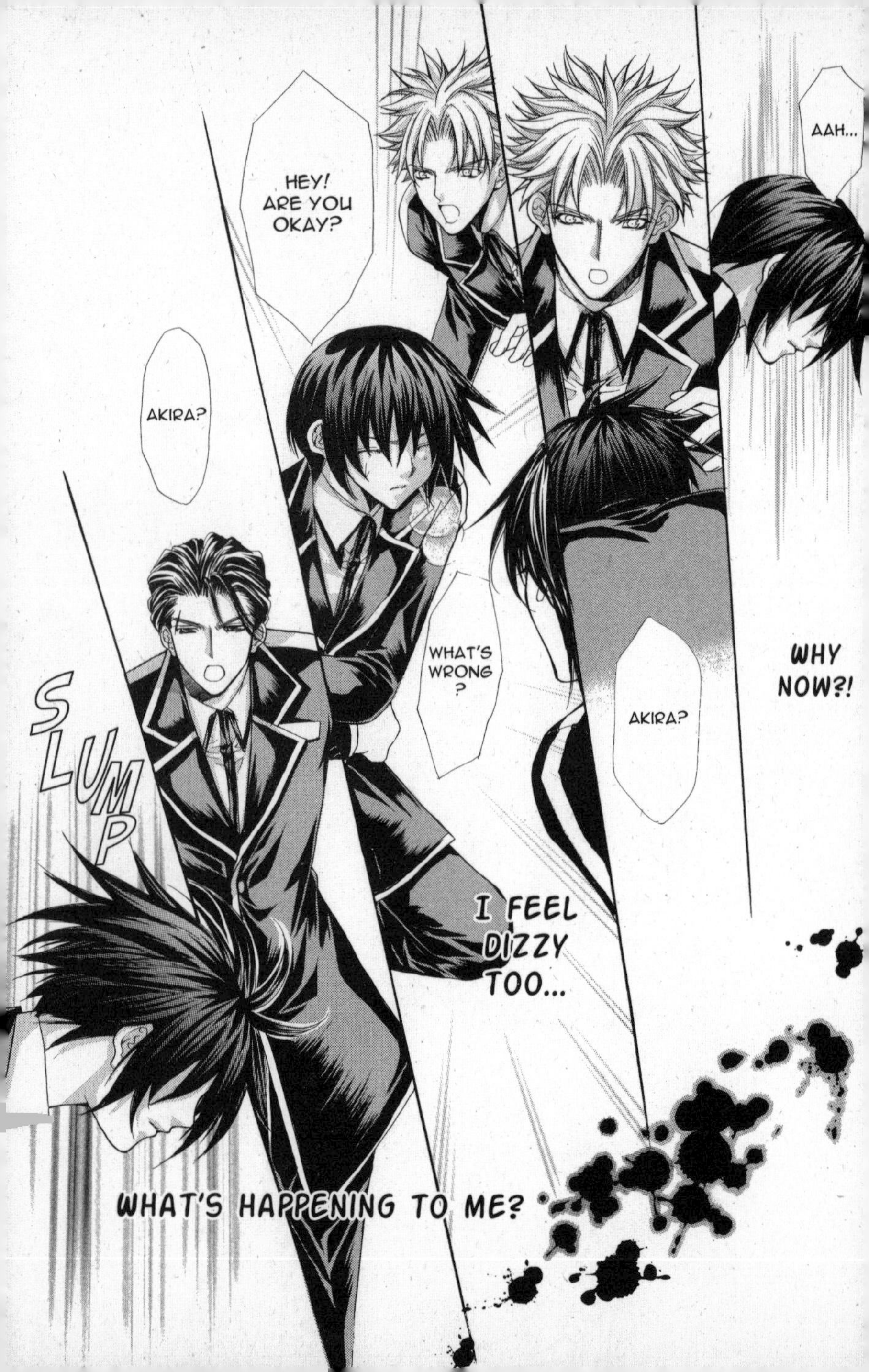

AAH...
WHY NOW?!
AKIRA?
HEY! ARE YOU OKAY?
WHAT'S WRONG?
I FEEL DIZZY TOO...
AKIRA?
SLUMP
WHAT'S HAPPENING TO ME?

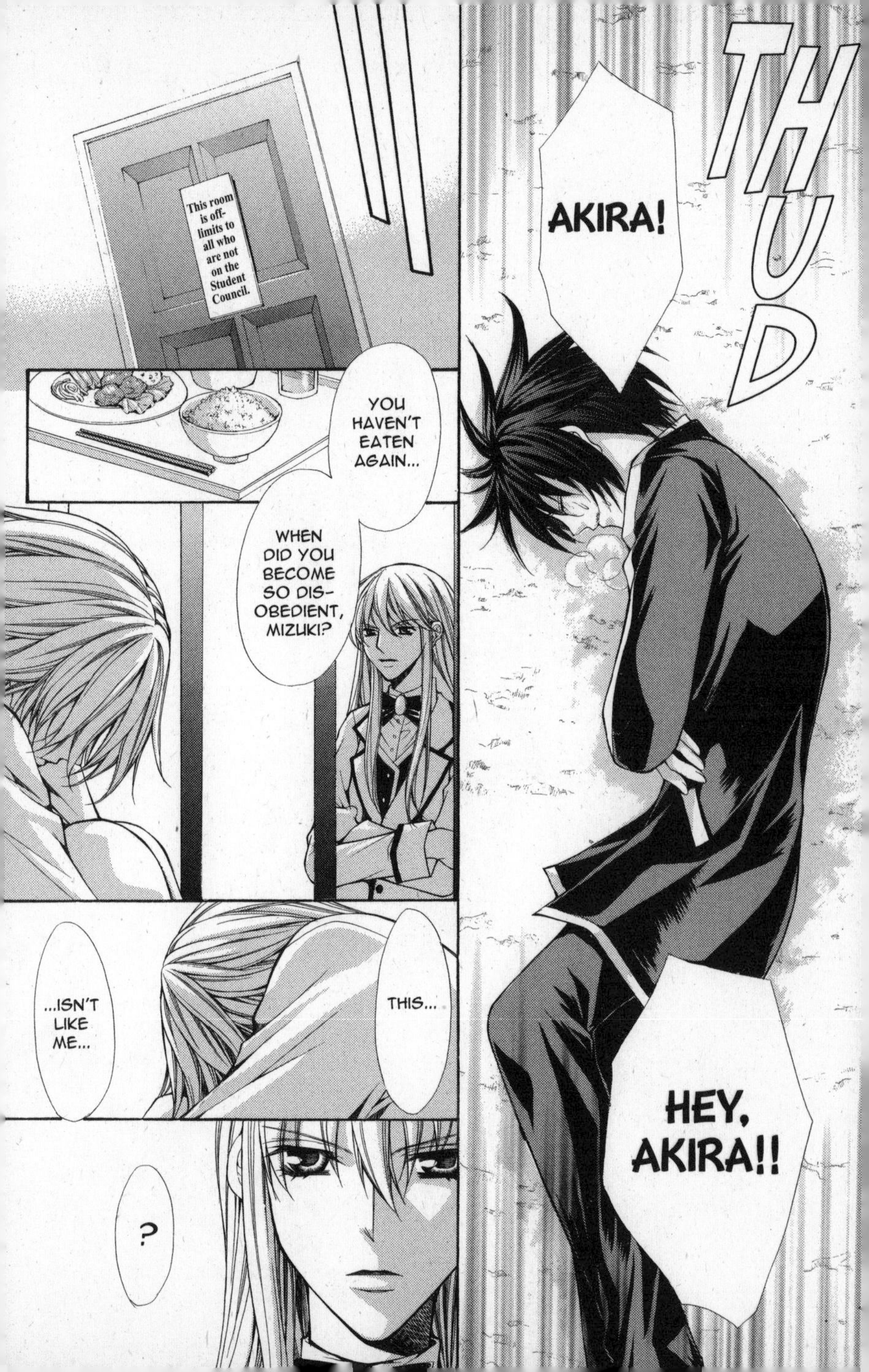
THUD
AKIRA!
HEY, AKIRA!!
This room is off-limits to all who are not on the Student Council.
YOU HAVEN'T EATEN AGAIN...
WHEN DID YOU BECOME SO DISOBEDIENT, MIZUKI?
THIS...
...ISN'T LIKE ME...
?

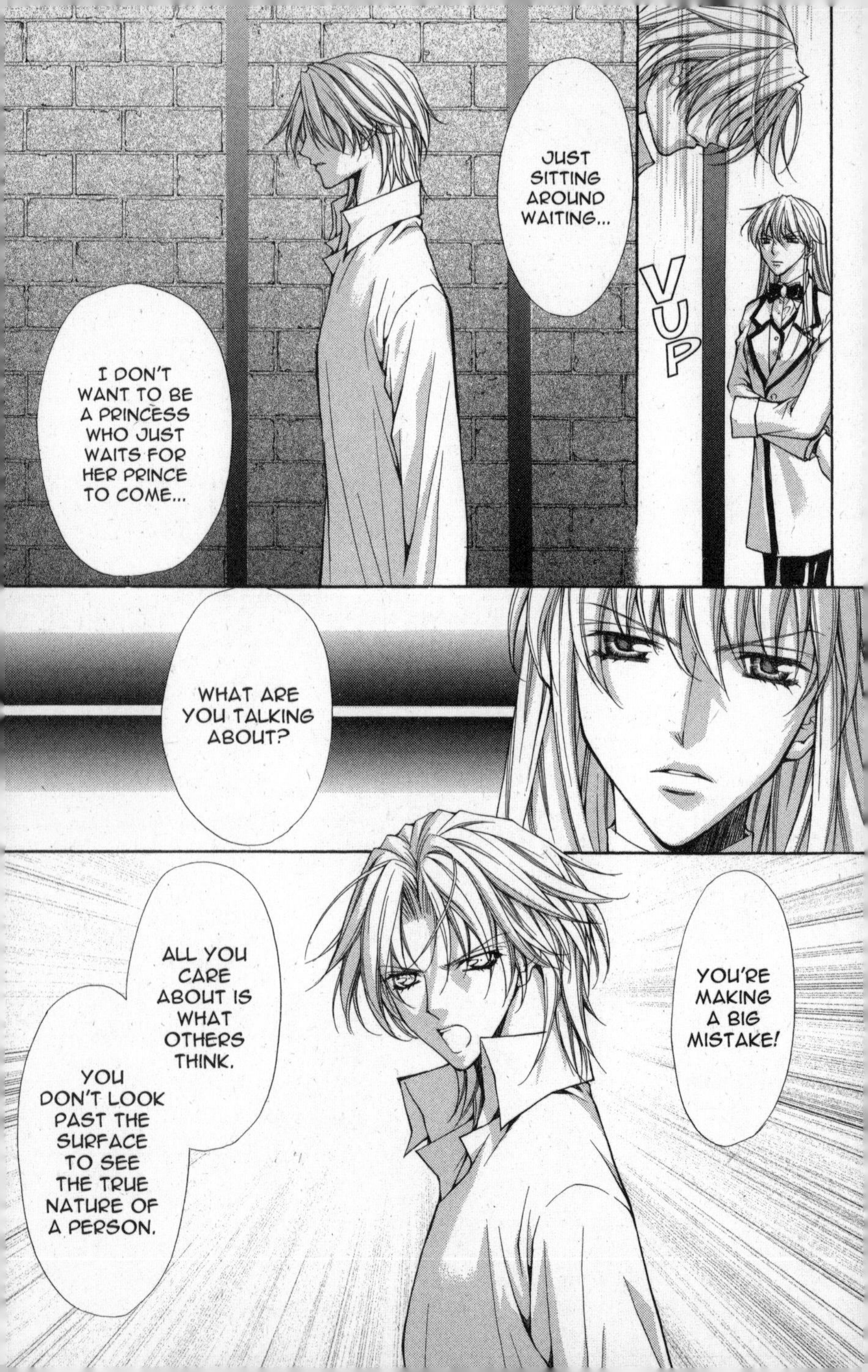
VUP
JUST SITTING AROUND WAITING...
I DON'T WANT TO BE A PRINCESS WHO JUST WAITS FOR HER PRINCE TO COME...
WHAT ARE YOU TALKING ABOUT?
YOU'RE MAKING A BIG MISTAKE!
ALL YOU CARE ABOUT IS WHAT OTHERS THINK.
YOU DON'T LOOK PAST THE SURFACE TO SEE THE TRUE NATURE OF A PERSON.

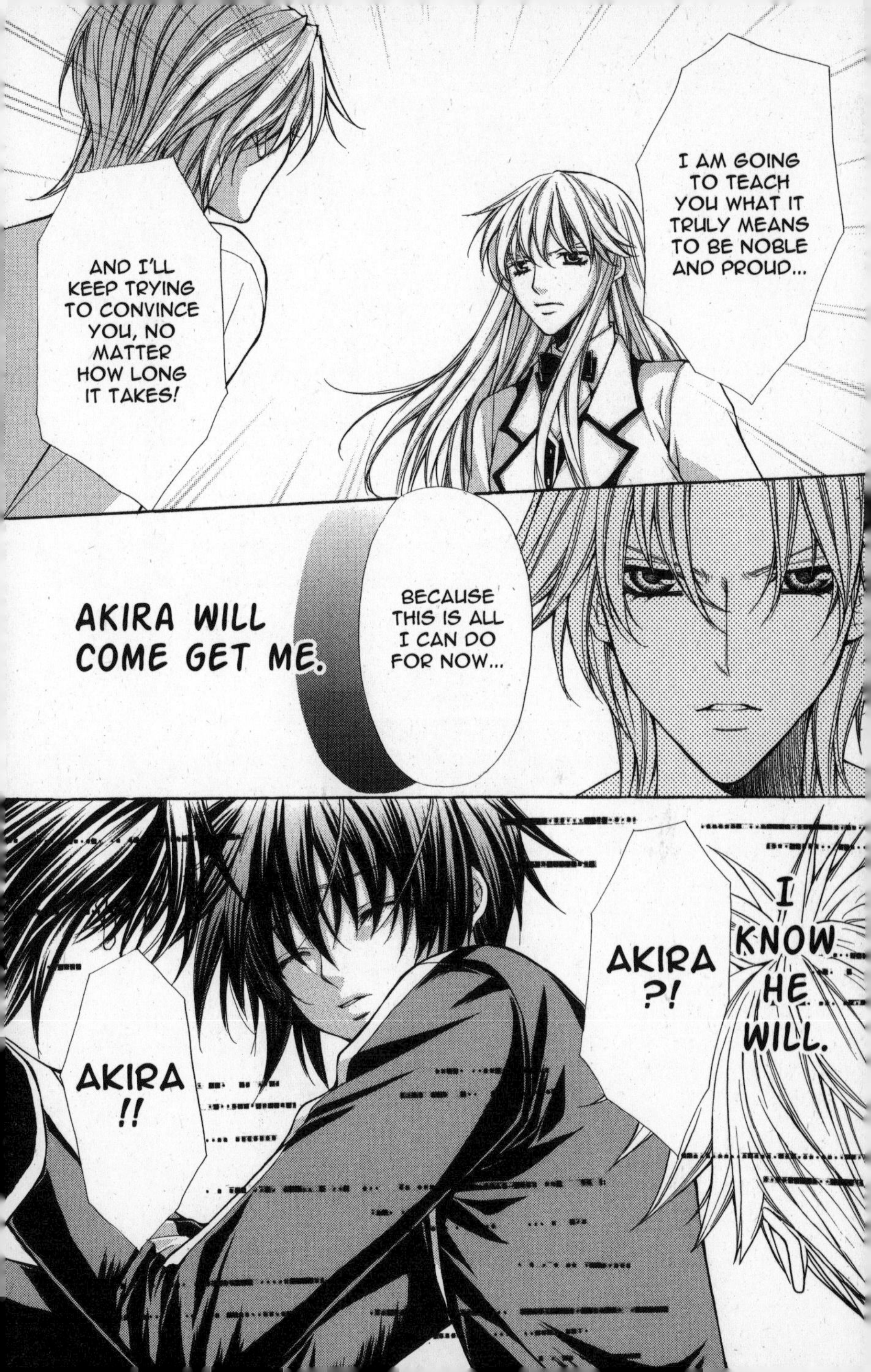
I AM GOING TO TEACH YOU WHAT IT TRULY MEANS TO BE NOBLE AND PROUD...
AND I'LL KEEP TRYING TO CONVINCE YOU, NO MATTER HOW LONG IT TAKES!
BECAUSE THIS IS ALL I CAN DO FOR NOW...
AKIRA WILL COME GET ME.
I KNOW HE WILL.
AKIRA?!
AKIRA!!

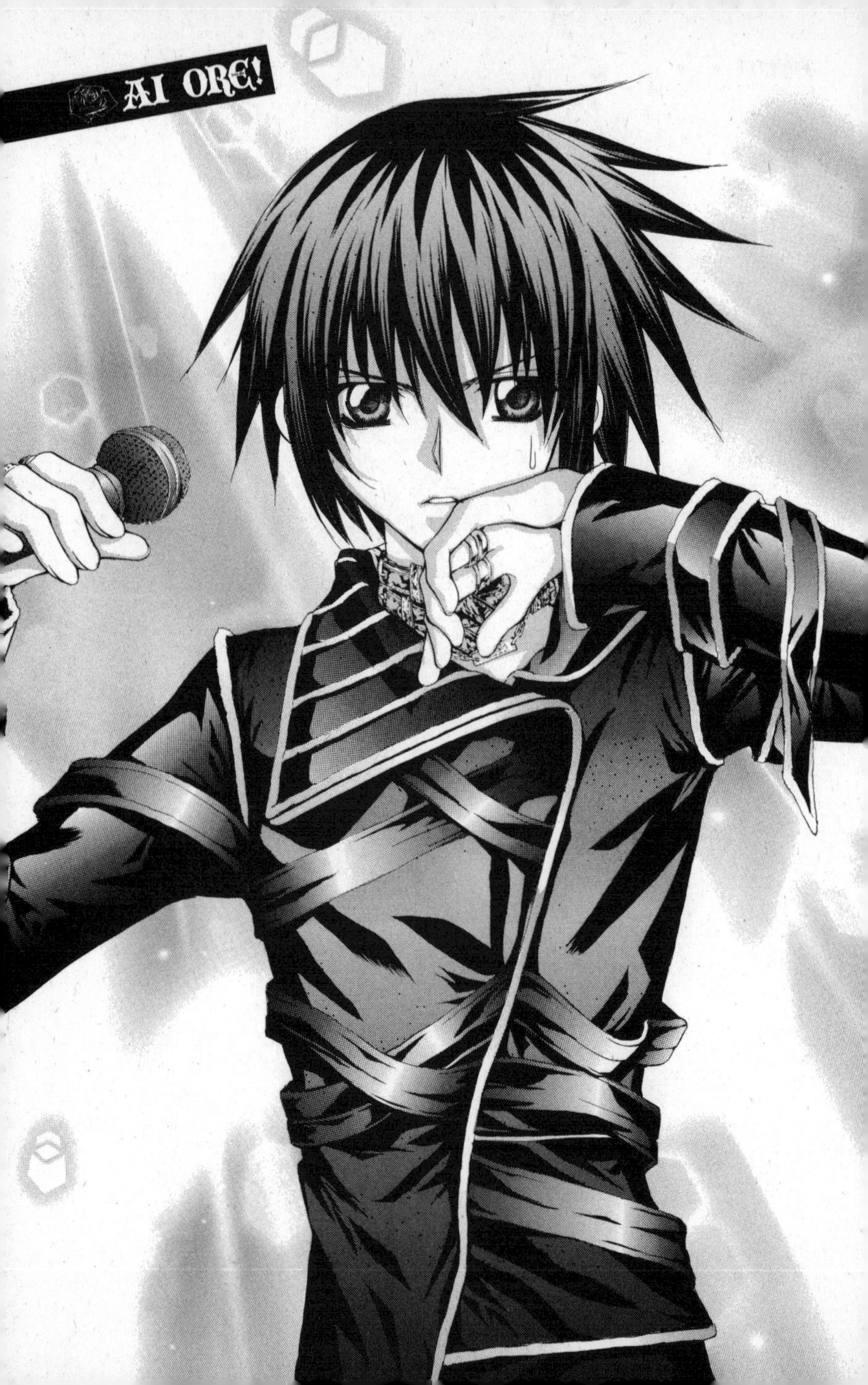
AI ORE!

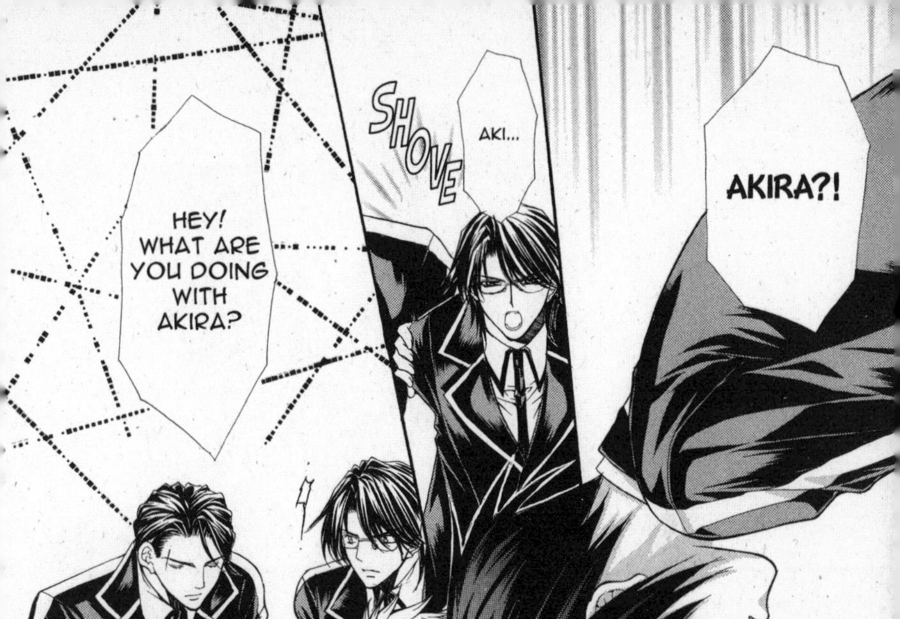
AKIRA?!
AKI...
SHOVE
HEY! WHAT ARE YOU DOING WITH AKIRA?
AKIRA!!

About Mizuki

I drew her with more manliness! And I added more tsundere* qualities!!
Mizuki is a female character I really respect. I want to continue making her a lot cooler and more of a lecher.
Well... I want to make every character a lecher, but maybe the word "lecher" is misleading. I mean sexy. But I'm thinking of something much sexier than the usual kind of sexiness.
(I just made it even harder to understand.) But I want to make her cuter than anyone else on the inside. She is a girl, after all.
It's so frustrating because the Mizuki in my head is such a cool character, and my drawing skills can't convey it!

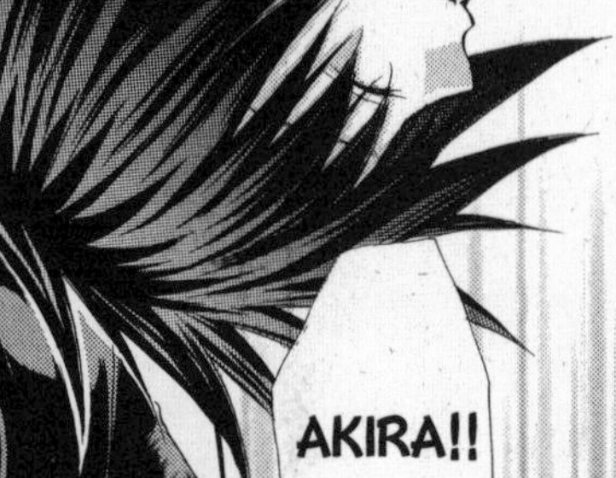
Hmph!! Idiot!

*Tsundere characters are prickly and standoffish at first, but then they become loving and devoted over time.

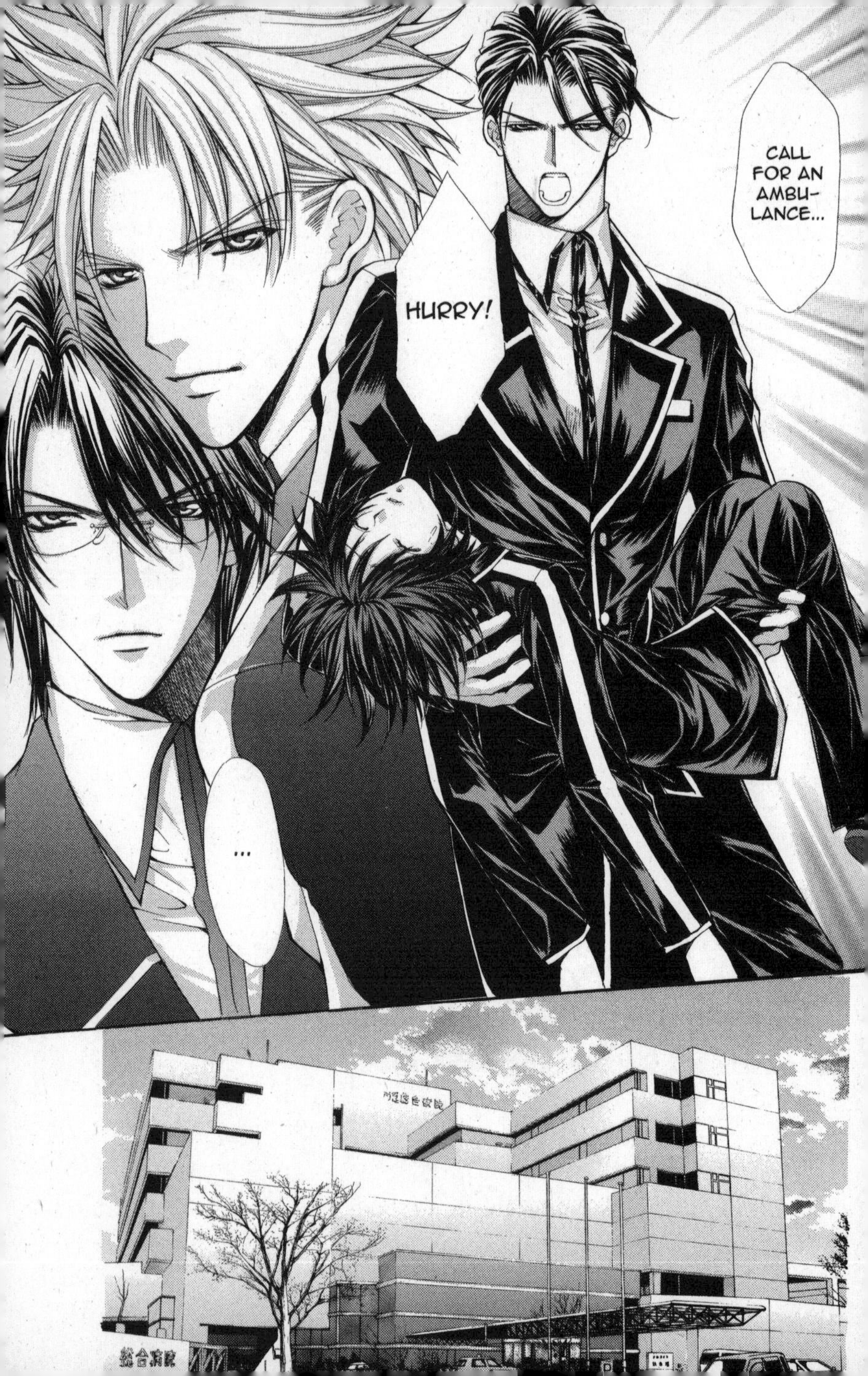
CALL FOR AN AMBULANCE...
HURRY!
...

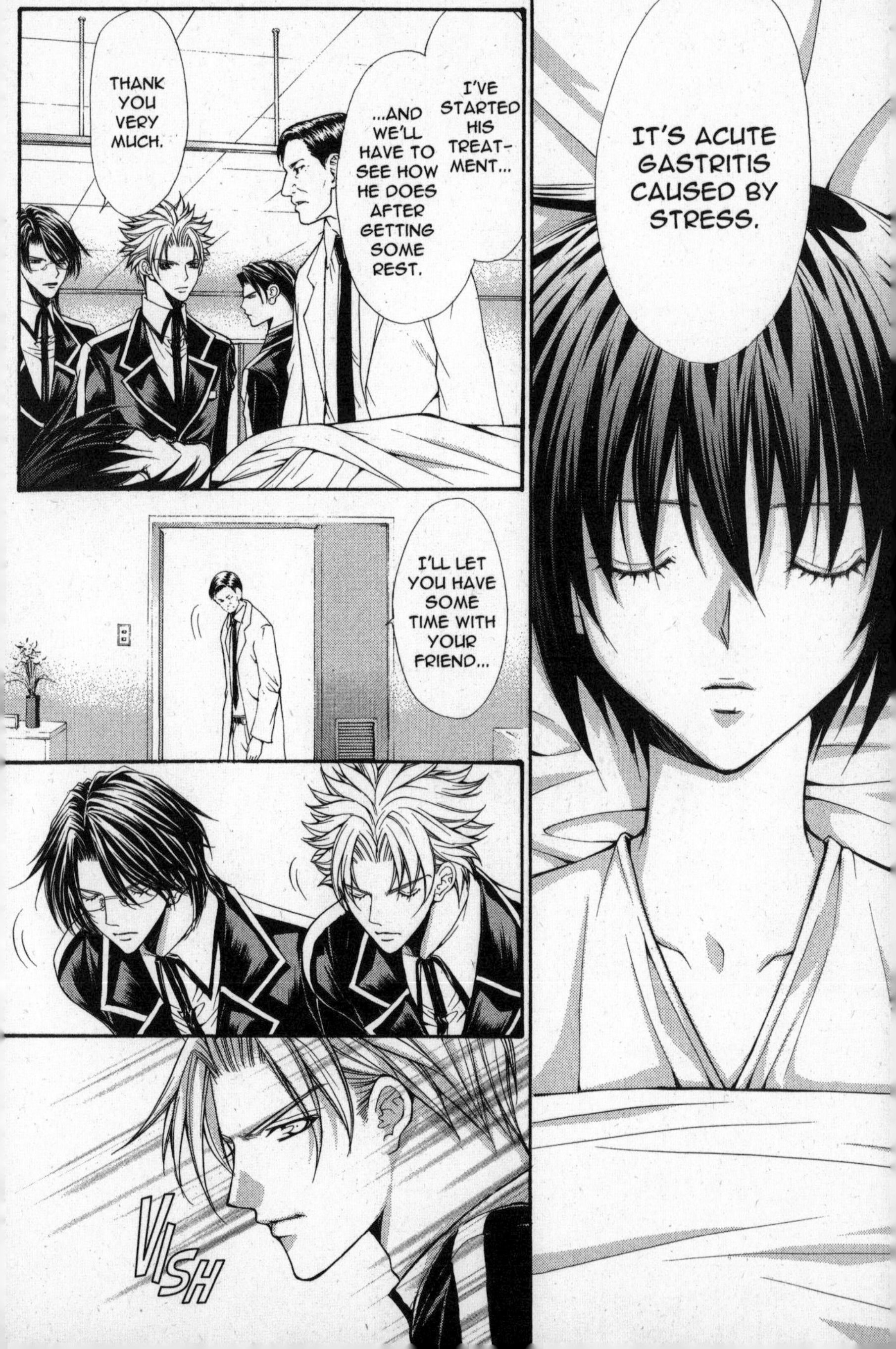
IT'S ACUTE GASTRITIS CAUSED BY STRESS.
I'VE STARTED HIS TREATMENT...
...AND WE'LL HAVE TO SEE HOW HE DOES AFTER GETTING SOME REST.
THANK YOU VERY MUCH.
I'LL LET YOU HAVE SOME TIME WITH YOUR FRIEND...
VISH

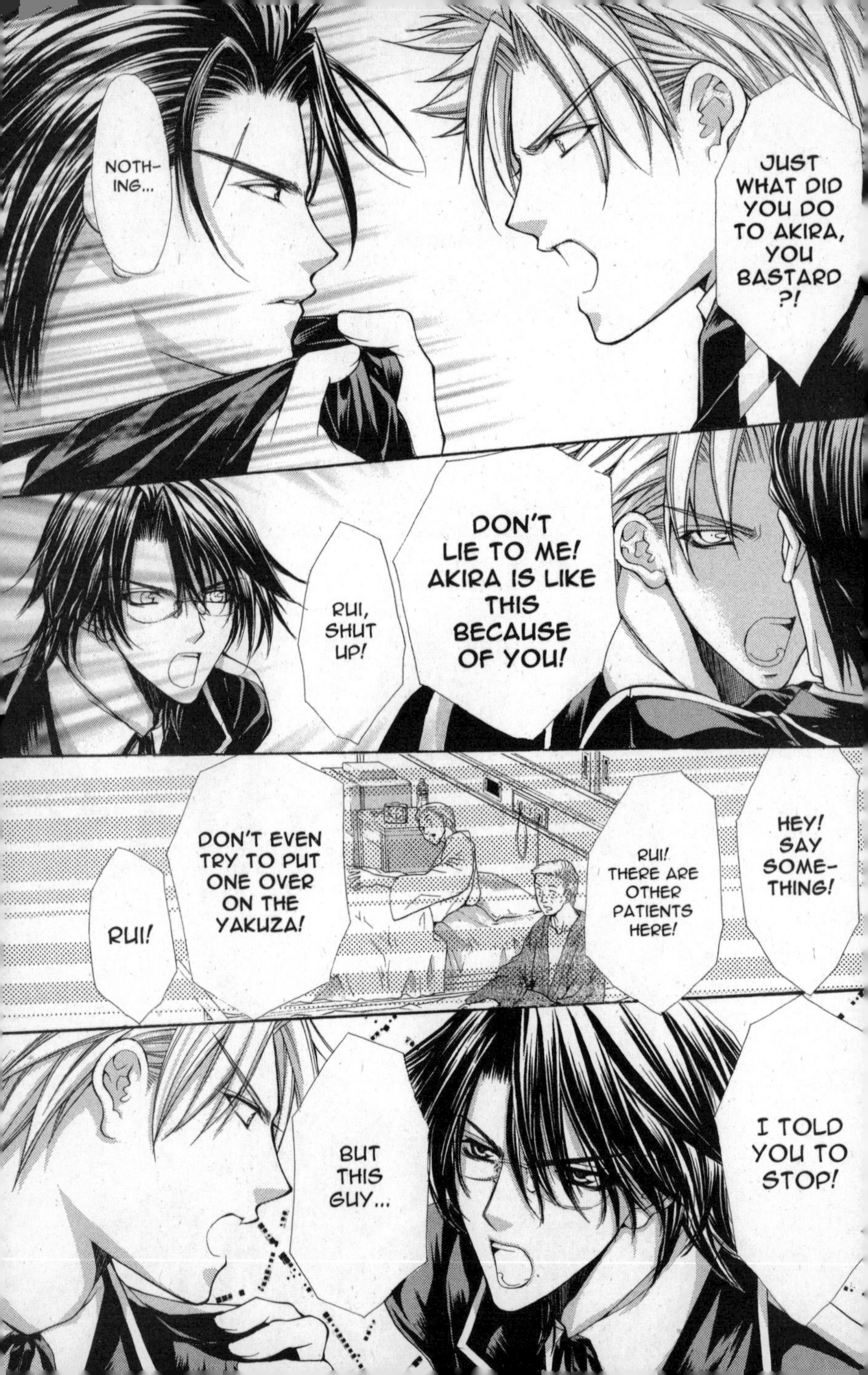
JUST WHAT DID YOU DO TO AKIRA, YOU BASTARD?!
NOTHING...
DON'T LIE TO ME! AKIRA IS LIKE THIS BECAUSE OF YOU!
RUI, SHUT UP!
HEY! SAY SOMETHING!
RUI! THERE ARE OTHER PATIENTS HERE!
DON'T EVEN TRY TO PUT ONE OVER ON THE YAKUZA!
RUI!
I TOLD YOU TO STOP!
BUT THIS GUY...

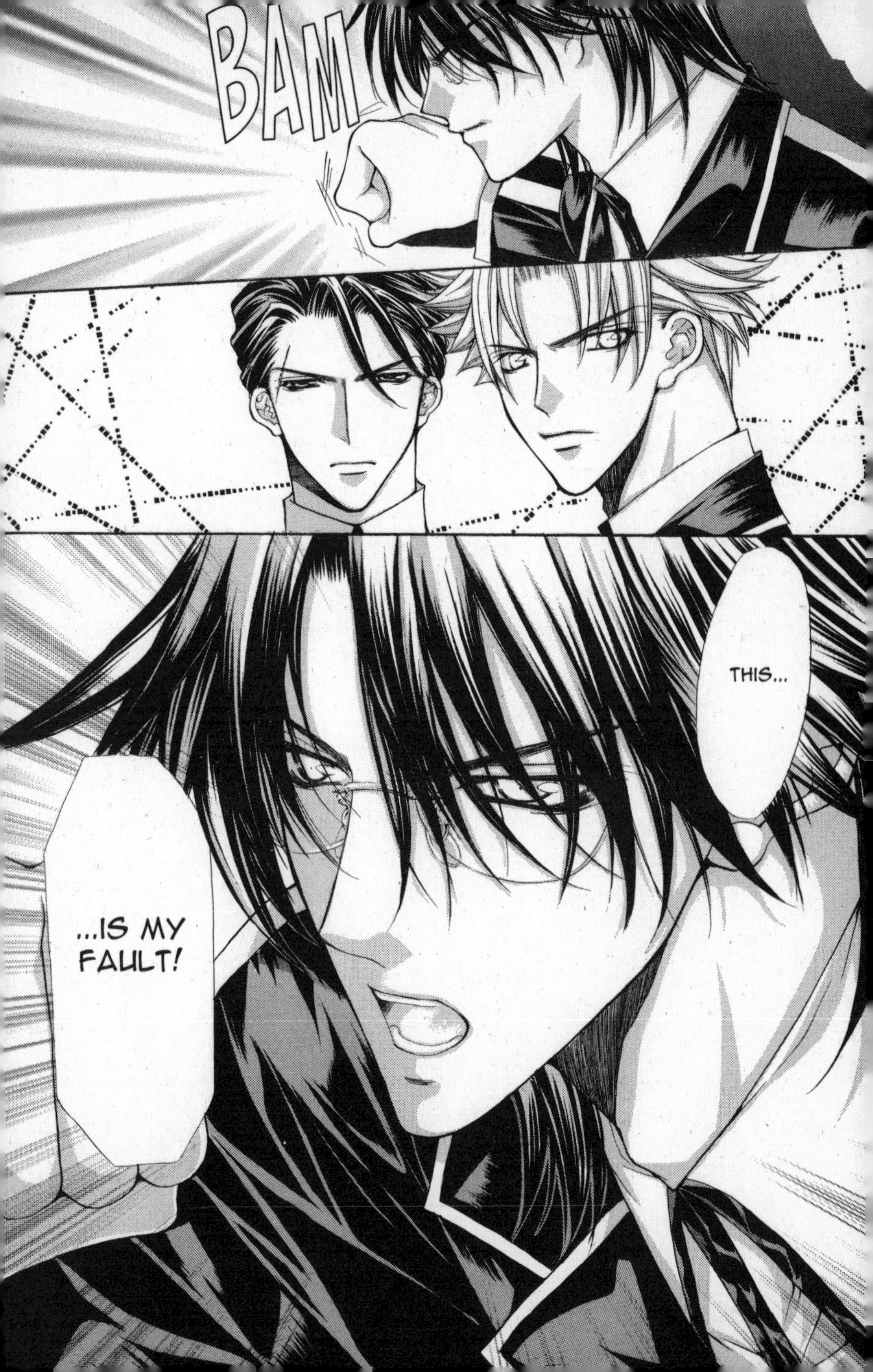
BAM
THIS...
...IS MY FAULT!

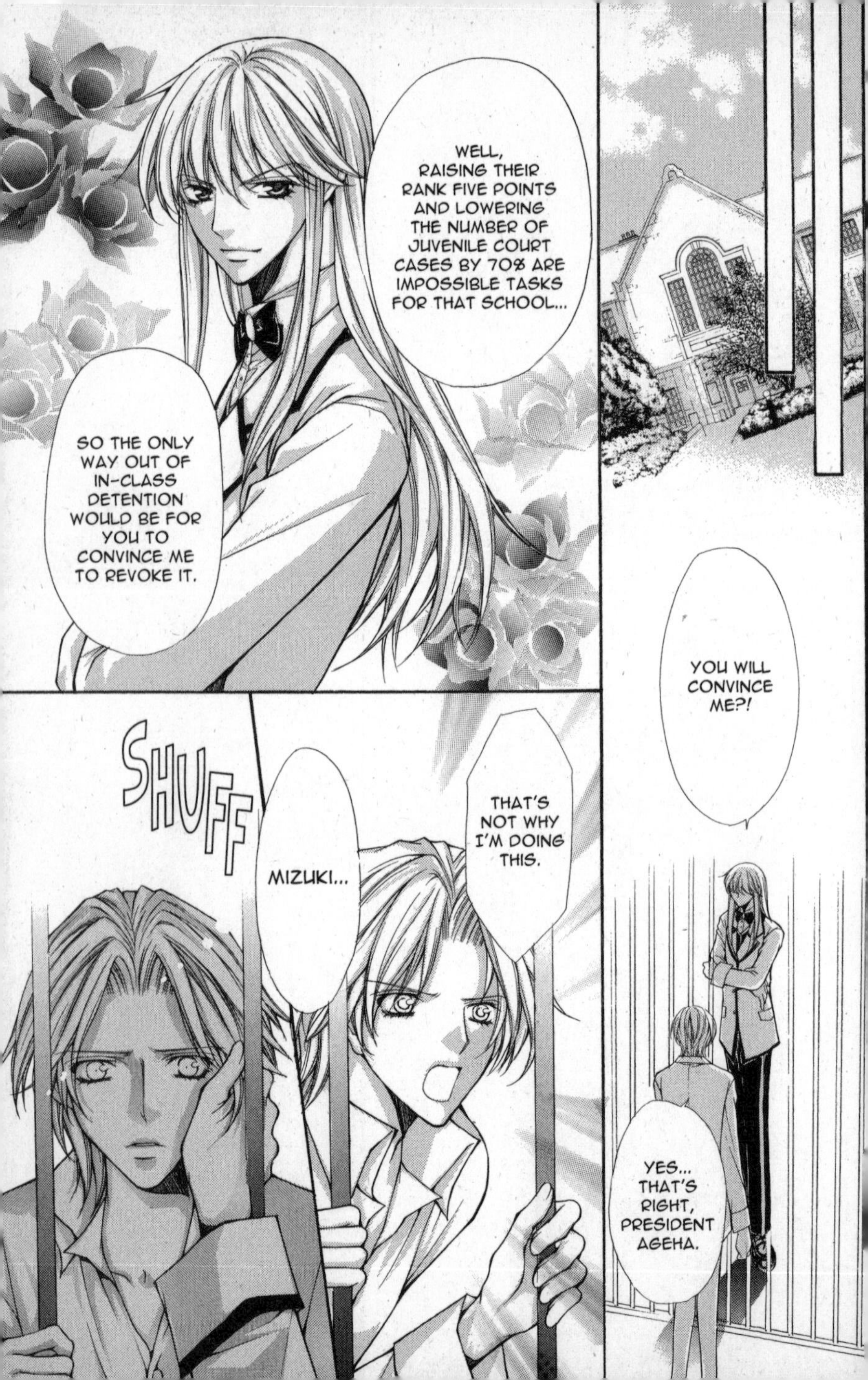
YOU WILL CONVINCE ME?!
YES... THAT'S RIGHT, PRESIDENT AGEHA.
WELL, RAISING THEIR RANK FIVE POINTS AND LOWERING THE NUMBER OF JUVENILE COURT CASES BY 70% ARE IMPOSSIBLE TASKS FOR THAT SCHOOL...
SO THE ONLY WAY OUT OF IN-CLASS DETENTION WOULD BE FOR YOU TO CONVINCE ME TO REVOKE IT.
SHUFF
THAT'S NOT WHY I'M DOING THIS.
MIZUKI...

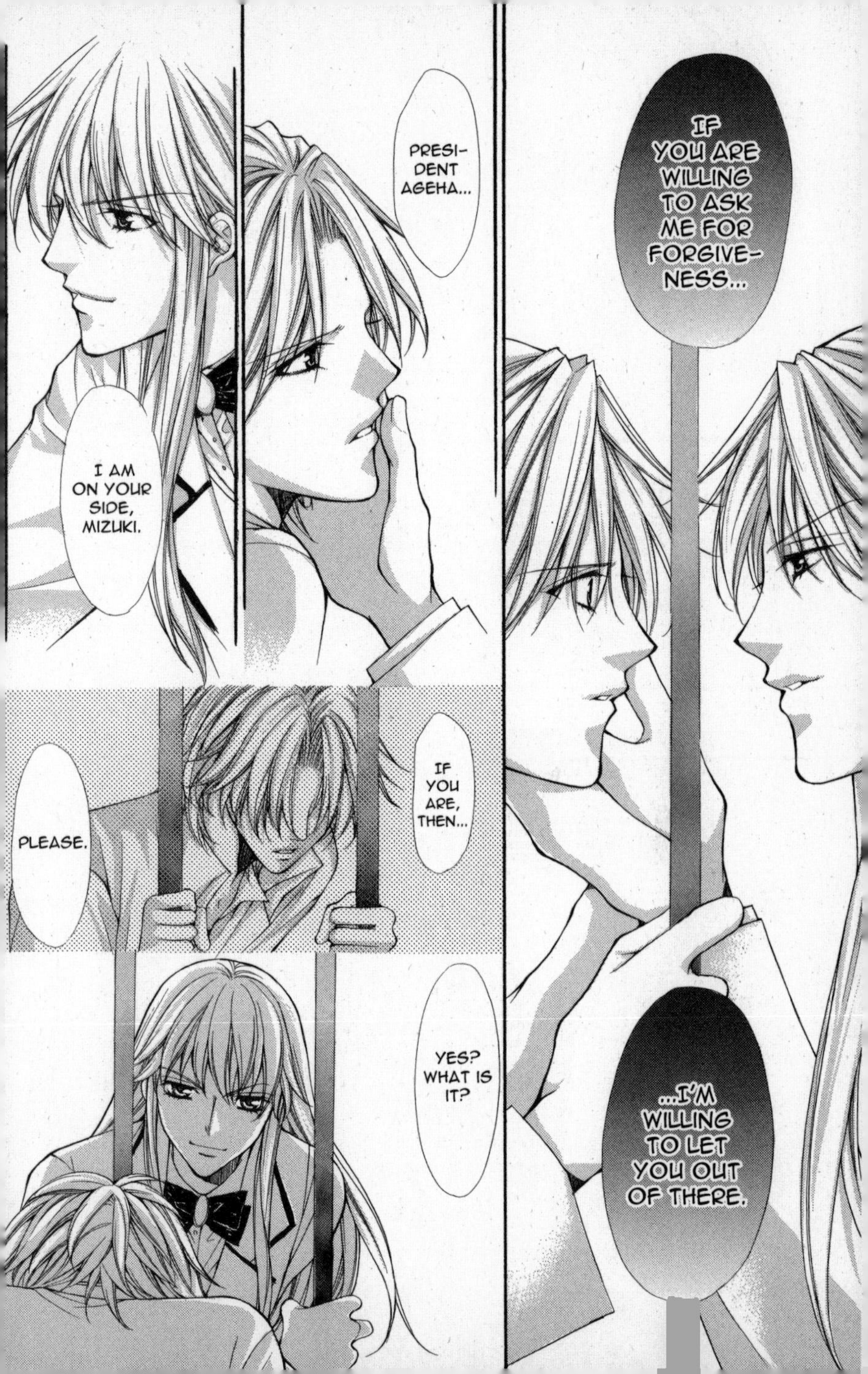
IF YOU ARE WILLING TO ASK ME FOR FORGIVE-NESS...
...I'M WILLING TO LET YOU OUT OF THERE.
PRESI-DENT AGEHA...
I AM ON YOUR SIDE, MIZUKI.
IF YOU ARE, THEN...
PLEASE.
YES? WHAT IS IT?

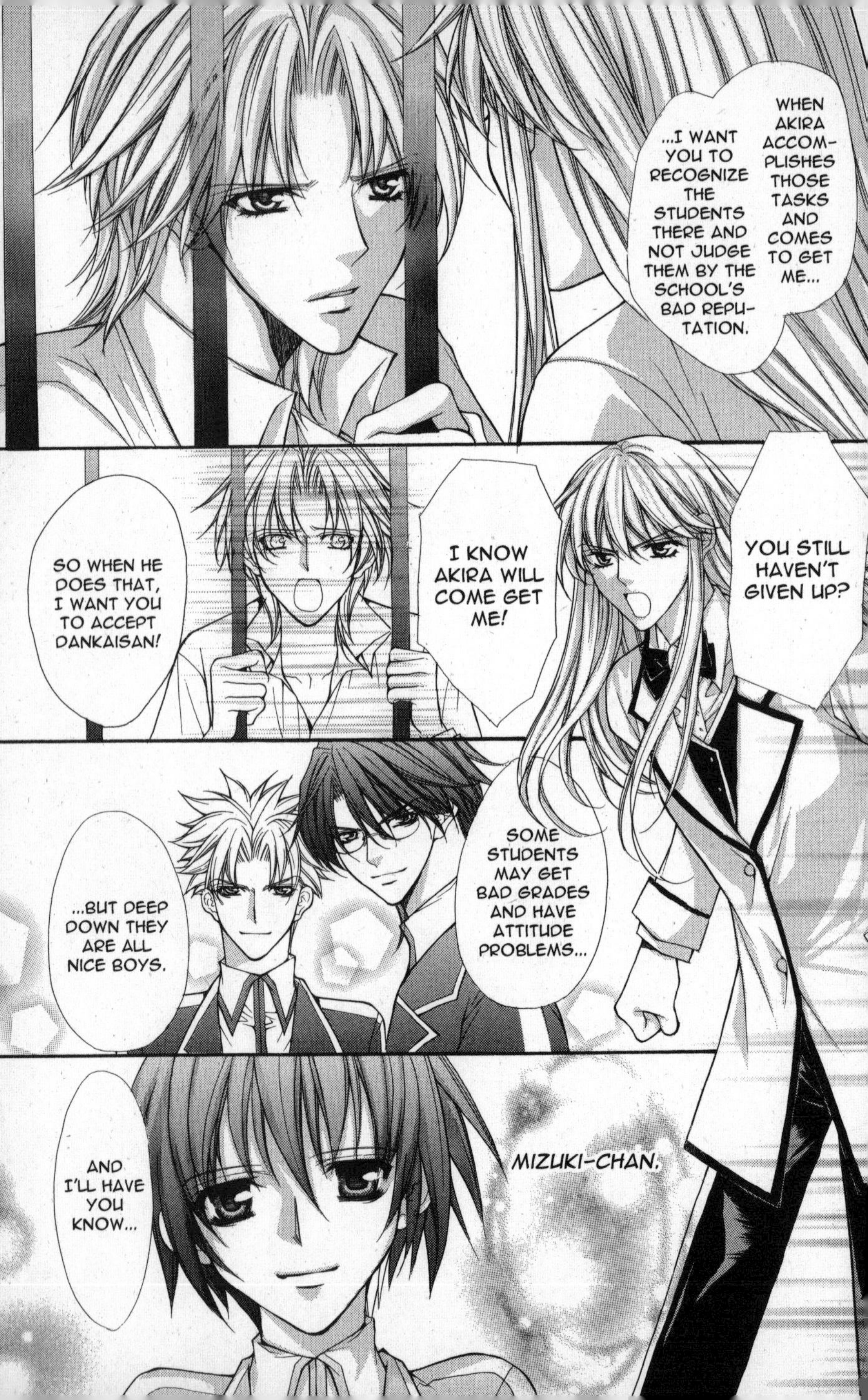
WHEN AKIRA ACCOMPLISHES THOSE TASKS AND COMES TO GET ME...
...I WANT YOU TO RECOGNIZE THE STUDENTS THERE AND NOT JUDGE THEM BY THE SCHOOL'S BAD REPUTATION.
YOU STILL HAVEN'T GIVEN UP?
I KNOW AKIRA WILL COME GET ME!
SO WHEN HE DOES THAT, I WANT YOU TO ACCEPT DANKAISAN!
SOME STUDENTS MAY GET BAD GRADES AND HAVE ATTITUDE PROBLEMS...
...BUT DEEP DOWN THEY ARE ALL NICE BOYS.
MIZUKI-CHAN.
AND I'LL HAVE YOU KNOW...

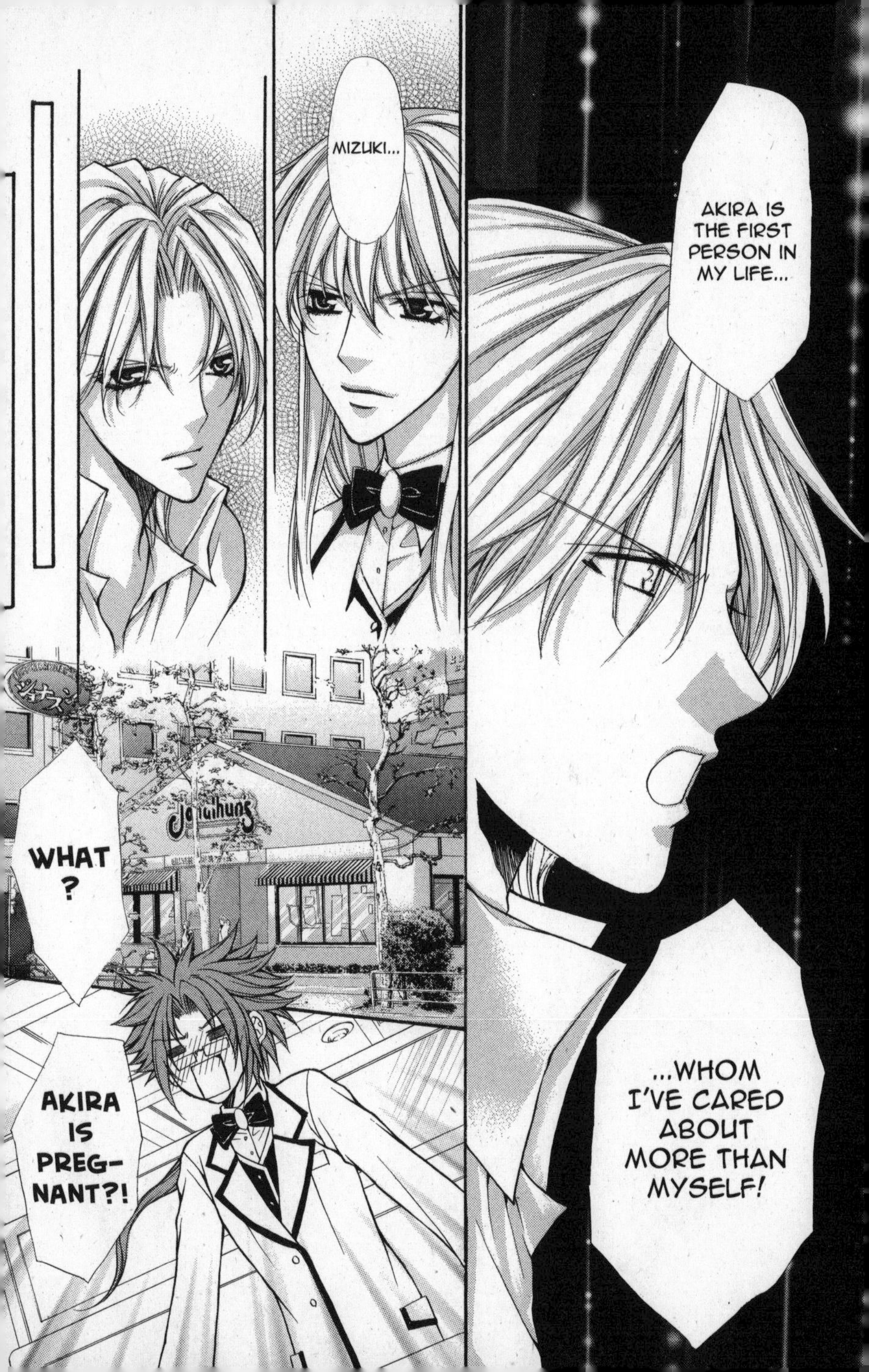
AKIRA IS THE FIRST PERSON IN MY LIFE...
...WHOM I'VE CARED ABOUT MORE THAN MYSELF!
MIZUKI...
WHAT?
AKIRA IS PREGNANT?!

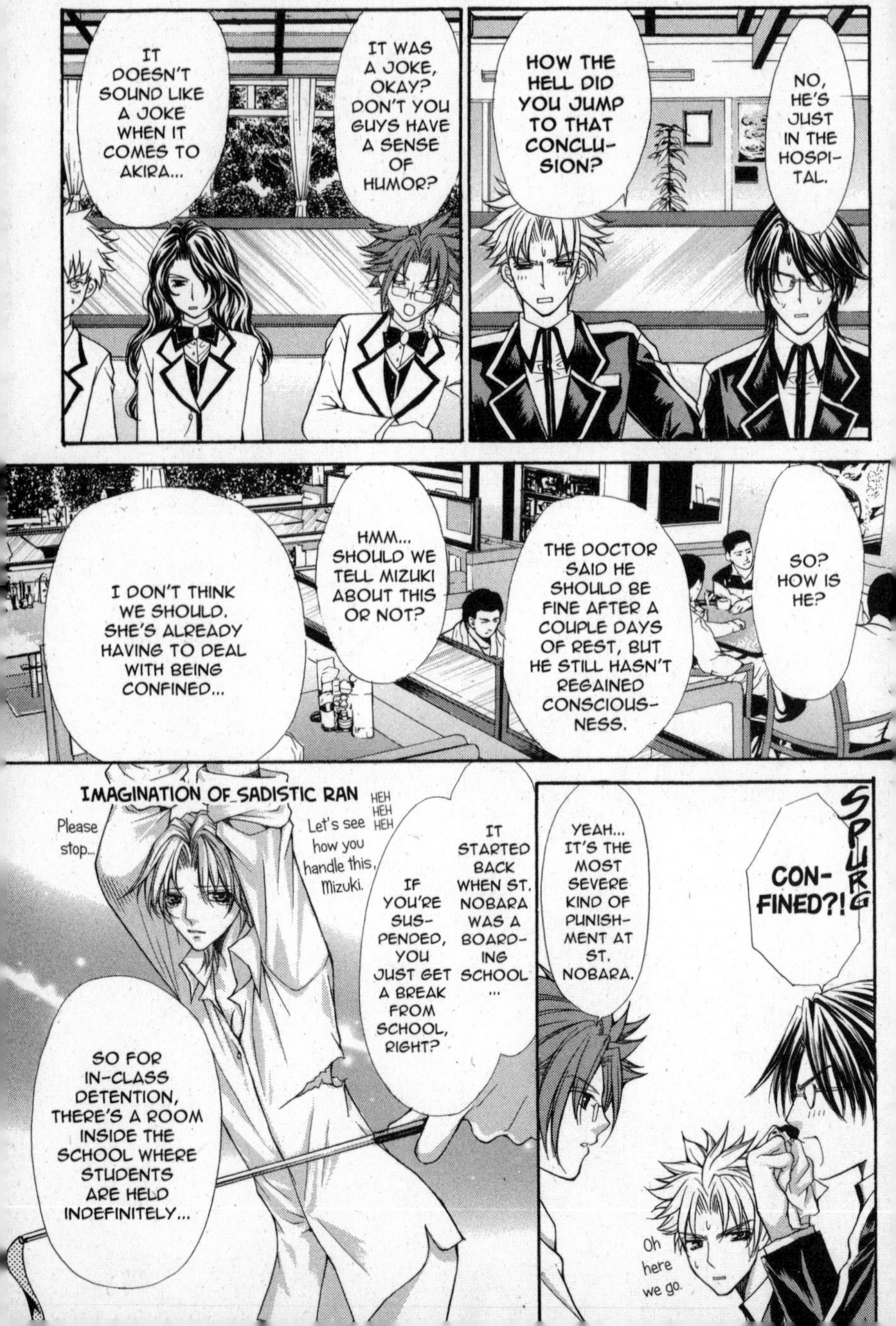
NO, HE'S JUST IN THE HOSPITAL.
HOW THE HELL DID YOU JUMP TO THAT CONCLUSION?
IT WAS A JOKE, OKAY? DON'T YOU GUYS HAVE A SENSE OF HUMOR?
IT DOESN'T SOUND LIKE A JOKE WHEN IT COMES TO AKIRA...
SO? HOW IS HE?
THE DOCTOR SAID HE SHOULD BE FINE AFTER A COUPLE DAYS OF REST, BUT HE STILL HASN'T REGAINED CONSCIOUSNESS.
HMM... SHOULD WE TELL MIZUKI ABOUT THIS OR NOT?
I DON'T THINK WE SHOULD. SHE'S ALREADY HAVING TO DEAL WITH BEING CONFINED...
SPURG
CON-FINED?!
YEAH... IT'S THE MOST SEVERE KIND OF PUNISHMENT AT ST. NOBARA.
Oh here we go.
IT STARTED BACK WHEN ST. NOBARA WAS A BOARDING SCHOOL...
IF YOU'RE SUSPENDED, YOU JUST GET A BREAK FROM SCHOOL, RIGHT?
IMAGINATION OF SADISTIC RAN
HEH HEH HEH
Let's see how you handle this, Mizuki.
Please stop...
SO FOR IN-CLASS DETENTION, THERE'S A ROOM INSIDE THE SCHOOL WHERE STUDENTS ARE HELD INDEFINITELY...

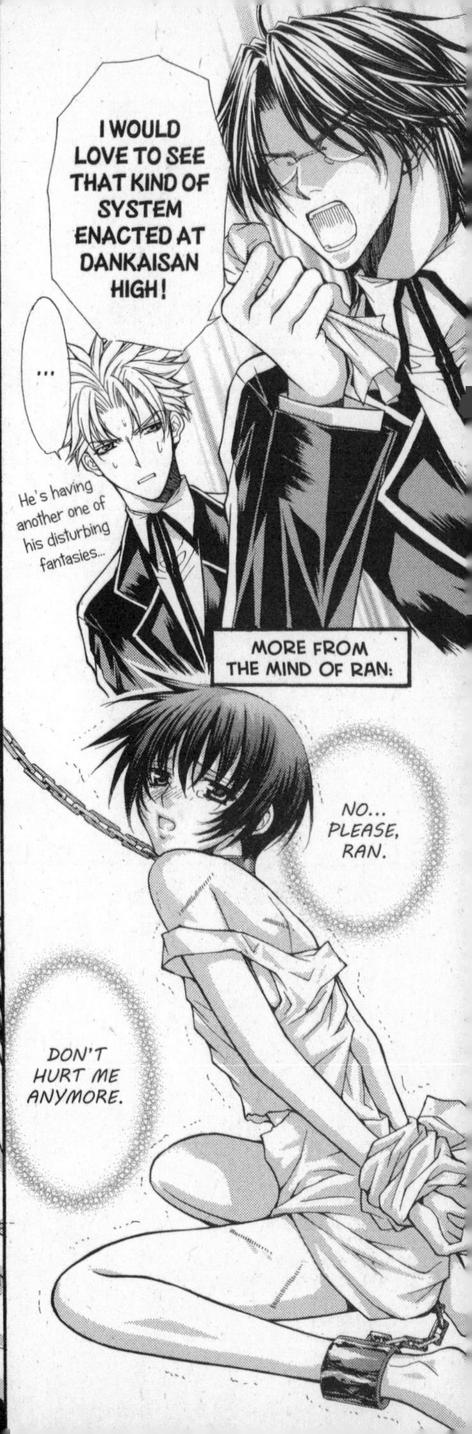
I WOULD LOVE TO SEE THAT KIND OF SYSTEM ENACTED AT DANKAISAN HIGH!
...
He's having another one of his disturbing fantasies...
MORE FROM THE MIND OF RAN:
NO... PLEASE, RAN.
DON'T HURT ME ANYMORE.

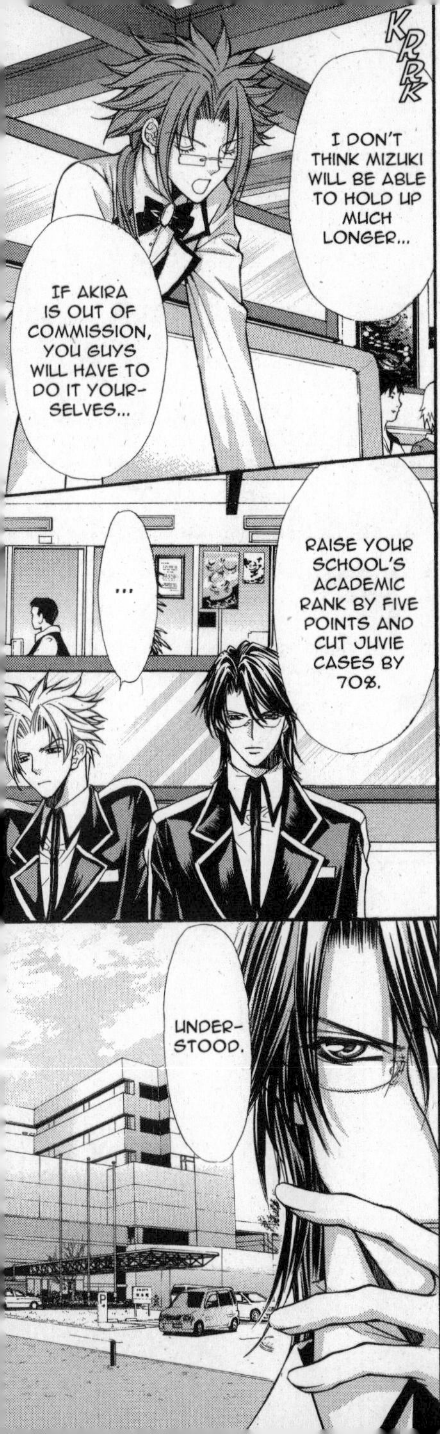
KRRK
I DON'T THINK MIZUKI WILL BE ABLE TO HOLD UP MUCH LONGER...
IF AKIRA IS OUT OF COMMISSION, YOU GUYS WILL HAVE TO DO IT YOUR-SELVES...
RAISE YOUR SCHOOL'S ACADEMIC RANK BY FIVE POINTS AND CUT JUVIE CASES BY 70%.
...
UNDER-STOOD.

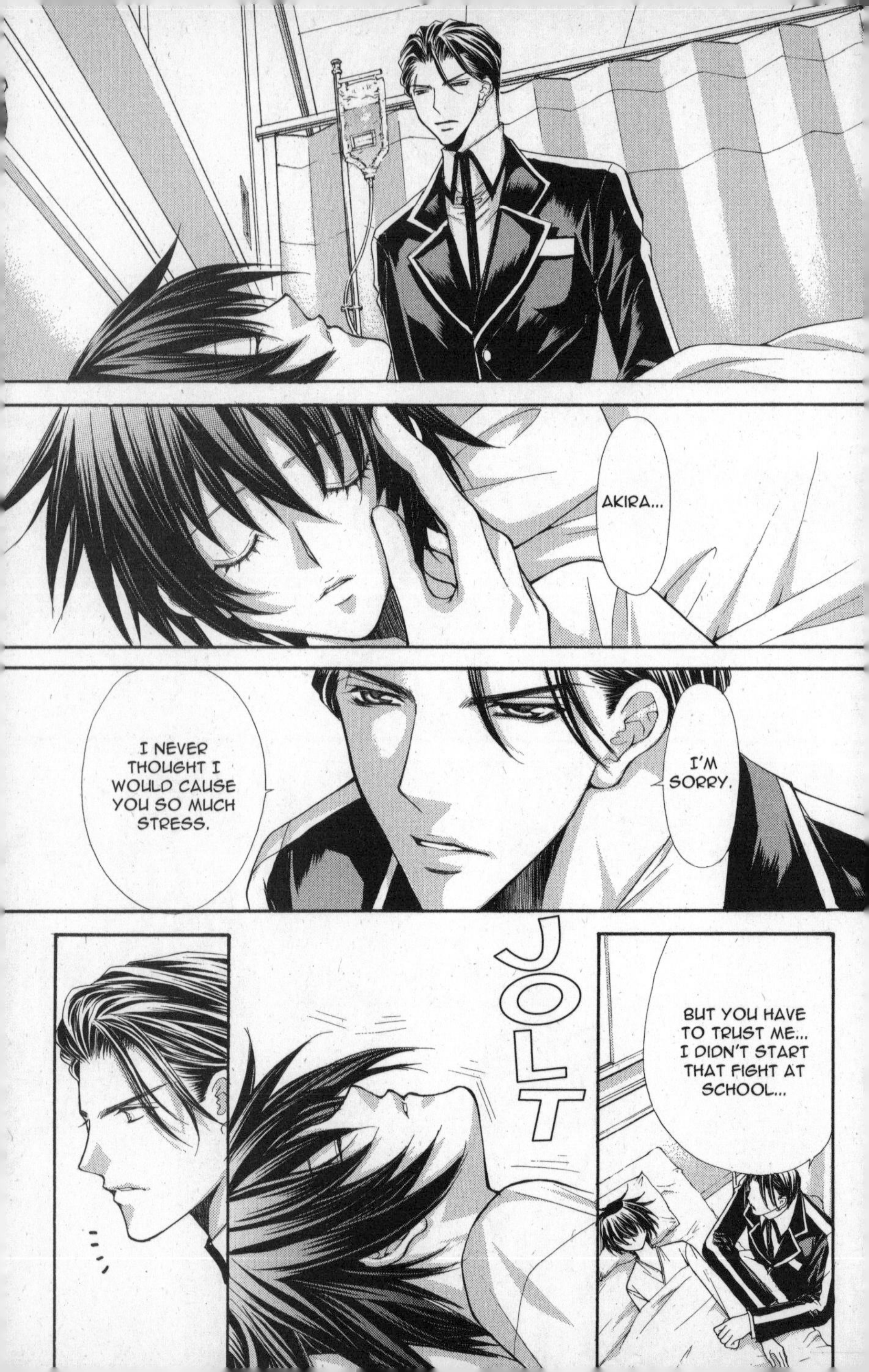
AKIRA...
I'M SORRY.
I NEVER THOUGHT I WOULD CAUSE YOU SO MUCH STRESS.
BUT YOU HAVE TO TRUST ME... I DIDN'T START THAT FIGHT AT SCHOOL...
JOLT

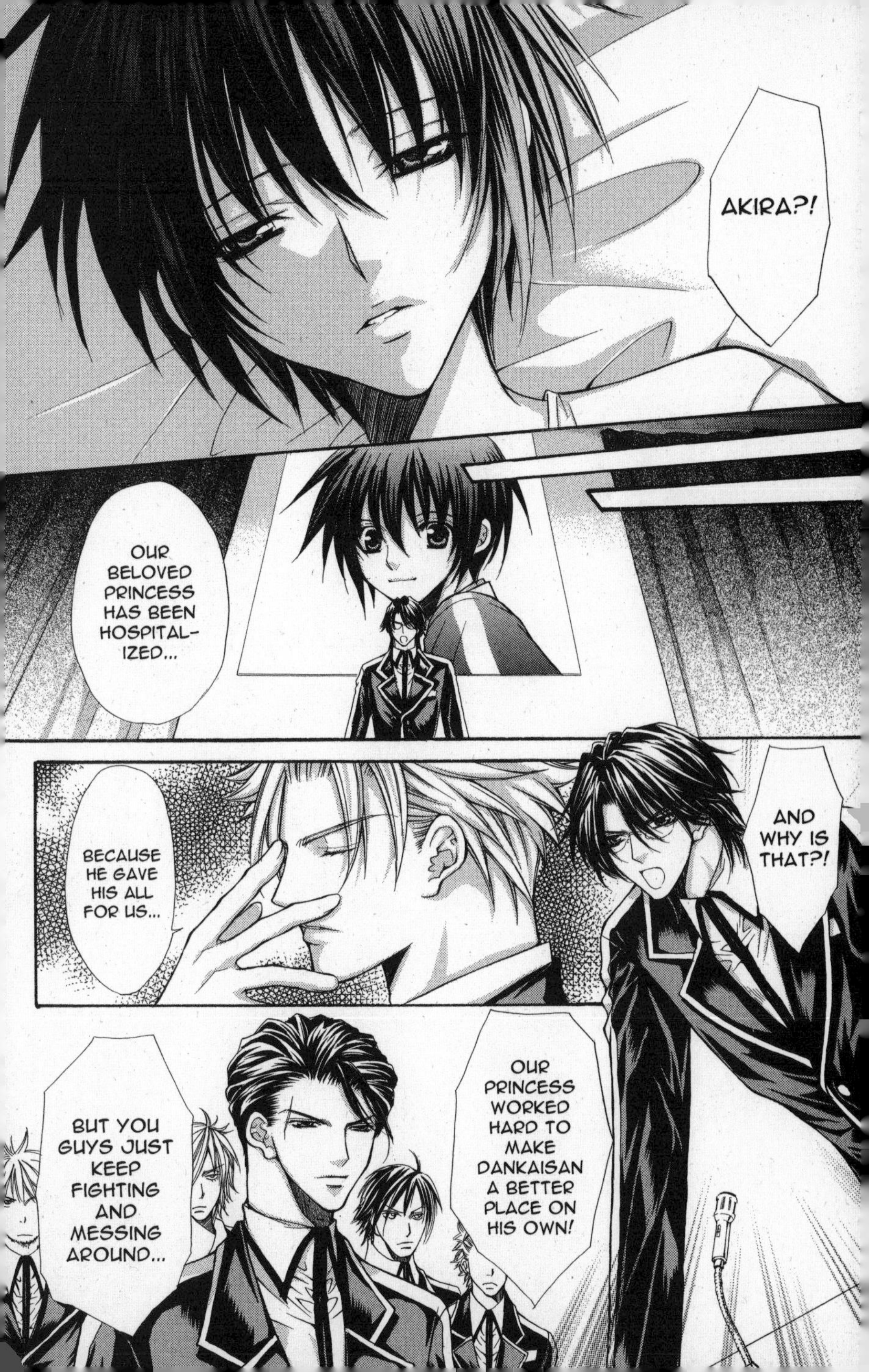
AKIRA?!
OUR BELOVED PRINCESS HAS BEEN HOSPITAL-IZED...
AND WHY IS THAT?!
BECAUSE HE GAVE HIS ALL FOR US...
OUR PRINCESS WORKED HARD TO MAKE DANKAISAN A BETTER PLACE ON HIS OWN!
BUT YOU GUYS JUST KEEP FIGHTING AND MESSING AROUND...

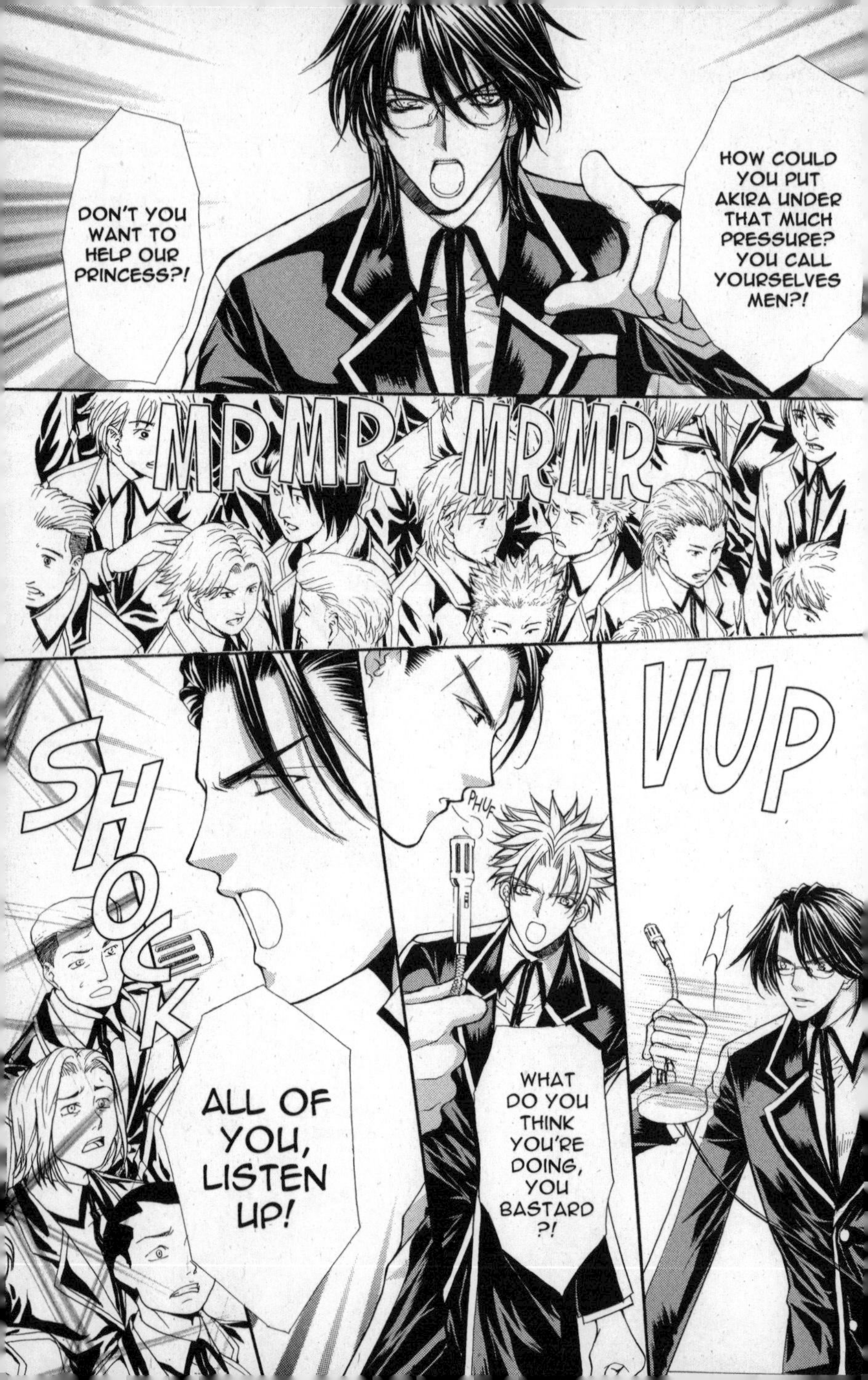
HOW COULD YOU PUT AKIRA UNDER THAT MUCH PRESSURE? YOU CALL YOURSELVES MEN?!
DON'T YOU WANT TO HELP OUR PRINCESS?!
MRMR
MRMR
VUP
PHUF
WHAT DO YOU THINK YOU'RE DOING, YOU BASTARD?!
SHOCK
ALL OF YOU, LISTEN UP!

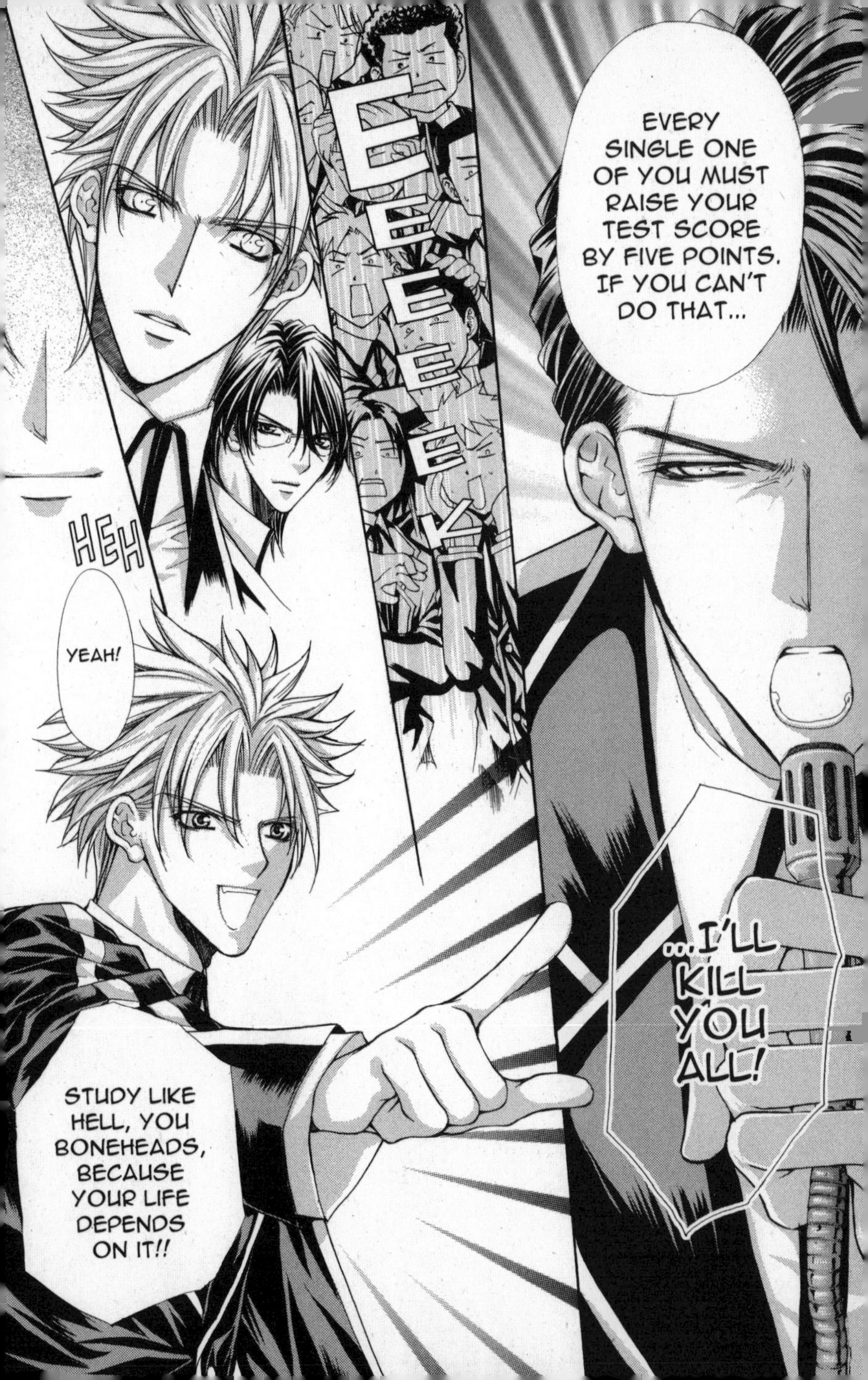
EVERY SINGLE ONE OF YOU MUST RAISE YOUR TEST SCORE BY FIVE POINTS. IF YOU CAN'T DO THAT...
...I'LL KILL YOU ALL!
EEEEEK
HEH
YEAH!
STUDY LIKE HELL, YOU BONEHEADS, BECAUSE YOUR LIFE DEPENDS ON IT!!

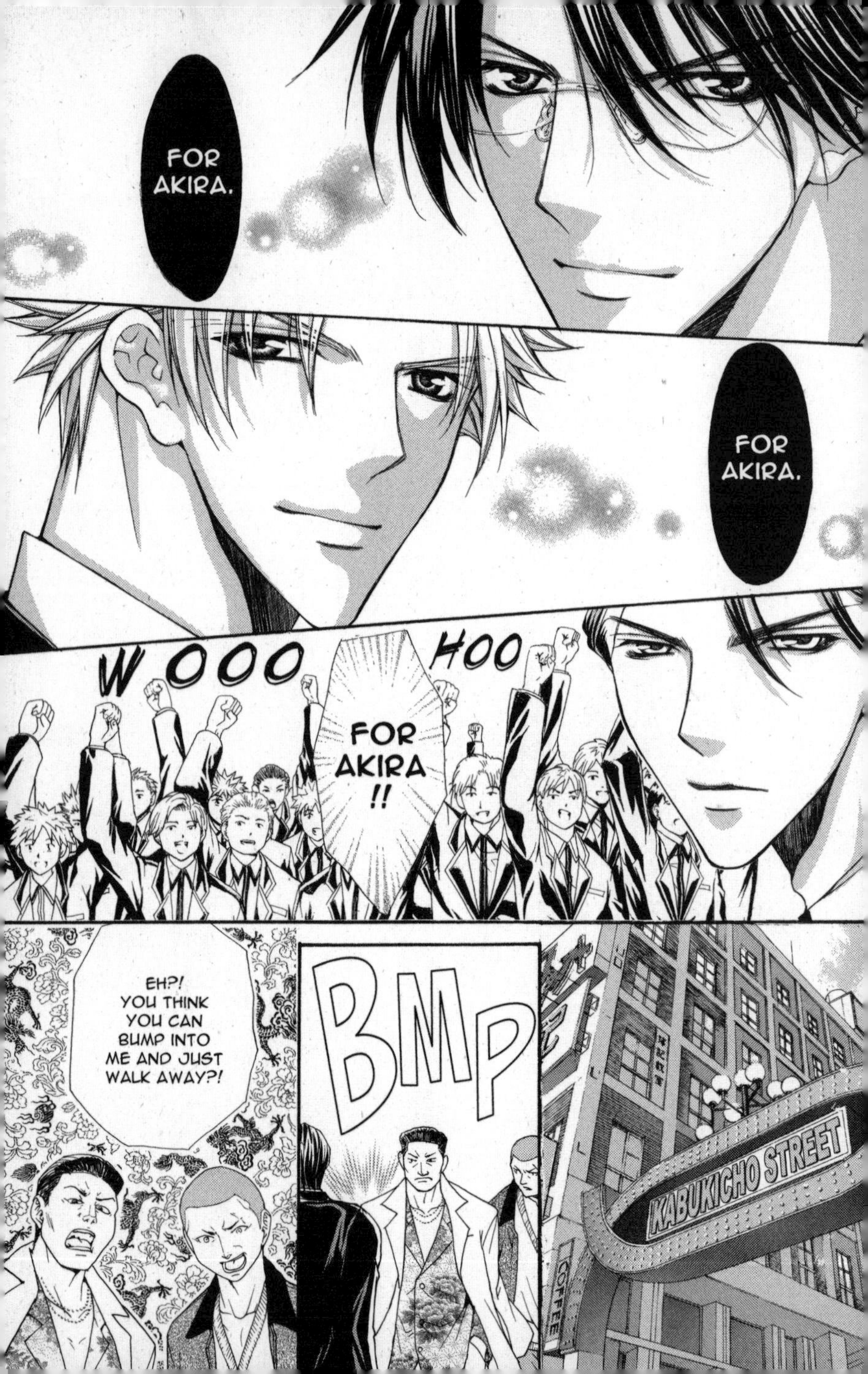
FOR AKIRA.
FOR AKIRA.
WOOO HOO
FOR AKIRA !!
KABUKICHO STREET
COFFEE
BMP
EH?! YOU THINK YOU CAN BUMP INTO ME AND JUST WALK AWAY?!

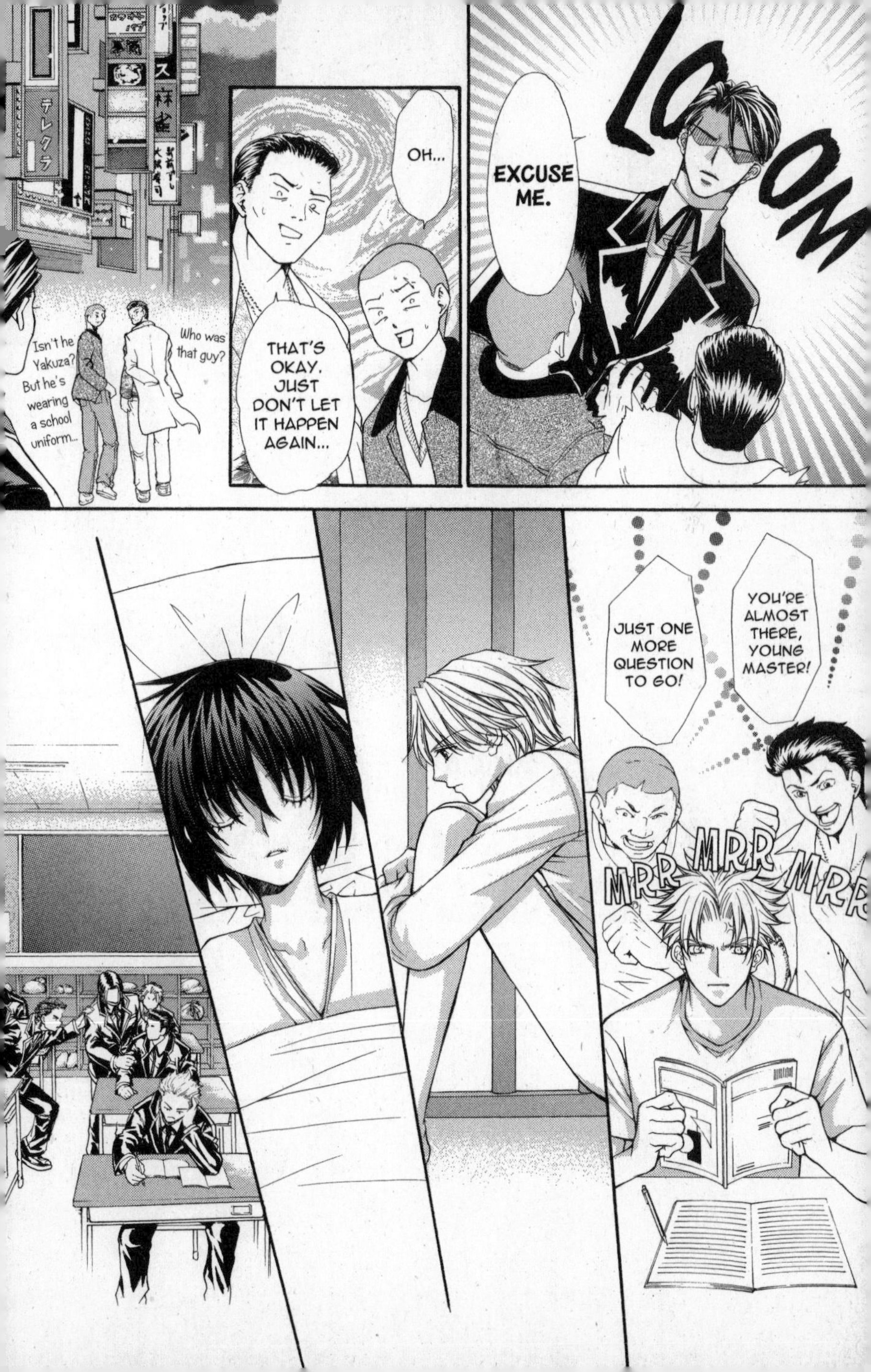
LOOM
EXCUSE ME.
OH...
THAT'S OKAY. JUST DON'T LET IT HAPPEN AGAIN...
Who was that guy?
Isn't he Yakuza? But he's wearing a school uniform...
YOU'RE ALMOST THERE, YOUNG MASTER!
JUST ONE MORE QUESTION TO GO!
MRR
MRR
MRR

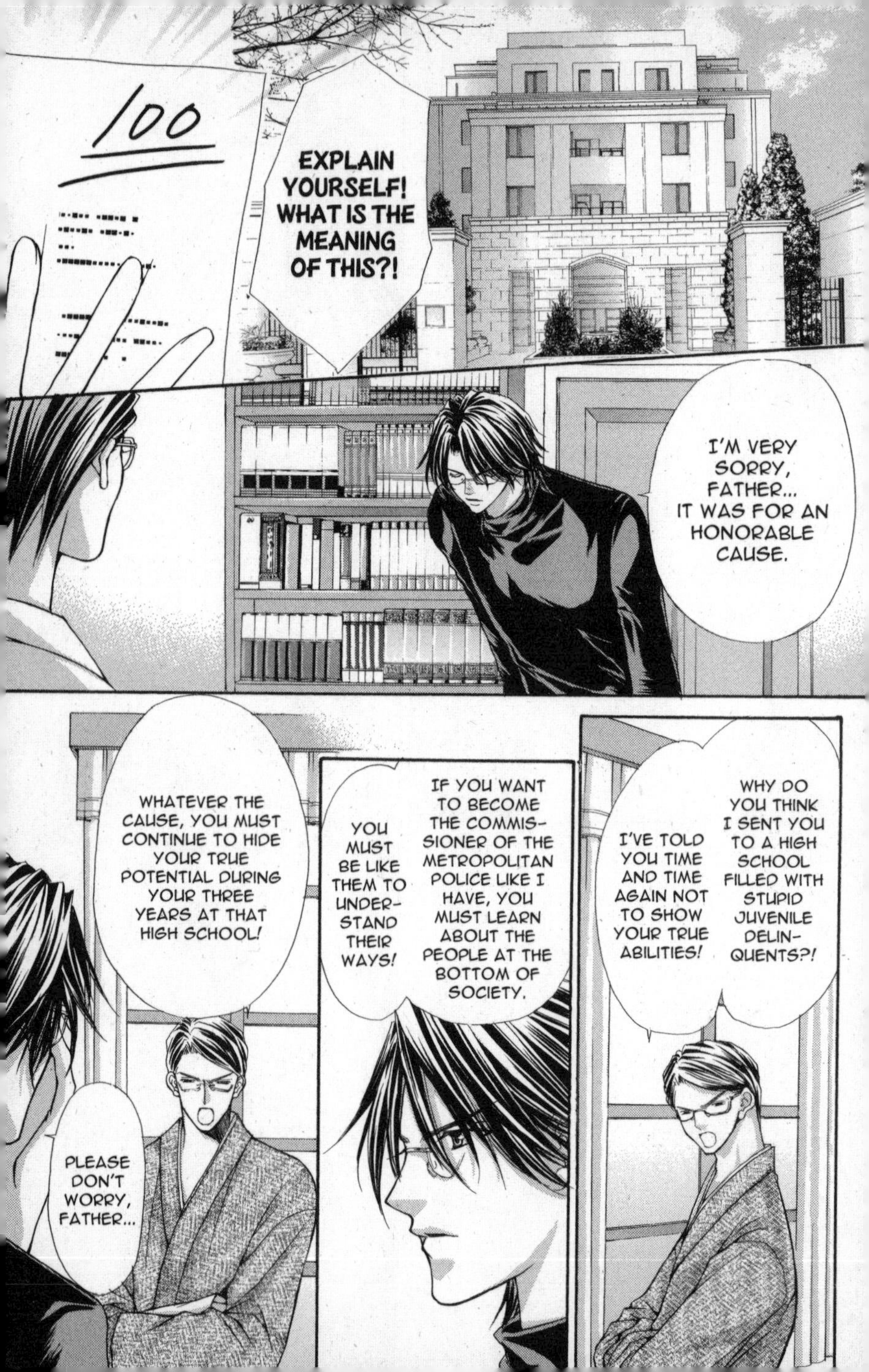
EXPLAIN YOURSELF! WHAT IS THE MEANING OF THIS?!
100
I'M VERY SORRY, FATHER... IT WAS FOR AN HONORABLE CAUSE.
WHY DO YOU THINK I SENT YOU TO A HIGH SCHOOL FILLED WITH STUPID JUVENILE DELIN-QUENTS?!
I'VE TOLD YOU TIME AND TIME AGAIN NOT TO SHOW YOUR TRUE ABILITIES!
IF YOU WANT TO BECOME THE COMMIS-SIONER OF THE METROPOLITAN POLICE LIKE I HAVE, YOU MUST LEARN ABOUT THE PEOPLE AT THE BOTTOM OF SOCIETY.
YOU MUST BE LIKE THEM TO UNDER-STAND THEIR WAYS!
WHATEVER THE CAUSE, YOU MUST CONTINUE TO HIDE YOUR TRUE POTENTIAL DURING YOUR THREE YEARS AT THAT HIGH SCHOOL!
PLEASE DON'T WORRY, FATHER...

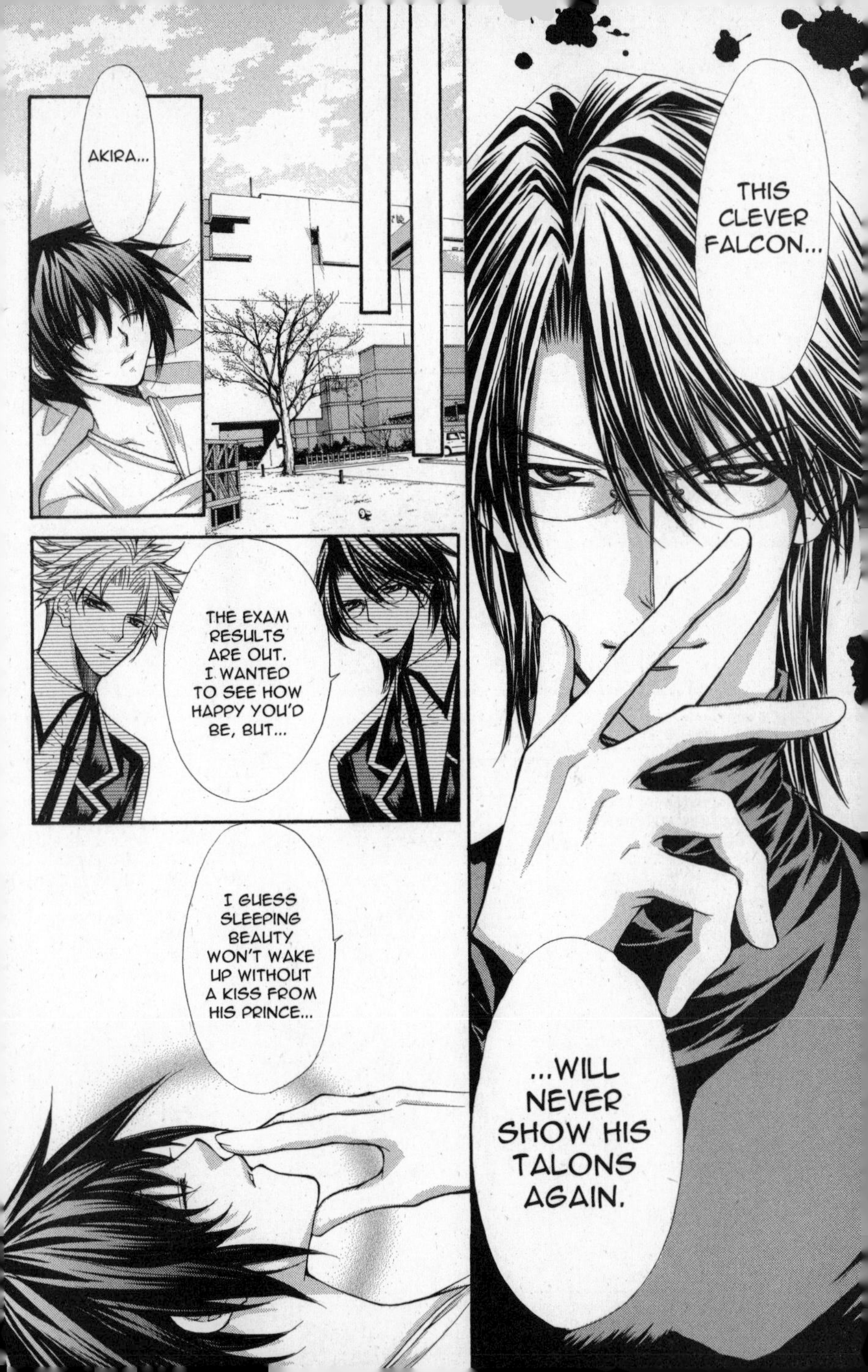
THIS CLEVER FALCON...
...WILL NEVER SHOW HIS TALONS AGAIN.
AKIRA...
THE EXAM RESULTS ARE OUT. I WANTED TO SEE HOW HAPPY YOU'D BE, BUT...
I GUESS SLEEPING BEAUTY WON'T WAKE UP WITHOUT A KISS FROM HIS PRINCE...

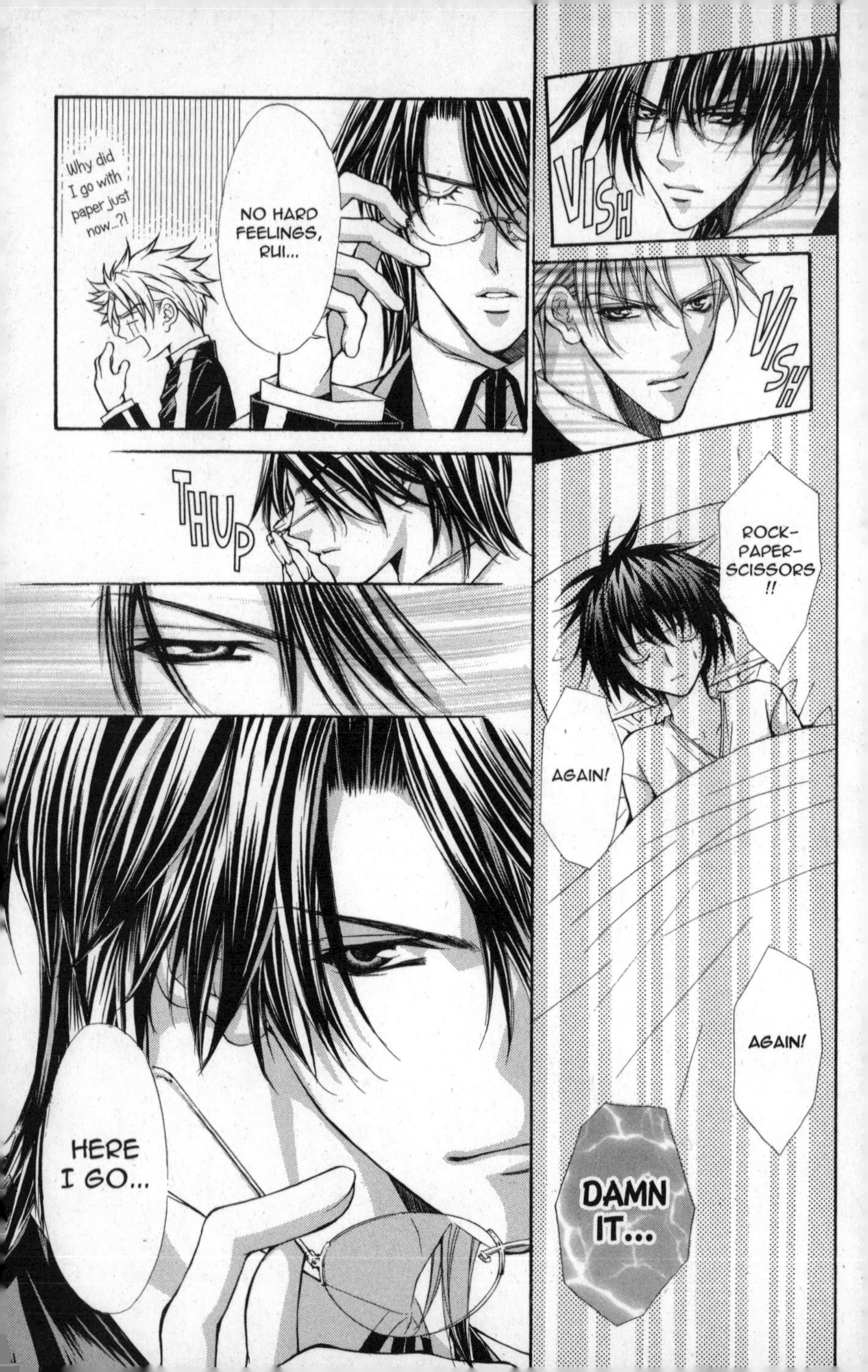
VISH
VISH
ROCK-PAPER-SCISSORS!!
AGAIN!
AGAIN!
DAMN IT...
NO HARD FEELINGS, RUI...
Why did I go with paper just now...?!
THUP
HERE I GO...

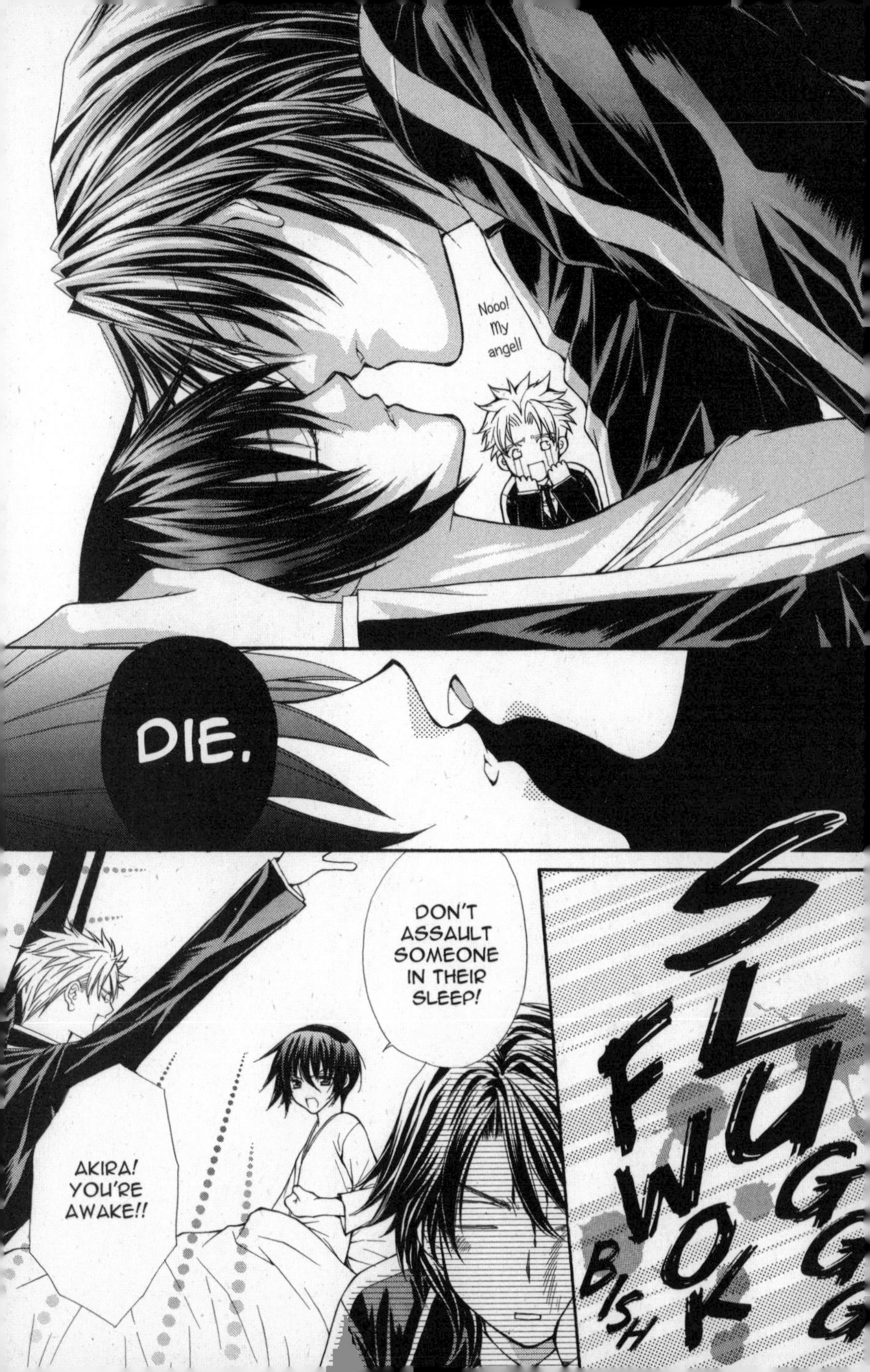
Nooo! My angel!
DIE.
SLUG
FWOK
BISH
GGGG
DON'T ASSAULT SOMEONE IN THEIR SLEEP!
AKIRA! YOU'RE AWAKE!!

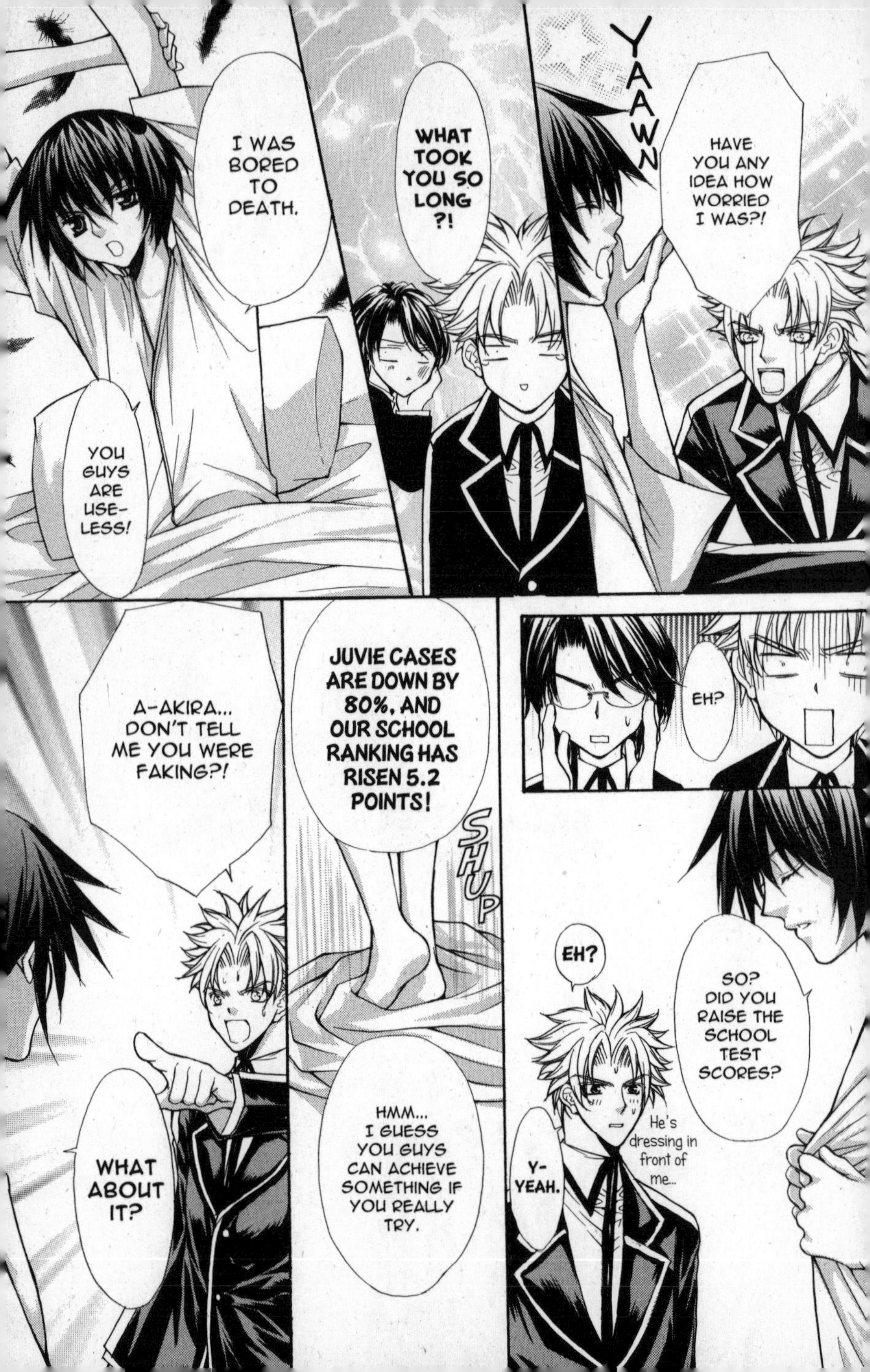
YAAWN
HAVE YOU ANY IDEA HOW WORRIED I WAS?!
WHAT TOOK YOU SO LONG?!
I WAS BORED TO DEATH.
YOU GUYS ARE USELESS!
EH?
SO? DID YOU RAISE THE SCHOOL TEST SCORES?
EH?
Y-YEAH.
He's dressing in front of me...
JUVIE CASES ARE DOWN BY 80%, AND OUR SCHOOL RANKING HAS RISEN 5.2 POINTS!
SHUP
HMM... I GUESS YOU GUYS CAN ACHIEVE SOMETHING IF YOU REALLY TRY.
A-AKIRA... DON'T TELL ME YOU WERE FAKING?!
WHAT ABOUT IT?

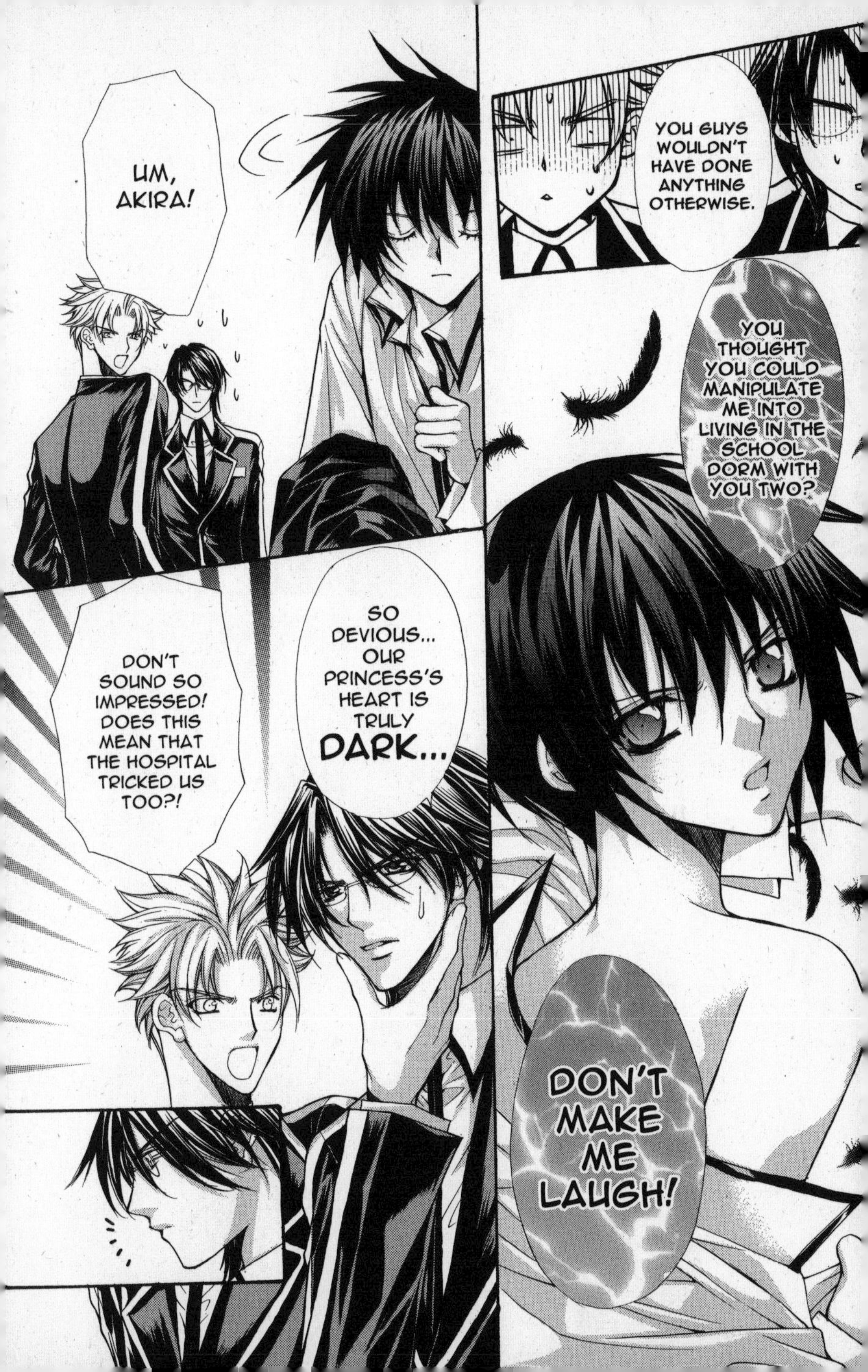
YOU GUYS WOULDN'T HAVE DONE ANYTHING OTHERWISE.
YOU THOUGHT YOU COULD MANIPULATE ME INTO LIVING IN THE SCHOOL DORM WITH YOU TWO?
DON'T MAKE ME LAUGH!
UM, AKIRA!
SO DEVIOUS... OUR PRINCESS'S HEART IS TRULY DARK...
DON'T SOUND SO IMPRESSED! DOES THIS MEAN THAT THE HOSPITAL TRICKED US TOO?!

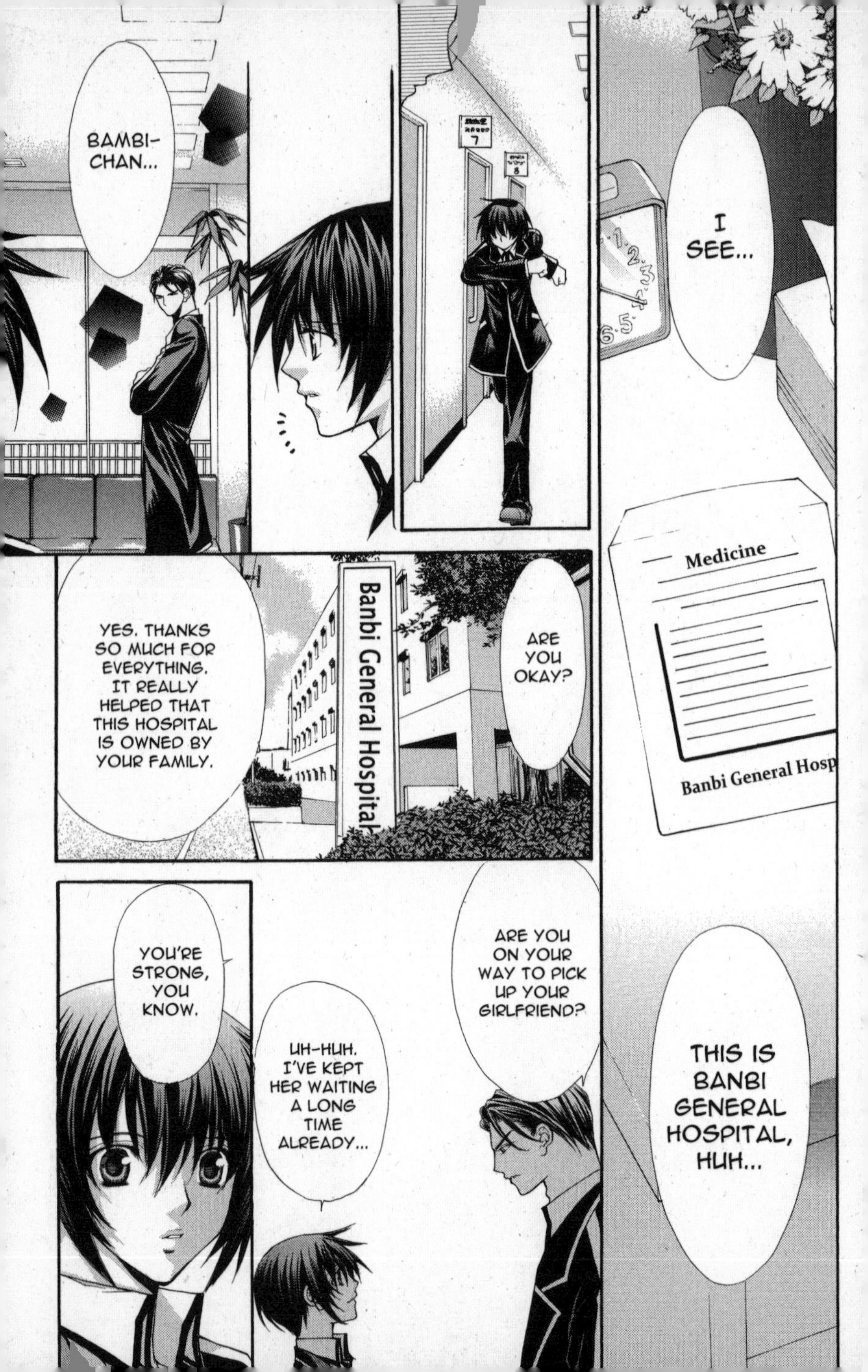
I SEE...
Medicine
Banbi General Hosp
THIS IS BANBI GENERAL HOSPITAL, HUH...
BAMBI-CHAN...
ARE YOU OKAY?
Banbi General Hospital
YES. THANKS SO MUCH FOR EVERYTHING. IT REALLY HELPED THAT THIS HOSPITAL IS OWNED BY YOUR FAMILY.
ARE YOU ON YOUR WAY TO PICK UP YOUR GIRLFRIEND?
UH-HUH. I'VE KEPT HER WAITING A LONG TIME ALREADY...
YOU'RE STRONG, YOU KNOW.

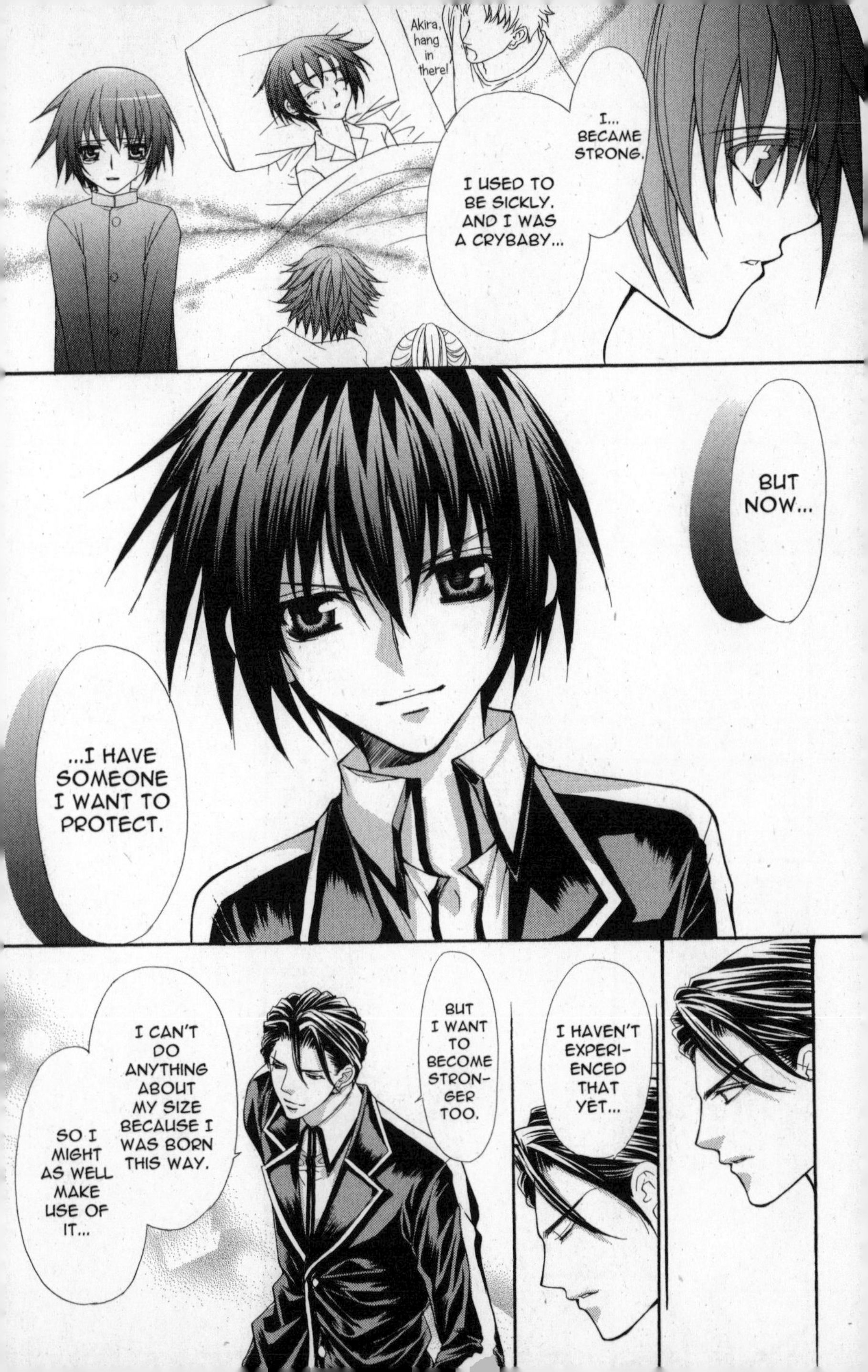
Akira, hang in there!
I... BECAME STRONG.
I USED TO BE SICKLY. AND I WAS A CRYBABY...
BUT NOW...
...I HAVE SOMEONE I WANT TO PROTECT.
I HAVEN'T EXPERI-ENCED THAT YET...
BUT I WANT TO BECOME STRON-GER TOO.
I CAN'T DO ANYTHING ABOUT MY SIZE BECAUSE I WAS BORN THIS WAY.
SO I MIGHT AS WELL MAKE USE OF IT...

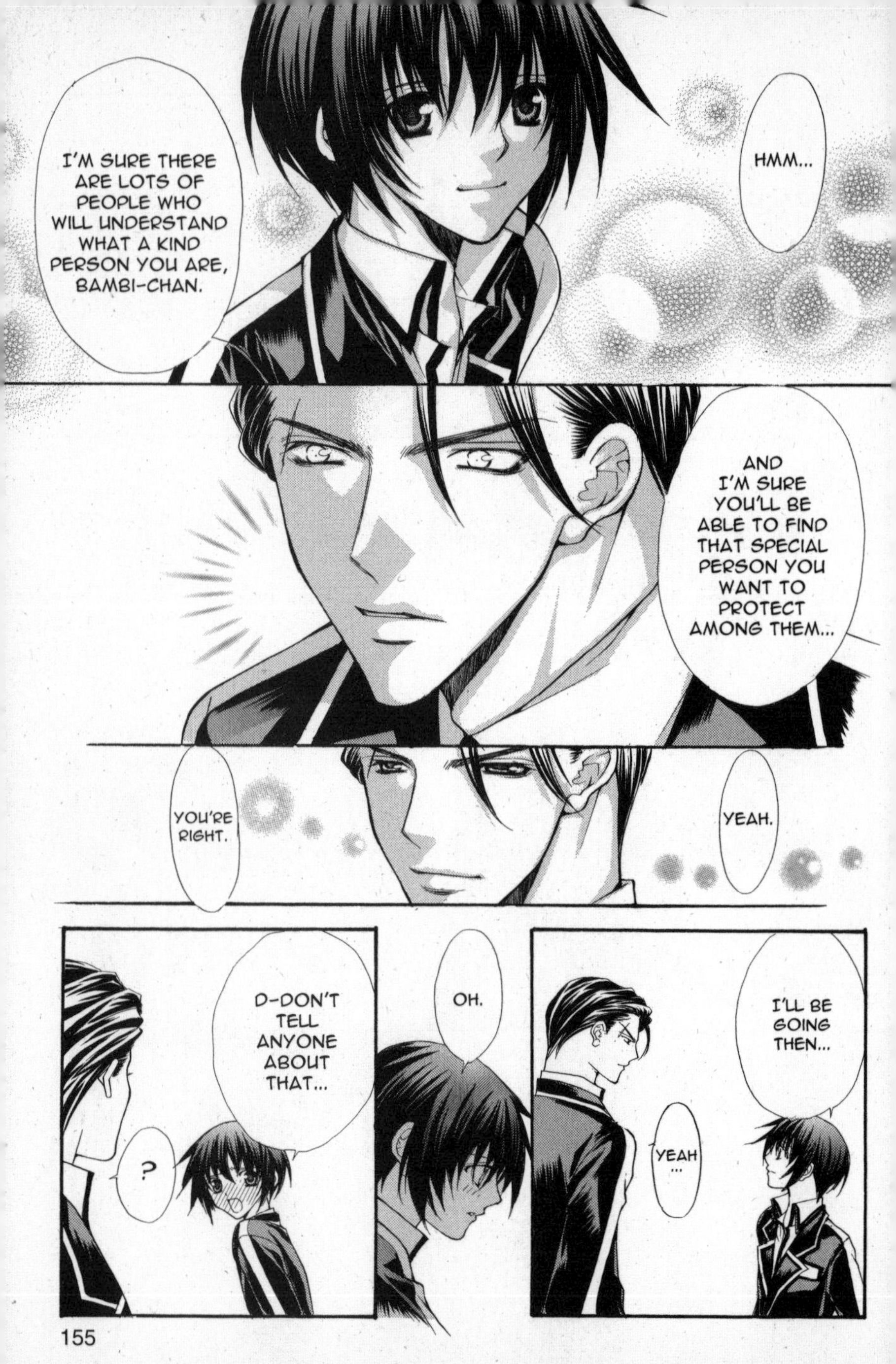
HMM...
I'M SURE THERE ARE LOTS OF PEOPLE WHO WILL UNDERSTAND WHAT A KIND PERSON YOU ARE, BAMBI-CHAN.
AND I'M SURE YOU'LL BE ABLE TO FIND THAT SPECIAL PERSON YOU WANT TO PROTECT AMONG THEM...
YEAH.
YOU'RE RIGHT.
I'LL BE GOING THEN...
YEAH ...
OH.
D-DON'T TELL ANYONE ABOUT THAT...
?

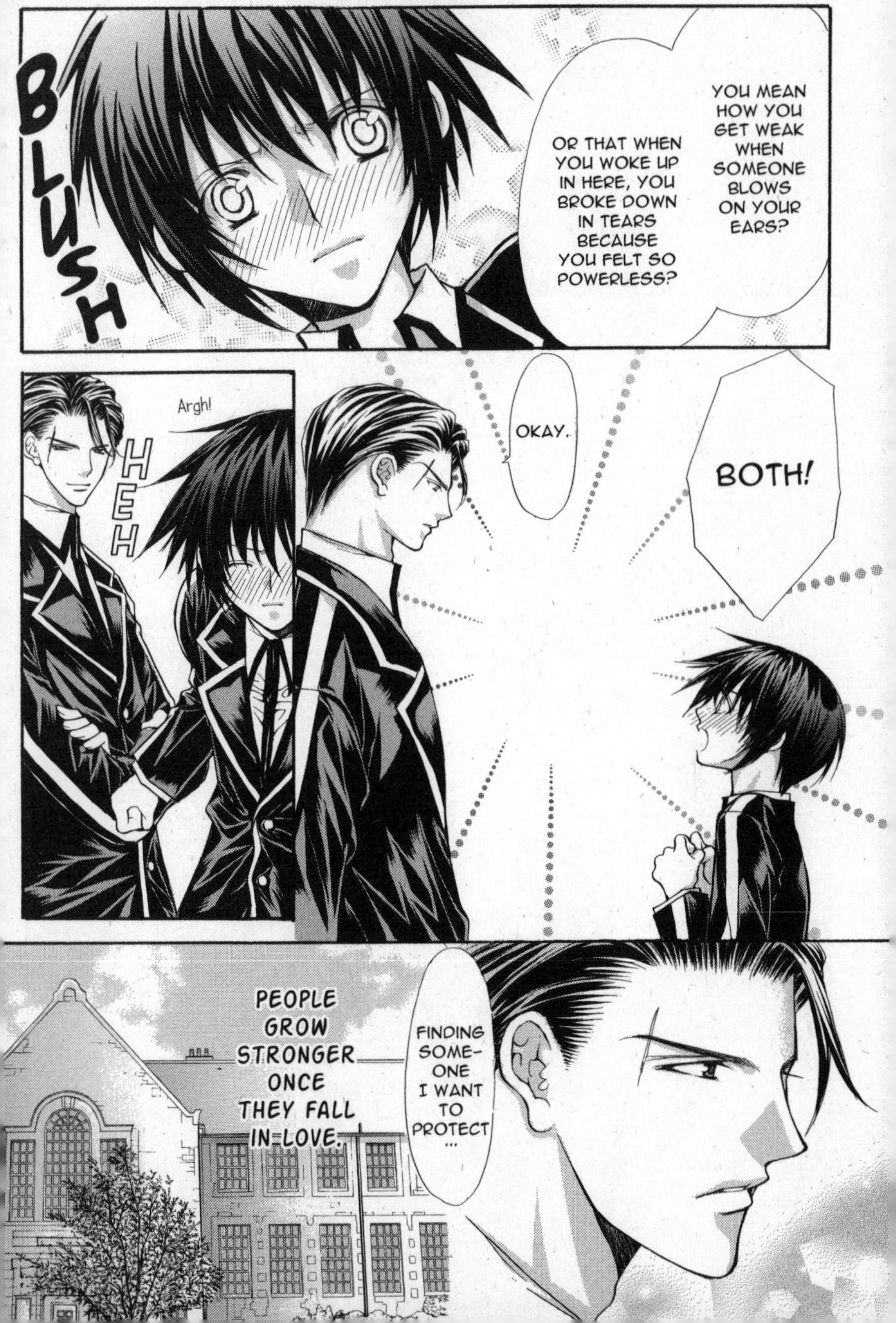
YOU MEAN HOW YOU GET WEAK WHEN SOMEONE BLOWS ON YOUR EARS?
OR THAT WHEN YOU WOKE UP IN HERE, YOU BROKE DOWN IN TEARS BECAUSE YOU FELT SO POWERLESS?
BLUSH
BOTH!
OKAY.
Argh!
HEH
FINDING SOME-ONE I WANT TO PROTECT...
PEOPLE GROW STRONGER ONCE THEY FALL IN LOVE.

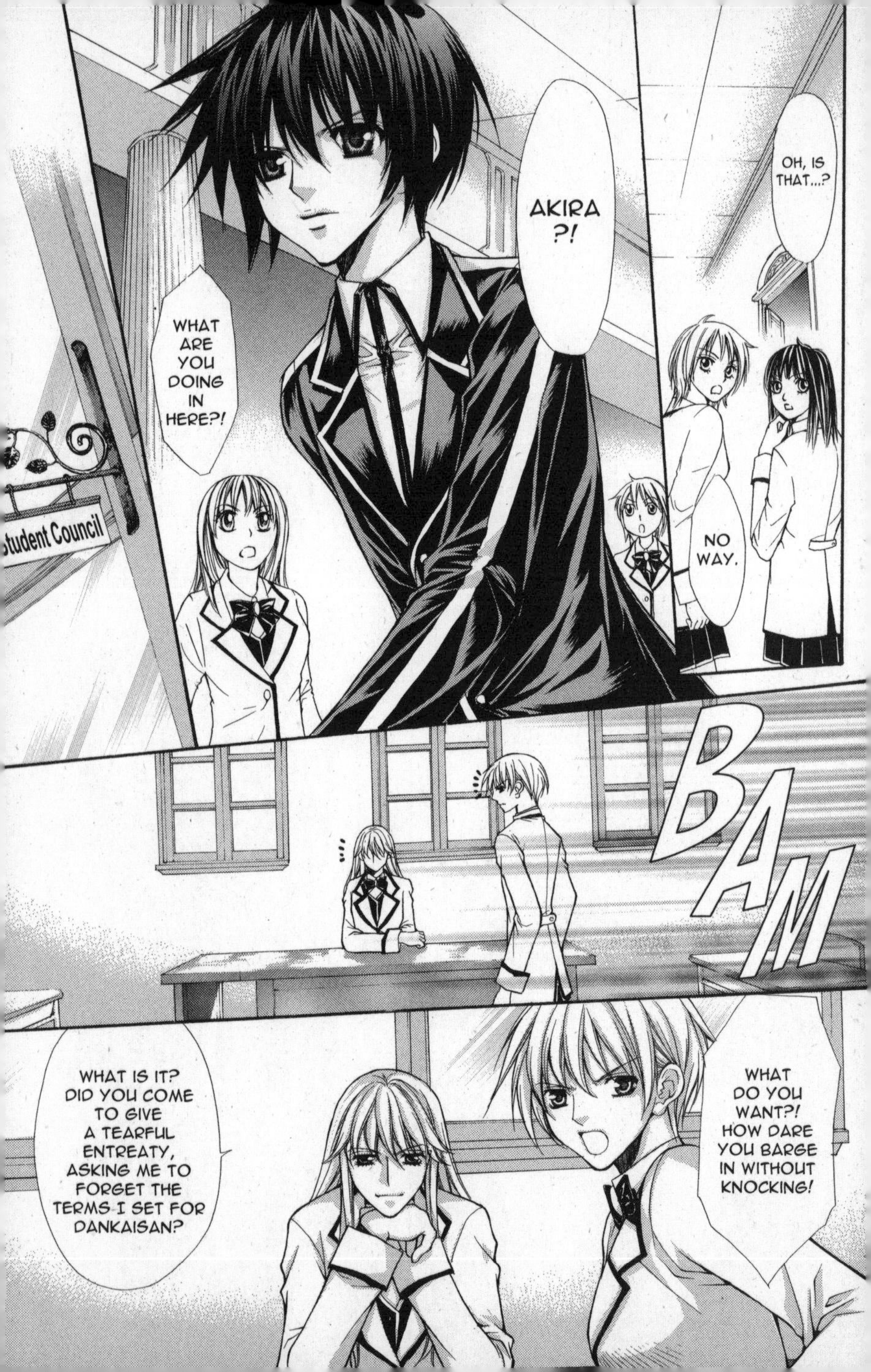
OH, IS THAT...?
NO WAY.
AKIRA ?!
WHAT ARE YOU DOING IN HERE?!
Student Council
BAM
WHAT DO YOU WANT?! HOW DARE YOU BARGE IN WITHOUT KNOCKING!
WHAT IS IT? DID YOU COME TO GIVE A TEARFUL ENTREATY, ASKING ME TO FORGET THE TERMS I SET FOR DANKAISAN?

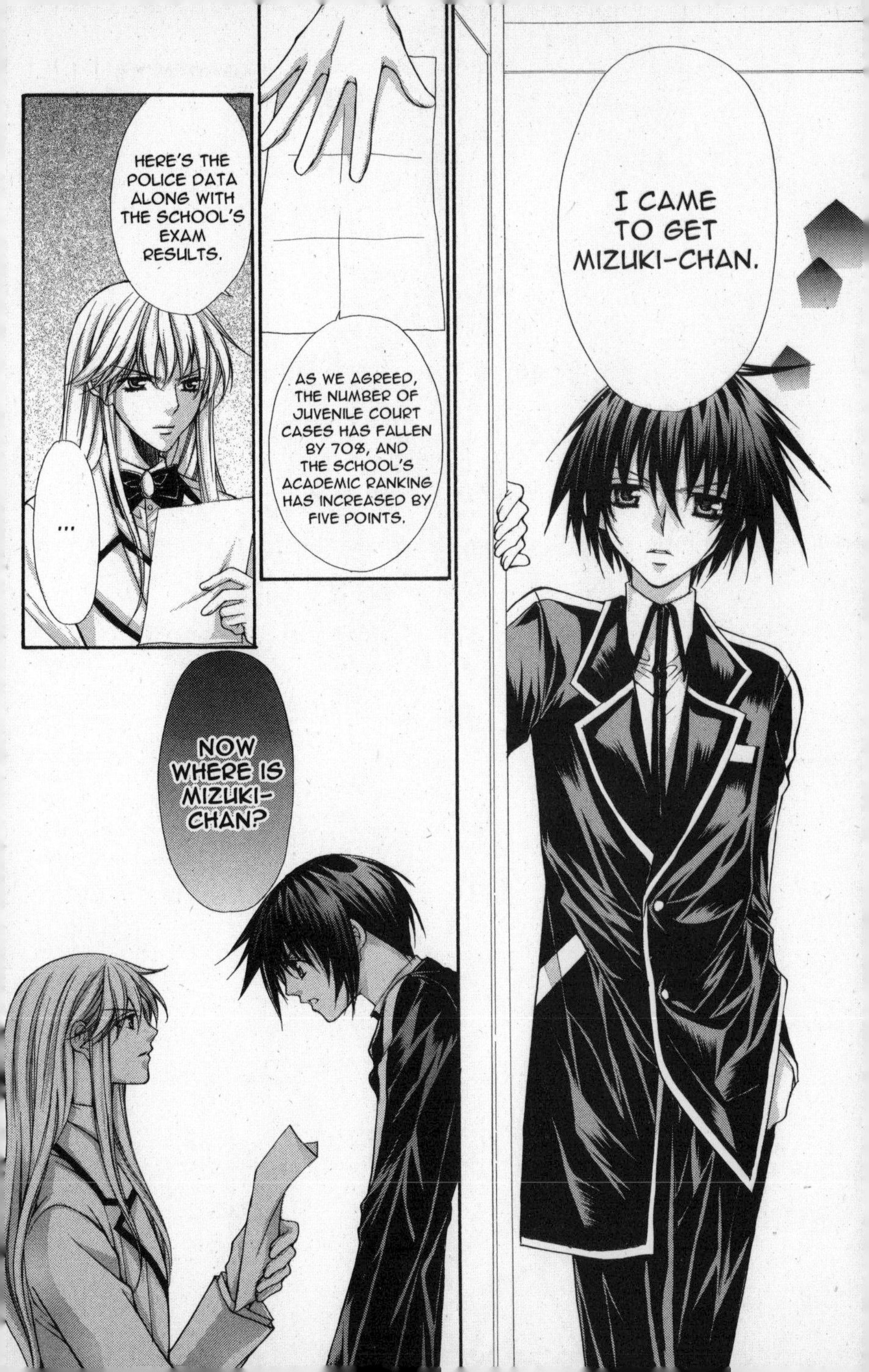
I CAME TO GET MIZUKI-CHAN.
AS WE AGREED, THE NUMBER OF JUVENILE COURT CASES HAS FALLEN BY 70%, AND THE SCHOOL'S ACADEMIC RANKING HAS INCREASED BY FIVE POINTS.
HERE'S THE POLICE DATA ALONG WITH THE SCHOOL'S EXAM RESULTS.
...
NOW WHERE IS MIZUKI-CHAN?

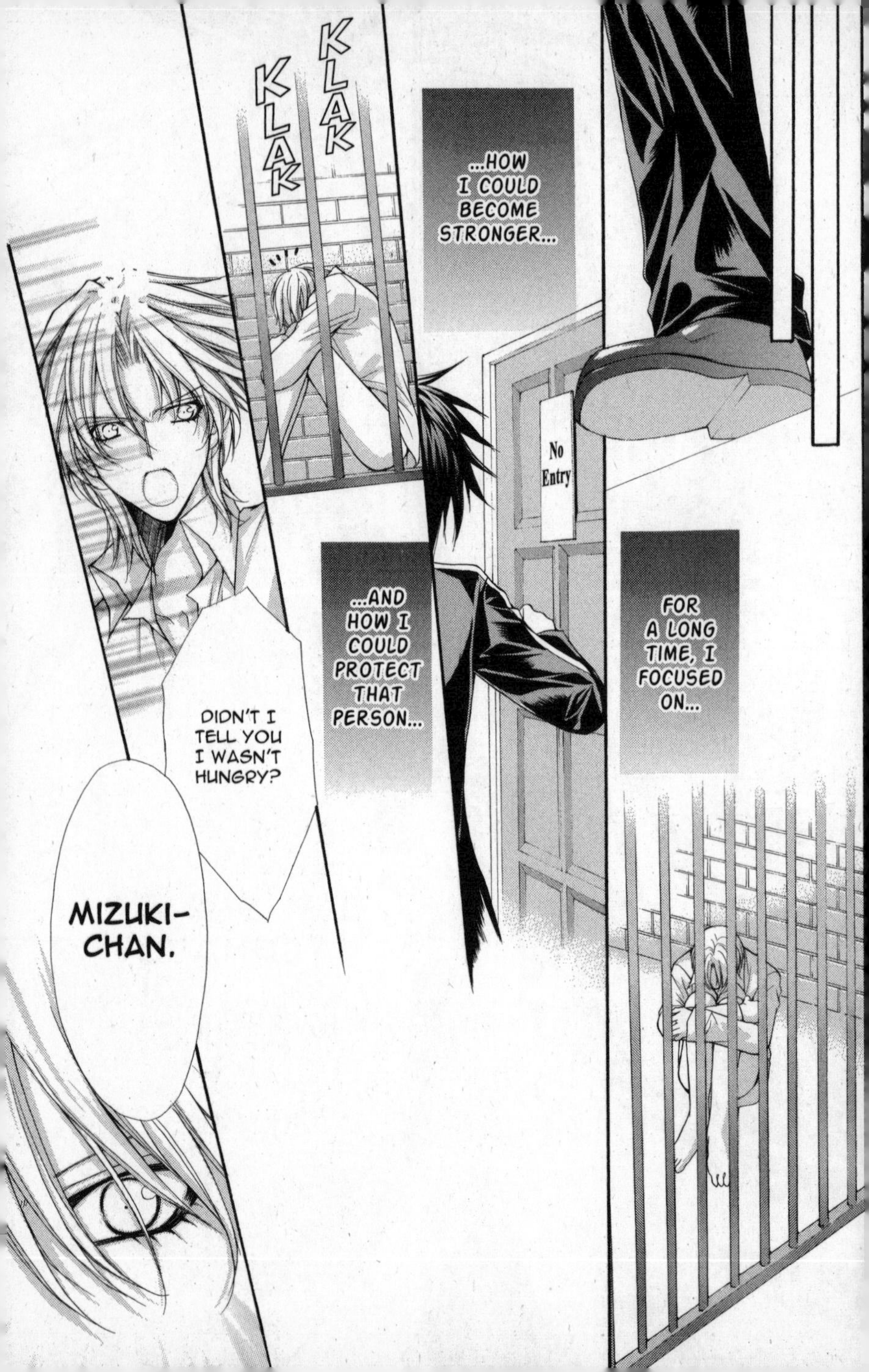
FOR A LONG TIME, I FOCUSED ON...
...HOW I COULD BECOME STRONGER...
...AND HOW I COULD PROTECT THAT PERSON...
No Entry
KLAK KLAK
DIDN'T I TELL YOU I WASN'T HUNGRY?
MIZUKI-CHAN.

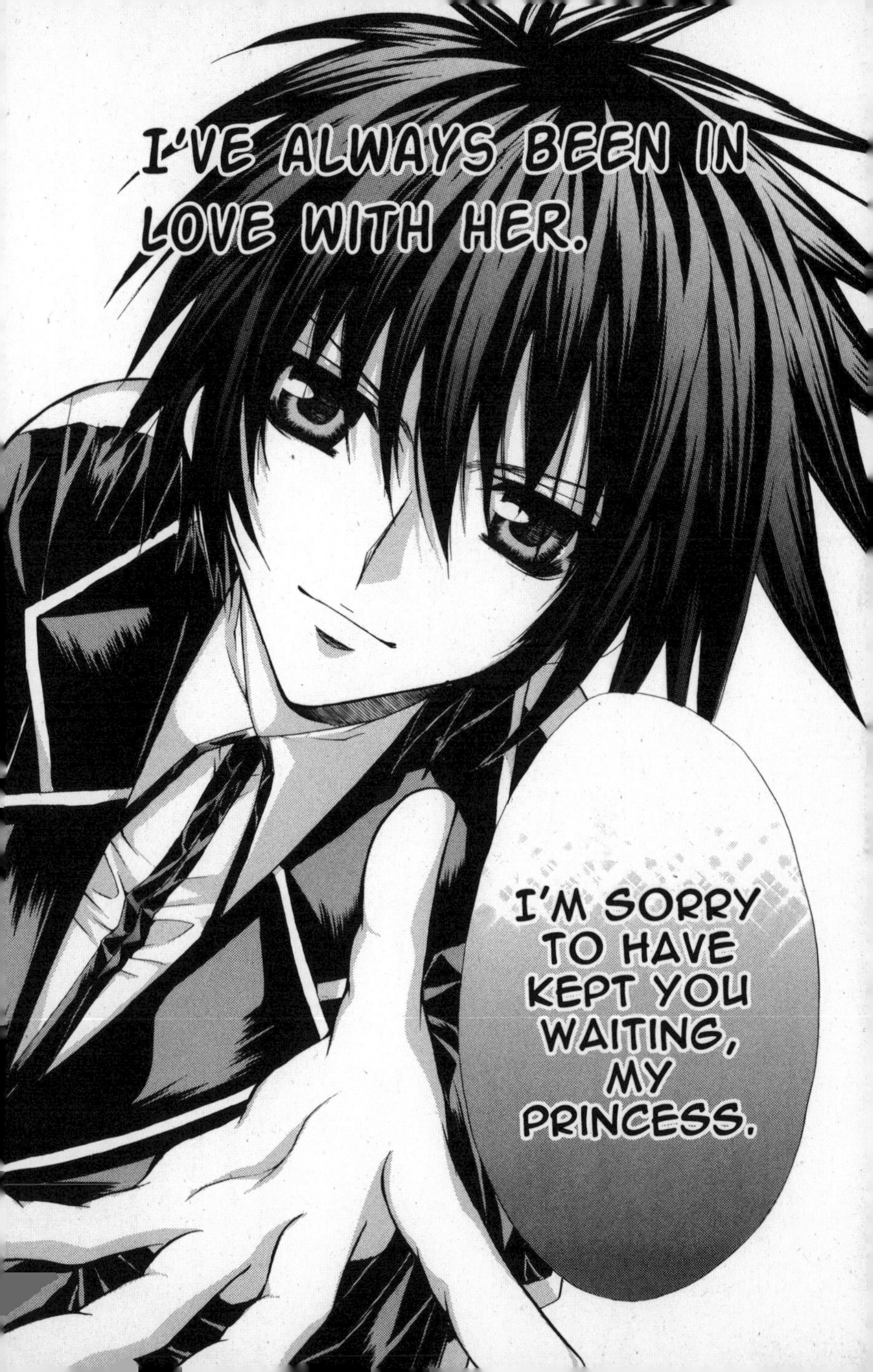
I'VE ALWAYS BEEN IN LOVE WITH HER.
I'M SORRY TO HAVE KEPT YOU WAITING, MY PRINCESS.

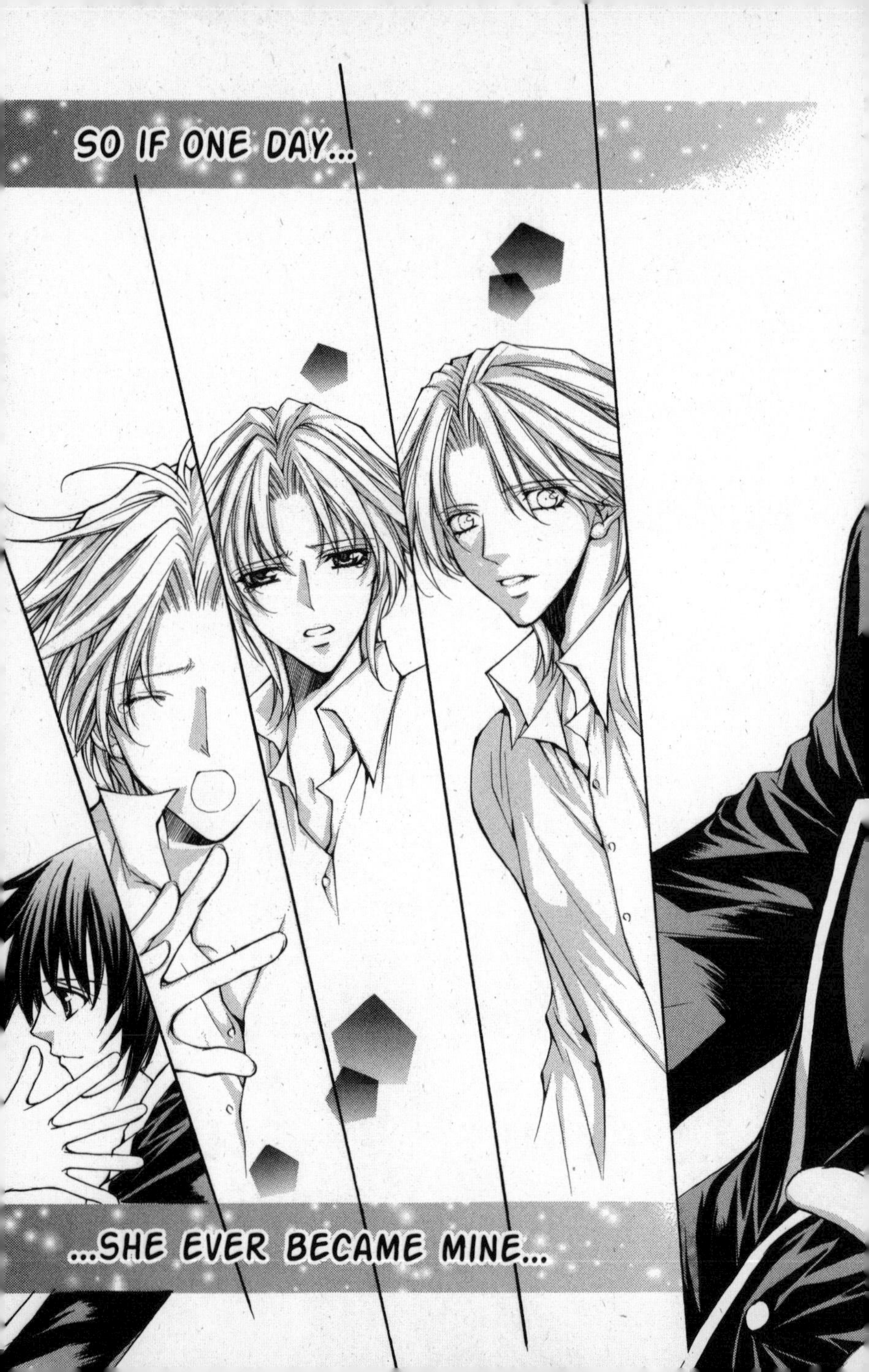
SO IF ONE DAY...
...SHE EVER BECAME MINE...

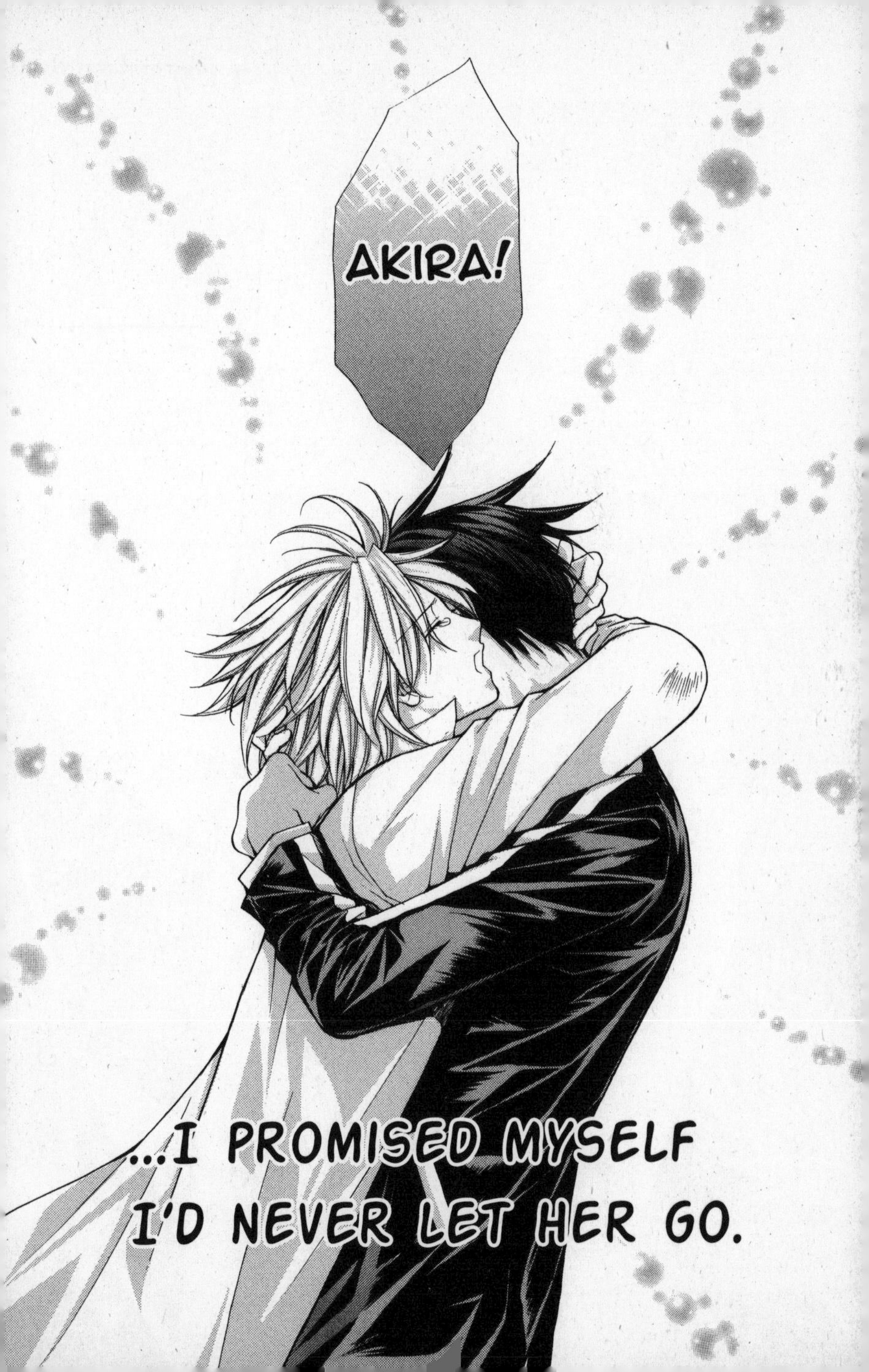
AKIRA!
...I PROMISED MYSELF I'D NEVER LET HER GO.

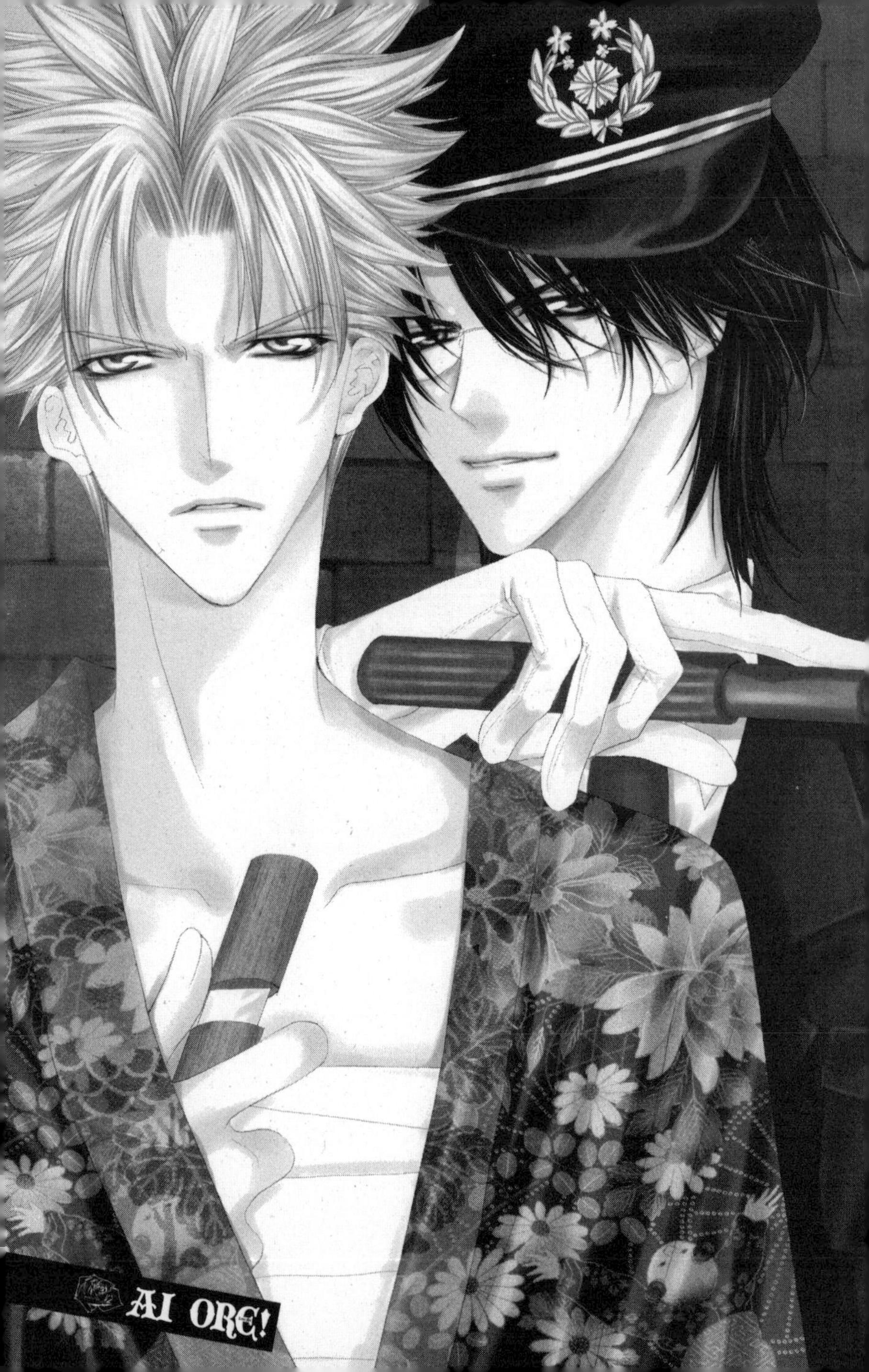
AI ORE!

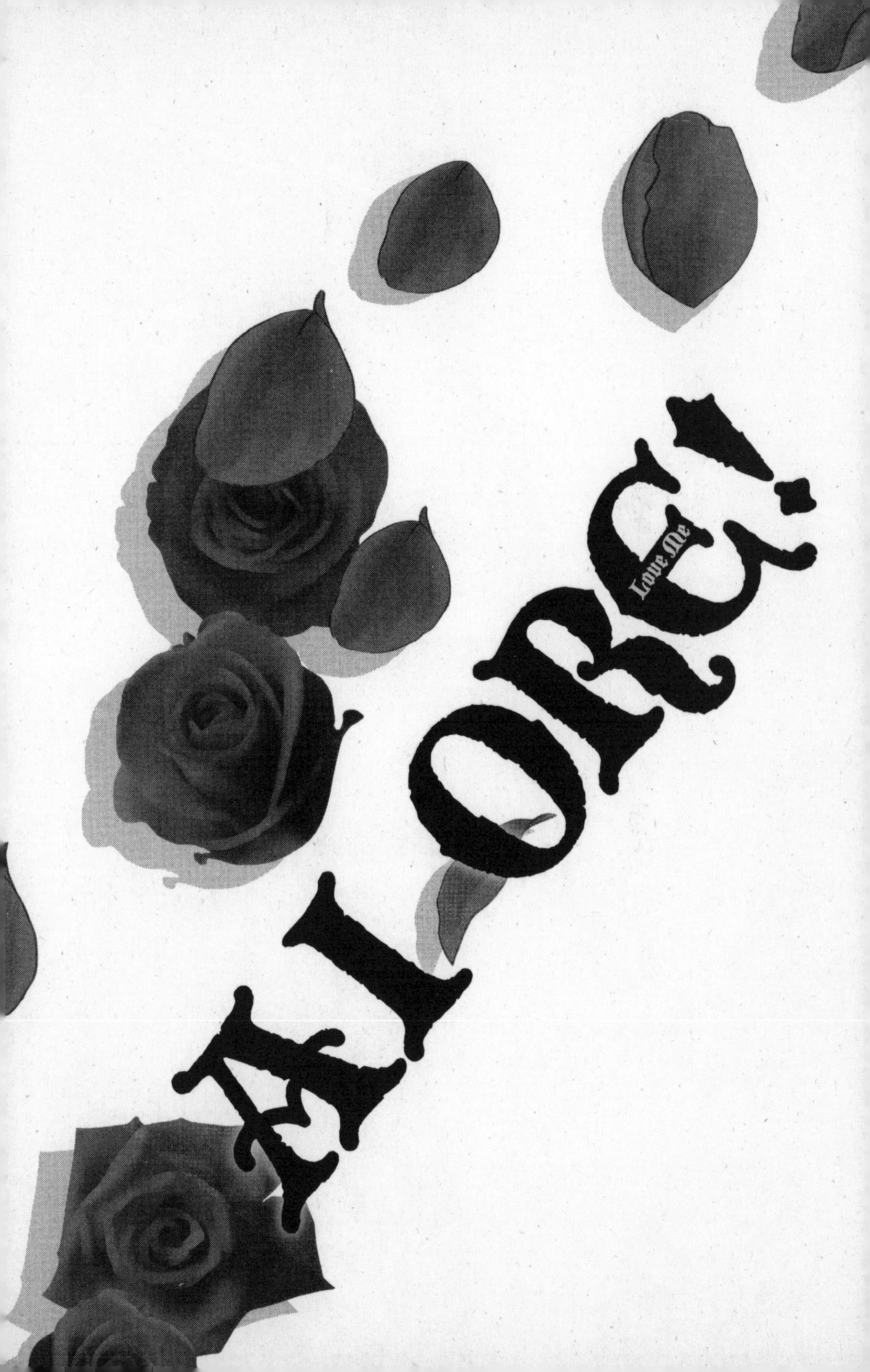
AMORE!
Love Me

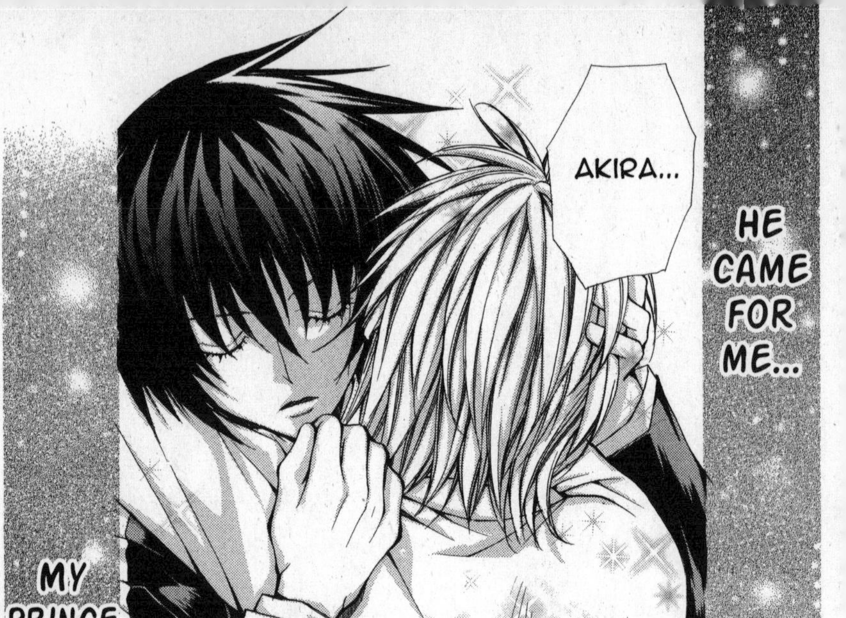
AKIRA...
HE CAME FOR ME...
MY PRINCE ...
AKIRA!

About the Supporting Characters

I think Rui and Ran's appearances have increased a lot.
In the past I had to cut out most of their scenes (TT), and there were also characters who would appear only once... This time I wanted to take better care of the supporting cast. Obviously the two main characters are important, but they can't be brought to life without the support of the other characters... I was very happy to be able to include many chapters about Rui and Ran. Banbi won't end up as a one-time character, and I'm looking forward to seeing how he will interact with the others.

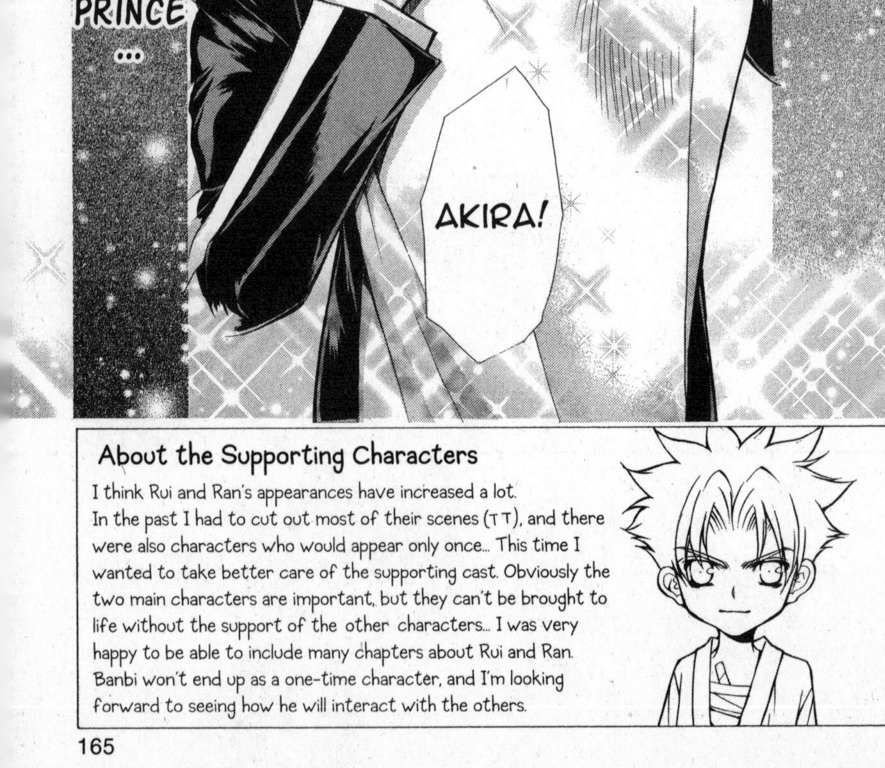

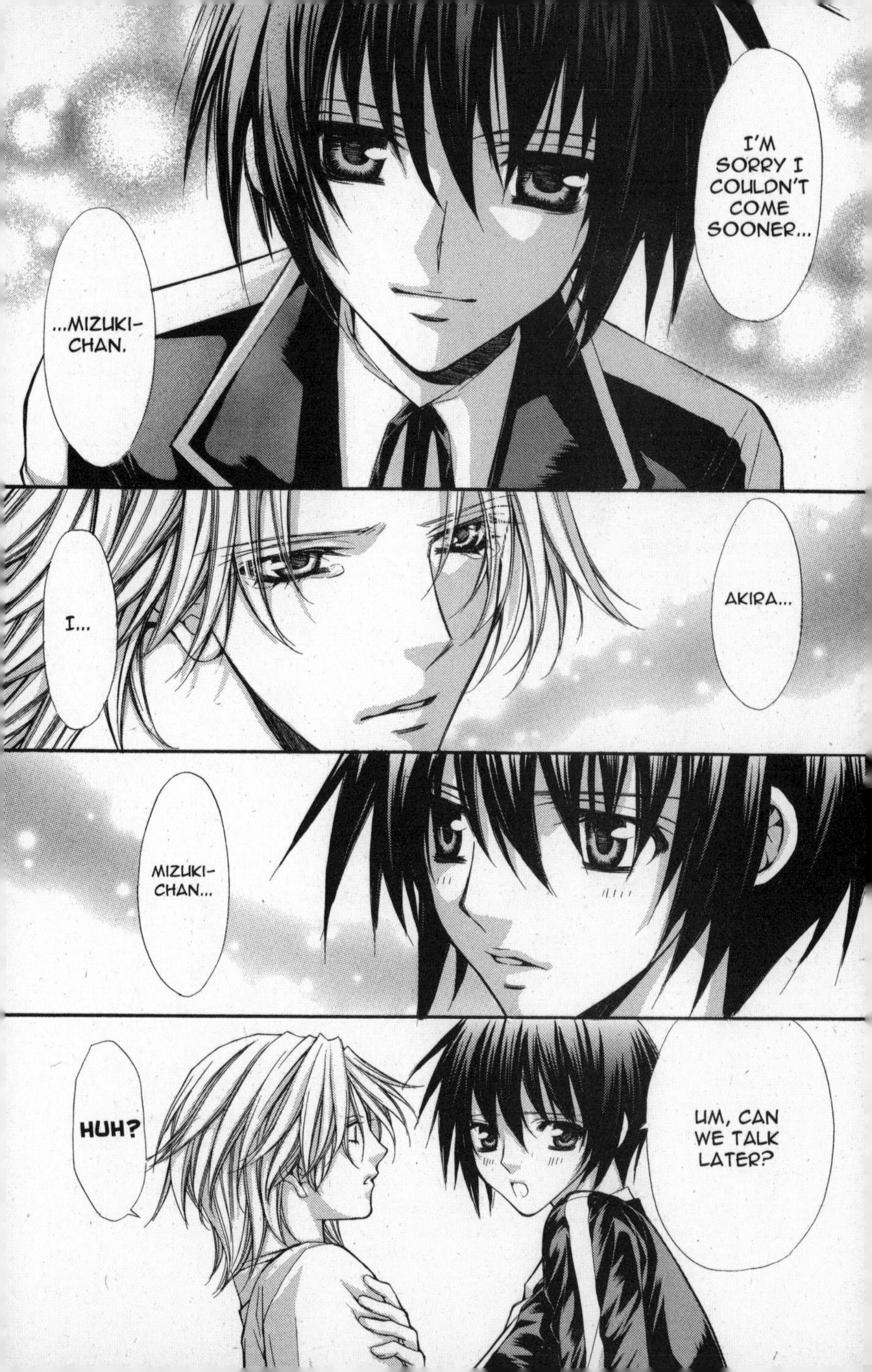
I'M SORRY I COULDN'T COME SOONER...
...MIZUKI-CHAN.
AKIRA...
I...
MIZUKI-CHAN...
UM, CAN WE TALK LATER?
HUH?

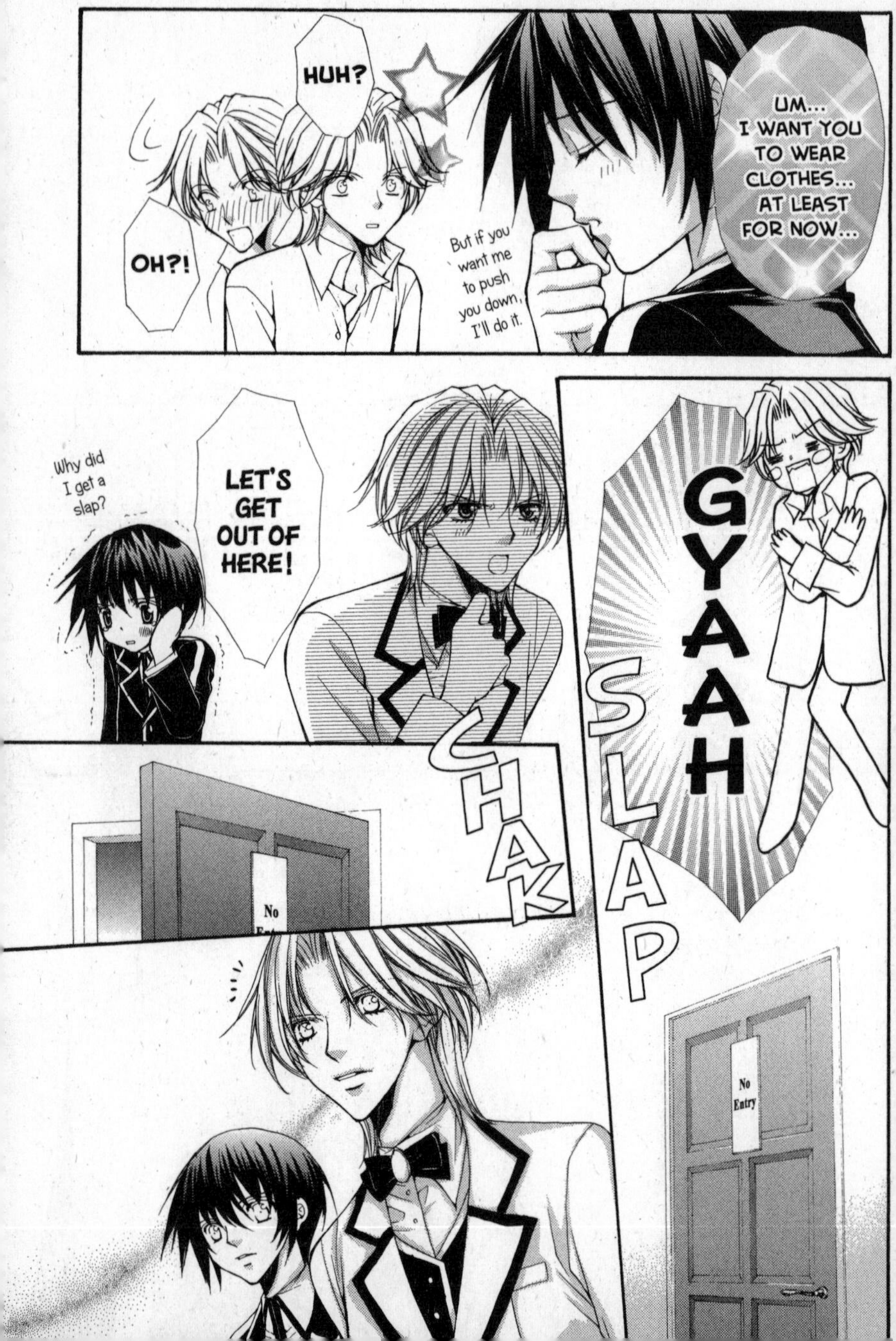
UM... I WANT YOU TO WEAR CLOTHES... AT LEAST FOR NOW...
But if you want me to push you down, I'll do it.
HUH?
OH?!
GYAAH
SLAP
LET'S GET OUT OF HERE!
Why did I get a slap?
CHAK
No Entry

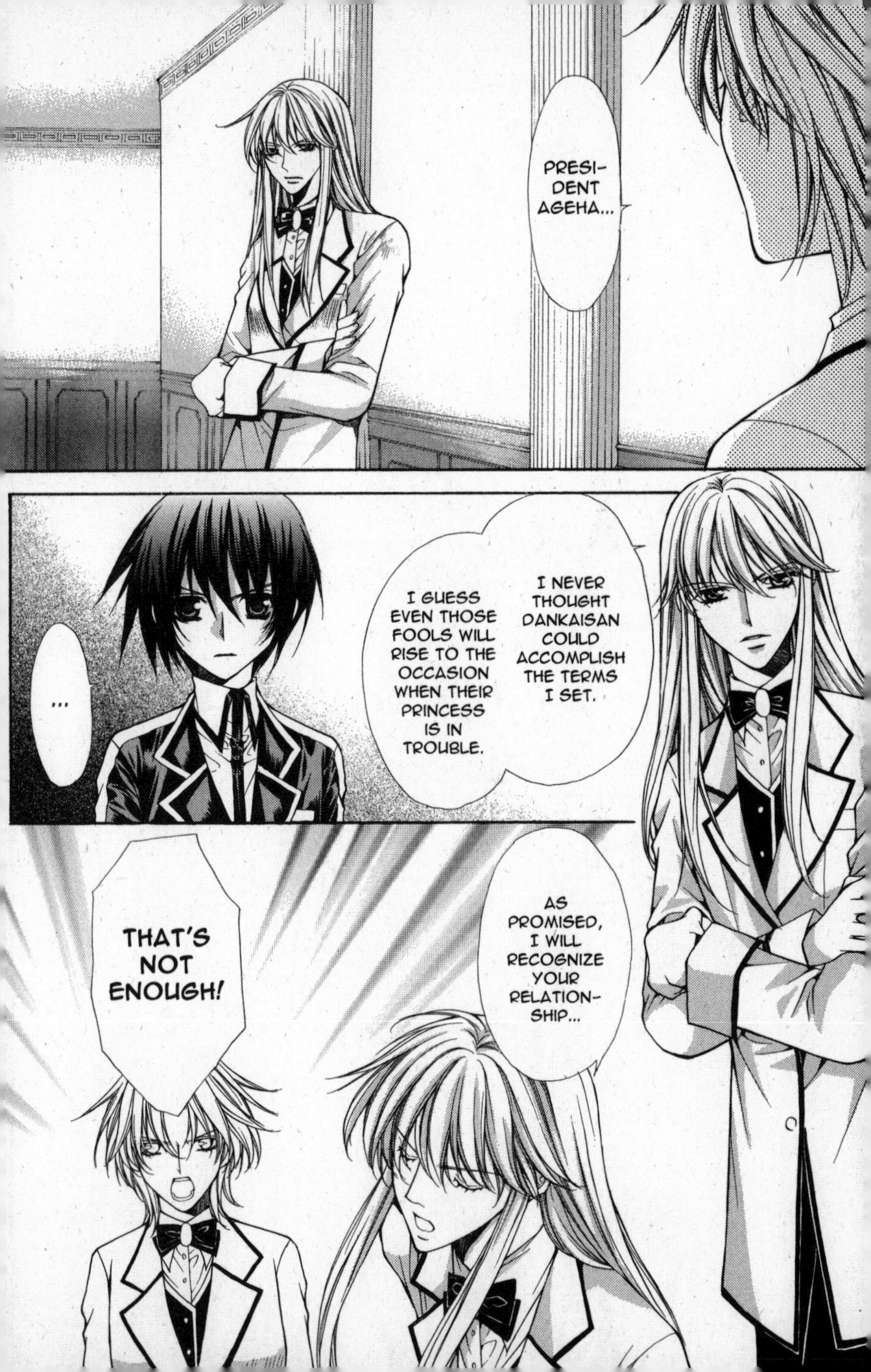
PRESI-
DENT
AGEHA...
I NEVER THOUGHT DANKAISAN COULD ACCOMPLISH THE TERMS I SET.
I GUESS EVEN THOSE FOOLS WILL RISE TO THE OCCASION WHEN THEIR PRINCESS IS IN TROUBLE.
...
AS PROMISED, I WILL RECOGNIZE YOUR RELATION-SHIP...
THAT'S NOT ENOUGH!

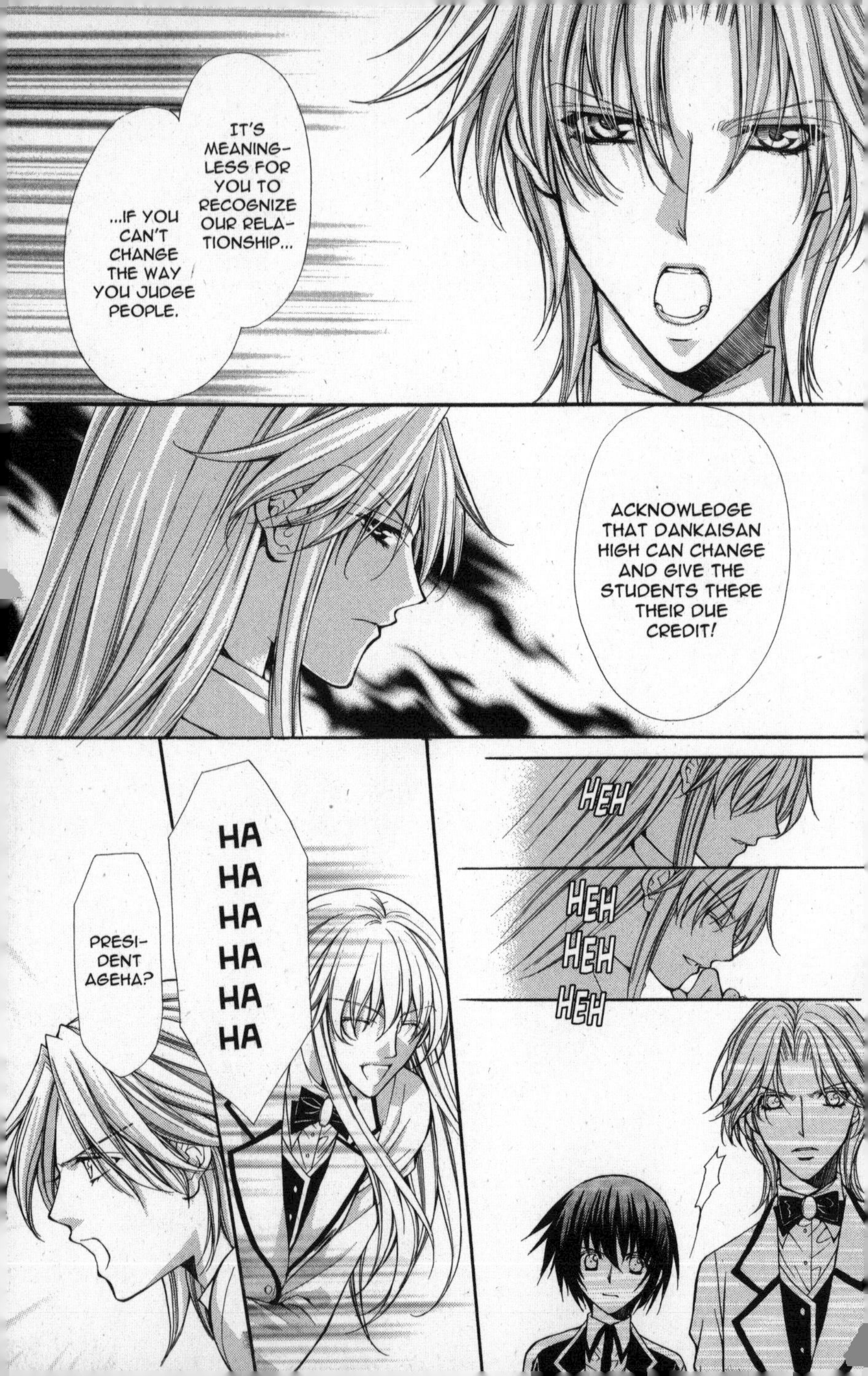
IT'S MEANINGLESS FOR YOU TO RECOGNIZE OUR RELATIONSHIP...
...IF YOU CAN'T CHANGE THE WAY YOU JUDGE PEOPLE.
ACKNOWLEDGE THAT DANKAISAN HIGH CAN CHANGE AND GIVE THE STUDENTS THERE THEIR DUE CREDIT!
HEH
HEH HEH HEH
HA HA HA HA HA HA
PRESIDENT AGEHA?

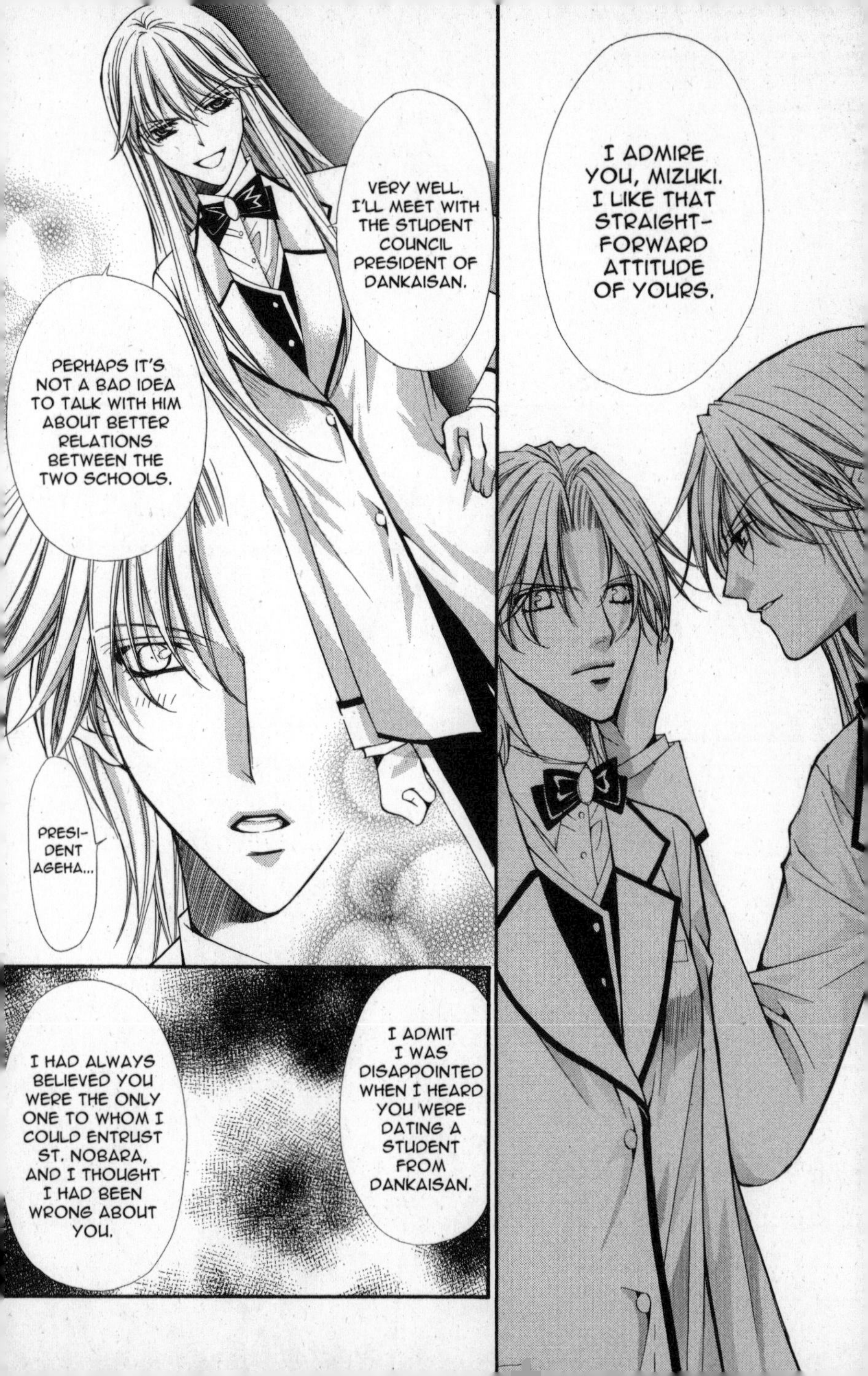
I ADMIRE YOU, MIZUKI. I LIKE THAT STRAIGHT-FORWARD ATTITUDE OF YOURS.
VERY WELL. I'LL MEET WITH THE STUDENT COUNCIL PRESIDENT OF DANKAISAN.
PERHAPS IT'S NOT A BAD IDEA TO TALK WITH HIM ABOUT BETTER RELATIONS BETWEEN THE TWO SCHOOLS.
PRESI-DENT AGEHA...
I ADMIT I WAS DISAPPOINTED WHEN I HEARD YOU WERE DATING A STUDENT FROM DANKAISAN.
I HAD ALWAYS BELIEVED YOU WERE THE ONLY ONE TO WHOM I COULD ENTRUST ST. NOBARA, AND I THOUGHT I HAD BEEN WRONG ABOUT YOU.

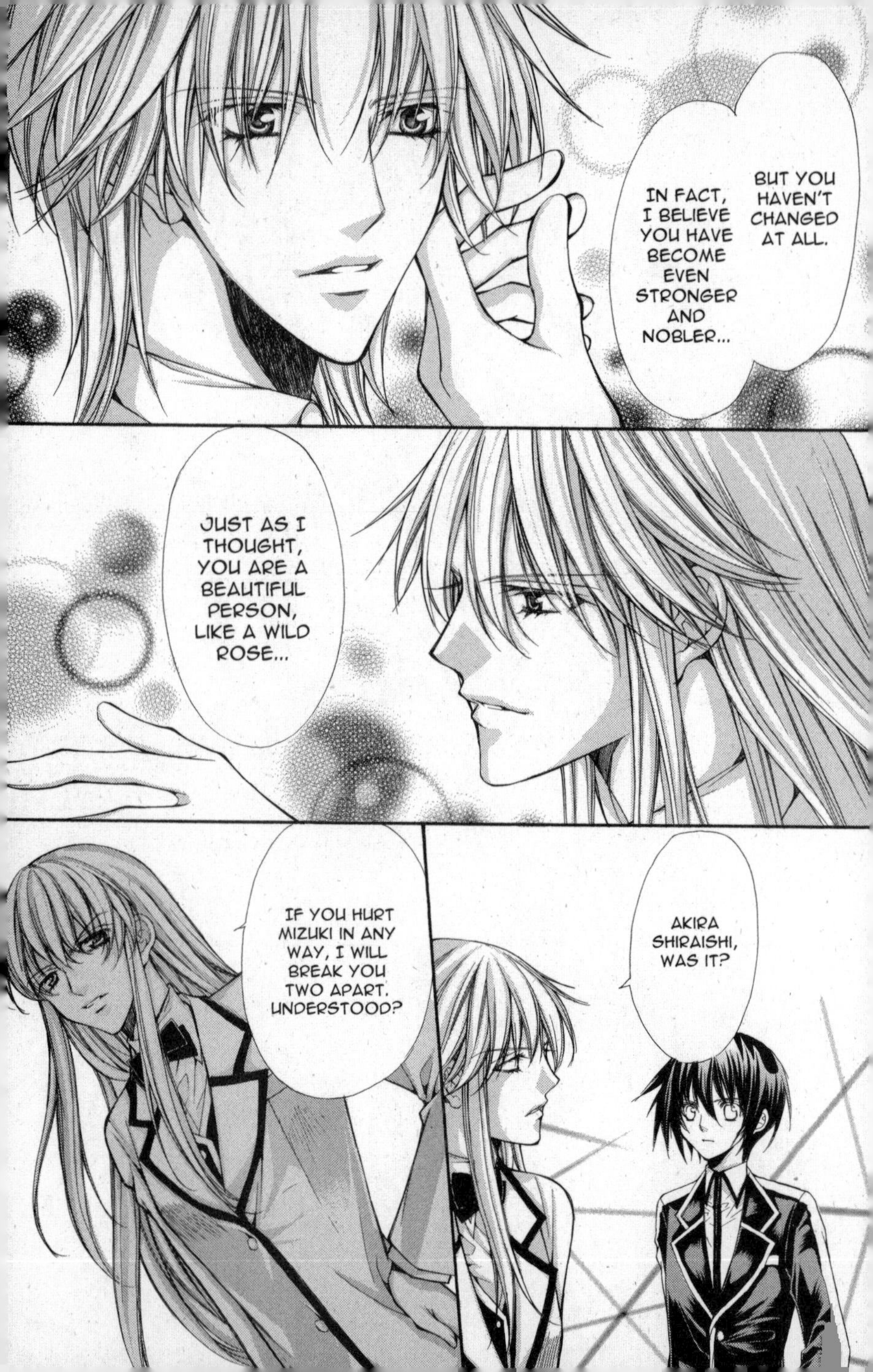
BUT YOU HAVEN'T CHANGED AT ALL.
IN FACT, I BELIEVE YOU HAVE BECOME EVEN STRONGER AND NOBLER...
JUST AS I THOUGHT, YOU ARE A BEAUTIFUL PERSON, LIKE A WILD ROSE...
AKIRA SHIRAISHI, WAS IT?
IF YOU HURT MIZUKI IN ANY WAY, I WILL BREAK YOU TWO APART. UNDERSTOOD?

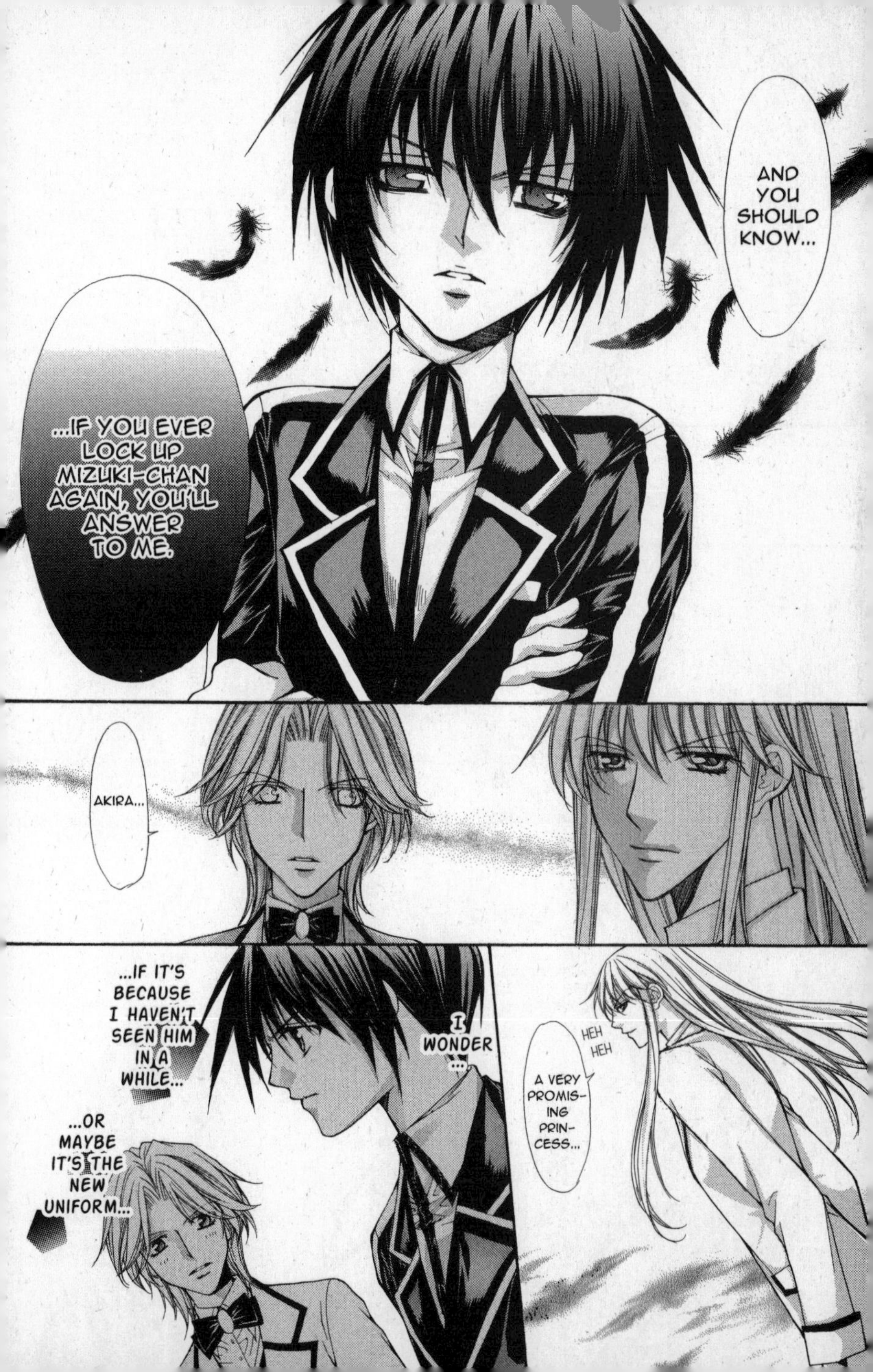
AND YOU SHOULD KNOW...
...IF YOU EVER LOCK UP MIZUKI-CHAN AGAIN, YOU'LL ANSWER TO ME.
AKIRA...
HEH HEH
A VERY PROMISING PRINCESS...
I WONDER...
...IF IT'S BECAUSE I HAVEN'T SEEN HIM IN A WHILE...
...OR MAYBE IT'S THE NEW UNIFORM...

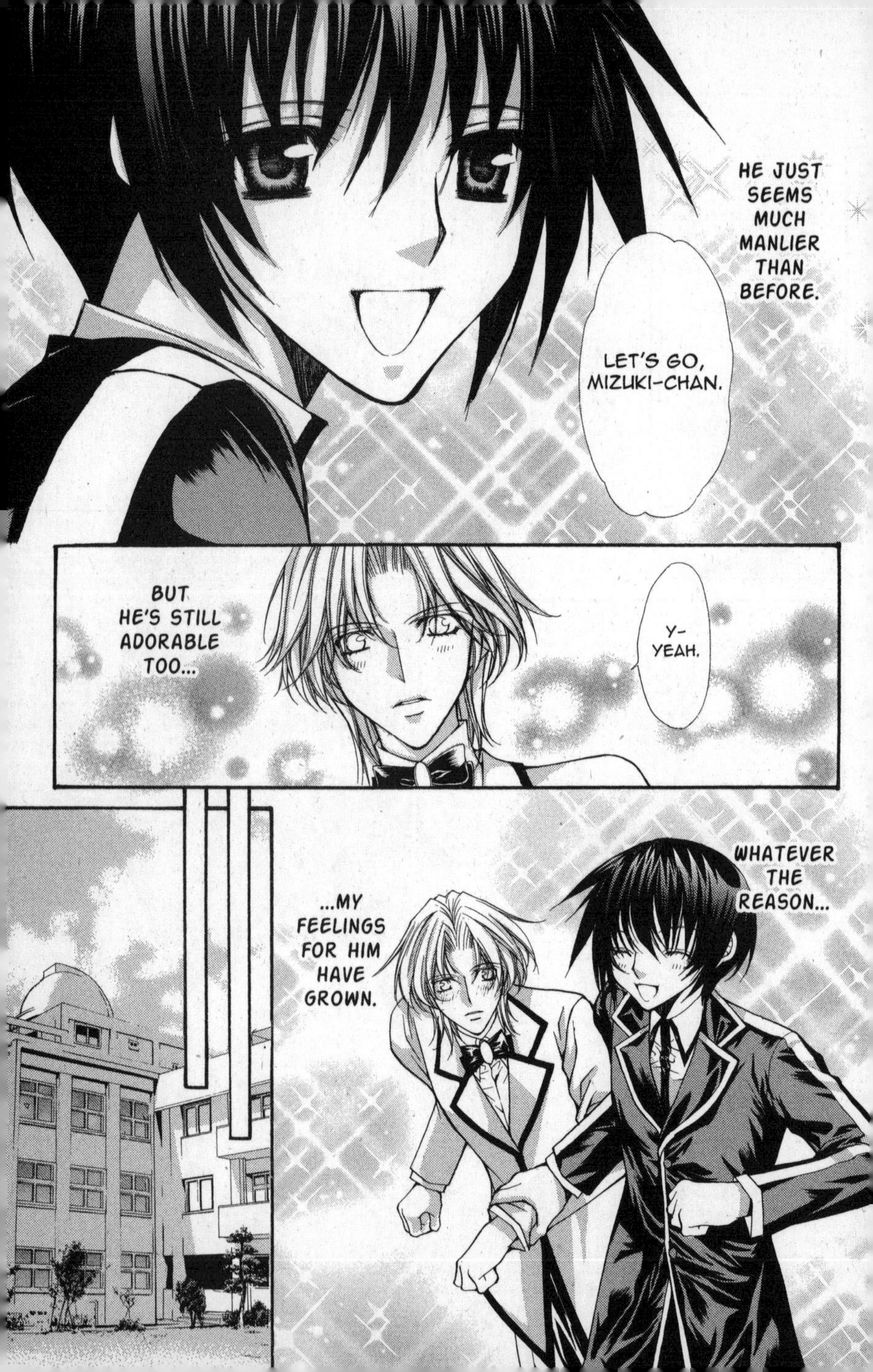
HE JUST SEEMS MUCH MANLIER THAN BEFORE.
LET'S GO, MIZUKI-CHAN.
Y-YEAH.
BUT HE'S STILL ADORABLE TOO...
WHATEVER THE REASON...
...MY FEELINGS FOR HIM HAVE GROWN.

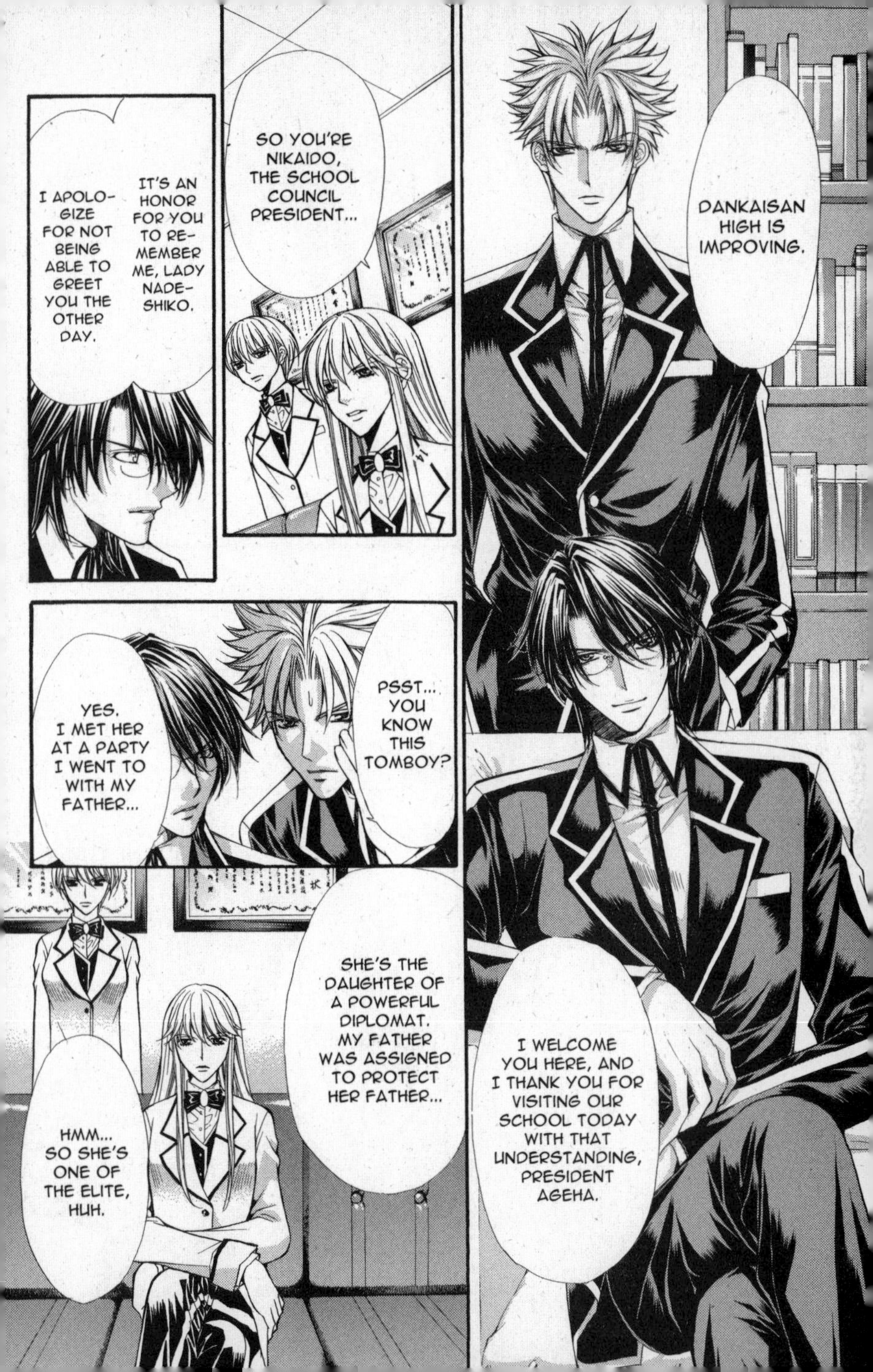
DANKAISAN HIGH IS IMPROVING.
I WELCOME YOU HERE, AND I THANK YOU FOR VISITING OUR SCHOOL TODAY WITH THAT UNDERSTANDING, PRESIDENT AGEHA.
SO YOU'RE NIKAIDO, THE SCHOOL COUNCIL PRESIDENT...
IT'S AN HONOR FOR YOU TO RE-MEMBER ME, LADY NADE-SHIKO.
I APOLO-GIZE FOR NOT BEING ABLE TO GREET YOU THE OTHER DAY.
PSST... YOU KNOW THIS TOMBOY?
YES. I MET HER AT A PARTY I WENT TO WITH MY FATHER...
SHE'S THE DAUGHTER OF A POWERFUL DIPLOMAT. MY FATHER WAS ASSIGNED TO PROTECT HER FATHER...
HMM... SO SHE'S ONE OF THE ELITE, HUH.

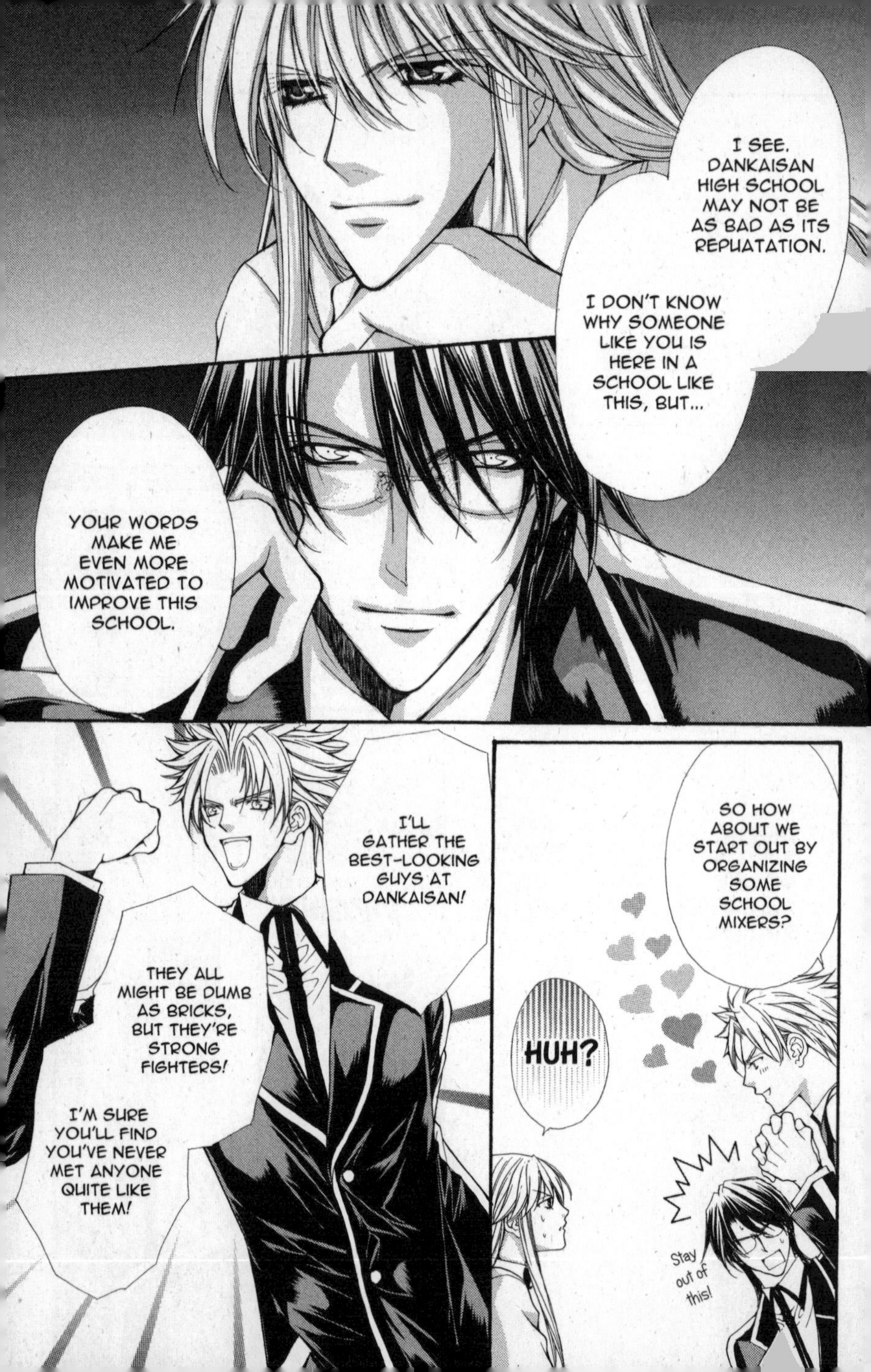
I SEE. DANKAISAN HIGH SCHOOL MAY NOT BE AS BAD AS ITS REPUATATION.
I DON'T KNOW WHY SOMEONE LIKE YOU IS HERE IN A SCHOOL LIKE THIS, BUT...
YOUR WORDS MAKE ME EVEN MORE MOTIVATED TO IMPROVE THIS SCHOOL.
I'LL GATHER THE BEST-LOOKING GUYS AT DANKAISAN!
THEY ALL MIGHT BE DUMB AS BRICKS, BUT THEY'RE STRONG FIGHTERS!
I'M SURE YOU'LL FIND YOU'VE NEVER MET ANYONE QUITE LIKE THEM!
SO HOW ABOUT WE START OUT BY ORGANIZING SOME SCHOOL MIXERS?
HUH?
Stay out of this!

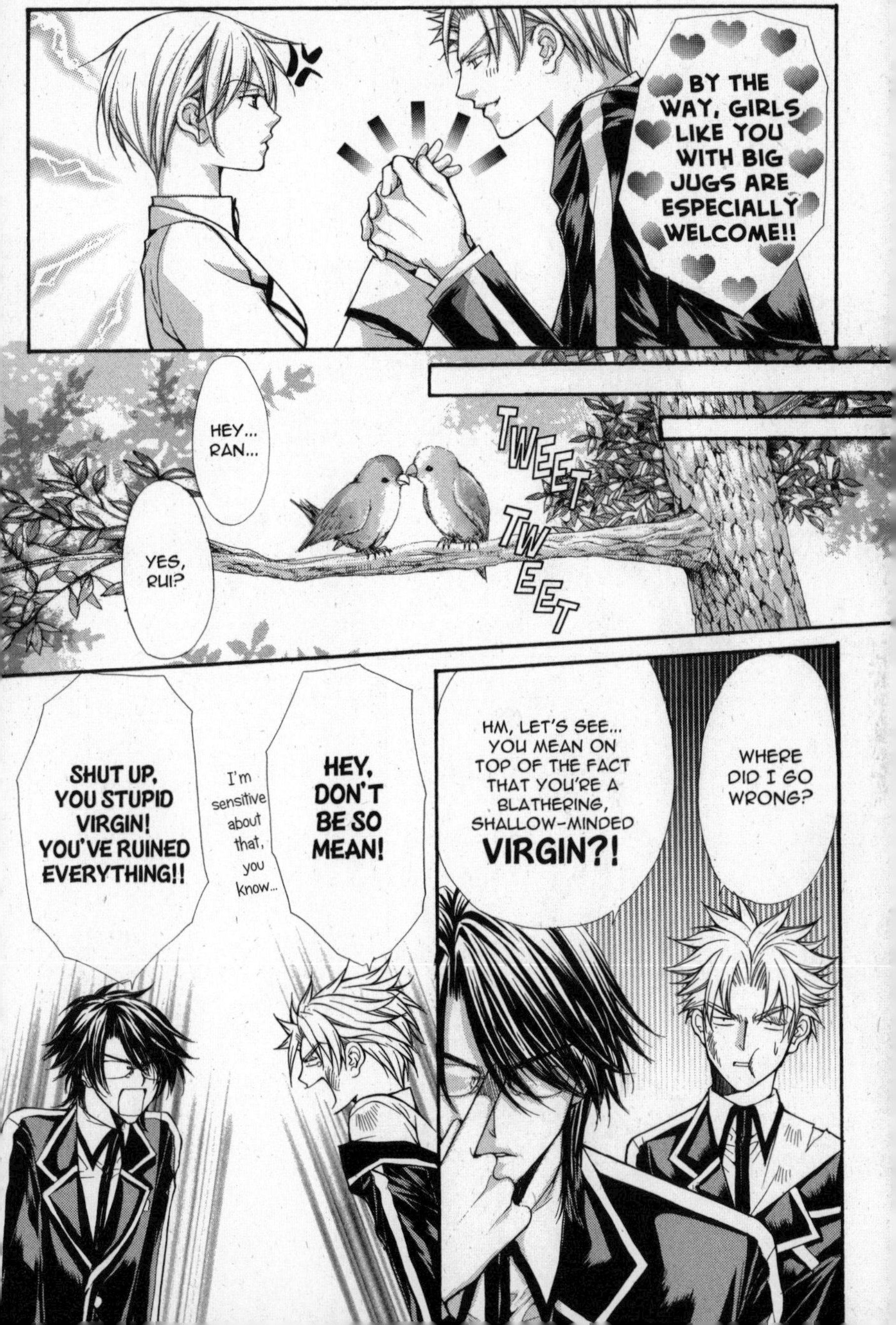
BY THE WAY, GIRLS LIKE YOU WITH BIG JUGS ARE ESPECIALLY WELCOME!!
TWEET
TWEET
HEY... RAN...
YES, RUI?
WHERE DID I GO WRONG?
HM, LET'S SEE... YOU MEAN ON TOP OF THE FACT THAT YOU'RE A BLATHERING, SHALLOW-MINDED VIRGIN?!
HEY, DON'T BE SO MEAN!
I'm sensitive about that, you know...
SHUT UP, YOU STUPID VIRGIN! YOU'VE RUINED EVERYTHING!!

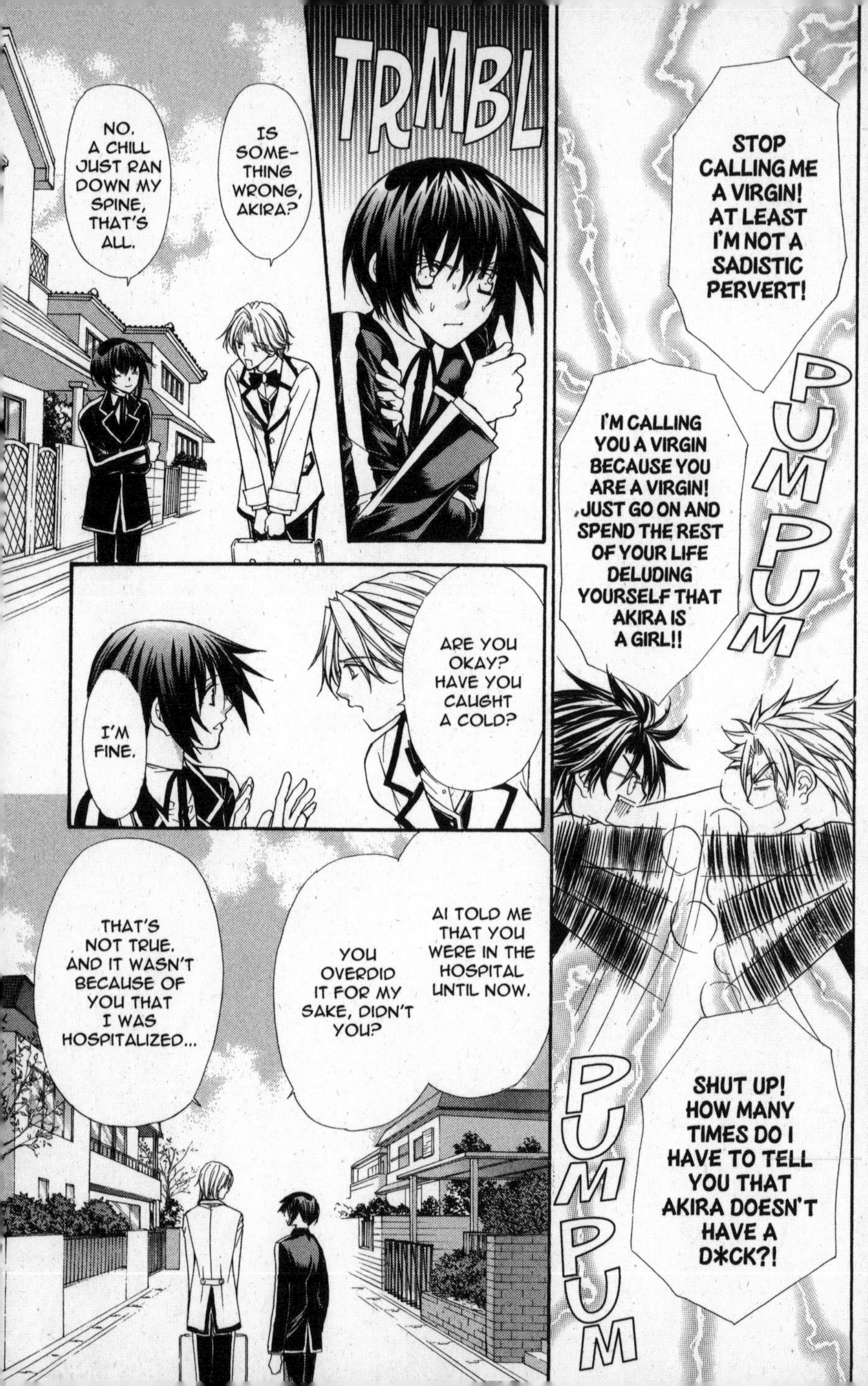
STOP CALLING ME A VIRGIN! AT LEAST I'M NOT A SADISTIC PERVERT!
PUMPUM
I'M CALLING YOU A VIRGIN BECAUSE YOU ARE A VIRGIN! JUST GO ON AND SPEND THE REST OF YOUR LIFE DELUDING YOURSELF THAT AKIRA IS A GIRL!!
SHUT UP! HOW MANY TIMES DO I HAVE TO TELL YOU THAT AKIRA DOESN'T HAVE A D*CK?!
PUMPUM
TRMBL
IS SOMETHING WRONG, AKIRA?
NO. A CHILL JUST RAN DOWN MY SPINE, THAT'S ALL.
ARE YOU OKAY? HAVE YOU CAUGHT A COLD?
I'M FINE.
AI TOLD ME THAT YOU WERE IN THE HOSPITAL UNTIL NOW.
YOU OVERDID IT FOR MY SAKE, DIDN'T YOU?
THAT'S NOT TRUE. AND IT WASN'T BECAUSE OF YOU THAT I WAS HOSPITALIZED...

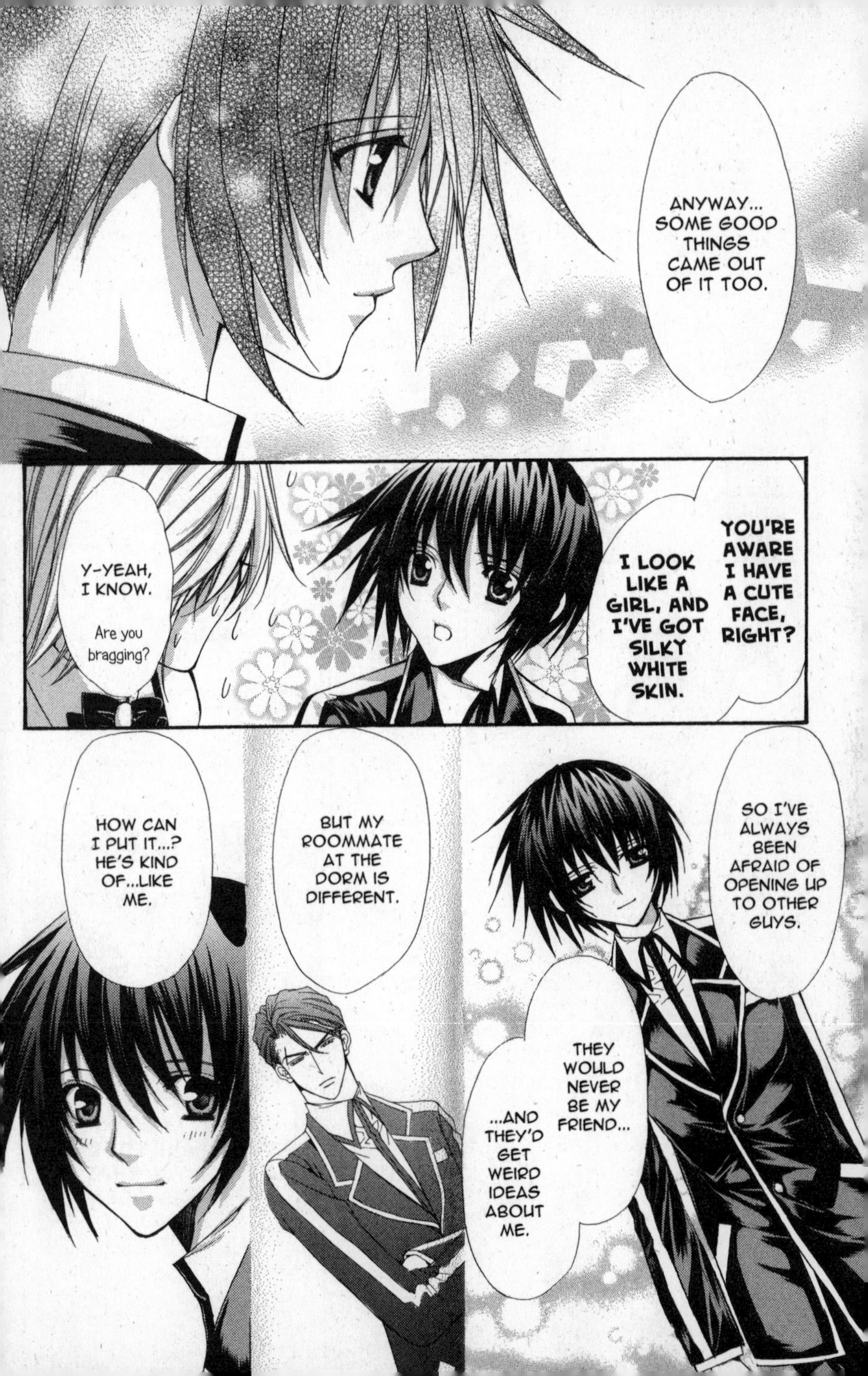
ANYWAY... SOME GOOD THINGS CAME OUT OF IT TOO.
YOU'RE AWARE I HAVE A CUTE FACE, RIGHT?
I LOOK LIKE A GIRL, AND I'VE GOT SILKY WHITE SKIN.
Y-YEAH, I KNOW.
Are you bragging?
SO I'VE ALWAYS BEEN AFRAID OF OPENING UP TO OTHER GUYS.
THEY WOULD NEVER BE MY FRIEND...
...AND THEY'D GET WEIRD IDEAS ABOUT ME.
BUT MY ROOMMATE AT THE DORM IS DIFFERENT.
HOW CAN I PUT IT...? HE'S KIND OF...LIKE ME.

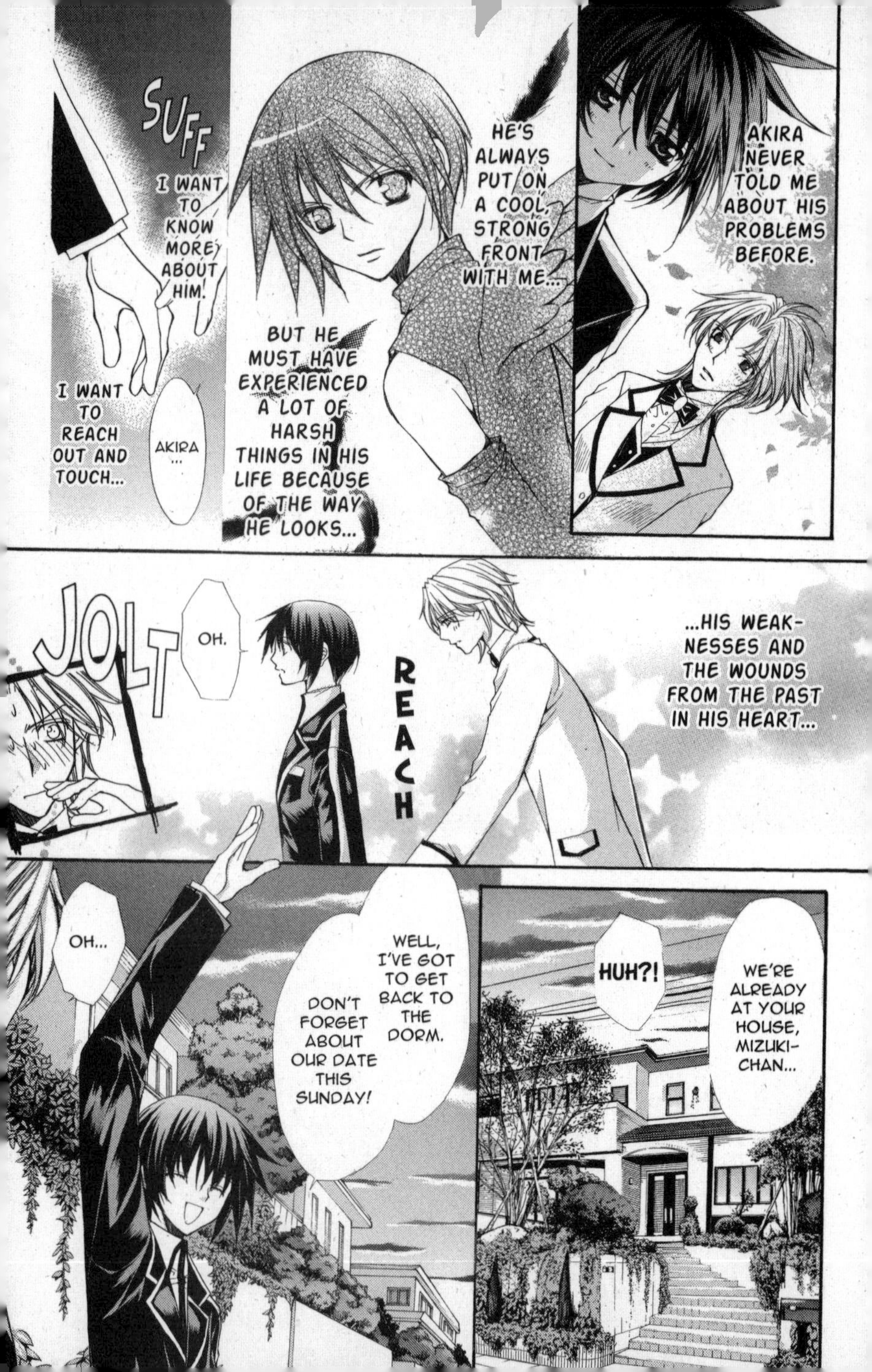
AKIRA NEVER TOLD ME ABOUT HIS PROBLEMS BEFORE.
HE'S ALWAYS PUT ON A COOL, STRONG FRONT WITH ME...
BUT HE MUST HAVE EXPERIENCED A LOT OF HARSH THINGS IN HIS LIFE BECAUSE OF THE WAY HE LOOKS...
SUFF
I WANT TO KNOW MORE ABOUT HIM.
AKIRA ...
I WANT TO REACH OUT AND TOUCH...
...HIS WEAKNESSES AND THE WOUNDS FROM THE PAST IN HIS HEART...
REACH
OH.
JOLT
WE'RE ALREADY AT YOUR HOUSE, MIZUKI-CHAN...
HUH?!
WELL, I'VE GOT TO GET BACK TO THE DORM.
DON'T FORGET ABOUT OUR DATE THIS SUNDAY!
OH...

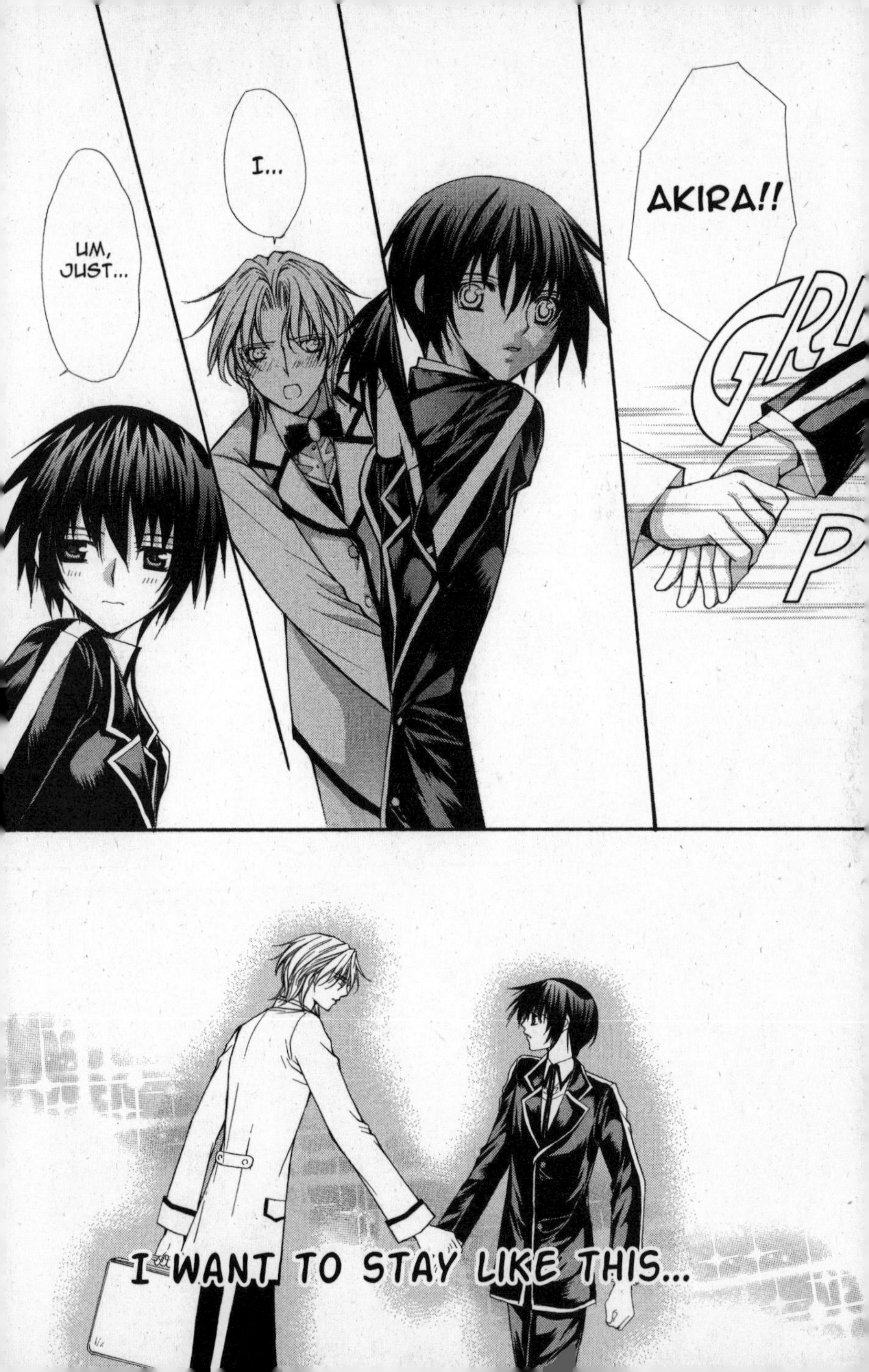
AKIRA!!
GRI
P
I...
UM, JUST...
I WANT TO STAY LIKE THIS...

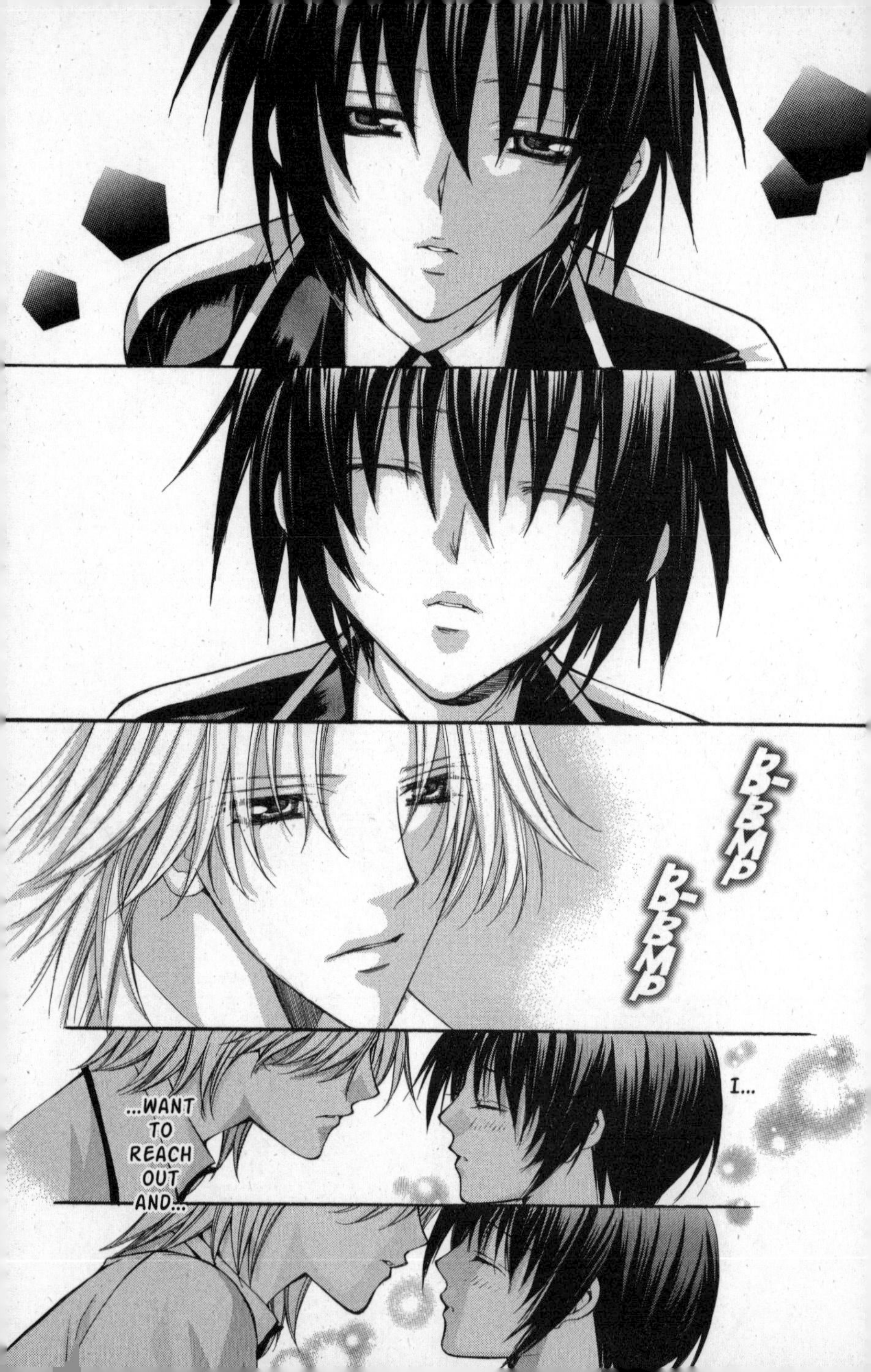
B-BUMP
B-BUMP
I...
...WANT TO REACH OUT AND...

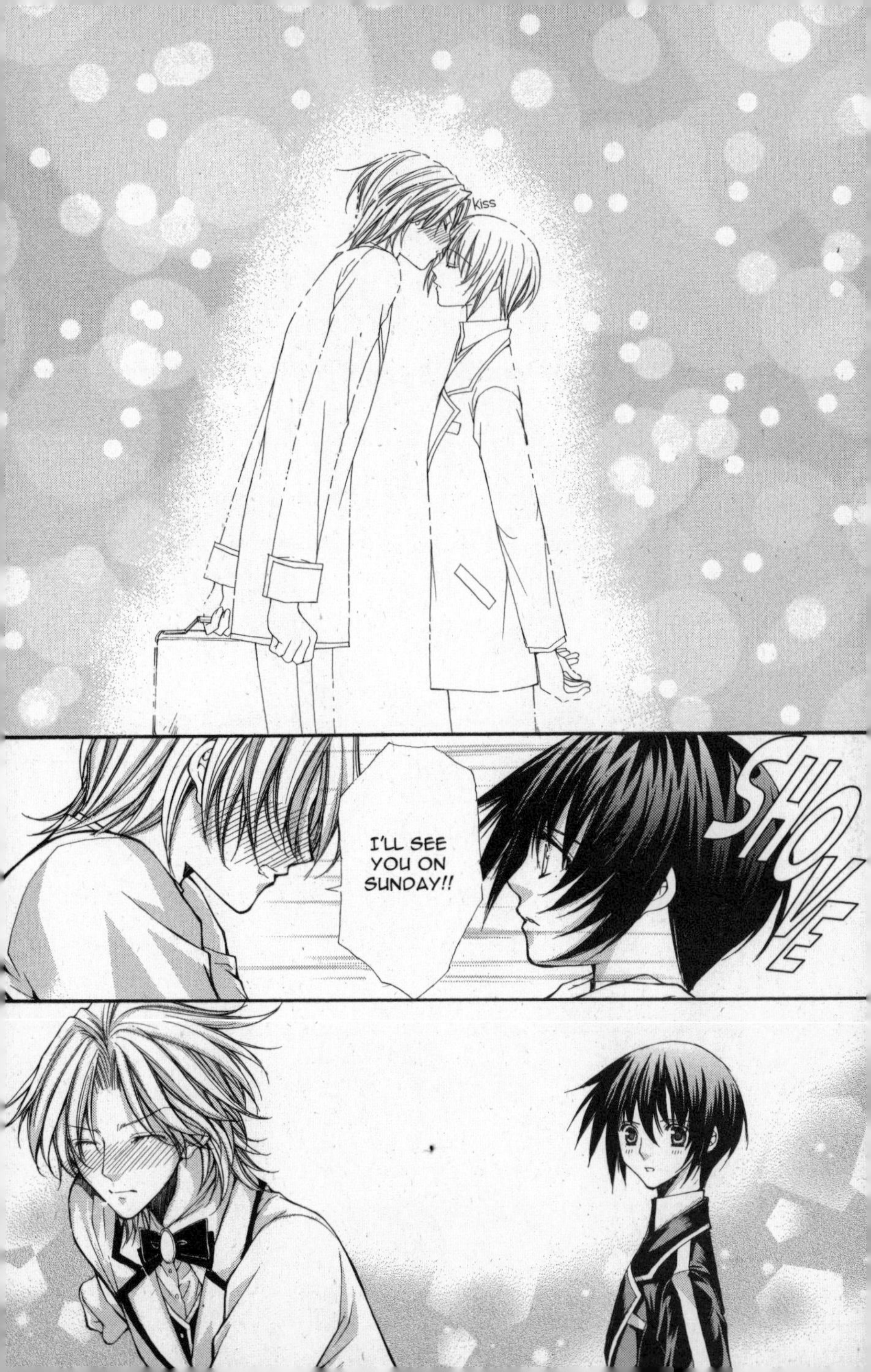
kiss
SHOVE
I'LL SEE YOU ON SUNDAY!!

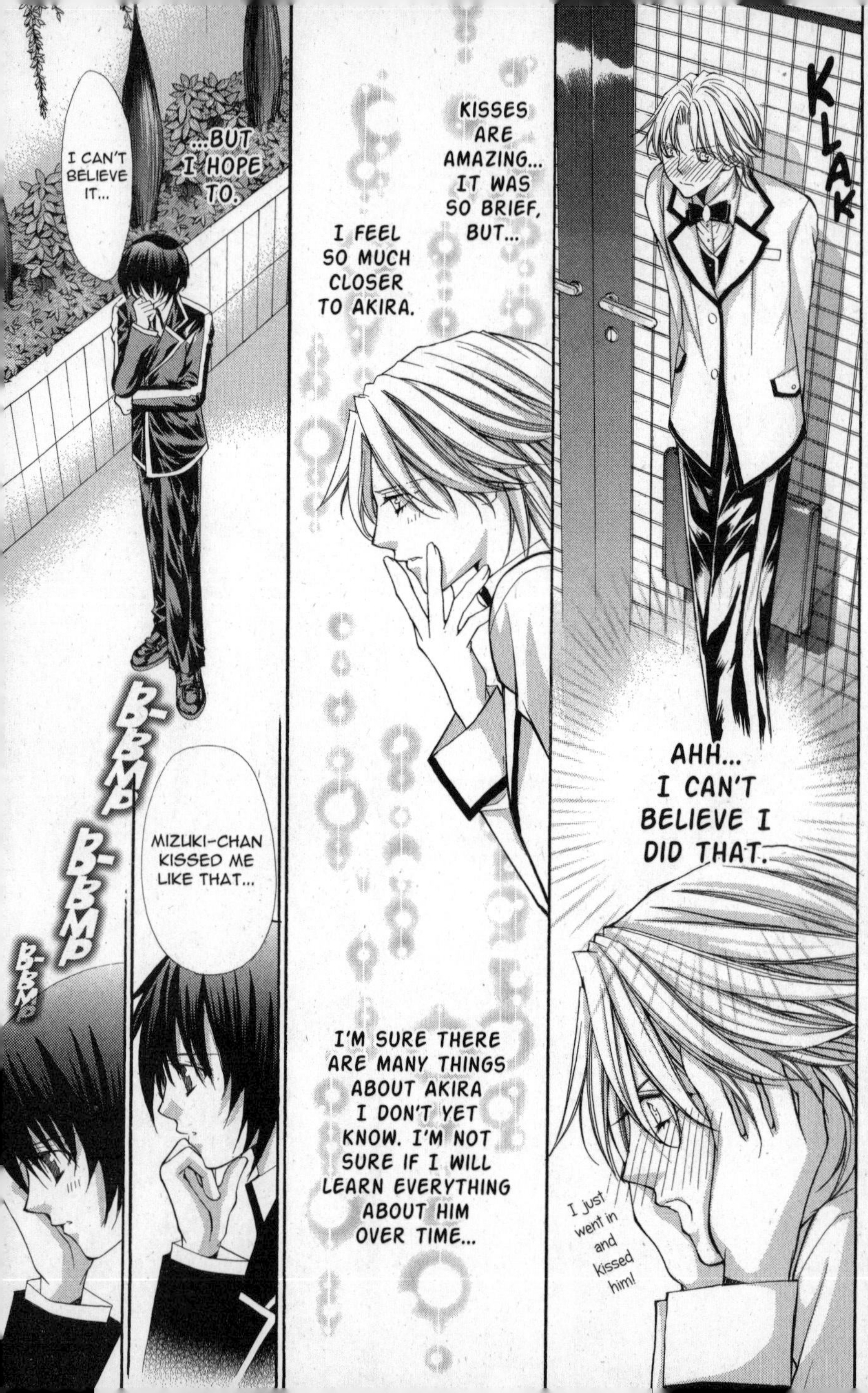
KLAK
AHH... I CAN'T BELIEVE I DID THAT.
I just went in and kissed him!
KISSES ARE AMAZING... IT WAS SO BRIEF, BUT...
I FEEL SO MUCH CLOSER TO AKIRA.
I'M SURE THERE ARE MANY THINGS ABOUT AKIRA I DON'T YET KNOW. I'M NOT SURE IF I WILL LEARN EVERYTHING ABOUT HIM OVER TIME...
...BUT I HOPE TO.
I CAN'T BELIEVE IT...
B-BMP B-BMP
MIZUKI-CHAN KISSED ME LIKE THAT...
B-BMP

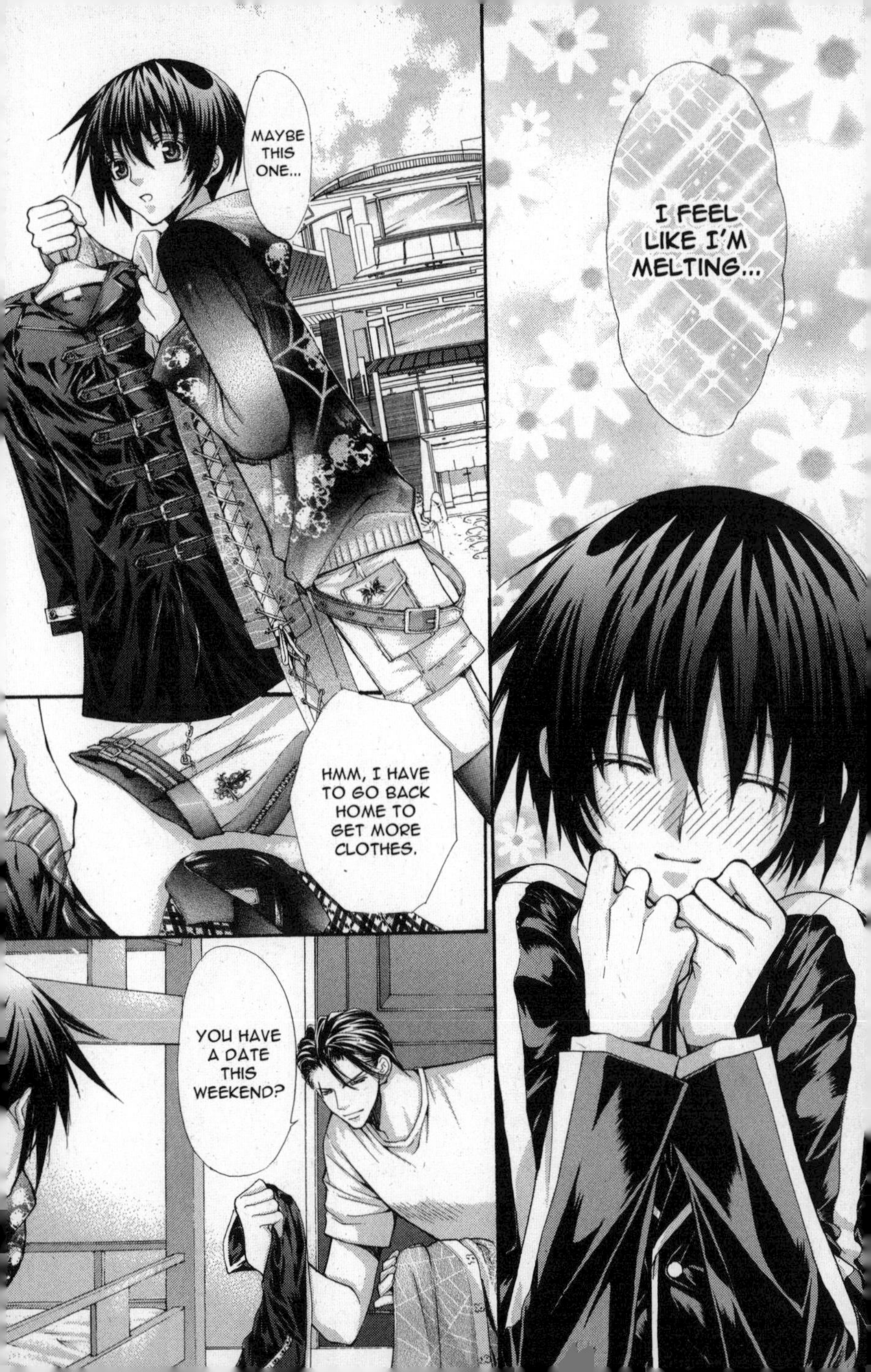
I FEEL LIKE I'M MELTING...
MAYBE THIS ONE...
HMM, I HAVE TO GO BACK HOME TO GET MORE CLOTHES.
YOU HAVE A DATE THIS WEEKEND?

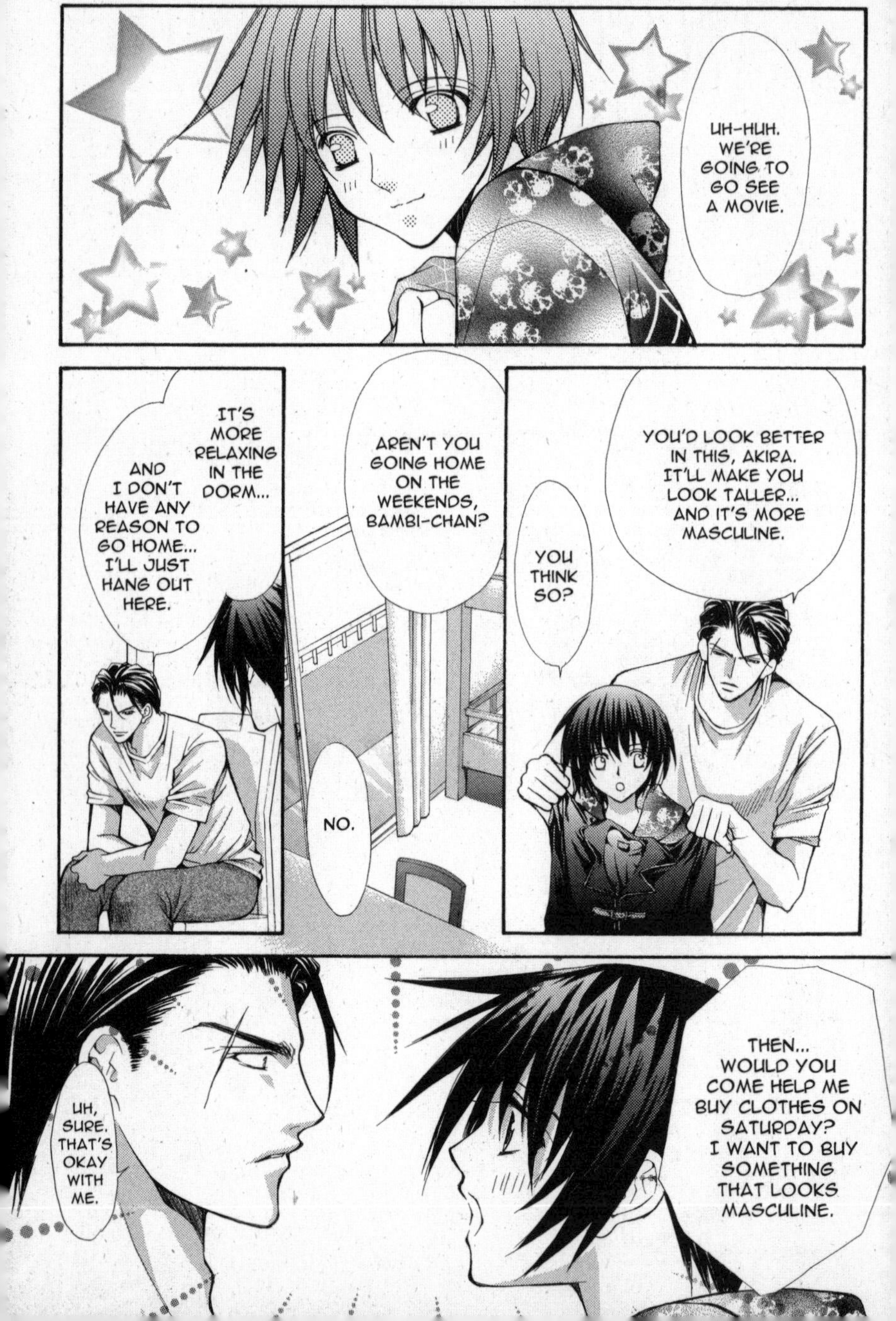
UH-HUH. WE'RE GOING TO GO SEE A MOVIE.
YOU'D LOOK BETTER IN THIS, AKIRA. IT'LL MAKE YOU LOOK TALLER... AND IT'S MORE MASCULINE.
YOU THINK SO?
AREN'T YOU GOING HOME ON THE WEEKENDS, BAMBI-CHAN?
NO.
IT'S MORE RELAXING IN THE DORM...
AND I DON'T HAVE ANY REASON TO GO HOME... I'LL JUST HANG OUT HERE.
THEN... WOULD YOU COME HELP ME BUY CLOTHES ON SATURDAY? I WANT TO BUY SOMETHING THAT LOOKS MASCULINE.
UH, SURE. THAT'S OKAY WITH ME.

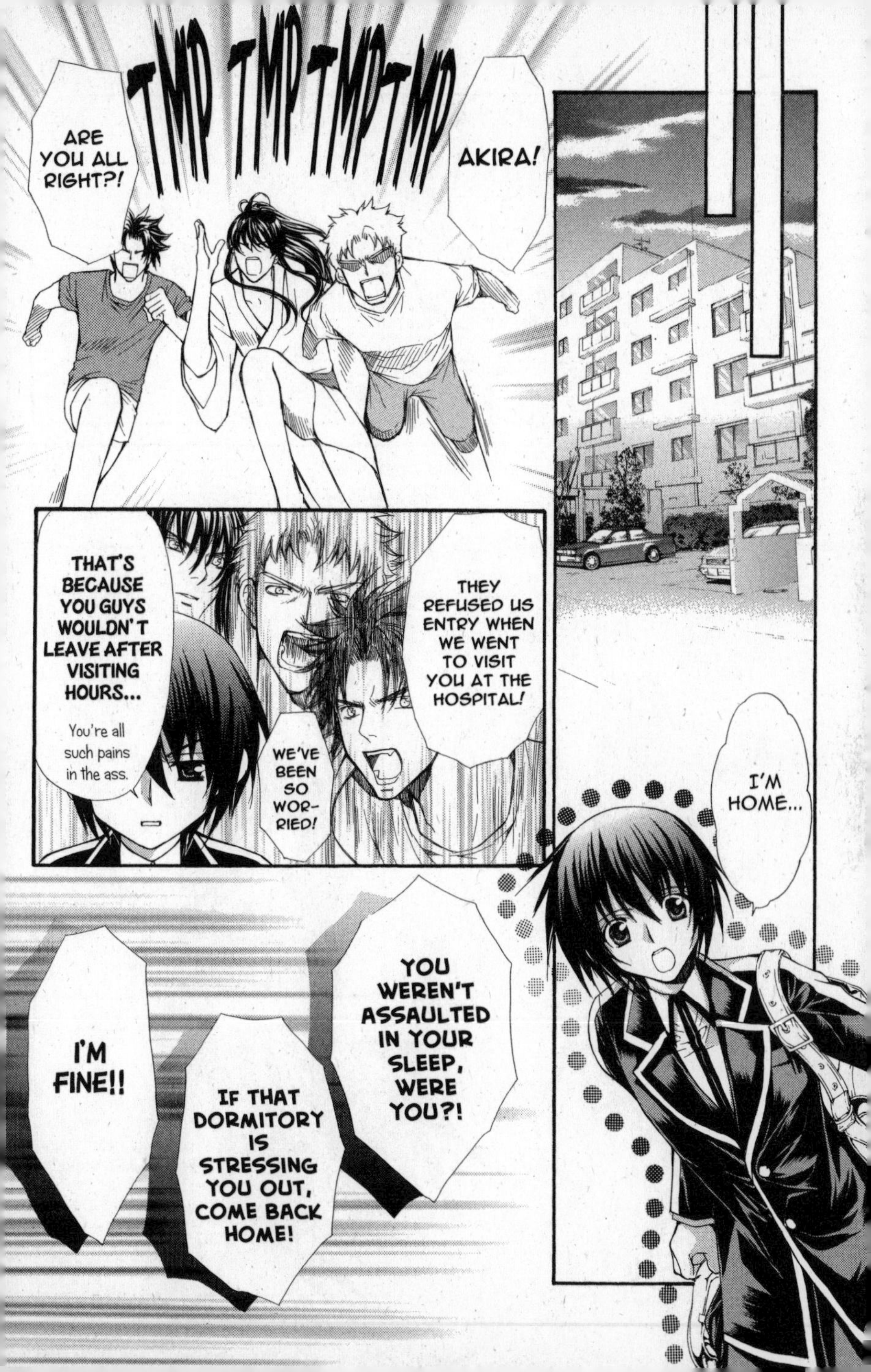
I'M HOME...
AKIRA!
TMP TMP TMP TMP
ARE YOU ALL RIGHT?!
THEY REFUSED US ENTRY WHEN WE WENT TO VISIT YOU AT THE HOSPITAL!
WE'VE BEEN SO WOR-RIED!
THAT'S BECAUSE YOU GUYS WOULDN'T LEAVE AFTER VISITING HOURS...
You're all such pains in the ass.
YOU WEREN'T ASSAULTED IN YOUR SLEEP, WERE YOU?!
IF THAT DORMITORY IS STRESSING YOU OUT, COME BACK HOME!
I'M FINE!!

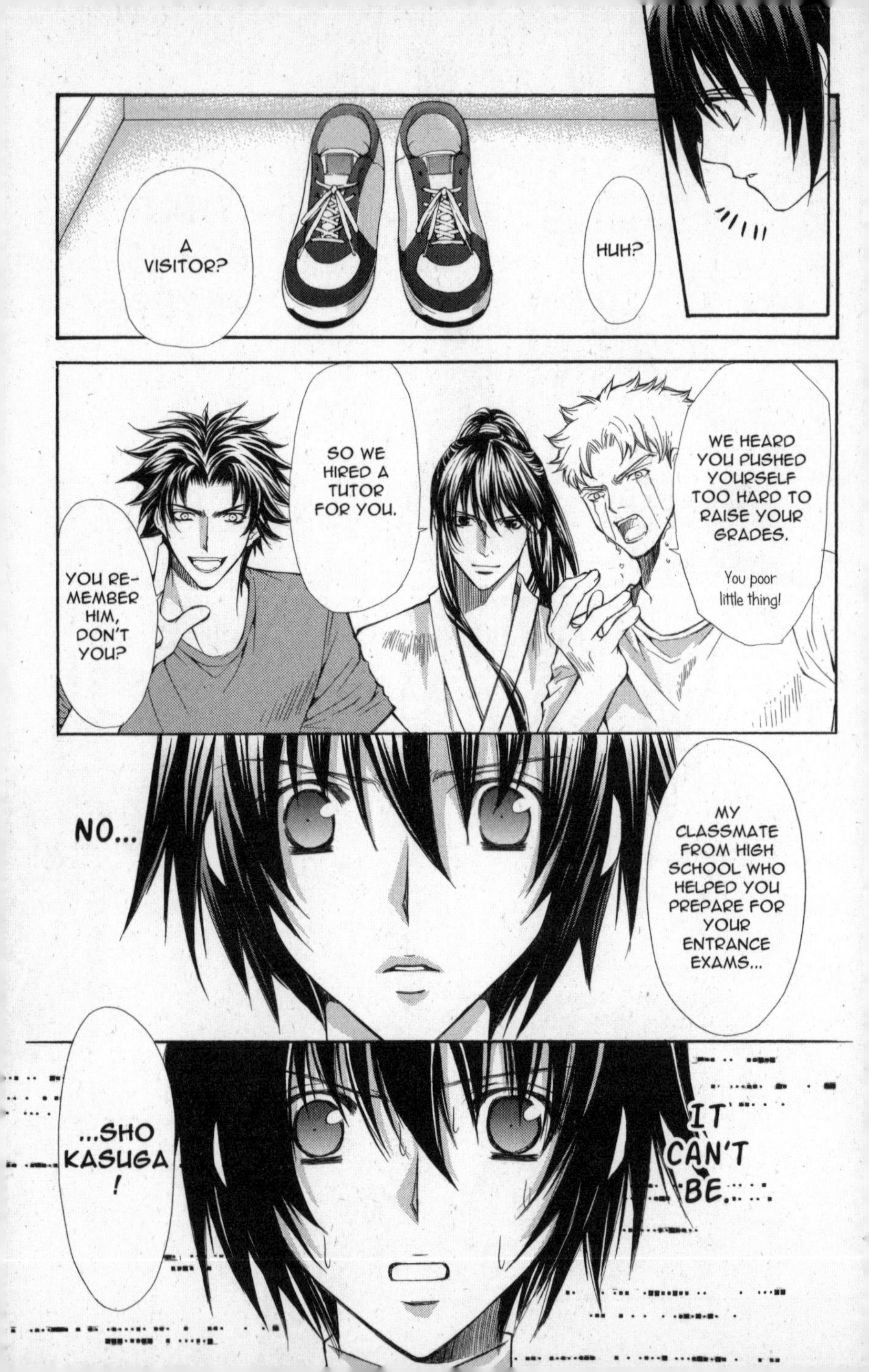
HUH?
A VISITOR?
WE HEARD YOU PUSHED YOURSELF TOO HARD TO RAISE YOUR GRADES.
You poor little thing!
SO WE HIRED A TUTOR FOR YOU.
YOU RE-MEMBER HIM, DON'T YOU?
MY CLASSMATE FROM HIGH SCHOOL WHO HELPED YOU PREPARE FOR YOUR ENTRANCE EXAMS...
NO...
IT CAN'T BE...
...SHO KASUGA!

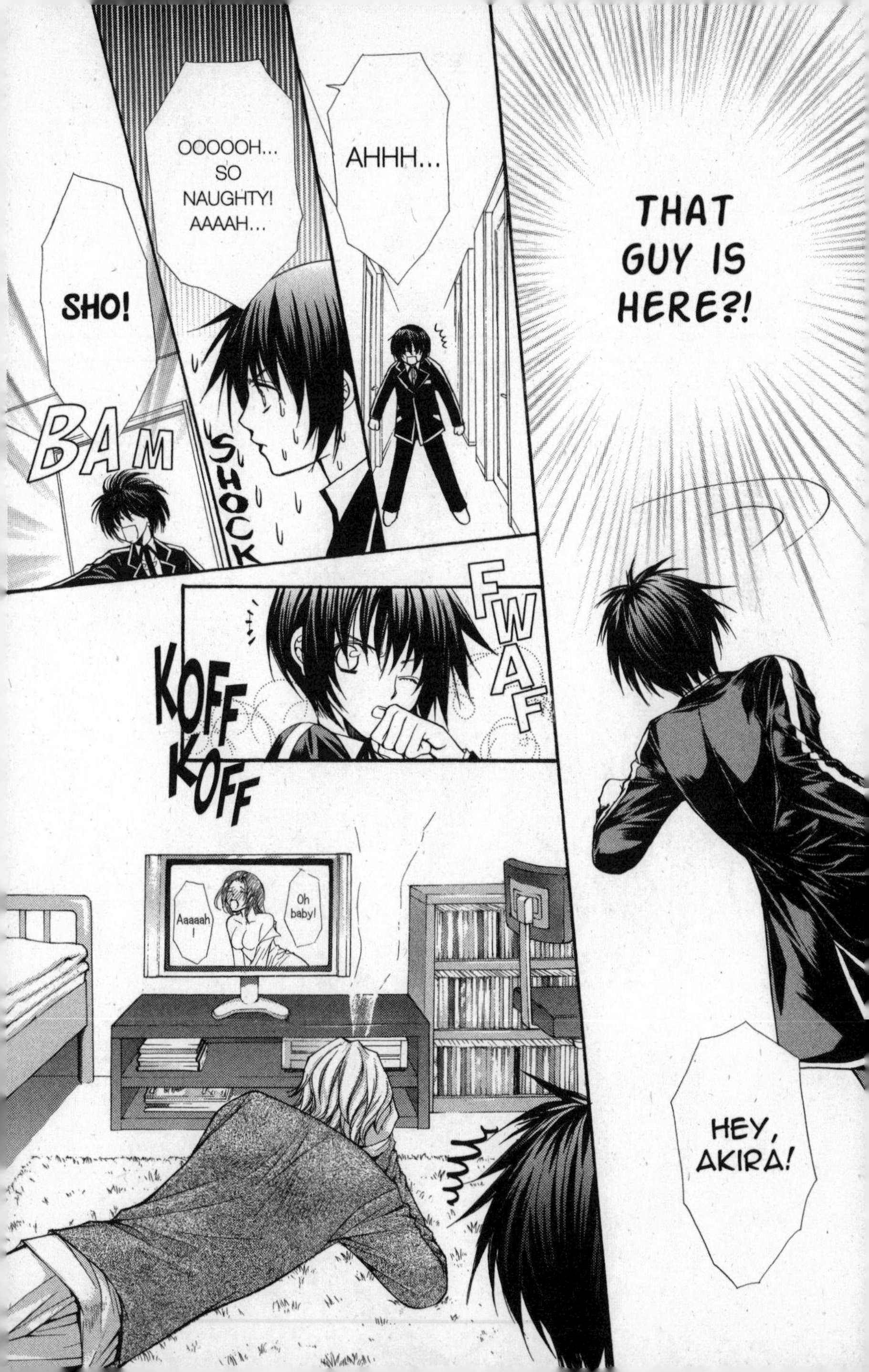
THAT GUY IS HERE?!
HEY, AKIRA!
AHHH...
OOOOOH... SO NAUGHTY! AAAAH...
SHOCK
SHO!
BAM
FWAF
KOFF KOFF
Oh baby!
Aaaaah!

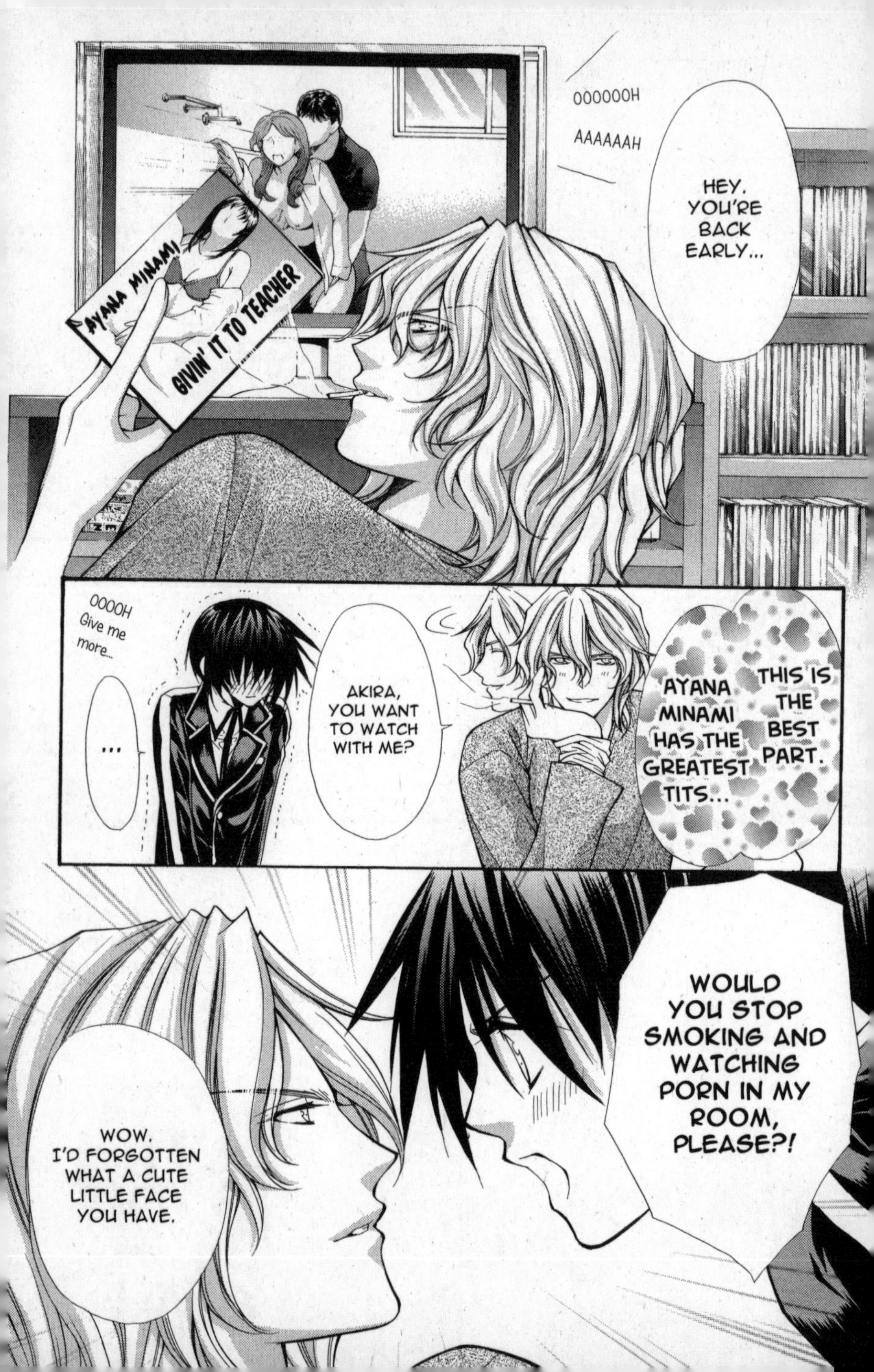
HEY. YOU'RE BACK EARLY...
OOOOOOH
AAAAAAH
AYANA MINAMI
GIVIN' IT TO TEACHER
THIS IS THE BEST PART.
AYANA MINAMI HAS THE GREATEST TITS...
AKIRA, YOU WANT TO WATCH WITH ME?
OOOOH Give me more...
...
WOULD YOU STOP SMOKING AND WATCHING PORN IN MY ROOM, PLEASE?!
WOW. I'D FORGOTTEN WHAT A CUTE LITTLE FACE YOU HAVE.

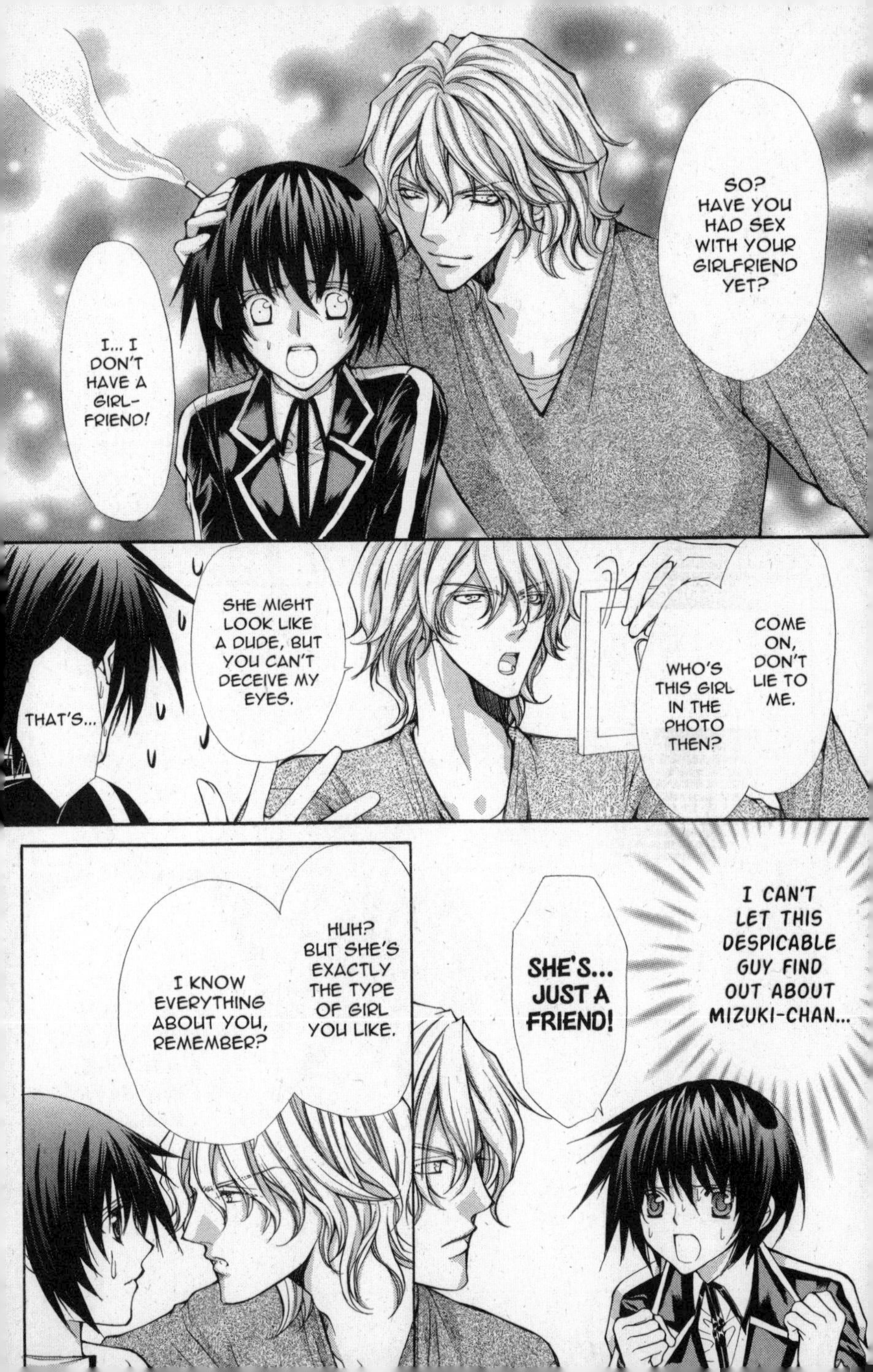
SO? HAVE YOU HAD SEX WITH YOUR GIRLFRIEND YET?
I... I DON'T HAVE A GIRL-FRIEND!
COME ON, DON'T LIE TO ME.
WHO'S THIS GIRL IN THE PHOTO THEN?
SHE MIGHT LOOK LIKE A DUDE, BUT YOU CAN'T DECEIVE MY EYES.
THAT'S...
I CAN'T LET THIS DESPICABLE GUY FIND OUT ABOUT MIZUKI-CHAN...
SHE'S... JUST A FRIEND!
HUH? BUT SHE'S EXACTLY THE TYPE OF GIRL YOU LIKE.
I KNOW EVERYTHING ABOUT YOU, REMEMBER?

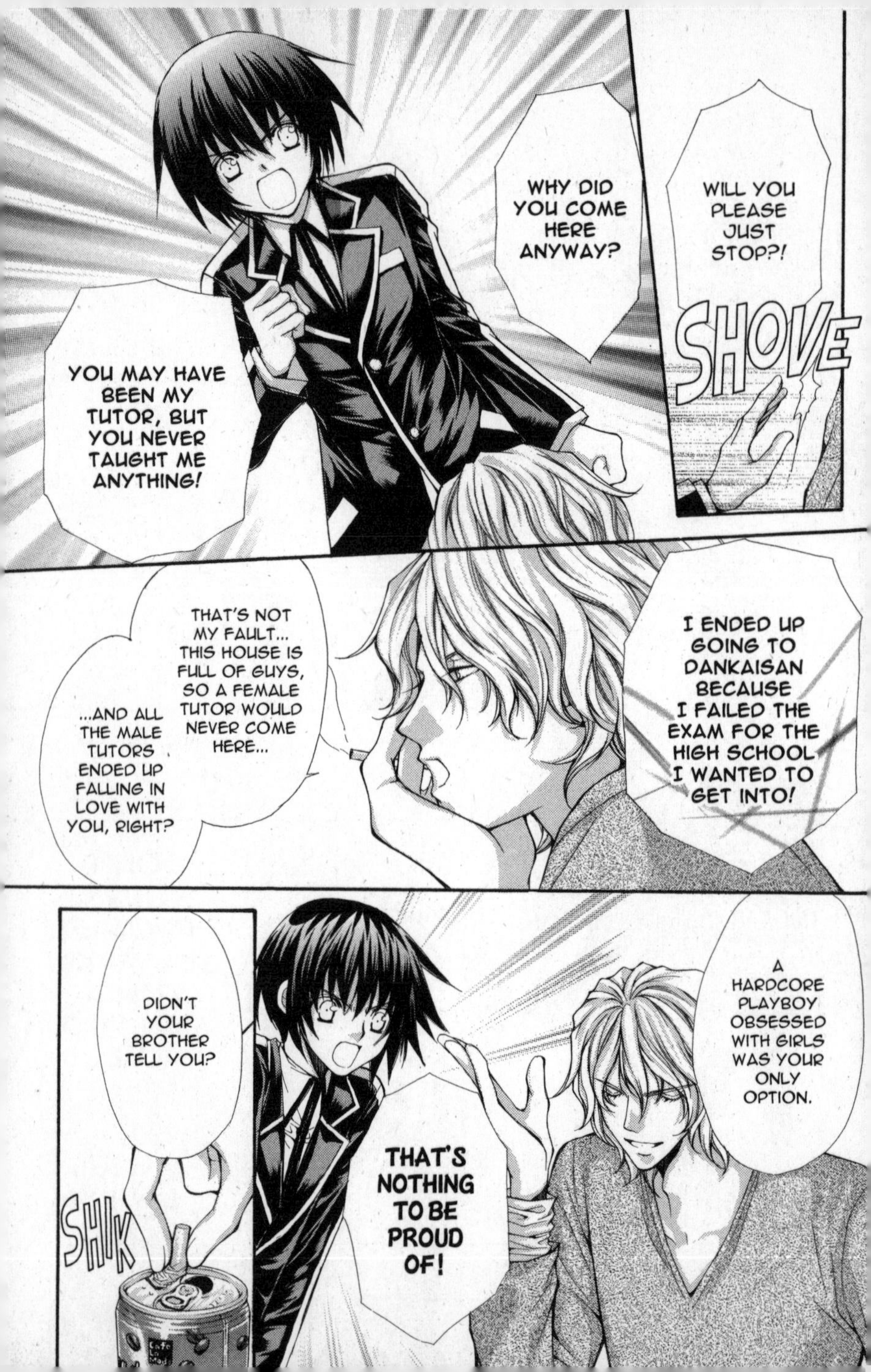
WILL YOU PLEASE JUST STOP?!
SHOVE
WHY DID YOU COME HERE ANYWAY?
YOU MAY HAVE BEEN MY TUTOR, BUT YOU NEVER TAUGHT ME ANYTHING!
I ENDED UP GOING TO DANKAISAN BECAUSE I FAILED THE EXAM FOR THE HIGH SCHOOL I WANTED TO GET INTO!
THAT'S NOT MY FAULT... THIS HOUSE IS FULL OF GUYS, SO A FEMALE TUTOR WOULD NEVER COME HERE...
...AND ALL THE MALE TUTORS ENDED UP FALLING IN LOVE WITH YOU, RIGHT?
A HARDCORE PLAYBOY OBSESSED WITH GIRLS WAS YOUR ONLY OPTION.
THAT'S NOTHING TO BE PROUD OF!
DIDN'T YOUR BROTHER TELL YOU?
SHIK

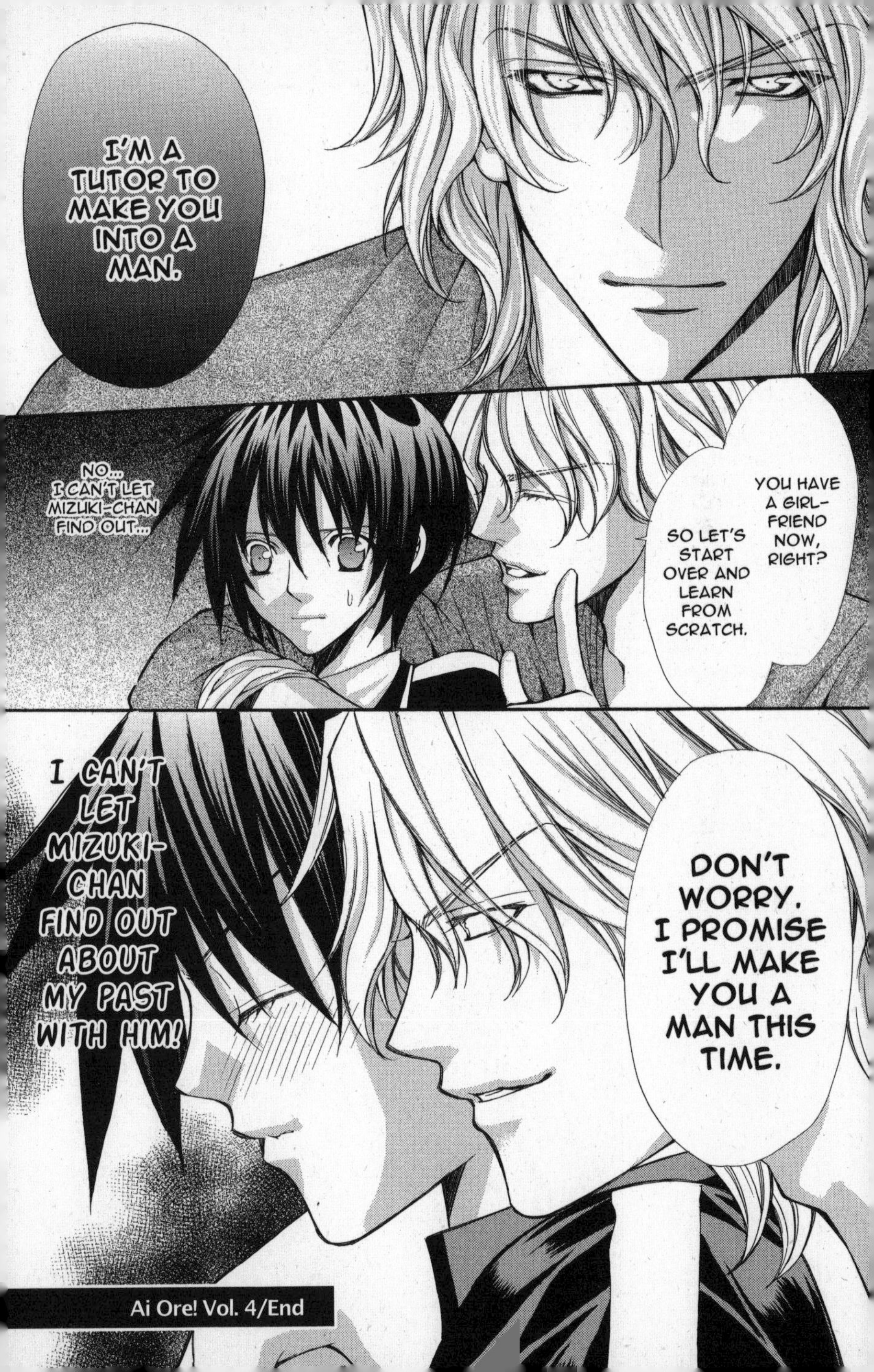
I'M A TUTOR TO MAKE YOU INTO A MAN.
YOU HAVE A GIRL-FRIEND NOW, RIGHT?
SO LET'S START OVER AND LEARN FROM SCRATCH.
NO... I CAN'T LET MIZUKI-CHAN FIND OUT...
DON'T WORRY. I PROMISE I'LL MAKE YOU A MAN THIS TIME.
I CAN'T LET MIZUKI-CHAN FIND OUT ABOUT MY PAST WITH HIM!
Ai Ore! Vol. 4/End

The Third Ai Ore! Drama CD Is Out!!

A Word from Shinjo

The moe aspect has been ramped up even more compared to the first and second CDs. You might think, "Huh? What else could happen?" but I'm telling you it's amazing!! The "Mixer Episode" is an original story I wrote. It's like... Bambi and Rui are...?! (I guess I didn't tell you anything... ♪) I've added more lines and stories from the actual manga, but those are literally like an "Explosion of Shinjo's Libido!!" So I added exciting new scenes with Mizuki and President Ageha, and also scenes with Bambi and Akira. I'd like to introduce my favorite line from this drama CD:

"Ah... Please, Ran. Don't hurt me anymore."

Aaargh, what's he doing to you, Akira...?!

I am so touched to be able to continue bringing this series to all my fans. This manga is packed with all kinds of feelings. I really enjoyed working on it, and I was able to do all the things I've wanted to do. I would like to express my appreciation to all the people who love this series. Thank you very much!

-Mayu Shinjo

Mayu Shinjo was born on January 26. She is a prolific writer of shojo manga, including the series *Sensual Phrase*. Her current series include *Ai-Ore!* and *Ayakashi Koi Emaki*. Her hobbies are cars, shopping and taking baths. Shinjo likes The Prodigy, Nirvana, U2 and Glay.

Ai Ore!

Volume 4
Shojo Beat Edition

STORY AND ART BY
MAYU SHINJO

Translation/Tetsuichiro Miyaki
Touch-up Art & Lettering/Inori Fukuda Trant
Design/Yukiko Whitley
Editor/Nancy Thistlethwaite

Ai Ore! ~Danshikou no Hime to Joshikou no Ouji~
Volume 1
© Mayu SHINJO 2008
First published in Japan in 2008 by KADOKAWA
SHOTEN Co., Ltd., Tokyo.
English translation rights arranged with
KADOKAWA SHOTEN Co., Ltd., Tokyo.

Printed in the U.S.A.

Published by VIZ Media, LLC
P.O. Box 77010
San Francisco, CA 94107

10 9 8 7 6 5 4 3 2 1
First printing, February 2012

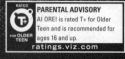

www.viz.com

www.shojobeat.com

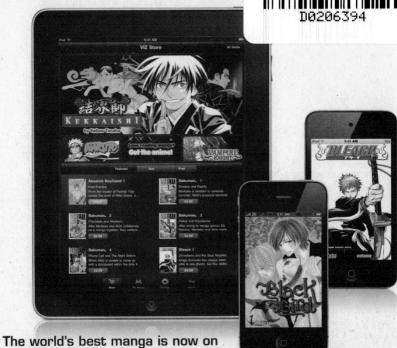
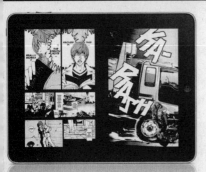